D0372310

MICHIGAN'S UPPER PENINSULA

JOSH BISHOP

Contents

Discover Michigan's Upper Peninsula

"That's north of the Mackinac Bridge and just south of Heaven, for those of ya that don't know nuthin'."

– Escanaba in da Moonlight

Things are different above the Bridge. If you're coming from the Lower Peninsula the change is noticeable the moment you get off the Mackinac Bridge and stop in St. Ignace. You're someplace special. Big cities, shopping malls, expansive parking lots – none of these exist across the Bridge. The Upper Peninsula offers a taste of a different lifestyle, shaped by a unique geography and natural seclusion of Michigan's upper third.

The Upper Peninsula is surrounded by water: Lake Superior to the north, Lake Michigan to the south, and Lake Huron and the St. Mary's River to the east. Most of the land is blanketed by heavy old-growth forest or younger trees that have erased the scars of heavy logging. There are more than 300 waterfalls, 4,300 lakes, 12,000 miles of streams, and 1,700 miles of Great Lakes shoreline. Living in the middle of nature's largely uncultivated splendor – one third of Michigan's land – is a mere three percent of the state population.

People come here to get away from it all. The U.P. is a land set aside for hiking, skiing, mountain biking, camping, fishing and much more.

There are cities, but even the biggest (Marquette, Sault Ste. Marie, Escanaba, Menominee) are rustic by most standards. There is no Upper Peninsula metropolis.

But that's part of the lure. You'll stop in towns that are little more than an intersection, cities where the local watering hole is the only bar in miles. Yoopers (read U.P.-ers) live by different rules. They even sound different above the bridge; most natives say things like "youse guys," "yoobecha," and end most sentences with "ya know?" or "eh?" Not surprisingly, it's a nasal, Midwest inflection with a linguistic nod to a Scandinavian past and a healthy dose of Canadian, ya know?

Yoopers value independence, solitude, self-sufficiency. Life moves slower up here, which may be what you'd expect from people who put up with long winters that drop more than 10 feet of snow. It tends to slow people down a bit.

Now the Upper Peninsula is earning a reputation as an uncommon cure for urban sprawl and traffic congestion. Pretty cool, eh?

Planning Your Trip

▶ WHERE TO GO

The five-mile Mackinac Bridge joins Michigan's Upper and Lower Peninsulas.

The Straits of Mackinac

The Straits of Mackinac see most of the Upper Peninsula's traffic. All of the traffic from the Lower Peninsula bottlenecks across the five-mile-long Mackinac Bridge and into the great north. It's here, too, where many travelers decide to stop. Picturesque **Mackinac Island** is one of America's more perfect getaways, while historic sites and state parks on and off the island bring the region's long history to life. Visit **Colonial Michilimackinac** in Mackinaw City and **Fort Mackinac** on the island.

Escanaba and the Lake Michigan Shore

The Lake Michigan shoreline makes for a pleasant drive with many worthy stops along the way. Sandy beaches off U.S. 2 invite travelers to pull over and dip their toes into the water. Head south into the Garden Peninsula, where **Fayette Historic State Park** memorializes the region's mining history. Detour south into **Escanaba** and **Menominee**, two of the Upper Peninsula's largest cities—each filled with

its own unique charm. An old mining town, Escanaba has seen better days, but don't let that keep you from the city's pleasant waterfront; tour the **Sand Point Lighthouse** and spend time in **Ludington Park.**

The Superior Upland

The western U.P. is best known for **downhill skiing** and **Porcupine Mountain National Park** (aka "the Porkies"). The area's relatively mountainous terrain and

IF YOU HAVE . . .

- **THREE DAYS:** Visit the Straits of Mackinac.

- **FIVE DAYS:** Add Marquette and the Lake Superior Shore.

- **ONE WEEK:** Add the Keweenaw Peninsula and Isle Royale.

- **TWO WEEKS:** Add Escanaba and the Lake Michigan Shore, and Whitefish Bay to the Lake Huron Shore.

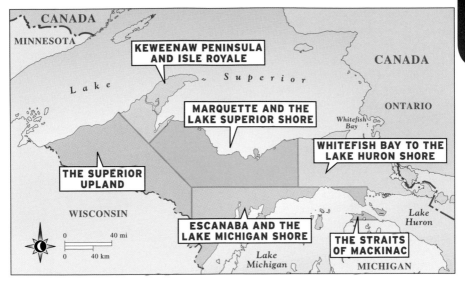

extreme levels of snowfall combine to make Ironwood and its environs the top downhill ski destination in the Midwest. Hit up Ski Brule, Big Powderhorn Mountain, or Blackjack Ski Resort. There's downhill skiing in the Porkies, too, but the real draw here are the miles and miles of hiking trails that wind through the pristine wilderness. When it comes to outdoor pursuits, only Isle Royale National Park outdoes the Porkies.

Keweenaw Peninsula and Isle Royale

Copper Harbor, at the top of the Keweenaw Peninsula, has a well-deserved reputation as the end of the road in Michigan. Stop in the twin cities of Houghton and Hancock on your way through—grab a brew at The Library or tour Quincy Mine. Also stop at the quaint, historic town of Calumet.

The island of Isle Royale would be Michigan's true end of the road if a road went there. The rugged Isle Royale National Park can be reached only by boat or plane.

Hike or paddle and watch for reclusive moose and wolves.

Marquette and the Lake Superior Shore

Lake Superior provides some of the nation's most beautiful scenery—tough pine, stony

Seen from above, Copper Harbor is an idyllic town carved out of the surrounding wilderness.

beaches, and craggy rocks carved into a dramatic panorama by relentless waves. Rent a **sea kayak** to get a proper look at the unique natural formations of the famous **Pictured Rocks National Lakeshore.** Spend time in **Marquette,** checking out the vibrant arts scene, historic downtown, and of course, **Presque Isle Park.** Check out **Munising,** a darling town located on a picturesque bay. Take the ferry to **Grand Island** or reserve a spot on a Pictured Rocks **boat cruise.**

Whitefish Bay to the Lake Huron Shore

Whitefish Bay offers natural protection from Lake Superior's wildly inclement weather. The bay drains south into the St. Mary's River like a giant funnel, guiding ships through the **Soo Locks** that connect Lakes Superior and Huron, providing the Great Lakes with an essential shipping lane. A visit to the Soo Locks is a must while visiting **Sault Ste. Marie,** a

The Les Cheneaux islands are a boater's paradise.

dynamic city, second only to Marquette in population and, perhaps, popularity. On the shore of Lake Huron, **Les Cheneaux** and **Drummond Island** are remote, quiet destinations forgotten by tourists yet perfect for relaxation.

▶ WHEN TO GO

Summers are capable of getting frightfully hot and humid. Still, this is when the outdoors come alive. Backwoods campers, hikers, mountain bikers, sea kayakers, and fishermen descend on the Upper Peninsula like a swarm of flies (speaking of which, do be aware of black fly season, usually in late June or early July). Hotel rates are highest on the weekends of July 4 and Labor Day, and only moderately lower during the months in between.

The Upper Peninsula comes alive in **autumn.** Nights cool down to a pleasant chill and the turning leaves color the forests in brilliant reds and yellows. Days are less humid, less hot, and less crowded than during the peak summer season. Many summertime

pursuits are more appealing after the summer heat and before the long winter settles in—you can hike the same trails, fish the same streams, and camp the same sites, but now they're surrounded by the changing deciduous colors.

In **winter,** much of the U.P. is covered in snow, making it an ideal destination for downhill and cross-country skiing, snowshoeing, and snowmobiling. The western U.P. is well-suited for winter recreation, with a handful of ski resorts and miles of cross-country ski and snowmobile trails. Double-check with your host while planning a winter trip since some accommodations and restaurants close down for the winter.

Spring days tend to be overcast or rainy,

FALL COLORS

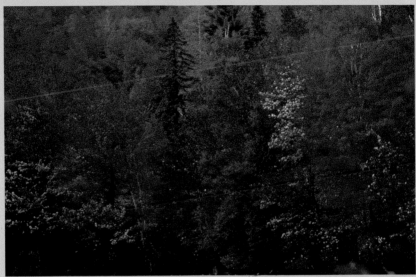

Upper Peninsula forests put on an amazing color display each autumn.

Odds are that when you're planning your fall color tour of Michigan's Upper Peninsula one of two things will happen: either you'll come a week early and be met with colors as exciting as the shades of green you see in your back lawn, or the colors will have turned before you get there and all you'll see are naked tree branches and a carpet of dead leaves. But if you hit it just right – oh, is it a sight to see! All you need to enjoy the glory of countless trees in their peak color is the will to get outside, whether it's on a hiking trail, in a kayak along the shoreline, or in a car on one of the main highways.

One of the finest routes in the U.P. is the circle formed between **Eagle River** and **Copper Harbor** by U.S. 41 and M-26, an hour-long 45-mile loop. It may be prettiest hour of your life, especially the stretch along U.S. 41/Copper Country Trail Scenic Byway. Visit the Keweenaw mid-September–early October to catch the best colors. The **Marquette-Negaunee-Au Train tour** will take you into the Huron Mountains on the way to Big Bay and back, as well as on a wider loop south and east of the city along M-35, U.S. 41, M-94, and M-28. There is a trail that follows Lake Michigan from Menominee through Escanaba and on toward Manistique, and another that includes Sault Ste. Marie, Drummond Island, and Hessel. All told, **Travel Michigan** (www.michigan.org) lists eight Upper Peninsula color trails on their website, including stops along the way and detailed maps for each tour.

snow often sticks around well into April, the trails get soggy and muddy, and the temperature can be chilly. On the other hand, it can be particularly impressive to watch Mother Nature shrug off her winter coat. Snowmelt overfills the rivers and streams, making this season especially attractive to waterfall watchers.

Frozen for the long winter, Tahquamenon Falls are a popular winter hiking destination.

▶ BEFORE YOU GO

Transportation

You can get to the Upper Peninsula by any manner of transportation: plane, boat, bus, bike, snowmobile, and foot. Though once you're there you're going to want a car. There's **little public transportation available,** and what little there is, is limited to stops along routes between the bigger cities. The U.P. is far bigger than most people assume; it can take several hours to drive from one city to the next. If you have any intentions of getting off the main, paved roads, **four-wheel drive** and a high clearance are *highly* recommended.

What to Take

The best way to see the U.P. is to throw a **tent** in the back of a pickup truck and hop from campsite to campsite across the peninsula. Pack the outdoors staple accessories: plenty of **bug spray,** sturdy shoes, and clothing for inclement weather. Take a small backpack for day trips or short hikes. And unless you're planning on dining at one of Marquette's finer restaurants or enjoying a formal dinner at the

Grand Hotel or another Mackinac Island resort (several places on the island have dress codes), don't bother packing nice clothes.

It is a good idea to get a **Michigan State Park sticker** ahead of time. The annual pass will get you in and out of some top spots without trouble. If you want to wander across the International Bridge into Canada, pack your **passport.**

If you're looking to get in touch with Upper Peninsula wilderness, camping is the way to go.

Explore Michigan's Upper Peninsula

▶ BEST OF MICHIGAN'S UPPER PENINSULA

The best of Michigan's Upper Peninsula is spread across a landmass that stretches some 320 miles across. To properly explore all that the Upper Peninsula has to offer requires at least two weeks, and even that might be pushing it. There's no way around it: to get from one city to the next requires a lot of driving. The route below will keep your car time limited to a couple hours for each stretch when possible, but for parts of the trip it's unavoidable. The following includes a selection of the U.P.'s best—lighthouses, historic sites, waterfalls, cities, and outdoor pursuits.

and find a cheap hotel) and catch an early ride on one of the ferries to **Mackinac Island.** The earliest is at 7:30 A.M. Spend the morning and early afternoon touring the island's historic sites: **Fort Mackinac** is a can't-miss, and several other sites—the **Biddle House** and **Benjamin Blacksmith Shop**—are also worth your while. Wind down your evening with a stroll through downtown—buy fudge at **Murdick's** or **Ryba's,** and nose around the quaint streets. Stay the night at an island hotel—**The Grand Hotel,** if your budget allows for it.

Day 1
Arrive in Mackinaw City or St. Ignace as early as you can (better still, arrive the night before

Day 2
Today, spend a little more time outside. It's time to get out into Mackinac Island State

CROSSING ICE BRIDGES

There are more than 3,000 miles of groomed snowmobile trails that crisscross the Upper Peninsula.

There are more than 3,000 miles of interconnected groomed snowmobile trails in the Upper Peninsula. Big deal. Sure, it's impressive – until you realize that a few of the unofficial trails take you off solid ground and across the frozen surface of the Great Lakes. When the lakes freeze over during the U.P.'s long, cold winters, one of the brave locals will venture out onto the ice . . . on a snowmobile. As soon as it's thick enough to hold, a trail of discarded Christmas trees marks the paths across Lake Huron in three different places. One trail leads to and from **Mackinac Island,** while two others cross international borders from **Drummond Island** to **St. Joseph Island** or **Thessalon, Ontario** (bring your passport and check in with customs). It's a thrill, yes, but it's also dangerous and done at your own substantial risk: If you plunge through the ice into Lake Huron, easy money says you aren't coming back up.

Park, which covers the majority of the island. Take a horse-drawn carriage, rent a bike, or hoof it yourself; the park's more than 2,000 acres are well-suited for any outdoor pursuit. Head for **Arch Rock** or **Devil's Kitchen.** Golfers can spend their time at the **Jewel.** Grab a quick lunch, then visit the Grand Hotel or stop by the **Mackinac Island Butterfly House.** Head back to the ferry docks before the last boat leaves. Stay the night in **St. Ignace** at the **Boardwalk Inn.**

Day 3

Spend the morning on U.S. 2 as it winds along the Lake Michigan shoreline. You're heading all the way to Menominee, but detour south into the **Garden Peninsula** where the historic ghost town at **Fayette Historic State Park** is worth a couple hours of your time. Double back to U.S. 2 and drive to **Escanaba,** Stop for lunch at **Hereford and Hops** on historic Ludington Avenue. After lunch, continue on to **Menominee** and spend the evening exploring the historic district or wandering the waterfront at the **Great Lakes Marina Park.** Stay the night in Menominee (try **Gehrke's Guesthaus**) or across state lines in Marinette, Wisconsin.

The Porcupine Mountains Wilderness State Park is the largest, wildest state park in Michigan.

Day 4

Today you'll continue traveling west. Travel through Iron Mountain to **Ironwood**, stopping at the **Iron Mountain Iron Mine.** Stop in **Iron River** for lunch at **The Depot Restaurant and Bakery,** then continue on to Ironwood for an afternoon excursion to the top of the **Copper Peak Adventure Ride.** You won't find a better view in all of the U.P. Head back to town for dinner at **Don and GG's.** Make the 20-minute drive out to **Little Girl's Point** to watch the sun set over Lake Superior before driving back to **Wakefield** and the **Regal Country Inn** for the night.

Day 5

It's time to see more of the Upper Peninsula's famous wilderness. Get back in the car and drive to **Porcupine Mountains Wilderness State Park.** Start early in order to spend as much time as possible in the park. Stop at the Visitor Center for maps and advice, then hit the secluded trails or the park's better-known locales. Don't miss the **Lake of the Clouds**

or the view from the observation tower at **Summit Peak.** Hunt down the waterfalls along South Boundary Road: **Manabezho Falls** are especially nice. If you packed a tent, stay the night in the park, otherwise book a room near **Ontonagon—Mountain View Lodges** will treat you right.

Arch Rock is one of the most immediately recognizable landmarks in Mackinac Island State Park.

MUSH! DOGSLEDDING IN THE U.P.?

The art and sport of mushing is a growing pasttime in places like Colorado's Rocky Mountains. In other places, such as Alaska, it's never really gone out of style. Here in the Midwest, it's still an uncommon pastime. Yet, not in the U.P. Thanks in part to the popularity of the **U.P. 200,** a mid-February sled dog race that begins and ends in Marquette, sled dog excursions have become something of an expected novelty. You can watch the race, but taking the leap from spectator to participant is something else all together. Contact one of the Upper Peninsula's kennels to see about taking a full-, half-, or multi-day trip. Contact **Triple Creek Kennels** (E5372 M-94, Munising, 877/275-7533) to arrange for a guided trip across the winter landscape.

Day 6

Spend the morning in Houghton and its sister city **Hancock**. There are plenty of shops, restaurants, and diversions among the cities' hilly streets. Tour the **Quincy Mine** for a look at the region's mining history. Grab a sandwich and brew from **The Library**. Take your time getting to **Copper Harbor**. Stop in quaint downtown **Calumet** and detour to the top of **Brockway**

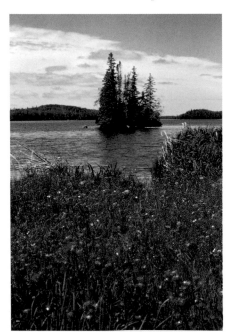

Isle Royale is the Upper Peninsula's most secluded park.

Mountain Drive. In Copper Harbor, visit **Fort Wilkins State Park** and explore the small downtown before turning in for the night at the **Keweenaw Mountain Lodge.**

Day 7

It's technically possible to visit **Isle Royale National Park** in one day, but it isn't recommended. No, if you want to go to the park, plan on taking at least three or four days. Take the three-hour journey on the *Isle Royale Queen IV* from Copper Harbor to the park. If you're don't want to camp, check into the **Rock Harbor Lodge** (you'll need reservations) and settle on a day hike. If you're planning to head into the island, grab a map, talk to the rangers, and start hoofing it up the trails. Preparation is key here, so make sure you've got everything you need before setting out.

Days 8-9

Congratulations. You've got a couple of days on the island. If you stayed at the Rock Harbor Lodge, you won't want for things to do. Take a few more **day hikes** along some of the shorter trails into the island—**Scoville Point** and **Lookout Louise** are good choices, and the view from **Ojibway Tower** is phenomenal. Look into a Park Service boat tour or rent a sea kayak and nose around the shoreline yourself. Pack your

Pictured Rocks National Lakeshore is the most striking stretch of the Lake Superior shoreline.

lunches and take them with you; dinners at the lodge are satisfying.

Backwoods campers and hikers will have 165 miles of trail beneath their feet. There's no way to hike it all in a few days, but a well-planned trip will have you walking from campsite to campsite while you keep a lookout for **moose.**

Day 10

Regardless of where you stayed last night, make sure you're back at the ferry dock by 2:45 P.M. for the ride back to Copper Harbor. You'll get into town a little before 6 P.M., just in time for dinner at the **Harbor Haus,** or hit the road right away for Marquette, which is about three hours away. Check in at the **Landmark Inn** for the evening.

Day 11

Waking up in **Marquette** means you have all day to explore the U.P.'s largest city. Start at **Presque Isle Park** on the west side of town. Taking a perimeter loop in your car can be done in no time at all—better to park the car and set off into the park on foot, bicycle, or cross-country skis. Wander along a footpath to the Lake Superior shore, and bring your camera with you. Head back into town for lunch. This college town has many unique shops—including two amazing bookstores (**Bookworld** and **Snowbound Books**)—to keep you occupied for the afternoon. Enjoy a fine dinner at the **Vierling Saloon** and check out any evening entertainment before heading to the hotel for the night.

Day 12

Spend the morning getting in a last look at some of Marquette's attractions before you leave town. If you didn't get a chance to visit its historic stops, try one of the many museums or head to the **Marquette Harbor Lighthouse** at the maritime museum.

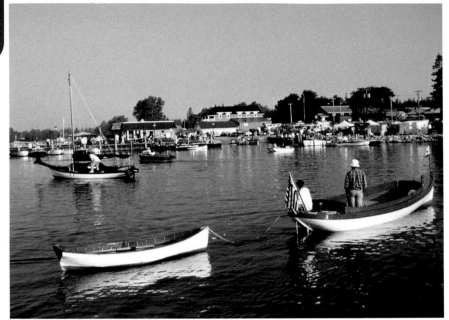
antique wooden boat show at Hessel

Midday will find you on the road again. This time you will follow the exceptionally beautiful Lake Superior shore on the way east to **Munising** in time to catch a boat cruise along **Pictured Rocks National Lakeshore** (or paddle it yourself in a kayak). Next, drive to **Tahquamenon Falls State Park**, where you'll see one of the Upper Peninsula's waterfall gems. Finish the day by driving to **Long Ships Motel** in Sault Ste. Marie.

Day 13

Sault Ste. Marie is most famous for the **Soo Locks**, which allow massive freighters to pass along the Saint Mary's River between Lakes Superior and Huron. It is easy to lose track of time watching the locks at work. For an even closer look, take a boat tour through the locks. Spend some time on **Portage Avenue**, too. Sure, it's a little touristy but it's also filled with small town charm. Duck into any of the local restaurants for dinner (**Freighters** is a good choice) and take it easy for the rest of the evening. Stay the night in Sault Ste. Marie.

Day 14

Head south of Sault Ste. Marie to **Les Cheneaux**, where boaters and fishermen are right at home among the area's more than 30 islands and countless channels on Lake Huron. This relaxing part of the U.P. is perfect for winding down at the end of the trip, especially with visits to **Cedarville**, **Hessel**, and **DeTour**. For some easy hiking and biking, **Drummond Island** is the place to do it. Otherwise, enjoy a slow pace for your final day in Michigan's Upper Peninsula before the hour drive to **St. Ignace** and back to the real world across the bridge.

▶ FOLLOWING THE LAKE SUPERIOR TRAIL

This trail features one of the most interesting aspects of Lake Superior: its natural history. The Lake Superior Trail is primarily concerned with Lake Superior's famously rugged shoreline, inland forests, and waterfalls. Lake Superior is unlike any of the other Great Lakes, not only because of its size, depth, temperature, and the ferocity of its water, but because its shoreline screams *wilderness*.

Grand Island National Recreation Area and Pictured Rocks National Park

Beginning in Munising, visit the Grand Island National Recreation Area, for some mild hiking or biking. Consider it a warm-up for the world-class hiking to come. From Munising, set out on one of the Upper Peninsula's finest hiking trails, which cut a path along Lake Superior into Pictured Rocks National Park. A good portion of the 90 miles of trails here are technically part of the North Country Trail. Backcountry campsites spaced between two and four miles apart mean you can spend several days walking and camping along the most stunning portion of Lake Superior shore. Look for seven named waterfalls,Munising, Bridalveil, Miners, Mosquito, Chapel, Spray, and Sable Falls, or hunt down Miner's Castle. The trails and campsites can get pretty busy during peak season, so plan accordingly.

Au Sable Point Light

You'll need a car to get to the next stop on the Lake Superior Trail, so you'll have to double back to Munising or have someone pick you up from inside the park (or in Grand Marais if you made it all the way across). Continuing east, the Au Sable Point Light. Parking is at the Lower Hurricane River Campground, and the lighthouse is a short hike along the lake. If you're there in the peak of the summer season, you can

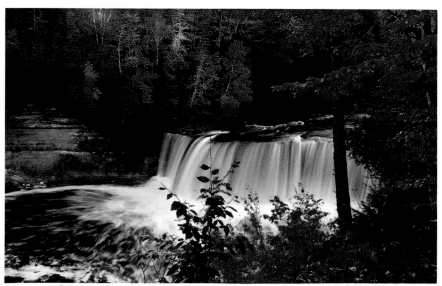

Tahquamenon Falls

take a guided tour. Otherwise, feel free to explore the site on your own. Stop at the **Crisp Point Lighthouse,** too.

Upper and Lower Tahquamenon Falls

Further along the trail is Tahquamenon Falls State Park. The Upper and Lower Tahquamenon Falls are located in Michigan's second-largest state park. One of the largest falls east of the Mississippi, the Upper Falls stretches more than 200 feet across and has an impressive drop of nearly 50 feet; the Lower Falls are comprised of five smaller, slightly less impressive drops. With plenty of **campsites** and some 40 miles of **hiking trails,** you can easily spend days exploring the park by foot before moving on.

Whitefish Point

At Whitefish Point, check out the **bird observatory,** the **Great Lakes Shipwreck Museum** and **Whitefish Point Light Station.** The 1849 light was one of the first on the lake. The museum offers public tours.

Other stops on the trail highlight the area's natural features—such as the mouth of the **Two-Hearted River**—along with a

As part of the Mackinac Historic State Parks, Old Mackinac Point Lighthouse is staffed by costumed interpreters.

smattering of lighthouses and other man-made destinations. For detailed information about the Lake Superior Trail, visit the **Eastern Upper Peninsula Nature Tourism Alliance** website (www.greatwaters.net).

▶ HISTORY COMES TO LIGHT

The U.P. has a wealth of natural attractions, but its history deserves a nod as well. Start in the Straits of Mackinac and follow the trail to the west, stopping at historic destinations and lighthouses along the way. This is one of the U.P.'s finest and most convenient trips.

Day 1

Mackinaw City is home to the impressive **Colonial Michilimackinac.** The reconstructed fort is staffed by costumed interpreters who demonstrate 1770s British life, including soldierly duties and domestic chores.

Spend several hours here forgetting the modern world. Don't miss the Redcoats' musket and cannon firing demonstrations. Break for lunch at the **Historic Depot Restaurant.**

While in Mackinaw City, stop by **Old Mackinac Point Lighthouse.** The late 19th-century lighthouse has since been restored and includes tours and hands-on exhibits. The inside of the lighthouse features period reconstructions—you can even try on a lighthouse keeper's clothing. Take a tour into the tower and lantern room for a birds-eye view of the Mackinac Bridge.

old cannon artillery at Fort Mackinac

Historic Mill Creek is home to an 18th-century water-powered sawmill. In addition to the sawmill, there's an Adventure Tour that makes Mill Creek an especially convenient stop for families with older children. We're talking a Forest Canopy Bridge in the treetops, a climbing wall, and a zip line. Stay the night at **Bell's Melody Motel** or, if you have kids, **Aqua-Grand Mackinaw Inn and Waterpark.**

Day 2

Moving on to Mackinac Island, the state historic park system continues with **Fort Mackinac.** The fort hosts interpreters who fire cannons and rifles, march in military formation, and generally showcase historic military life. Lunch at the fort's **Tea Room Restaurant** in the 1780 Officers' Stone Quarters.

Historic Downtown Mackinac Island contains many buildings that outline the island's history all the way back to fur trader John Jacob Astor. Packaged admission at reduced rates are available from Mackinac Historic State Parks.

By this point, you've spent all day exploring historic sites, and another one just might be the last thing you want. But the **Grand Hotel** is more than the island's most famous Victorian destination: it's a pretty comfy bed, too. Get a room for the night—it'll cost you a pretty penny, but it's worthwhile.

Day 3

Heading west of the Straits, make a stop at the **St. Helena Island Lighthouse.** Built in 1873, the 71-foot light is open to the public by appointment. You'll need a boat to get to the island, of course, but if you'd rather admire from a distance, you can see it from the shoreline in **Gros Cap,** some six miles west of St. Ignace.

Visit the museum and gift shop at the 1895 **Seul Choix Point Lighthouse,** located about 14 miles east of **Manistique.** The museum displays any number of interesting items—and, of course, a visit to the keeper's

Fayette Historic State Park is the site of a well-preserved ghost town.

dwelling and the top of the 80-foot tower is worthwhile.

The elegantly preserved ghost town of **Fayette Historic State Park** is one of the most diverting historic stops in the U.P. Plan on spending several hours here. Explore some of the trails and natural features of the park as well as the town.

At the end of the Stonington Peninsula and directly across Little Bay de Noc from Escanaba, the 1865 **Peninsula Point Lighthouse** has been reduced by fire—only the tower remains. It's well-preserved, though, and the hike to the top of the spiral stairway will give you a great view of Green Bay and the Bays de Noc.

In the evening, continue to Escanaba, where another historic hotel waits for the night. The **House of Ludington** was built

in the late 1800s, and still carries the impressions of yesteryear.

Day 4

After breakfast at the sublime **Swedish Pantry,** head to the **Delta County Historical Museum.** With displays about logging, shipping, railroads, and other aspects of local and U.P. history, the museum has preserved a chronicle of Delta County's past.

Finish the tour with a visit to the **Historic Sand Point Lighthouse,** located on the museum grounds. The keeper's house has been restored, giving you an intimate glimpse of the life and times of the keeper and his family. Take a climb to the top of the tower and have a look around before leaving for lunch in downtown **Escanaba** at **Hereford and Hops.**

▶ ECHOES OF THE *EDMUND FITZGERALD*

This tour follows the general route taken by the tragic freighter made famous by folk singer Gordon Lightfoot, as well as another ship, the *Arthur M. Anderson,* that was on the lake that fateful night. This trip is perfect for anyone with a passion or passing interest in maritime history.

Day 1

Begin in Marquette. The **Marquette Maritime Museum** is an excellent introduction to Lake Superior's maritime heritage. Next, tour the **Marquette Harbor Lighthouse,** which is part of the maritime museum. Tours of the building—which preserves the life of a keeper—and its grounds are offered by museum staff. Dinner tonight is at **Upfront and Company.** Book a room at the historic **Landmark Inn.**

Day 2

This morning, take M-28 east into **Munising,** where you have a choice of two boat tours. A glass-bottom boat **Shipwreck Tour** will take you on a two-hour boat ride through Munising Bay above a series of shipwrecks visible through the clear water. **Pictured Rocks Cruises** offers boat cruises along the stunning Pictured Rocks National Lakeshore. The cruise lasts three hours, and follows the sandstone cliffs, wave-carved formations, and sand beaches of the shoreline. Spend the evening exploring Munising. Have dinner at **Sydney's** and stay the night at **Sunset Motel on the Bay.**

Day 3

It's time to get another look at **Pictured Rocks National Lakeshore,** this time from land. Lace up your hiking boots and hit the trails that wind through the park. Try the hike from Munising Falls Interpretive Center to Miners Beach, or consider any one of several day hikes. Take County Road H-58 and Chapel Road to a trailhead that has short hikes to Mosquito Falls, Mosquito Beach, Chapel Falls, Chapel Rock, and Chapel Beach. Continue to Grand Marais for dinner (try the **Lake Superior Brewing Company**). Your room tonight is at the **Beach Park Motel.**

Day 4

In the morning, visit the **Grand Marais Maritime Museum.** Your next stop is the **Au Sable Point Lighthouse and Maritime Museum.** The 1874 light is open to the public for guided tours throughout the summer. Return to Grand Marais and spend the evening relaxing in town before spending a second night at your motel.

Sable Falls in the Pictured Rocks National Lakeshore

two freighters in the Soo Locks

Day 5

Follow M-77 south to M-28 west, then take M-123 north to **Tahquamenon Falls State Park.** The waterfalls here are stunning and there are several hiking trails. But don't linger too long—more maritime history waits at Whitefish Point. Visit the **Great Lakes Shipwreck Museum** and **Whitefish Point Light Station** to view a film about the mysterious sinking as well as a few items from the ship. Dine at the **Tahquamenon Falls Brewery and Pub** and stay the night at **Paradise Inn.**

Day 6

Head south along M-123 to M-28 and take the highway east to I-75 and Sault Ste. Marie. Explore the **Museum Ship Valley Camp,** a maritime museum housed in a historic 1917 steam-powered freighter. Exhibits include lifeboats from the *Edmund Fitzgerald* and other displays—including the ship itself. Explore the ship's engine room, pilot house, and other rooms. Save your appetite for a sunset dinner cruise with **Soo Locks Boat Tours and Dinner Cruises.** and an insider's look at the famous Soo Locks. Check in to the **Long Ships Motel** for the night.

Day 7

Complete the tour with a look at the Soo Locks from the other side at the **Soo Locks Visitor Center.** In addition to an informative 30-minute movie and displays about the history and construction of the locks, you can watch from viewing platforms as the impossibly large ships pass through the locks.

Visit **Travel Michigan's** website (www .michigan.org) for more details about the tour, contact information for each site, and an overview of how the route relates to the history of the *Edmund Fitzgerald.*

SHIPWRECK DIVES

When the weather is warmer, you can spend some time beneath the surface of the Great Lakes, diving among shipwrecks in a sport more common to ocean waters. Lake Superior has been known to harbor a surprising anger against several of the ships that have plied the Great Lakes shipping lanes throughout the years. Many of the wrecks are waiting beneath the surface at five underwater diving preserves.

Dive with scuba gear and full wetsuits (these waters are cold, especially well below the surface) at preserves in Alger, Whitefish Point, Marquette, Keweenaw, and the Straits of Mackinac. One of the finest is **Alger Underwater Preserve,** which features the wreckage of seven ships at depths ranging from 12 to 105 feet. The Straits of Mackinac Shipwreck Preserve has 15 wrecks, but they're spread farther apart than in Alger, and they tend to be deeper, too – some in excess of 200 feet below the surface.

THE STRAITS OF MACKINAC

The Straits of Mackinac have long separated the Yoopers from the Trolls. Yoopers get their nickname from the U.P. (say "U.P.-ers"), while "Trolls" is a good-natured name for Michiganders who live to the south, "under the bridge."

Five miles wide at their narrowest point, the Straits are largely responsible for the Upper Peninsula's isolation. Before the completion of the Mackinac Bridge in 1957, passenger cars waited in miles-long lines for a spot on one of the ferries that crisscrossed the Straits each day. Now, thanks to the bridge, the only ferries crissing or crossing are headed for Mackinac Island.

If the Mackinac Bridge is how tourists bypass the Straits, then Mackinac Island is why they come. Resting smack dab in the middle of the Straits, between Lake Michigan and Lake Huron, between the Upper and Lower Peninsulas, the island has been a favorite destination since it became Mackinac National Park in 1875—the United States' second national park, after Yellowstone. The park, which has since been transferred to state control, covers some 80 percent of the island.

Visitors to the island will notice a conspicuous lack of automobiles; they've been banned since the 1920s. As a result, Mackinac Island really does seem frozen *Somewhere in Time,* which just happens to be the name of a semifamous movie, starring Christopher Reeve and Jane Seymour, that was filmed on the island. The Victorian atmosphere draws families, romantics, and anyone looking for a good old-fashioned horse-and-buggy taxi ride.

© TRAVEL MICHIGAN

HIGHLIGHTS

◖ Fudge: Fudge wasn't invented on the island, but it has since become its most popular confection. But is it really all that good? Yoobetcha (page 31).

◖ Grand Hotel: The 1887 hotel is the most famous on the island, with 385 rooms and the world's longest front porch. Jane Seymour circa 1980 didn't hurt, either (page 31).

◖ Fort Mackinac: British and American troops fought over the fort during the War of 1812. Today, Fort Mackinac's costumed interpreters bring its glory days to life (page 32).

◖ Lilac Festival: Of all the times to visit Mackinac Island, this 10-day festival in early June is the best (page 34).

◖ Mackinac Bridge: Drive across Michigan's pride and joy, the five-mile long "Mighty Mac" suspension bridge or stop at Mackinac Bridge View Park to take pictures of this amazing feat of engineering (page 40).

◖ Colonial Michilimackinac State Park: The site of the original fort, built in 1715, is the location of a 50-year-long archaeological dig, summertime reenactments, and a big, wooden, stockaded replica fort (page 51).

LOOK FOR ◖ TO FIND RECOMMENDED SIGHTS, ACTIVITIES, DINING, AND LODGING.

Oh, and try not to be offended when you hear locals refer to you as a "Fudgie," probably under their breath, but usually in good humor. While fudge wasn't invented on Mackinac, the island has since become famous for it. Odds are you'll be buying at least a sliver of fudge while you're here, which is why residents have dubbed you and the millions of other visitors with the endearing nickname. Get used to it.

St. Ignace in the U.P. and Mackinaw City in the Lower Peninsula bookend the bridge and have carved out reputations worthy of the high traffic passing through. Stop in Mackinaw for the fudge, St. Ignace for the auto shows, and both for the history. Museums in each city interpret the region's distinct history from native peoples to today.

Travelers looking for a good base for hub-and-spoke day trips to other U.P. locations can take advantage of the area's copious lodging and restaurants. Of course, if you're coming to the Straits, try not to embarrass yourself: Regardless of how it's spelled, it's pronounced "MACK-i-*naw*," never "MACK-i-*nack*."

PLANNING YOUR TIME

Travelers coming north across the bridge have no choice but to pass through the cities on either end of the five-mile stretch. Sure, you may be on the way to Copper Harbor for some kayaking or driving west for Ironwood's downhill skiing, but it's worth your time to get off the highway and spend some time in the Straits.

Although two days will be enough time to see the best of the Straits, the region's natural

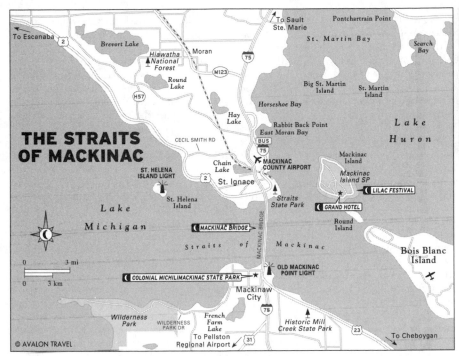

beauty and Mackinac Island's unique atmosphere often entice people to stay longer. Plan on spending a full day on the island. Lodging tends to be cheaper on the mainland, but if you don't mind digging a little deeper into the pocketbook, a stay on Mackinac (particularly at the costly Grand Hotel) is worth it. Mackinaw City and St. Ignace can both be tackled in a single day.

Summers are the busiest (and the best) season for visiting, and Mackinac Island draws the largest crowd, while St. Ignace tends to be best for outdoor activities. If you're interested in the area's history, you'll want to make an afternoon of Mackinaw City's historical sites.

HISTORY

Native Americans knew of the abundant hunting and fishing resources in the Straits area long before the French or British caught wind of them. Originally called Michilimackinac (Land of the Great Turtle), the island was considered sacred by the Anishinaabe-Ojibwe, who thought it was populated by the first people and home of the Great Spirit Gitchie Manitou. In addition to using the island as a tribal gathering place, Ojibwa, Ottawa, and other tribes hunted on Mackinac Island and neighboring Bois Blanc Island. They did a good job of it, too, trading some of their catch to tribes farther south in exchange for veggies and grain.

The French caught on before too long. The first Europeans to visit the area were French Jesuits who arrived in the 1670s to both take advantage of the fur trade and convert the Native Americans to Christianity. Jacques Marquette, a priest and an explorer, founded a town and mission at St. Ignace in 1671, naming it after the founder of the Jesuit Society, Saint Ignatius of Loyola. It was quickly followed by a trading post and later Fort Michilimackinac.

The British and French skirmished over the land, with the fort periodically changing hands between them until the Treaty of

Paris gave it—and all French land east of the Mississippi—to the British in 1763. Seven years later, the British commander abandoned the fort for a more easily defendable position on Mackinac Island, where the British would overstay their welcome even after the land was given to the United States after the American Revolution.

American soldiers took over Fort Mackinac in 1796 and managed to hang on to it for almost twenty years. Enter the War of 1812. The British retook the fort by sneaking onto the island at night and surprising the American soldiers, who turned over the fort without a fight. The British were in charge of things for two years, and the island saw plenty of fighting as Americans tried to retake the fort; in 1814 the Treaty of Ghent returned the island to the United States.

Throughout it all, the fur trade remained strong. Europeans traded canoe-loads of goods for pelts from beaver and other animals that had been trapped by the Native Americans. Mackinac Island became one of the country's most valuable trading posts during the 1820s, making way for America's first millionaire, John Jacob Astor. His American Fur Company was the leader in Mackinac's thriving fur trade. Eventually, the trade in overhunted furs gave way to commercial fishing.

After all the military skirmishes settled down, the island began earning a reputation as one of the Victorian era's most popular summer getaways. An American soldier wrote, "The air up here is so healthy, you have to go somewhere else to die." The vacation spot grew more and more famous, drawing vacationers from the Midwest and beyond. A growing interest during the second half of the 19th century culminated in the 1890s as lumbermen, railroad barons, and other wealthy Americans began building cottages on the island.

Cars were banned on the island in the 1920s, and things have more or less stayed the same ever since. There are somewhere around 600 horses on the island in the summertime, though that number dwindles to a few handfuls in the winter, when most horses stay on the mainland. The horses, carriages, carts, and well-kept Victorian homes and hotels combine to give Mackinac its timeless charm, and have made it one of the most popular vacation destinations in the Midwest.

THE FRENCH FUR TRADE

In the beginning, the economy of New France was driven in large part by the fur trade. European demand for animal pelts combined with the abundance of New World animal life – particularly the beaver – to create a nearly perfect arrangement of supply and demand. But the fur trade didn't just open up the cash flow – it helped spur Canada's westward expansion.

The fur trade was a highly regulated business at first, but before too long, illegal traders, known as *coureurs de bois* or "runners of the woods," traveled away from the settlements and deep into Native American territory, where they traded European goods like rifles, blankets, and fishing gear for canoe-loads of fur. The *coureurs* traded, worked, and lived among the native peoples, often marrying native women and integrating into their communities. They learned the skills necessary to survive in the wilderness and they adopted native clothing, food, and transportation.

Not much time passed before the French government realized that the unchecked illegal fur trade was bad for business, so they created a system of permits to separate legal *coureurs*, called *voyageurs*, from illegal ones. The *voyageurs* worked as laborers, interpreters, and guides, pushing deeper and deeper into the continent, taking New France with them.

It was the push by these fur traders that, along with Jesuit missionaries, greatly accelerated the expansion of France's territory; they've since become legendary folk heroes, particularly in French Canada.

Mackinac Island

During its peak tourism season, Mackinac Island draws some 15,000 people each day, and you'll want to prioritize it as one of the Upper Peninsula's quintessential destinations. There's plenty of history on this little island: Native Americans, French traders, and British soldiers eventually gave way to Victorian resorts, then everything sort of stopped. Fort Mackinac stands above a town that really does seem frozen in time.

Much of the downtown area can feel a little kitschy and is often packed with tourists, but there are plenty of treasures here for those willing to spend some time looking. Besides, most of the island—80 percent of it—is undeveloped state land, so if you need to get away from the crowds, there's plenty of open space available.

SIGHTS
Downtown
You'll be dropped off at the ferry docks. If you stick around for a while, you can get a taste of the day-to-day goings on of Mackinac Island's grunt work. At the Arnold Line Dock, you can sneak a peek at workers unloading carton after carton of vegetables from the ferry and reloading them by hand onto drays (wagons) for delivery to local restaurants. Even the UPS man does his route on bicycle, pulling a cart loaded with packages.

After spending a little time at the four blocks of shops and restaurants on Main Street, make the most of your visit by getting off the main drag. For an overview of what the island has to offer, take a carriage tour with **Mackinac Island Carriage Tours** (906/847-3307, www.mict.com, $23 adults, $9 children), located across from the Arnold Line ferry dock next to the chamber of commerce. The pleasant narrated tour takes about two hours, rambling along at a relaxing pace past the Grand Hotel, Arch Rock, Skull Cave, Fort Mackinac, and most of the island's other key sites. This locally owned business is the world's largest horse and

buggy livery, with more than 300 horses, mostly crosses of beefy Percherons, Belgians, and Clydesdales. Seasonal peak hours (mid-June through Labor Day) are from 9 A.M.–5 P.M., with slightly shorter hours from early May to mid-June and after Labor Day through the end of October, weather permitting.

One block inland from Main, some of Mackinac's original residences line up on **Market Street.** Much quieter than frenetic Main, Market has several interesting stops for visitors. The headquarters of the American Fur Company, John Jacob Astor's empire, is now the **Robert Stuart House Museum** (906/847-3307, May–Oct., $1.50–$3.50, free with Mackinac Island Carriage Tour ticket). The 1817 building retains many of its original furnishings, including fur company ledgers, fur weighing scales, and other artifacts.

A block west, knowledgeable interpreters demonstrate spinning at **Biddle House** and smithing at the **Benjamin Blacksmith Shop.** These and other historic buildings are part of the state park, and are included with the admission ticket to Fort Mackinac. They have shorter hours than the fort, though, open from 11 A.M.–6 P.M. For current information, stop by the park visitors center across from Marquette Park on Huron Street, or contact Mackinac State Historic Parks (231/436-4100, www.mackinacparks.com).

From Marquette Park, follow Fort Street up the hill to the **Governor's Residence** at the corner of Fort and East Bluff Road. The state purchased the "cottage" in the 1940s. It's the official residence of the state governor, though the amount of time actually spent here varies from governor to governor. The house is open for tours on Wednesday mornings.

Some of the island's more impressive "cottages" line up along **East Bluff.** Wander east from the governor's mansion to see some of these Victorian marvels. Happily, most survived the Depression era—when they could be purchased for pennies on the dollar, of course.

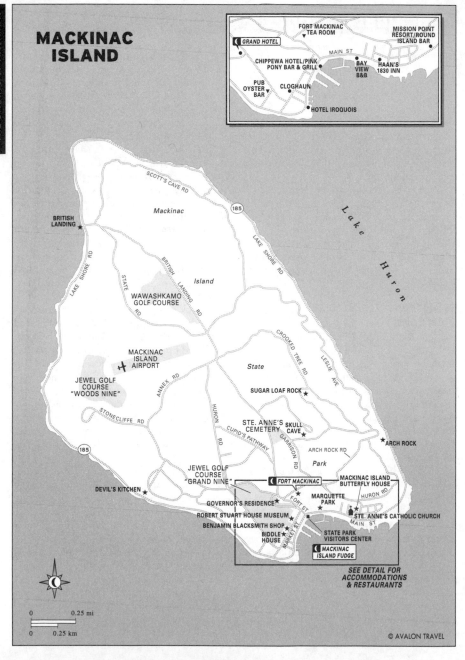

MACKINAC ISLAND

FORT MACKINAC
TEA ROOM

GRAND HOTEL

MISSION POINT
RESORT/ROUND
ISLAND BAR

MAIN ST

CHIPPEWA HOTEL/PINK
PONY BAR & GRILL

BAY
VIEW
B&B

HAAN'S
1830 INN

PUB
OYSTER
BAR

CLOGHAUN

HOTEL IROQUOIS

SCOTT'S CAVE RD

Mackinac

185

L a k e

BRITISH
LANDING

LAKE SHORE RD

H u r o n

LAKE SHORE RD

BRITISH LANDING RD

STATE

Island

RD

WAWASHKAMO
GOLF COURSE

CROOKED TREE RD

MACKINAC
ISLAND
AIRPORT

State

LESLIE AVE

JEWEL GOLF
COURSE
"WOODS NINE"

ANNEX RD

SUGAR LOAF ROCK

STONECLIFFE RD

HURON RD

STE. ANNE'S
CEMETERY

SKULL
CAVE

185

CUPID'S PATHWAY

GARRISON RD

ARCH ROCK RD

ARCH ROCK

JEWEL GOLF
COURSE
"GRAND NINE"

Park

DEVIL'S KITCHEN

FORT MACKINAC

MACKINAC ISLAND
BUTTERFLY HOUSE

GOVERNOR'S RESIDENCE

FORT ST

MARQUETTE
PARK

HURON RD

ROBERT STUART HOUSE MUSEUM

BENJAMIN BLACKSMITH SHOP

STE. ANNE'S CATHOLIC CHURCH

MARKET ST

MAIN ST

BIDDLE
HOUSE

STATE PARK
VISITORS CENTER

MACKINAC
ISLAND FUDGE

SEE DETAIL FOR
ACCOMMODATIONS
& RESTAURANTS

0   0.25 mi

0   0.25 km

© AVALON TRAVEL

Today, they're well cared for and worth more than $1 million. (And remember, most are summer homes only!)

Work your way down one of the sets of public steps to the lakefront, where Main Street becomes Huron Street. Continue your walk east, passing smaller but no less appealing cottages and homes. Many are skirted with geraniums and lilacs, the island's signature flowers.

Tucked away on McGulpin Street is the **Mackinac Island Butterfly House** (906/847-3972, www.originalbutterflyhouse.com, 10 A.M.–7 P.M., $7 adults, $4 children). Owner Doug Beardsley used to use his greenhouses to grow thousands of geraniums for the Grand Hotel and other clients. He relied on biodynamic growing methods, releasing beneficial insects to care for his plants instead of using chemical sprays. When economics made his small greenhouse less viable, he stuck with his insects. After hearing about a butterfly house in Europe, Beardsley added some different plants and began ordering pupae from around the world. Now hundreds of butterflies flutter by freely in his greenhouse/atrium, some nearly six inches long. You can observe them up close on walls and plants, or sit still long enough and they'll land on you.

(FUDGE

You knew it was coming. Sooner or later you'll succumb to Mackinac Island's famous fudge. A visitor treat since Victorian tourism days, the confection can be found in shops lining Main Street. Two of the oldest, **Murdick's** (906/847-3530, http://mackinac.murdicks.com) and **Ryba's** (906/847-3347, www.ryba.com), have multiple island locations. You can buy a sizeable slab to take or mail home, or just a small sliver to nibble. (A little goes a long way—it's very rich stuff, and you'll regret it later if you overdo it.)

Ste. Anne's Catholic Church

You'll find the oldest church on Mackinac Island near the butterfly house. It's worth a visit, even if it is a quick one, for its architecture and history. A testimony to the island's long history of Roman Catholicism (remember,

Jesuits were the first non-natives to set foot here), Ste. Anne's Church has been serving the community since the 1740s.

The church continues to serve the community: in addition to daily mass, you'll find a community square dance on the spacious front porch once a week. The basement hosts a small museum that preserves and interprets the religious history of Mackinac Island. A number of religious articles and church records (baptismal, marriage, and death records) date as far back as 1695.

Ste. Anne's gift shop has a number of Ste. Anne's souvenirs and collectibles, as well as the typical religious items. There isn't much else to do here, though if you're into old cemeteries you'll want to check out Ste. Anne's Cemetery, up the hill behind Fort Mackinac and on the way to Fort Holmes.

The museum and gift shop are open Monday–Friday 10 A.M.–4 P.M., Saturday until 6 P.M., and Sunday 9 A.M.–3:30 P.M. Call 906/847-3507 or visit www.steanneschurch.org for more information.

(Grand Hotel

The iconic Grand Hotel, a gracious edifice built on a truly grand scale, has become practically synonymous with Mackinac Island. It is one of the largest summer resorts in the world, operating from early April through late October. Its famous 660-foot-long covered front porch gets decked out each spring with 2,500 geraniums planted in seven tons of potting soil. Its 12 restaurants and bars serve as many as 4,000 meals a day. The resort's impeccable grounds offer guests every amenity, from saddle horses to designer golf to boccie ball to swimming in the outdoor pool made famous by 1940s actress Esther Williams, who filmed *This Time for Keeps* here.

But opulence is what the railroads and steamships were after when they formed a consortium and built the Grand Hotel in 1887, dragging construction materials across the frozen waters by horse and mule. The wealthiest of all Mackinac Island visitors stayed here, of course, high on the hill.

© BALTHAZAR KORAB / TRAVEL MICHIGAN

The Grand Hotel has been a Mackinac Island landmark since the late 1880s.

Yet unlike other turn-of-the-century resorts that burned to the ground or grew dog-eared and faded, the Grand Hotel has managed to maintain its grace and dignity over the years. It still hosts all manner of celebrities and politicians—five U.S. presidents to date—and still offers a sip of the Gilded Age with high tea in the parlor each afternoon and demitasse served after dinner each evening. Room rates still include a five-course dinner in the soaring main dining room, and jackets and ties or skirts or dresses are still the required attire after 6 P.M.

The Grand Hotel's time-capsule setting prompted director Jeannot Szwarc to choose it as the location for the 1980 film *Somewhere in Time*, starring Christopher Reeve, Jane Seymour, and Christopher Plummer. For whatever reason, the movie has developed a huge following; its fan club reunites at the hotel each year in late October.

While room rates can get outright absurd ($675-plus per night, with doubles starting at $450), they include breakfast and dinner, and perhaps can be considered a worthwhile splurge

if you like this kind of thing. A more affordable option is to stay just one night for the experience and then book a room at a cheaper on- or off-island lodging for the rest of your visit.

What the heck—take tea, loll in the beautifully landscaped pool, or dance to the swing orchestra in the Terrace Room. Nonguests can sneak a peek at the hotel's public areas and grounds for a mildly unreasonable $15 ($7.50 for children, free for those younger than five). It's needed to thin the sightseers more than anything. Highly recommended are a stroll through the grounds, filled with Victorian gardens—25,000 tulips in spring!—and a visit to the snazzy Cupola Bar, with views halfway to Wisconsin.

Each of the 385 rooms is decorated differently, and, as of 2007 (and for the first time in more than 120 years), the entire hotel is air-conditioned. For availability and rates, contact the **Grand Hotel** (800/334-7263, www.grand hotel.com).

🌙 Fort Mackinac

Located at the crest of the bluff, whitewashed Fort Mackinac is worth a visit for the views alone, presiding over—as forts do—the downtown, the marina, and Lake Huron. But there's also plenty to see at this military outpost, which the British and Americans haggled over for nearly 40 years.

Along with peering over the parapets, you can wander in and out of 14 buildings within the fort. The barracks, officers' quarters, post hospital, and other buildings are filled with interpretive displays and decorated in period style. Costumed guides lead all sorts of reenactments, including musket firing and cannon salutes. A short audiovisual presentation, "The Heritage of Mackinac," does a good job of presenting basic history.

Admission to the fort is $10 adults, $6.25 children 5–17, and also includes admission to several other historic buildings on the island. If you're planning on visiting Colonial Michilimackinac, Old Mackinac Point Lighthouse or Historic Mill Creek State Park on the mainland, the combination ticket is

SOMEWHERE IN TIME

Beyond fantasy. Beyond obsession. Beyond time itself . . . he will find her.

Somewhere in Time

Your reaction to the tagline for *Somewhere in Time*, a 1980 movie starring Christopher Reeve and Jane Seymour and filmed at the Grand Hotel, is a pretty good indication of whether you'll love or hate the movie. If you find it hopelessly romantic, a bit old-fashioned, and somewhat endearing – go rent the movie now. But if you thought it was too sweet and you shuddered a little, it isn't worth your time.

The film tells the story of Richard Collier, a writer who, after a strange encounter with an old woman who pleads, "Come back to me," tries to figure out who she was. While staying at the Grand Hotel, he learns she was a turn-of-the-century actress named Elise McKenna,

and he becomes infatuated with her. He manages to travel back in time, where (when?) he meets her and the two fall in love. But will Richard be able to stay in 1912?

Mackinac Island's Victorian setting, and in particular the Grand Hotel, made it a natural location for the film. Unfortunately, when the movie was released it was much maligned by film critics, and its only Oscar nod was for Best Costume Design. Still, it's found a passionate following among people who are enthralled by its story of timeless love and old-fashioned values. In fact, the *Somewhere in Time* fan club has met at the Grand Hotel for a weekend each October since 1991.

It really is a decent, if affected, movie that's perfect for Valentine's Day or a first date, and it's a great way to relive your Grand Hotel stay – or to peek inside if you never make it there in person.

---

your best deal, giving you seven-day admission to three of the four parks for $22 adults, $13.50 children 5–17. The park is open early May–mid-October, with different times for each season: 9 A.M.–4:30 P.M. May 6–June 6, 9:30 A.M.–6 P.M. June 7–August 23 and 9:30 A.M.–4:30 P.M. August 24–October 12.

For information, stop by the park visitors center across from Marquette Park on Huron Street, or contact **Mackinac State Historic Parks** (231/436-4100, www.mackinacparks.com).

The Park

Too often overshadowed by other visitor attractions, Mackinac Island's natural history has drawn scientific interest for nearly 200 years. In the early 19th century, botanists discovered several species completely new to science, including the dwarf lake iris, still found only in the Straits of Mackinac region.

The island's landscape is made up of fields, meadows, marshes, coastline, swamps, bogs, and boreal forest. Early scientists marveled at the island's distinctive geography, especially the brecciated limestone that has been

sculpted by eons of wind and waves. The result is some dramatic rock formations, like the giant inland slab of limestone called **Sugar Loaf Rock,** the lakeside caves of **Devil's Kitchen,** and impressive **Arch Rock,** which rises nearly 150 feet above the eastern shore and spans some 50 feet.

In recognition of the park's distinctive "natural curiosities" and growing tourism, the U.S. government created Mackinac National Park in 1875—following Yellowstone as the country's second national park. Twenty years later, it was returned to Michigan and became Mackinac Island State Park, Michigan's first state park.

Walk, run, or bike, but make sure you get out of downtown to really see Mackinac Island. You'll be surprised how quickly you can leave any crowds behind as you set out on the paved eight-mile path that circles the island. The trail never wanders far from the pleasant shoreline and passes many of the island's natural features, which are well marked. Traveling clockwise, the first you'll reach is Devil's Kitchen; heading in the opposite direction you'll arrive

THE STRAITS OF MACKINAC

© TRAVEL MICHIGAN

Arch Rock is one of the most immediately recognizable landmarks in Mackinac Island State Park.

first at Arch Rock, the most dramatic of all Mackinac limestone oddities.

About halfway around, on the island's northwestern side, lies **British Landing,** where British soldiers sneaked onto the island in 1812. They hiked across Mackinac's interior, totally surprising the American garrison stationed at the fort (and apparently looking the other way), and recaptured the island. There's a small **nature center** here, staffed in summer months by a helpful naturalist. Hike the short **nature trail,** which has several interpretive signs as it weaves up a bluff.

British Landing is also a good spot from which to head inland and explore the island's interior. British Landing Road bisects the island and links up with Garrison Road near **Skull Cave,** leading to the fort. It's a hilly, three-mile trip from shore to shore. British Landing Road is considered a "major road" by Mackinac standards, meaning you'll have to share it with carriages.

Lighthouses

The **Round Island Lighthouse** was built in 1895 to guide ships among the shoals and channels between Mackinac Island and uninhabited Round Island, where it was built. Though unmanned, the Round Island light still guides ships through the Straits today. Your best bet to see it is the eastbound lighthouse cruise offered out of Mackinaw City by Shepler's Ferry (see *Mackinac City* in this chapter).

ENTERTAINMENT

For the best of the island's **live music,** you'll want to check out the Grand Hotel, which offers plenty of live entertainment nightly. Catch live music at the Jockey Club at the Grand Strand, listen to the Grand Hotel Orchestra in the Terrace Room, or hear live bands at the Gate House. You can also find live entertainment at the Cupola Bar and at Woods. You'll find acoustic music at Mission Point Resort's Round Island Bar and Grill. Downtown, Patrick Sinclair's Irish Pub entertains crowds with live Irish music, DJs, karaoke, and '70s night.

It's easy to understand why **pub crawls** are so popular on the island—it's hard to get a drunk driving infraction if no one can drive. Free from having to give up their keys, visitors participate in designated pub crawls. Local retailers join in the game, too, selling t-shirts commemorating the experience (you might not remember it otherwise). Take it easy and finish a crawl over the course of a few nights.

FESTIVALS AND EVENTS
◖ Lilac Festival

For 10 days in early June, Mackinac Island celebrates the Mackinac Island Lilac Festival. During the festival, visitors can enjoy live music; A Taste of Mackinac, which showcases the talents of local chefs; and the Feast of Epona, the Roman and Celtic goddess of horses. The event culminates with the Grand Parade, one of North America's only all–hitch horse parades. Other events include a dog and pony show, the Blessing of the Animals, and a 10K run. It's not exactly Labor Day, but the

10 days get pretty busy. Still, this is Mackinac at its best.

Other Festivals

August is a big month for Mackinac Island. Early in the month, the **Mackinac Island Horse Show** celebrates the island's love of all things equestrian with events like showmanship and grooming, English and Western equestrian, and barrel racing. The **Mackinac Island Music Festival** is held annually toward the end of August, featuring a wide variety of live musical performances. During the **Mackinac Island Fudge Festival,** late in the month, the Fudgies finally get their due as the entire island turns out to celebrate the estimated 10,000 pounds of fudge that get made each season.

SUMMER SPORTS AND RECREATION
Trails

At last count, Mackinac Island State Park had more than 2,250 acres with over 70 miles of trails and footpaths, suitable for exploration on bike or foot. Pick up a free *Mackinac Island Map,* available all over town, and venture off. The map marks the location of old cemeteries, rock formations, and such, but it's even more appealing to just explore the smaller trails on your own and discover pretty, peaceful Mackinac. Everything's well marked, and you can't really get lost anyway—you're on a small island, after all.

For walking or biking tours, join **Doc Crain** as he shares local legends on the way through the island's boreal forest trails. Hiking tours meet Monday–Saturday at 2 P.M. at the Father Marquette Statue, while biking tours meet at Mackinac Wheels Monday–Saturday at 10 A.M. Friday and Saturday sunset bike tours depart at 7 P.M. Doc won't charge you a fee for the tours, but be generous and leave him a good-sized tip.

Runners can participate in the **Lilac Festival 10K** in early June, the **Mackinac Island Eight Mile** in September, or October's **Great Turtle Half Marathon.**

There are plenty of shops that offer hourly **bicycle rentals** on any variety of bike: single speeds, mountain bikes, bikes for children, tagalongs, buggies, or tandems for the hopeless romantic in all of us. Most rentals can be had for about $6/hour or $30/day. Equipment varies, so look before you pay. If you plan to do much cycling, you'll be happier bringing your own bike, since you can transport it on the ferry for about $7.50 round-trip. You'll want a hybrid or mountain bike to negotiate most interior trails.

On the Water

Open water sailing excursions are available on the **Mackinaw Breeze** (906/847-8669, www .mackinawbreeze.com, $30 adults, $15 children eight and younger), a custom-built catamaran that can accommodate up to 26 passengers. The most typical (and affordable) trips last about an hour and a half and feature as many views—including lighthouses, surrounding islands, and Arch Rock—as wind conditions allow. Contact Mackinaw Breeze for information about chartering half- and full-day cruises.

Mackinac Island's beautiful coastline is perfect for relaxation and picnicking, and often irresistibly tempting for those looking to take a dip, especially children. The east side of the island is best for the little ones, but be warned: the rocky shores require swimming shoes or sandals and there are no lifeguards, so swim at your own risk. Besides, the water can be pretty chilly even late in the season.

Of course, you can always bring a rod and reel and fish off the rocks on Mackinac Island's shore, but the lure of the Great Lakes makes deep-water **fishing** one of the island's most popular summer activities. There are no charter services based on the island itself, but, as with **parasailing,** a few boats dock here.

Horses

With more than 600 horses calling the island their summertime home, you won't be able to turn a corner without bumping noses with these beautiful animals. But to be honest, who would want it otherwise? It isn't every day you get the chance to ride a carriage down Main Street or take a buggy on an island circuit.

Carriage tours can be had with the island's largest livery, Mackinac Island Carriage Tours, which has been operating since 1869. You'll be able to take the reins during a drive-it-yourself buggy tour from **Jack's Livery Stable** (906/847-3391, www.jackslivery stable.com, $54/hour for two passengers, $66/hour for four passengers, May–Oct.). After gauging your skill with horses, one of the livery's professionals will give you driving instructions before setting you loose on the town with a free map. At **Cindy's Riding Stable** (906/847-3572, www.cindysridingstable.com, $35/hour, May–Oct.), you can take one of their 30-plus saddle horses into the island on your own.

Golf

In addition to a pleasant afternoon on the links, golfing Mackinac brings with it a cheap thrill: golf carts are the only powered vehicles allowed on the island. So while other visitors are struggling to rein in an unruly horse or hoofing it across the island, you'll be smoking a cigar as you drive something that actually has an engine in it.

Mackinac is the proud home of the oldest continuously played golf course in Michigan, **Wawashkamo** (906/847-3871, www.wawash kamo.com). Vacationers have been golfing the course's nine holes since 1898, and the second set of tee placements makes it possible to play a full 18 holes on rough natural terrain, which includes traditionally Scottish thistle and heather. Wawashkamo, which means "walk a crooked trail," is built on a former War of 1812 battlefield, adding to its historic appeal. Plan on paying $65 for 18 holes and a cart, $50 if you leave the wheels behind. Nine holes are $45 with cart, $35 without.

The Grand Hotel's 18 holes, known as **The Jewel** (906/847-3331, www.grandhotel.com), consists of two nine-hole courses—the Grand Nine, across the street from the hotel, and the Woods Nine in the island's interior. Horse-

drawn transportation is provided between the two courses. Eighteen holes cost hotel guests $85 ($115 for nonguests) and nine holes will run guests $49 (nonguests pay $59).

Mission Point Resort presents **The Greens at Mackinac** (906/847-3312, www.mission point.com), 18 holes of executive putting greens where even the most experienced putters can hone their skills or try out the merchandise from the pro shop selection of putters.

Other Activities

Three sets of **tennis courts** are available on Mackinac Island—there are public courts behind Fort Mackinac, and courts are available to guests at the Grand Hotel and Mission Point Resort.

WINTER SPORTS AND RECREATION
Ski and Snowshoe Trails

The island is a bit trickier to get to once the Straits freeze over, but for those willing to go through the extra effort, a winter paradise awaits. The 70-plus miles of trails that bring out the hikers, bikers, and runners in summertime are converted to cross-country ski and snowshoe trails. Mackinac Island Ski Club volunteers team up with the state park to maintain a series of groomed winter trails. As an added bonus, the island is considerably less crowded (read: not at all crowded), so it'll feel like you have the place to yourself.

The Balsam Shop (906/847-3591, www .balsamshop.com) is open winter weekends and holidays for cross-country ski and snowshoe rentals. Since most of the island shuts down well before the snows come, winter lodging is limited. Check out **Bogan Lane Inn** (906/847-3439, www.boganlaneinn.com, $85–120), **Pontiac Lodge** (906/847-3364, www.pontiac lodge.com, $85–350), or **Harbor Place Studio Suites** (800/626-6304, www.harborplace studiosuites.com, $75–200) for rooms.

Horse-drawn taxis (bundle up!) are available from Mackinac Island Carriage Tours (906/847-3323, www.mict.com) with reservations. **Mackinac Island Airport** is the only way on and off the island once the ferries stop running.

ACCOMMODATIONS

Along with the **Grand Hotel,** there are many other grand places to stay on Mackinac Island. Yes, rates can be high, and as you'll see below, the range of prices can be astoundingly wide even within one particular property. (You'll pay dearly for a water view.) But don't dismiss staying on Mackinac; you can find reasonable rates at smaller B&Bs and apartments, the latter of which often have good deals for week-long stays. The options below tip both ends of the scale. For information on more island accommodations, including rates and photos, visit www.mackinacisland.org.

Unfortunately, there is no camping on Mackinac Island.

Hotels and Motels

The **Chippewa Hotel** (800/241-3341, www .chippewahotel.com, $95–545) is a venerable old Mackinac hotel that had a $3 million renovation several years back. The result is a classy and comfortable place to stay, with a location at the heart of the island, on Main Street, overlooking the marina. The 24-person lakeside hot tub alone may be worth the stay.

Two separate buildings—Cudahy Manor and the Summer House—make up the **Inn at Stonecliffe** (906/847-3355, www.theinnat stonecliffe.com, May–Oct., $85–275 Cudahy Manor, $195–385 Summer House). More than 100 years old, the inn has been completely remodeled and restored. The Cudahy Manor is more B&B than hotel, a turn-of-the-century Tudor manor with 16 rooms, the more expensive of which have views of the Straits of Mackinac and the bridge. The Summer House has 33 studio suites.

One of the island's most striking buildings, the **Hotel Iroquois** (906/847-3321, www .iroquoishotel.com, $205–445 rooms, $375– 985 suites), was built in 1900 as a home for the island blacksmith. It's since been converted into a 46-room hotel with a fine dining restaurant ($28–40 entrées) and a private sunbathing deck. Hotel Iroquois is a Condé Nast Traveler Gold List hotel and earned a perfect score for its location. Still, with suite rates a couple hundred dollars more expensive than even the Grand Hotel's luxury rooms, you'll be better off sticking with Hotel Iroquois's competitively priced regular rooms.

Bed-and-Breakfasts

Cloghaun (906/847-3885, www.cloghaun.com, May–Oct., $105–190 high season, $75–155 off season, including breakfast) was built in 1884 by Thomas and Bridgette Donnelly, who left their homeland during the Irish Potato Famine and followed a relative to Mackinac Island. Today, this grand Victorian (it's pronounced CLA-hahn) with large grounds is still owned by their descendents. It's located on Market Street, next to some of the island's historic attractions and just one block from Main. Eight rooms have private baths; two others share.

Below East Bluff near Ste. Anne's Church, **Haan's 1830 Inn** (906/847-6244, www .mackinac.com/haans, May 15–Oct. 11, $58–195) is a Greek Revival built by Colonel Preston, one of the last officers to preside over Fort Mackinac. Just try to drag yourself out of the wicker chairs on the big front porch. Four of the seven rooms have private baths; one suite includes a full kitchen.

Only a five or ten minute walk from the ferry docks, **Bay View Bed & Breakfast** (906/847-3295, www.mackinacbayview.com, May–Oct., $95–425) has exactly that: a great view of the bay. If you spend a little extra cash for a room with a view, you'll find yourself overlooking the yacht harbor. Breakfast is served on the veranda; make sure you try the custom Bay View Blend Coffee.

Other Lodging

◖ Mission Point Resort (6633 Main St., 906/847-3312, www.missionpoint.com) may have the island's very best location, spread across 18 acres at the island's southeastern tip. Though not Victorian era—it was built in the 1950s by the Moral Re-Armament movement, a post–World War II patriotic group—the sprawling, bright-white resort is attractive and well-kept, with beautiful lawns lined with Adirondack chairs. Amenities include an outdoor pool, tennis and volleyball courts, and loads of kids' activities.

In addition to the professional putting green, bicycle rentals, lawn bowling, croquet, tennis, and professional spa, Mission Point Resort offers hayrides around Mackinac Island. The resort's Tower Museum, eight stories up, provides a striking panoramic view of the island and the Straits. Interpretive displays on each floor present fascinating looks at topics such as maritime shipping history, Native American heritage, and building the Mackinac Bridge.

You'll have your choice of four restaurants while at the resort. Lakeside Marketplace can provide you with a picnic lunch on your way out to explore the island, while the Epicurean is the place for elegant dining and an impressive selection of wines. Rooms start at $149–309, but you can expect them to skyrocket at the height of summer.

FOOD

One of the finest dining deals on the island is the **Fort Mackinac Tea Room** (906/847-3331, www.grandhotel.com), located in the lower level of the Officer's Stone Quarters within the fort itself. Surrounded by thick masonry walls, the tearoom serves up both a great atmosphere and great food prepared by Grand Hotel chefs. Moderately priced entrées can climb into the $30 range, but good soups, salads, and sandwiches can be had for around $10. Opt for a spot on the terrace since the high setting is outstanding, and forts weren't exactly designed for expansive views.

Everyone has to hit the **((Pink Pony Bar & Grill** (906/847-3341, www.chippewahotel .com) at least sometime during a Mackinac visit. Located in the Chippewa Hotel, overlooking the marina, this is *the* party place following the famed Chicago-to-Mac yacht race. The food's great, too, with good burgers, whitefish sandwiches and such on the lunch menu, and steaks, seafood, and ribs for dinner.

MACKINAC ISLAND FUDGE

Mackinac's most famous sweet wasn't invented on the island at all. No one is really sure exactly how it happened, but it's commonly accepted that the sugary goodness was the result of a screwed up, or "fudged," batch of caramels.

Fudge was first made on the island in the late 1800s by Newton Jerome "Rome" Murdick, who began selling the candy to resorters who came to the island and the just-opened Grand Hotel. Now in the fifth generation of the family, Murdick's Fudge is still selling the stuff on the island, in Mackinaw City, and at a few other locations. Rome Murdick began making his fudge on a marble slab, which gave summer tourists incredible fudge, and a show to boot.

Of course, Murdick's isn't the only place that sells fudge. It isn't even the only place that sells *great* fudge. There are currently 15 fudge shops on Mackinac Island, and each one is worth a visit (though if you visit all of them, you'll end up with the stomachache of a lifetime).

Before long, Mackinac earned a reputation. It wouldn't be fair to say that people come for the fudge, but while they're here they buy it by the pound – no, by the *ton*. The tourists' relentless appetite for fudge has earned them the nickname "Fudgies."

Dinner entrées average around $23. Outdoor patio dining is available in season.

The **Round Island Bar and Grill** (906/847-3312, www.missionpoint.com, 7 A.M.–9 P.M.) at Mission Point Resort, has sandwiches and salads in a casual setting overlooking the Straits and neighboring Round Island. Sample some of Michigan's best regional beers and wines.

The island's best fine dining is found at the high-end hotels and resorts. Try the **1852 Grill Room** at the Island House Hotel (906/847-3347, www.theislandhouse.com), the Hotel Iroquois's **Carriage House Dining Room**

(906/847-3321, www.iroquoishotel.com), and the Grand Hotel's **Main Dining Room** and **Woods Restaurant** (906/847-3331, www.grandhotel.com).

INFORMATION

For help with accommodations and other information ahead of time, contact the **Mackinac Island Chamber of Commerce & Tourism Bureau** (877/847-0086, www.mackinacisland.org). You can also get a visitors guide with maps of the state park at the **Mackinac Island State Park Visitor Center,** located on Main Street across from the island's Marquette Park and open from early May to mid-October.

GETTING THERE AND AROUND

Don't even think about bringing a car. The only motorized transportation allowed on the island are golf carts and a few public service vehicles—a fire truck, an ambulance, and the like. Of course,

Since the 1920s, cars have been banned on Mackinac Island. Instead, horses are the transportation of choice.

© TERRY W. PHIPPS/MACKINAC ISLAND TOURISM BUREAU

you're welcome to drive to Mackinaw City or St. Ignace and catch a ferry to the island, but you'll have to leave your car behind.

Boat

Three ferry lines offer service to Mackinac Island: **Arnold Transit Company** (906/847-3351, www.arnoldline.com, $21 adults, $10.50 children 5–12), **Shepler's Mackinac Island Ferry** (231/436-5023, www.sheplersferry.com, $20 adults, $10 children 5–12), and the **Star Line** (800/638-9892, www.mackinawferry.com, $22 adults, $11 children 5–12). Ferries run, in general, from Mackinaw City between May and October, and from St. Ignace April through November. Free parking is available for day-trippers; overnight guests will have to pay.

If you're sailing your own boat, you can contact the **Mackinac Island State Harbor** (906/847-3561, www.michigan.gov/dnr) for reservations up to six months in advance of your stay. The marina's 76 slips are available from late May to mid-September. You can contact the marina on radio channel 9. It's located at 45° 50.40 N, 84° 36.42 W.

Air

Mackinac Island Airport (MCD) is the only way to get to the island in the winter, and it's always an option in the summer, too. Year-round flights are available from St. Ignace through Great Lakes Air (906/643-7165, www.greatlakesair.net, $25 adults, $17.50 children under 12) by reservation only. Northwest Airlines offers flights in season from Pellston Regional Airport (PLN), south of Mackinaw City. Horse-drawn taxi service is available from the airport to your hotel; contact **Mackinac Island Carriage Tours** (906/847-3323, www.mict.com).

Getting Around

While on the island, horses are certainly the most unique means of getting around. Taxis can be hired at **Mackinac Island Carriage Tours** (906/847-3323, www.mict.com). If you enjoy walking and hiking, you can get around Mackinac Island on foot; the island is about eight miles in circumference. Mackinac is a wonderful place for casual strolls and all-day hikes.

The island is also a great place to cycle. **Mackinac Island Bike Shop** (906/847-6337, www.mackinacislandbikes.com) at the Lake View Hotel has an excellent selection. For single and double strollers, as well as electric wheelchairs, stop by **Ryba's Bicycle Rentals** (906/847-3208, www.rybabikes.com). There are a number of other bicycle rentals on the island, most of which offer competitive prices, or you can bring your own across on the ferry for about $7.50.

St. Ignace

St. Ignace is directly at the north end of the Mackinac Bridge, and is worthwhile for both its history and its off-island lodging. It's made a reputation of its own: with an annual auto show and plenty of tourist draws, this city (the first off the bridge) is often a traveler's introduction to the Upper Peninsula. It doesn't have all the glam of Mackinac Island's resorts, but it doesn't have as much of an overwhelmingly touristy feel as Mackinaw City either. Good news for campers, hikers, and the like: its access to Hiawatha National Forest makes St. Ignace the Strait's best area for out-of-doors activity.

SIGHTS
◖ Mackinac Bridge
You can't miss it: it's that massive bridge. Its total length is 26,372 feet. At midspan, the roadway is 200 feet above water. It has 42,000 miles of wire in the main cables. It's big.

Known as "Mighty Mac" or simply "The Bridge," this is Michigan's pride and joy. Stretching across nearly five miles of open water, Mighty Mac has the third longest total suspension of any bridge in the world, and ranks as number one in the Western Hemisphere. There are other ways of measuring suspension—the length of the main span between towers, for example—that put the Bridge farther down the list, but try telling that to a Michigander.

There are good photo spots on either end of the bridge; just find a bit of St. Ignace's southern shore and you can't miss it (try Straits State Park or Mackinac Bridge View Park just west of the toll plaza). Driving the bridge is different from looking at it, and if you can manage the approximately 10-minute-long and oddly exciting drive you should do it. If you can't bring yourself to stay behind the wheel—and a lot of people can't—bridge personnel will drive your car across while you lie down in the back seat with your eyes closed. Pedestrians, bicyclists, and snowmobilers aren't permitted to cross—transportation is provided for a fee of $2/person, including a bike, and $10 for a snowmobile and driver.

Father Marquette National Memorial and New France Discovery Center
High above the open Straits of Mackinac, this largely open-air site commemorates French explorer and Jesuit missionary Jacques Marquette. In the 1660s and 1670s, Marquette paddled through the Great Lakes, founding dozens of cities—including Sault Ste. Marie and St. Ignace—along the way. Next, Marquette linked up with Louis Jolliet and paddled another several thousand miles to become the first European explorer of the Mississippi.

Walking trails feature interpretive signs that discuss Marquette's Great Lakes travels and the impact the area's geography had on settlement. Little emphasis is given to the effect Marquette's missionary work had on Native Americans, thousands of whom Marquette converted to Christianity. A small museum on site burned down several years ago, but it's still worth a visit for the National Memorial, the outdoor trail, and the panoramic view of the Mackinac Bridge.

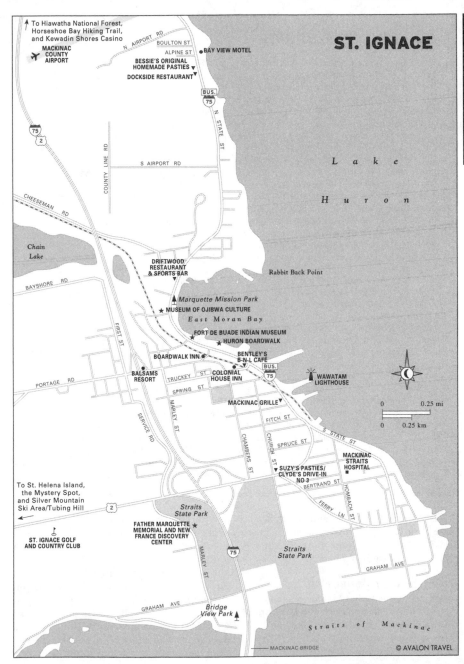

THE STRAITS OF MACKINAC

ST. IGNACE

To Hiawatha National Forest, Horseshoe Bay Hiking Trail, and Kewadin Shores Casino

MACKINAC COUNTY AIRPORT

N AIRPORT RD
BOULTON ST
ALPINE ST
BAY VIEW MOTEL
BESSIE'S ORIGINAL HOMEMADE PASTIES
DOCKSIDE RESTAURANT

BUS. 75

N STATE ST

75
2

COUNTY LINE RD
S AIRPORT RD

CHEESEMAN RD

Lake
Huron

Chain Lake

DRIFTWOOD RESTAURANT & SPORTS BAR

BAYSHORE RD

Rabbit Back Point

Marquette Mission Park
MUSEUM OF OJIBWA CULTURE
East Moran Bay

FORT DE BUADE INDIAN MUSEUM
HURON BOARDWALK

FIRST ST

BOARDWALK INN
BENTLEY'S B-N-L CAFE
BUS. 75

BALSAMS RESORT
PORTAGE RD
TRUCKEY ST
COLONIAL HOUSE INN
SPRING ST

WAWATAM LIGHTHOUSE

MARLEY ST
SERVICE RD

MACKINAC GRILLE

FITCH ST

0   0.25 mi
0   0.25 km

CHURCH ST
SPRUCE ST

CHAMBERS ST

S STATE ST

MACKINAC STRAITS HOSPITAL

SUZY'S PASTIES/ CLYDE'S DRIVE-IN NO 3
BERTRAND ST

To St. Helena Island, the Mystery Spot, and Silver Mountain Ski Area/Tubing Hill

2

ST. IGNACE GOLF AND COUNTRY CLUB

Straits State Park

FATHER MARQUETTE MEMORIAL AND NEW FRANCE DISCOVERY CENTER

FERRY LN
HOMBACH ST

75

Straits State Park

MARLEY ST

GRAHAM AVE

GRAHAM AVE

Bridge View Park

Straits of Mackinac

MACKINAC BRIDGE

© AVALON TRAVEL

BUILDING THE BRIDGE

It was an impossible dream, but one that had been kept alive since 1884, when a story in the *Grand Traverse Herald* reported that ferry service had failed as a means of traversing the Straits. The only way, it said, was by a tunnel or a bridge.

Since the beginning, Michigan had been cut in two by the Straits of Mackinac – one third, isolated and rugged, to the north; two thirds below. As early as 1897 and as late as the 1970s, there was talk – serious talk – of the Upper Peninsula seceding from Michigan and forming its own state: The Superior State. It seems that the physical separation led to an ideological separation; even today, many Yoopers are Yoopers first and Michiganders second. The Straits were more than a pain to get across, with ferry lines stretching for miles. They were a problem.

After years of planning and failure to get financial backing, bridge construction officially began in May 1954. At the time, it was the biggest bridge construction fleet ever assembled, and when the bridge was finally finished and open to traffic in 1957, designer David B. Steinman wrote that "the people of Michigan built the world's greatest bridge."

"They built it in the face of discouragement," he wrote, "of faintheartedness on the part of many of their leaders, of warnings that the rocks in the Straits were too soft, the ice too thick, the winds too strong, the rates of interest on the bonds too high, and the whole concept too big." It wasn't too big, but it wasn't easy either. It took three years of construction and $99 million dollars, and it regrettably cost five men their lives: Frank Pepper, James R. LeSarge, Albert Abbot, Jack C. Baker, and Robert Koppen. It's a steep cost for one of the world's finest engineering marvels.

"Mighty Mac" is five miles long, with a center span between the main towers of 3,800 feet. The main towers stand 552 feet above the water; the roadway itself is some 200 feet up. It weighs 1,024,500 pounds, has 4,851,700 steel rivets and 1,016,600 steel bolts, and can withstand winds up to an amazing 600 miles per hour. The suspended bridge is capable of moving as much as 35 feet east-to-west in high winds, but they shut the roadways down long before the swaying reaches that point.

The cost of operating and maintaining the bridge is taken from the few bucks you'll pay as a crossing toll, and the maintenance it takes to keep a more-than 50 year old bridge safe for traffic is a staggering and unending job. But it's worth it – as frightening as it can be to drive across the bridge (it bows visibly in the wind, and you're 200 feet high), it's safe.

Michiganders are proud of their bridge, and they should be. On the down side, it does mean that you'll be shelling out obscene amounts of money for a room with a bridge view, but on the up side – look at the thing. It's gorgeous. And it's convenient, too. Without it, travelers from the south would be waiting in an hours-long queue for the ferries; with it, access to the entire Upper Peninsula is as easy as keeping your eyes on the road and your hands on the wheel.

The Memorial is on the grounds of Straits State Park (906/643-8620, Memorial Day–mid-Sept.), west of I-75 and south of U.S. 2. A park sticker is required for entry.

Downtown St. Ignace

In contrast to the Father Marquette memorial, the **Marquette Mission Park and Museum of Ojibwa Culture** (500 N. State St., 906/643-9161, www.stignace.com, $2 adults, $1 children, $5 families) tells the story of the Ojibwa

and the effect the European explorers had on their culture. The museum is also the presumed site of Father Marquette's grave and the site of his Jesuit mission.

Displays housed in a former Catholic church include artifacts from archaeological digs on the grounds (some dating to 6000 B.C.), explanations of how the Ojibwa adapted and survived in the area's often harsh climate, and a discussion of how they allied with the French fur traders, though it greatly diminished their traditional way of life. Don't miss the museum's adjacent gift shop, featuring authentic, locally made crafts such as ash baskets, quill jewelry, and more. It also offers an excellent selection of books on both Native American and French Straits history. During peak season (late June–Labor Day), the museum is open 10 A.M.–8 P.M. Monday–Saturday and noon–8 P.M. Sunday. Early and late season hours are shorter (daily 11 A.M.–5 P.M. Memorial Day–June and 11 A.M.–6 P.M. Labor Day–early Oct.).

Fort deBaude Indian Museum (334 N. State St., 906/643-6622) interprets pre-contact Native, French, English, and American periods. With more than 6,700 square feet, the museum has one of the city's largest collections, including historical Native American and military weapons. Unfortunately, it's also one of St. Ignace's least visited museums.

The **Huron Boardwalk** follows the shoreline for a mile, with interpretive signs explaining the role of the bay in the area's settlement. Outdoor displays explore the Straits of Mackinac history and include a rudder from a wooden steamer sunk in 1894 and the windlass from an 1891 shipwreck.

Castle Rock

Three miles north of St. Ignace, you'll come across one of those tourist spots that is hopelessly, almost embarrassingly irresistible. Castle Rock (Castle Rock Road, 906/643-8268, www.stignace.com, $0.50 admission, daily early May–mid-Oct.) is a vertical tower that rises nearly 200 feet and provides unparalleled views of Mackinac Island, the Straits, and Lake Huron. The oversized Paul Bunyan and Babe, his blue ox, is an exciting photo opportunity for children or adults with a certain sense of humor, but most people just head to the 170-step climb without looking twice. The gift shop is pretty kitschy, too.

The Mystery Spot

This would hardly bear mentioning if it wasn't for the billboards you've seen around town and are no doubt wondering about. In

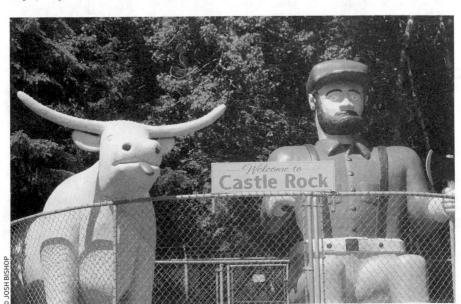

© JOSH BISHOP

Located just off I-75, Castle Rock is part tourist trap and part historic, scenic lookout.

the early 1950s, some surveyors apparently stumbled across an area where their equipment stopped working correctly. The laws of physics don't seem to apply here: tall people seem smaller, chairs balance with two legs in the air, and you'll be able to walk up a wall without falling. If you're the sort of person who pulls off the highway for UFO lookout towers and giant yarn balls, it can be fun and the optical illusions will probably make for some interesting photos. **The Mystery Spot** (150 Martin Lake Rd., 906/643-8322, http://mysteryspotstignace.com) is open 9 A.M.–8 P.M. May 15–June 15, and 8 A.M.–9 P.M. June 16–Labor Day. Late-season hours are the most limited: 9 A.M.–7 P.M. Labor Day–late October.

Lighthouses

As far as historic lighthouses go, there aren't many to be had in St. Ignace. The closest historic lighthouse is on **St. Helena Island,** a few miles west of the city in the Straits of Mackinac. Built in 1873, the 71-foot tower and attached keeper's quarters fell into disrepair after the lighthouse was automated in the 1920s. It's gotten quite a bit of restoration during the past several years, and it's open to the public by appointment (313/436-9150). The island is accessible by boat, but landlubbers can get a decent view from a U.S. 2 pull-off in Gros Cap, six miles west of St. Ignace. Downtown's **Wawatam Lighthouse,** just off the Huron Boardwalk, looks handsome enough, but it's only a few years old.

ENTERTAINMENT

The Upper Peninsula isn't much for metropolitan entertainment—nightclubs and lounges are almost nonexistent—but it does manage to get gaming right, though tending to leave out the flash of, say, Atlantic City's high-rolling casinos. **Kewadin Shores Casino** (3039 Mackinac Trail, 800/539-2346, www.kewadin .com, open year-round), more commonly called "The Shores," has 25,000 square feet of space for games such as blackjack, poker, and roulette and more than 900 slot machines. The Northern Pines lounge features live entertainment every

Friday and Saturday, and Wednesday night is comedy night every week.

Eighty-one rooms are available at the hotel, which is located on the shores of Lake Huron. Visitors can also enjoy the pool, fitness center, and game room. Dining options include **Horseshoe Bay Restaurant** (7 A.M.–10 P.M. Sun.–Thurs., 7 A.M.–midnight Fri.–Sat.) and the **Whitetail Bar and Grill** (11 A.M.–10 P.M. daily).

FESTIVALS AND EVENTS

One of the best ways to learn about the Upper Peninsula's Native Americans is to attend a powwow. Powwows celebrate a tribe's heritage through colorful dancing, feasting, ancient stories, and ceremonies. Many are open to the public and can be wonderful learning experiences. Understand that powwows and many other Native American cultural events have a spiritual element to them. Halter tops, bare chests, pets, drinking, smoking, and certain

© TRAVEL MICHIGAN

For one day, during the Annual Mackinac Bridge Walk, pedestrians can walk across Mighty Mac.

other behavior is out of place here. Look around and see how others are acting or dressing, or ask questions of tribal representatives.

On Labor Day, the Mackinac Bridge Authority throws its no pedestrian policy out the window for the **Annual Mackinac Bridge Walk.** During the walk, which begins in St. Ignace and ends in Mackinaw City, the bridge's east lanes are closed to traffic. Walking begins at 7 A.M., and no walkers are allowed to start after 11 A.M., so make sure you get there on time or, better still, early. It takes about two hours to make the five-mile walk, and there are no restrooms on the bridge, so you'd better be able to hold it. Transportation is provided from Mackinaw City to St. Ignace for $5.

Auto Shows

St. Ignace's claim to fame is the **Straits Area Auto Show,** which draws some 3,000 cars and 100,000 spectators the last weekend of June. Most tend to be 1950s and '60s muscle cars, which cruise the streets à la *American Graffiti.* Based on the success of this auto show, St. Ignace has added a variety of other automotive shows throughout the summer, featuring antiques, classics, trucks, and whatever else with wheels they can come up with. These include the **Antiques & Classics on the Bay** in June, the ridiculously longwinded **On the Waterfront Car/Small Truck Show/Pedal Cars & Swap Meet** in September, and, also in September, the **Richard Crane Memorial Truck Show.**

SUMMER SPORTS AND RECREATION
Hiawatha National Forest

Named after "The Song of Hiawatha," a poem by Henry Wadsworth Longfellow that tells the story of the 16th-century Iroquois chief, the Hiawatha National Forest is a swath of protected land stretching all the way from St. Ignace north to the Lake Superior shore. Many of the forest's 860,000 acres are found in the central U.P., but the eastern side of the forest is where you'll find many of St. Ignace's summer recreation opportunities.

© RANDALL MCCUNE / TRAVEL MICHIGAN

Off-road vehicles can be used on plenty of trails and roads in the Upper Peninsula.

Trails

Thirty-five miles of the **North Country National Scenic Trail** lie in the St. Ignace District of Hiawatha National Forest. When the trail is completed, it will stretch from New York state to North Dakota. Off-limits to horses and motor vehicles, the trail is perfect for hikers, who will pass through cedar, aspen, pine, and northern hardwood. The flat-to-rolling trail is fully marked, but not all sections have been brought to trail standards. The **Horseshoe Bay Hiking Trail** is a short, two-mile (round-trip) trail that leads from Foley Creek Campground to a secluded, sandy Lake Huron beach and back. Only three miles from St. Ignace, the trail takes you through northern white cedar lowlands, where you're likely to spot ducks and great blue herons in the numerous ponds.

Hiawatha National Forest has more than 2,000 miles of forest road available for motor vehicle use, plenty of which is within easy reach of St. Ignace. Detailed maps of **ATV/ORV** trails are available. Rules are strict, so make sure you double-check before setting out.

You'll want to contact Hiawatha National Forest's St. Ignace Ranger District office (1900 West U.S. 2, 906/643-7900, 8 A.M.–4:30 P.M. Mon.–Fri.) for detailed information, trail maps, and information on other recreation opportunities.

Fishing

If you're into deep-water fishing, you could do a lot worse than the Great Lakes—here you'll find salmon, perch, walleye, whitefish, herring, pike, and more. Contact **E.U.P. Fishing Charters** (724 Cheeseman Rd., 877/475-3474, catchfish@lighthouse.net) or **Dream Seaker Charters & Tours** (888/634-3419, www.dreamseaker.com) for information on charters into the Straits.

Inland fishing is abundant in the area. Inland lakes, rivers, and streams provide famously good fishing from April right up to December's freeze. You'll need a Michigan Department of Natural Resources (DNR) fishing license; temporary nonresident licenses are available online at www.mdnr-elicense.com.

Other Water Sports

Like the rest of the U.P., St. Ignace can be a summertime paradise. In particular, visitors have come to love the sandy **beaches** and the relatively warm waters, which offer plenty of relaxing recreation. You'll find suitable swimming spots at **Straits State Park** (720 Church St., 906/643-8620, www.michigan.gov/dnr) or any number of smaller beaches along the Lake Huron and Lake Michigan shores.

If you thought the Straits were beautiful at eye level, imagine seeing them from a harness attached to a parachute and a 600-foot cable. Parasailing excursions are available from **Mackinaw Parasailing** (866/436-7144, $55 or $65 single, $100 or $120 tandem), which docks at the Star Line Railroad Dock in St. Ignace. Mackinaw Parasailing has been giving tourists a new perspective for years from a custom boat that allows for easy flight deck takeoffs and landings. You can also catch a ride from Mackinac Island and Mackinaw City.

Golf

For some stunning scenery, the **St. Ignace Golf and Country Club** (223 U.S. 2, 906/643-8071) offers nine holes with views of the Mackinac Bridge, Lake Huron, and the Straits of Mackinac. Rental clubs and power carts are available. The golf course is located off of U.S. 2, a short distance west of I-75, next to the Big Boy.

WINTER SPORTS AND RECREATION

Ski and Snowshoe Trails

The miles of hiking trails in St. Ignace don't go away in the winter, they just get covered with snow, perfect for **cross-country skiing** and **snowshoeing.** The North Country National Scenic Trail's 35 St. Ignace miles are popular with skiers. There's a warming cabin at the trailhead to Sand Dunes Ski Trail, which has seven groomed trails suitable for every ski level. Trails range between 1.5 and 7.6 miles. While on Loop A, look for claw marks left by black bears climbing the trees in the fall (remember, bears hibernate in the winter). For more information, contact Hiawatha National Forest's **St. Ignace Ranger District office** (1900 West U.S. 2, 906/643-7900, 8 A.M.–4:30 P.M. Mon.–Fri.).

Downhill Skiing

Believe it or not, you can actually find downhill skiing west of town, at **Silver Mountain Ski Area/Tubing Hill** (Cheeseman Rd. and U.S. 2 West, 906/643-6083). It isn't much of a ski area, mind you, but there are a few runs for beginning and intermediate skiers and snowboarders, as well as snow tubing with rope tow, paddle towing, and groomed runs. Serious skiers will want to head west to the Iron Mountain area for some of the U.P.'s best downhill skiing, but Silver Mountain is an entertaining diversion for families.

Snowmobiling

There are about 3,000 miles of snowmobile trails that spread across Michigan's Upper Peninsula, and a few of the trailheads are right here in St. Ignace. Bundle up and hit the trails to pristine winter wilderness or popular destinations like Tahquamenon Falls. The local snowmobile club maintains many of the trails, and snowmobiles can be rented from the **Econo Lodge** (680 West U.S. 2, 906/643-9688) or **Quality Inn** (913 Boulevard Dr., 800/906-4656). If you're bringing your own, be aware that snowmobile crossings aren't allowed on the Mackinac Bridge; transportation is provided by the **Mackinac Bridge Authority** (906/643-7600) for $10 per sled.

As a fairly important side note, remember that snowmobiling in the Upper Peninsula can be remarkably dangerous, especially for newcomers. Every year there are snowmobile-related deaths as reckless enthusiasts drive after a few drinks or plunge through the ice—stay on marked trails and stay *off* rivers and lakes. One particularly popular trail is the ice bridge to Mackinac Island,

marked by a line of discarded Christmas trees stretching across Lake Huron. If you'd like to make the trip, talk to locals who know what's going on, check trail conditions with the **Straits Area Snowmobile Club** (www.straitsareasnowmobileclub.com), and consider the risks carefully.

ACCOMMODATIONS

St. Ignace is jam-packed with lodging, which draws tourists who want to visit Mackinac Island without paying island prices. Unfortunately, many of St. Ignace's accommodations are run-of-the-mill and utilitarian. Don't expect to find the glitz of high-end lodging or expensive resorts like the island's Grand Hotel—you are in Michigan's Upper Peninsula, after all—but that doesn't mean you have to settle for a chintzy room, either.

Hotels and Motels

Billed as St. Ignace's oldest lodging establishment, the **Boardwalk Inn** (316 North State St., 800/254 5408, www.boardwalkinn.com, $47–150) was built in 1928, and the lobby has 1929 desk registers to prove it. The historic hotel is, as its name implies, located across the street from the Huron Boardwalk, putting it smack in the middle of St. Ignace's goings on. From here, it's an easy walk to most any attraction, including ferries to Mackinac Island. The hotel fills up quickly, especially during the Labor Day Bridge Walk and St. Ignace's annual car show, so book your rooms well in advance.

Considering the smashing views of Lake Huron and waterfront access to a private beach and boardwalk, the **Bay View Motel** (1133 North State St., 906/643-9444, http://bayview.franklinsites.com, $32–76 late Apr.–Oct.) is surprisingly cheap. Don't expect much from the Spartan rooms, of course, but what this motel lacks in decor it makes up for in its thrifty appeal and scenic location. Expect rates to jump during holidays and festivals.

Bed-and-Breakfasts

Although it has seven adjoining motel rooms,

the [(Colonial House Inn (90 North State St., 906/643-6900, www.colonial-house-inn .com, $59–155) is first and foremost a bed-and-breakfast, and St. Ignace's only one at that. The Victorian-style home overlooks the Straits of Mackinac and features a wraparound veranda and second-floor balcony. Each of the B&B's seven rooms is distinctively and individually decorated, and has a double or queen size bed and a private bath. Occupancy is limited to two people per room, so families will have to stay in the adjacent motel or find rooms elsewhere.

Camping

Of St. Ignace's many campgrounds, the most popular is Straits State Park (720 Church St., 906/643-8620, $16–28). With 275 campsites, many with electrical service and all with access to modern restrooms, the park's popularity is driven by a number of can't-say-no perks, including Lake Huron waterfront access, stunning views of the bridge, and the Father Marquette memorial and interpretive trail, which are located here. Close to town, the campground is right in the thick of it, and with easy access to Mackinac Island ferries and other attractions, it's almost worth putting up with the summertime crowds. Of the four modern campgrounds, aim for East Loop or West Loop, which have nicely wooded sites right on the Straits.

Smaller crowds can be found at Brevort Lake Campground ($16) in the Hiawatha National Forest some 20 miles west of St. Ignace. The 4,233-acre lake has about 70 large, forested campsites with tables and fire rings. Campers have access to the lake for boating, fishing, and swimming, and three hiking trails explore the surrounding forest. You'll find boat and canoe rentals, as well as groceries and other necessities, at a small store adjacent to the campground. You might also want to try one of the 54 sites at Foley Creek Campground ($14). Although still in Hiawatha National Forest, Foley Creek is only six miles outside town. Smaller and more secluded than Straits State Park, this campground is close enough to the St. Ignace

tourist scene to use as a home base. Private campsites are set among large shade trees; Lake Huron beach access is a one-mile hike up Horseshoe Bay Trail. Contact Hiawatha National Forest's St. Ignace Ranger District office (1900 W. U.S. 2, 906/643-7900, 8 A.M.–4:30 P.M. Mon.–Fri.) for additional information about both campgrounds.

Other Lodging

The cabins at Balsams Resort (1464 West U.S. 2, 906/643-9121 June–Labor Day, 313/791-8026 rest of the year, www.balsams resort.com, $110 daily, $655 weekly) are cozy, fully furnished homes away from home. Balsams Resort can put you up in a one- or two-bedroom log cabin, where you can prepare your own meals in the kitchen, relax in front of the fireplace, or wander over the streams and through the 40-acre woods. You won't be able to see Lake Michigan from all of its nine cabins, but the motel (which isn't quite as quaint) affords a decent view and guests have access to a private beach.

Several area cabins and cottages are available for rent on a nightly or weekly basis, which is an attractive option for families or vacationers looking for an extended, comfortable stay. With a wide range of rooms, locations, and availability, prices can be as low as $100 a night and can easily surpass $1,000 for weeklong rentals. For information and availability, contact the St. Ignace Visitors Bureau (6 Spring St., Ste. 100, 800/338-6660, www .stignace.com).

FOOD

It's not impossible to visit the U.P. without sinking your teeth into the crust of at least one pasty (say PASS-tee; a PACE-tee is an accessory for strippers), but it's pretty near sacrilegious if you don't at least try one. Stop by Bessie's Original Homemade Pasties (1106 North State St., 906/643-8487) for the traditional Yooper nosh, a potpie creation of beef (or chicken), potatoes, onions, rutabagas, and other vegetables. Bessie's also serves deli subs, pizza, old-fashioned ice cream, and smoked fish. **Suzy's Pasties** (1020 West U.S. 2, 906/643-7007) makes a mean pasty, too.

Clyde's Drive-In No. 3 (U.S. 2, just west of the bridge, 906/643-8303) is another perennial St. Ignace favorite. Known throughout the U.P. as home of the best burgers you'll find on either side of the bridge, Clyde's Drive-In is not only an authentic curbside restaurant, but it's also the best place for a meal a little on the cheaper side. You can choose to eat in if you prefer, but it gets pretty cramped. Clyde's menu includes fried shrimp, chicken, and perch, light breakfasts, old-fashioned malts and shakes, and the famous three-quarter-pound C Burger. Oh, in case you were wondering, Nos. 1 and 2 are in Sault Ste. Marie and Manistique, respectively.

You'll find more old-fashioned dining at **Bentley's B-n-L Cafe** (62 North State St., 906/643-7910), a fourth-generation diner that has a vintage soda fountain look.

Some of the town's best pizza, as well as steak, seafood, and sandwiches, can be found at **Driftwood Restaurant & Sports Bar** (590 North State St., 906/643-9133, 8 A.M.– 12:30 A.M., bar until 2 A.M.), a family restaurant and sports bar. Opening early for breakfast, the restaurant also offers a great lunch special for less than six bucks. Dinner entrées can climb as high as $22, a little steep for family dining, but more moderately priced plates can be had for around $10.

For the best of St. Ignace's fine dining scene—which manages to stay stubbornly unpretentious—grab a table at **◖ Dockside Restaurant** (1101 North State St., 906/643-7911) for an impressive view of Lake Huron. The **Mackinac Grille Restaurant & Waterfront Patio Bar** (251 South State St., 906/643-7482, $5–8 lunch, $10–15 dinner) specializes in locally caught whitefish. The restaurant is located on the marina and has views of the Straits, Mackinac Island, and the Star Line ferry dock. Mackinac Grille is open 11 A.M.–midnight Monday–Saturday and 9 A.M.–midnight Sunday during the summer tourist season. Off-season hours are 11 A.M.–9 P.M. Monday–Saturday and 9 A.M.–2 P.M. Sunday.

INFORMATION

For traveling assistance and information, contact the **St. Ignace Visitors Bureau** (6 Spring St., Ste. 100, 800/338-6660) or the **St. Ignace Chamber of Commerce** (560 North State St., 800/970-8717). Both can be found online at www.stignace.com. More particulars on the trails, camping, and recreation available in Hiawatha National Forest are available from the **St. Ignace Ranger District** office (1900 West U.S. 2, 906/643-7900, 8 A.M.–4:30 P.M.).

GETTING THERE AND AROUND
Car

Traveling from the south, follow I-75 north across the bridge to St. Ignace. From the north, I-75 drops into St. Ignace from Sault Ste. Marie, while travelers coming east from Wisconsin can take U.S. 2 into the city. If you're crossing the bridge from Mackinaw City, the 2009 passenger vehicle toll is $3, with an additional $1.50 for each axle if you're pulling a trailer. Tolls will increase every few years until they reach $4.50 in 2015; additional axles will bump up to $2.25. Motor homes will be on an incremental toll schedule, too: the $3.50/axle toll will jump up every few years until it reaches $6/axle in 2014.

Air

The two closest airports with regularly scheduled service are **Pellston Regional Airport (PLN),** south of Mackinaw City in the Lower Peninsula, and **Chippewa County International Airport (CIU)** in Sault Ste. Marie. For information on shuttles and car rentals, see *Mackinaw City* or *Sault Ste. Marie.*

If you'd rather fly into St. Ignace's Mackinac County Airport directly, you can charter a flight through **Great Lakes Air** (906/643-7165, www.greatlakesair.net) from a number of nearby locations, including Detroit and Chicago Midway or O'Hare, but it can be very costly.

Boat

Boaters can make reservations at one of the

120 slips at **St. Ignace Marina** (906/643-8131, www.michigan.gov/dnr). The harbormaster is on duty from mid-May through late September; you can reach the marina on radio channel 9. The location is 45° 51.58 N, 84° 43.06 W.

Public Transportation

Greyhound (800/231-2222, www.greyhound .com) has a bus terminal just across from the ferry docks, providing service to St. Ignace from all points across the country. **Amtrak** (800/872-7245, www.amtrak.com) has partnered with Greyhound to provide transportation to St. Ignace from several major cities in southwest Michigan. Indian Trails (800/292-3831, www.indiantrails.com) offers motor coach service to St. Ignace from Chicago and a number of Michigan cities.

Getting Around

Since you're in St. Ignace, odds are you'll want to head across to Mackinac Island before too long. You can catch a ride on a ferry at Arnold Transit Company (906/847-3351, www.arnold line.com), Shepler's Mackinac Island Ferry (231/436-5023, www.sheplersferry.com), or the Star Line (800/638-9892, www.mackinaw ferry.com).

Mackinaw City

To be completely honest, there isn't a whole lot to see in Mackinaw City unless you're a fan of strip malls and souvenir shopping. The few notable exceptions are several of Michigan's excellent historic parks—and, of course, the always beautiful Great Lakes view. You can find some good food and lodging here, but the city is most often used as a place for travelers to set up camp for their day trips to the island, and with good reason.

SIGHTS
Mackinac Historic State Parks

With a history as long and rich as Mackinac's, it isn't surprising to find a collection of historic sites that, together with Mackinac Island's Fort Mackinac and historic downtown, explore nearly 300 years of Michigan history. If you'd like to explore the park's lighthouse, sawmill, blacksmith shop, churches, homes, and two forts (and you really should), your best bet is going to be the combination ticket, which gives you seven-day admission to three of the four parks (Fort Mackinac, Colonial Michilimackinac, Old Mackinac Point Lighthouse, and Historic Mill Creek) for $22 adults, $13.50 children 5–17. Families might want to take advantage of the Mackinac Family Heritage Membership for season-long unlimited entry to all of the sites for up to two adults and all dependent children or grandchildren 17 or younger. The $59 membership includes 15 percent off museum store purchases. See individual listings below for single site admission rates.

Historic Mill Creek Discovery Park (9001 South U.S. 23, 231/436-4100, www.mackinac parks.com, $7.50 adults, $4.50 children 5–17) is an exceptionally pretty glen and rushing stream that creates a pleasant oasis for visitors, but it was once an innovative industrial site. When the British made plans to move from Fort Michilimackinac to Mackinac Island, Scotsman Robert Campbell recognized their imminent need for lumber. He purchased 640 acres of land surrounding the only waterway in the area with enough flow to power a sawmill. He built the mill in 1790 and later added a blacksmith shop and gristmill.

The site was no longer profitable when the fort ceased operation, so it was abandoned in the mid-1800s. Archaeologists and historians have worked together since the 1970s to recreate the water-powered sawmill on its original site. Today, visitors can see the splashing waterwheel in action and visit the Orientation Center, which has an audiovisual presentation and displays on other artifacts uncovered during the dig. Make sure to walk the park's 3.5 miles of trails, which wind through three kinds of forest or along the creek and mill pond, rising up to scenic overlooks with views of the Straits and Mackinac Island.

An extra $5 will gain you access to the park's new Treetop Discovery Tour, where you can stroll through the treetops on a canopy bridge, fly over a pond on a 350-foot zip line, or scale a climbing wall. Children have access to the Water Power Station and the Forest Friends Children's Play Area. Mill Creek is located just southeast of Mackinaw City, and is open from early May through mid-October 9 A.M.–4 P.M., until 5 P.M. early June to late August.

Old Mackinac Point Lighthouse (550 North Huron Ave., 231/436-4100, www.mackinac parks.com, $6 adults, $3.50 children 5–17) is Mackinaw City's third historic state park. Located on a point just east of the Mackinac Bridge, this 1892 cream-brick light guided ships through the busy Straits of Mackinac for nearly 70 years. When the Mackinac Bridge was completed in 1957, it became obsolete, since vessels could range on the bridge's high lights instead of this diminutive 50-foot tower. Today this charming lighthouse, topped with a cherry-red roof, houses a maritime museum, complete with hands-on exhibits, a tour to the top of the tower led by a costumed interpreter, and historic images. The lighthouse grounds serve as their own delightful little park, with impressive views of the Mackinac Bridge as well as picnic tables scattered across the tidy lawn.

◖ Colonial Michilimackinac State Park

Believed to be the nation's longest-running archaeological dig, the site of Colonial Michilimackinac State Park (102 Straits Ave.,

PONTIAC'S REBELLION

At the end of the French and Indian War, the Treaty of Paris gave the Great Lakes region to the British, who had a very different way of dealing with Native Americans. While the French had, for the most part, cultivated alliances with the tribes, giving them gifts and engaging in trade, the British were openly hostile – they saw Native Americans as a conquered people instead of as allies.

Native American resentment increased and came to a head in Detroit and throughout the Great Lakes area in 1763. An uprising was planned. The tribes passed messages in war belts made of wampum, encouraging the Native Americans to band together and push the British out of the region. Pontiac, the Ottawa chief who eventually gave the war its name, laid siege to Fort Detroit in May 1763, effectively beginning the war. The conflict quickly spread to other British forts in the region, including Fort Michilimackinac, one of the eight forts successfully taken.

On June 2, 1763, local Chippewa played a match of baggatiway, an early form of lacrosse, against visiting Sac just outside the fort. Soldiers watched the entertainment, unaware that the Chippewa had a violent surprise planned. One of the men threw an errant ball into the fort; when the players chased after it, they grabbed hidden weapons that had been smuggled in by Native American women and turned on the unsuspecting British, killing 16 soldiers within minutes. Five others were tortured to death after the fighting had subsided.

The Native American victory was short-lived. Just over a year later, the British returned to Fort Michilimackinac. Pontiac's siege of Fort Detroit, which ended in October 1763, ended even sooner. Today, Pontiac's Rebellion is considered a draw of sorts: the Native Americans failed to push the British out, but neither could the British conquer them. And, insofar as it forced the British to change their policies toward Native Americans, it was at least a partial success.

231/436-4100, www.mackinacparks.com, $10 adults, $6.25 children 5–17) has provided archaeologists with treasures since 1959. The 18th-century military outpost and fur-trading village is the finest of the Mackinac Historic State Parks. The site was long a well-traveled Native American hunting and trading ground; the French built a post here in 1715. The French exploited the Native Americans, bribing them with gifts and alcohol and encouraging them to work in the fur trade. Though the unfortunate relationship led many Native Americans to abandon their traditional ways of life, the two groups rarely fought. Instead, the French feuded with the British, who sought to expand their landholding in the region. For the next 65 years, the fort along the Straits alternately fell under French and British control.

The fort's most violent episode occurred while it was under British rule. In 1763, Pontiac, the Ottawa war chief, ordered an attack on British posts all over Michigan, an attempt to drive the growing British population out of Ottawa native land. While Pontiac laid siege to Detroit, local Ojibwa stormed the fort, killing all but 13 soldiers. In the end, though, it was the feisty colonists who sent the British fleeing from Fort Michilimackinac. They dismantled what they could and burned the rest to the ground in 1780, opting for a new, more-defensible post on nearby Mackinac Island.

Today, Colonial Michilimackinac State Park portrays the lives of both the Native Americans and the European settlers, with costumed interpreters reenacting daily life at a Native American encampment and a stockaded fort. Displays include many of the artifacts excavated by archaeologists. Interpreters demonstrate various crafts and skills, from cooking and weaving to cleaning weapons. They're quite knowledgeable and able to answer most visitors' questions. Don't miss the underground archaeological tunnel exhibit, "Treasures from the Sand." Colonial Michilimackinac is open from early May through mid-October 9 A.M.–4 P.M., until 6 P.M. early June to late August.

Mackinac Bridgemen Museum

It's not slick or fancy, but this small museum is loaded with tidbits and artifacts on the construction of the $100-million Mackinac Bridge. A very well done video documents the bridge's design and construction. The original museum (231/436-5937, May 1–Oct. 30 8 A.M.–midnight, free) was destroyed by a fire in 2005—it's since been rebuilt a mile south of Mackinaw City at 13922 Old U.S. 31.

Icebreaker Mackinaw Maritime Museum

When the United States Coast Guard Cutter *Mackinaw* was retired in 2006, ending 62 winters of clearing shipping lanes through the Great Lakes shipping channel, it was transferred to the Mackinaw Maritime Museum and docked in Mackinaw City. Built to help boost wartime production in the early 1940s, the ship was the most cutting-edge icebreaker in the world. Located at the old railroad dock (131 South Huron Ave., 231/436-9825, www.themackinaw

Mackinaw Crossings is the center of downtown's shopping and dining scene.

© BECCA BISHOP

THE STRAITS OF MACKINAC

.org), it's now open for tours from the end of May through August 10 A.M.–8 P.M. and September 10 A.M.–6 P.M.

Downtown

Mackinaw City's downtown is what many people refer to as a "tourist trap." Despite the genuine destinations offered elsewhere in the city, downtown seems overrun by tourists and tacky shops. Sure, there are moments when it can seem quaint, but those moments can be hard to find. You will, of course, want to find one or two of the city's innumerable **fudge shops,** and **Mackinaw Crossings** (248 South Huron Ave., 231/436-5030, www.mackinawcrossings.com) is an outdoor mall with some good stores and restaurants. The **Mackinaw Trolley Company** (231/436-7812) offers tours of Mackinaw City as well as a historical tour that crosses the bridge into St. Ignace. Tours are offered from early May through mid-October and cost around $20 for adults, depending on the tour (prices range $7–15 for children 5–12).

Lighthouses

Mackinaw City is a mixed bag for lighthouse lovers. On the one hand, **Old Mackinac Point Lighthouse** is the only light open to the public. The city's second lighthouse, **McGulpin's Point Lighthouse,** a few miles east, is a private residence and off-limits to tourists. On the other hand, there are enough historic light stations nearby to make the **lighthouse cruises** offered by Shepler's Ferry (556 East Central Ave., 231/436-5023, www.sheplers ferry.com, $49.50 adults, $37.50 children 5–12) one of the city's more popular attractions. Choose between cruising east into Lake Huron or west into Lake Michigan; either way, you'll pass below the Mackinac Bridge for a rare glimpse of its underside and get close enough to at least four historic lights to snap some photos. The trips last about three hours and are narrated by members of the Great Lakes Lighthouse Keepers Association. Historic lights include Mackinac Island's Round Island Light Station

© BECCA BISHOP

As part of the Mackinac Historic State Parks, Old Mackinac Point Lighthouse is staffed by costumed interpreters.

and Round Island Passage Light; St. Helena Island Light west of St. Ignace; and the White Shoal and Waugoshance lighthouses. Cruises are offered between June 9 and September 17, though not every day, so be sure to call ahead for a schedule.

FESTIVALS AND EVENTS

Hundreds of actors participate in Memorial Day weekend's **Colonial Michilimackinac Pageant,** which re-creates historical events from the 1700s, including the famous 1763 attack. Perhaps taking a cue from St. Ignace's auto shows, Corvette enthusiasts gather at the **Corvette Crossroads Auto Show** in late August.

Mackinaw City's biggest event is Labor Day's **Annual Mackinac Bridge Walk,** which begins in St. Ignace and ends here. A few days later, in early September, thousands of people turn out for **Hopps of Fun,** the city's annual beer and wine festival, featuring more than 50 microbrews and 60 Michigan wines.

Winter events include an annual **Winterfest** in early January (you need to see the outhouse races, if nothing else), and during the **Mackinaw Mush Sled Dog Race,** mushers compete for the purse in a number of events.

SUMMER SPORTS AND RECREATION
On the Water

One of the more popular **fishing** spots is the Mackinaw City Fishing Pier, built specifically for angling, and where you may have some luck with perch, bass, salmon, or trout. Cheboygan State Park (4490 Beach Rd., 231/627-2811, www.michigan.gov/dnr), some 20 miles east of the city, is a favorite among anglers.

St. Ignace's **E.U.P. Fishing Charters** (724 Cheeseman Rd., 877/475-3474, catchfish@ lighthouse.net) docks in Mackinaw City for offshore fishing trips with views of Mackinac Island and the bridge. For **parasailing** excursions into the Straits, contact Mackinaw Parasailing (866/436-7144, $55 or $65 single, $100 or $120 tandem).

Beaches

There are miles of shoreline in and around the city, much of it with beaches. About four miles west of Mackinaw City on Wilderness Park Road, Lake Michigan curves into Cecil Bay, with sandy shores and shallow water. Public restrooms are available.

Golf

South of the city, the **Mackinaw Club** (11891 North Mackinaw Hwy., Carp Lake, 231/537-4955, http://mackinawclub.com, May 10–October 31, $12–25 9 holes, $20–40 18 holes) was built on the site of an emergency World War II landing strip for B-25 bombers. Today, its 18 holes and driving range are open to the public.

Skydiving

You wouldn't know it from the name, but **Mackinaw City Skydiving** (1040 Arbor St., Harbor Springs, 231/330-3483, www.skydive harborsprings.com, spring–fall, $229 18 and older, discount for groups of four or more) isn't in Mackinaw City (it's actually a short drive in the opposite direction of the bridge, and is operated by Skydive Harbor Springs). Still, it has the best view of the bridge. Whether you jump on your own or in a tandem flight, you'll be able to see both peninsulas during one of the most exhilarating experiences in the region.

ACCOMMODATIONS

With the Straits as a major tourism draw, Mackinaw City alone has more than 3,000 rooms. There's nothing quite as extravagant as the island's Grand Hotel or Mission Point Resort, but the city has plenty of lodging at affordable rates.

Hotels and Motels

Families will probably find the prospect of staying at the **Aqua Grand Mackinaw Inn and Waterpark** (907 S. Huron Ave., 231/838-9032, www.aquagrand.com) irresistible. The new 5,000-square-foot water park, built in 2004, has plenty of room for the kiddies to splash and play with water cannons, waterfalls,

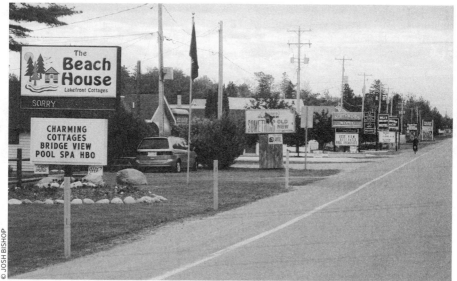

© JOSH BISHOP

Mackinaw City is filled with affordable mom-and-pop motels.

buckets, and other toys that douse them with more than 1,700 gallons of water each minute. There's also plenty of private Lake Huron beach. The four floors of guest rooms and two- or three-bedroom suites can accommodate families of any size. That said, if you don't have any little ones, you'll definitely want to find rooms somewhere else. Guest rooms begin at $69 and can climb as high as $259 for in-season suites.

Parkside Inn Bridgeview (771 N. Huron Ave., 800/827-8301, www.parksideinn.com) is a very nice hotel located just shy of the bridge, which means that you should be able to get what everyone wants when they stay here—a room with a view—but you'll pay for it, too. Double-occupancy rooms begin at $109 for midsummer weeknights and jump up from there. If you're lucky, you can snag a discount rate and squeeze in for less than $100, but don't plan on it.

If you're not too picky, there are plenty of no-frills motels offering basic rooms that won't exactly strain your budget. Try **Sunrise Beach** (11416 W. U.S. 23, 231/436-5461), **Bell's Melody Motel** (11460 W. U.S. 23,

231/436-5463, www.bellsmelodymotel.com), or **Northwinds Motel** (11472 W. U.S. 23, 231/436-7434, www.mackinawcitymotels .com). Like a lot of Mackinaw City lodging, you won't be too impressed, but they're about as cheap as they come—you can pay as little as $50, but expect prices some rooms to go as high as $125 during the busy summer months.

Bed-and-Breakfasts

Located in one of Mackinaw City's oldest homes, the **Deer Head Inn** (109 Henry St., 231/436-3337, www.deerhead.com, $80–225) was built in 1913. The five rooms each try to capture the rustic Northern Michigan spirit, with names like "Hemingway," "Wilderness," and "Hiawatha," and decorations that include bear skins, caribou and fox pelts, and mission furniture. Don't worry—the B&B doesn't lose any elegance for its woodsy charm. Deer Head Inn is open year-round, and room rates rise and fall seasonally.

The **(** **Brigadoon Bed & Breakfast** (207 Langlade St., 231/436-8882, www.mackinaw brigadoon.com, May–early Nov., $175–255) is located across the street from Huron Avenue, the Lake Huron shore, and the ferry docks. Its eight rooms mix modern appointments with a taste of the Old World. If you stay in the elegant butter-yellow building you'll find king or queen poster beds, heated marble floors in the private baths, and signature breakfasts on the veranda.

Camping

Mackinaw Mill Creek Camping (9730 U.S. 23, 231/436-5584, www.campmackinaw.com, May–Oct.) has more than 600 sites, including full hookups for RVs, tenting sites, cabins, and a mile of shoreline. The amenity-rich campground (free Wi-Fi!) is great for families. Sites range from $19 to $41, while cabin rates swing wildly according to seasonal and holiday demand.

The nearest state campground is 12 miles west at wonderful **Wilderness State Park** (898 Wilderness Park Dr., 231/436-5381, www.michigan.gov/dnr, Apr.–Dec.), located at the end of a point. It offers 250 modern campsites, rustic cabins, and bunkhouses. The park has two campgrounds, one on the lakeshore and another tucked away in a grove of mature pines. Twenty miles east of Mackinaw City, **Cheboygan State Park** (4490 Beach Rd., 231/627-2811, www.michigan.gov/dnr) has modern sites near Lake Huron's Duncan Bay. (None are directly on the water.)

Other Lodging

Private, individual cottages are the draw at **The Beach House** (11490 West U.S. 23, 231/436-5353, www.mackinawcitybeachhouse.com, mid-May–mid-Oct.). While rooms are clean and well kept, they're nothing to write home about—you'll want to stay here for the 250 feet of beach, the view of the bridge (only a mile away), and the cottagey feel, not so much for the decor. The rooms sleep between one and five people, with kitchenettes available.

FOOD

The **Historic Depot Restaurant** (248 South Huron Ave., 231/436-7060, www.mackinaw crossings.com) in Mackinaw Crossings is a casual dining restaurant with nightly entertainment, a full bar, and usually a pretty long wait time for a table. As its name implies, the restaurant channels the bygone days of train travel.

The two-story 🄲 **Dixie Saloon** (401 East Central Ave., 231/436-5449, www.dixiesaloon.com) was a Mackinaw City mainstay in the 1890s. The newly-renovated cedar building is wide open on the inside and features good all-American steak, ribs, and burgers. Stop by the Dixie Saloon on weekends for year-round live entertainment; the restaurant also features a full bar and weekly karaoke.

Fudge

If you put on a blindfold and walked into a random building, odds are it'll be a fudge shop. They're all over the place here. The first Murdick's Fudge Store was opened on Mackinac Island in 1887, and **Fran Murdick's Fudge** (222 Central Ave., 888/436-5415, www.franmurdicksfudge.com) is continuing the tradition more than 130 years later. Other fudge shops include **Joann's Fudge** (2 Main St., 303 East Central Ave., 231/436-5611, www.joannsfudge.com), **Marshall's Fudge Shop** (308 East Central Ave., 231/436-5082, www.marshallsfudge.com), and two **Kilwin's** locations (226 East Central Ave., 231/436-5939, and 176 South Huron Ave., 231/436-7200, www.kilwins.com).

INFORMATION

The **Mackinaw Area Visitors Bureau** (10800 West U.S. 23, 231/436-5664, www.mackinaw city.com) can be reached for helpful information, adventure guides, or brochures. Another option is the **Mackinaw City Chamber of Commerce** (216 East Central Ave., 231/436-5574, www.mackinawchamber.com), which offers plenty of visitor information, a comprehensive calendar of events, and additional community information.

GETTING THERE AND AROUND
Car

Mackinaw City is accessed by I-75, north from

Lansing or south from Sault Ste. Marie. If you're driving east from Wisconsin, take U.S. 2 to St. Ignace and join I-75 south across the bridge. The 2009 passenger vehicle toll is $3, with an additional $1.50 for each axle if you're pulling a trailer. Tolls will increase every few years until they reach $4.50 in 2015; additional axles will bump up to $2.25. Motor homes will be on an incremental toll schedule, too: the $3.50/axle toll will jump up every few years until it reaches $6/axle in 2014.

Air

Northwest Airlines currently schedules several flights daily to Pellston Regional Airport (PLN), about 15 miles south of Mackinaw City. Shuttle transportation is available from Wolverine Stages (800/825-1450, www.wolverinestages.com, reservations preferred) and Mackinaw Shuttle (888/349-8294, www.mackinawshuttle.com). Make sure you call ahead for reservations and current rates. Top of the Hill Taxi (231/330-0575) provides taxi service, or you can rent a car through Avis (231/539-8302, www.avis.com) or Hertz (231/539-8404, www.hertz.com).

Boat

The Mackinaw City Municipal Marina (231/436-5269, www.michigan.gov/dnr) has a total of 104 slips and can be reached on radio channels 9 and 16. The harbormaster is on duty from May 1–October 10, from 7 A.M.–9 P.M. The marina is located at 45° 46.55 N, 84° 43.12 W.

Public Transportation

Although Greyhound (800/231-2222, www.greyhound.com) offers limited service stops to Mackinaw City, there is no public transportation and no rental services in the city itself, so if you arrive without your own vehicle you'll have a tough time getting around. Amtrak (800/872-7245, www.amtrak.com) has partnered with Greyhound to provide service from some cities in southwest Michigan.

Getting Around

To book a spot on one of the three **ferries** with service from Mackinaw City to Mackinac Island, contact Arnold Transit Company (906/847-3351, www.arnoldline.com), Shepler's Mackinac Island Ferry (231/436-5023, www.sheplersferry.com), or the Star Line (800/638-9892, www.mackinawferry.com).

aerial view of the Mackinac Bridge

© TRAVEL MICHIGAN

ESCANABA AND THE LAKE MICHIGAN SHORE

U.S. 2, the main road that heads west from St. Ignace and hugs the Lake Michigan shoreline, has plenty of places to pull over and admire the lake. The beaches here are sandier than Lake Superior's, and the water is warm enough in the summer to take a chilly swim if the spirit moves you. Visitors taking a small detour to the north will find that the Seney National Wildlife Refuge is an ideal place for hunting, fishing, and berry picking in the summer and, in the winter, Nordic skiing and snowshoeing.

Like most U.P. towns, Manistique isn't quite the booming city it used to be. Since its heyday as a lumber port in the early 1900s, Manistique has shrunk to a town of just over 3,000 people. It's a quaint little town—the Manistique River flows through the center of town and into Lake

Michigan, and the scenic boardwalk is worth strolling when the weather is behaving. Just past Manistique, the Garden Peninsula drops south into Lake Michigan, framing the northern reaches of Green Bay.

Garden, the largest city in the Garden Peninsula, is really only worth driving through on your way to Fayette, the Upper Peninsula's most famous ghost town. You'll want to set aside an entire morning or afternoon to explore the once-bustling production town where pig iron was smelted during the Civil War.

The Green Bay shoreline, west of the Garden Peninsula, is known for its mild climate and relatively sympathetic winters, which average just over four feet of snowfall each year. That's little more than a dusting to Yoopers. The temperate weather year-round make the last bit of

© DAVID F. WISSE / TRAVEL MICHIGAN

HIGHLIGHTS

🌙 **Driving U.S. 2:** The few small towns, scenic pull-offs, and other diversions found along U.S. 2 are nothing compared to the drive along the lake (page 61).

🌙 **Indian Lake State Park:** One of the U.P.'s largest lakes is also one of its most popular recreation destinations – stop here for boating, fishing, hunting, skiing, swimming, and hiking (page 64).

🌙 **Fayette Historic State Park:** This historic townsite is one of the U.P.'s most famous ghost towns and a convenient metaphor

for the regional rise and fall of big industry. Incidentally, it's a great park, too (page 69).

🌙 **Bays de Noc:** With more than 200 miles of shoreline and 120,000 acres of water (or thereabouts), these bays have irresistible walleye fishing (page 71).

🌙 **Hiawatha National Forest:** The eastern part of the national forest spreads north from U.S. 2 all the way to Lake Superior. If you're looking for wilderness, you've found it here (page 77).

THE LAKE MICHIGAN SHORE

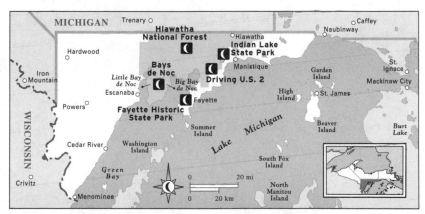

LOOK FOR 🌙 TO FIND RECOMMENDED SIGHTS, ACTIVITIES, DINING, AND LODGING.

Lake Michigan shoreline a favorite destination for outdoor enthusiasts. The cities of Escanaba and Menominee (the U.P.'s third and fourth largest, respectively) make this region better than most for dining and lodging selection.

PLANNING YOUR TIME

There's plenty of scenic driving along the lakeshore and a few worthwhile stops along the way. Like most U.P. cities, Escanaba, Menominee, and Manistique aren't exactly metropolises, but they are on the larger side. You'll find more options here than in the peninsula's smaller towns, but there still isn't

much to keep travelers here, unless, of course, you came for the fishing. Winter visitors will find miles of snowmobile trails packed into the small region. Still, unless you're spending a week at one of the forest campgrounds, a day or two to visit the cities or head north to inland recreation will be plenty of time for most tourists.

HISTORY

The cities along the Lake Michigan shore have shared the fate of many Upper Peninsula towns: Native American communities gave way to the mining and logging industries, which

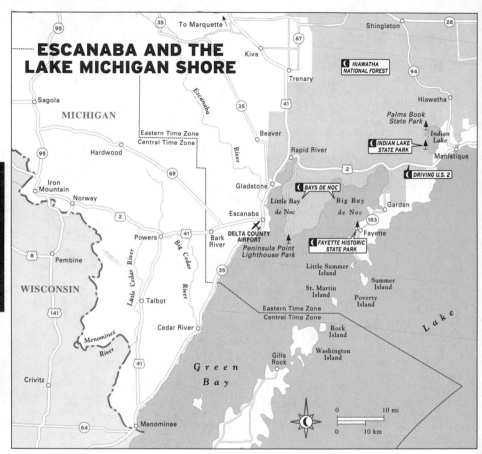

in turn collapsed as the natural resources became depleted and demand began to wane. Manistique was a thriving port city central to the timber industry, while Escanaba flourished as a conduit for iron ore shipping. Historic Fayette Townsite is a testimony to what could have happened to these once-bustling communities—it's been reduced to a ghost town. But Escanaba Manistique, and Menominee are still thriving communities, with economies that are supported in no small part by the U.P.'s enduring appeal as a tourism destination.

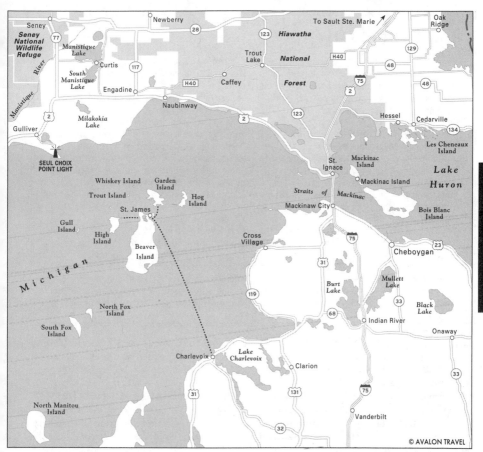

© AVALON TRAVEL

THE LAKE MICHIGAN SHORE

St. Ignace to Manistique

SIGHTS
【 Driving U.S. 2

U.S. 2 is one of the main east–west thoroughfares in the Upper Peninsula. There's not much entertainment or lodging along the shore, but the road to Manistique is lined with scenic pull-offs, beaches, and other detours. You'll definitely want to hit one or two of the scenic pull-offs for a stunning view of Lake Michigan, but there's no need to stop at all of them—even

the most beautiful views tend to get repetitive after a while, and as a general rule you can't go wrong by stopping at the first one you see.

Heading west along U.S. 2, you'll breeze through Brevort, Epoufette, and Naubinway. There's no real reason to stop, although if you want to poke around a little it certainly won't hurt. You can usually find a short hiking trail or two, a sandy beach, or a decent restaurant for a touch of local color and off-the-beaten-

LAKE MICHIGAN

There's no way around it: The Great Lakes are pretty impressive. Carved away by receding glaciers several thousand years ago, the five lakes are more than beautiful, useful, or recreational – they're downright huge. According to the Great Lakes Information Network, these lakes (Michigan, Superior, Huron, Erie, and Ontario) cover more than 94,000 square miles and hold an estimated 6 *quadrillion* gallons of water. That's six thousand million million gallons (6,000,000,000,000,000). That's about one-fifth of the Earth's fresh water, and it could cover the 48 contiguous states to a depth of nearly 10 feet.

Compared to numbers like that, Lake Michigan itself seems small. But the second largest lake in the United States (Lake Superior is the biggest) and the only Great Lake entirely within the United States' borders is no laughing matter. Lake Michigan is 307 miles long and 118 miles wide and holds just shy of 1,180 cubic *miles* of water. With an average depth of 279 feet, Lake Michigan is some 925 feet deep at its deepest point. Its surface area is 22,300 square miles, and it has more than 1,600 miles of shoreline. It's big.

Scientists who study these things will tell you that Lake Michigan and Lake Huron are "hydrologically inseparable" from each other, which roughly means that they've got the same surface elevation and aren't separated by a river. The Straits of Mackinac, spanned by Mighty Mac, connect the two lakes that are, for all purposes except the most technical, two separate bodies of water.

The southern end of Lake Michigan is the warmest and most swimmable, but there are plenty of sandy beaches in the U.P., too, and when compared to frigid Lake Superior, Lake Michigan is warm. You'll find plenty of good sailing and boating, world-renowned fishing, and sunsets that'll knock you off your feet.

path dining. A trip north on Highway 33 will bring you to the town of Curtis, nestled between **Big Manistique Lake** and **South Manistique Lake** and home to plenty of outdoor activities. Take a small southern detour along County Road 432 for a glimpse of Seul Choix Point Light. The road reconnects to U.S. 2 after passing between **McDonald Lake** and **Gulliver Lake,** two good-sized inland lakes.

Siphon Bridge and Water Tower

Although it isn't nearly as big as Mighty Mac (and not half as impressive, either), Manistique's siphon bridge, which crosses the Manistique River, may very well be the Upper Peninsula's second most interesting bridge. A strange engineering feat, the 1919 bridge is partially supported by the water underneath it; the roadway is actually sited four feet below water level. Its construction was prompted by a paper mill upstream, which needed to dam the river for its water needs, thus raising the river. You'll want to stop at the historic water tower for a taste of regional history, too. The 200-foot brick tower is located on the site of the Schoolcraft County Historical Park, which also includes a small historical museum.

Thompson State Fish Hatchery

In Thompson, just a few miles west of Manistique, you'll find a working fish hatchery, which produces a number of different fish for the Great Lakes and inland lakes. It isn't the prettiest stop on a tour of the U.P., but a relatively new interpretive center provides plenty of information about the importance of hatcheries and fisheries, small tributaries to the Great Lakes, and how watersheds work. The Thompson State Fish Hatchery (944 South State Highway M-149, 906/341-5587, 7:30 A.M.–3:30 P.M. daily, free) offers self-guided tours; you'll be able to read informative signs that help explain what you'll see, and you can watch staff working with the fish in the ponds.

Palms Brook State Park and Kitch-Iti-Kipi

Located on Indian Lake's western shore, north

and west of town, Palms Brook State Park (State Highway M-149, 906/341-2355) guards one of the U.P.'s most remarkable natural attractions. Kitch-Iti-Kipi, or "Big Spring," looks like a deep, dark pool tucked away in a grove of cedars—until you get up close. Then you discover it's an enormous spring, where gin-clear water bubbles out of the earth at a staggering 10,000–16,000 gallons per minute.

The park maintains a nifty raft, so you can propel yourself across the 200-foot-long spring with the help of a hand-powered cable. It's an amazing view, peering 45 feet down into its eerie emerald waters and erupting sand bottom, where lunker brown trout glide among the skeletons of downed trees. The spring is a popular attraction, so come in the early morning or, better yet, midwinter. (The spring never freezes over.) You'll have to hike 100 yards or so up the park's gated and unplowed entrance road, but Kitch-Iti-Kipi is the kind of magical place best appreciated in solitude.

Lighthouses

Ten miles south of Blaney Park at Gulliver, 14 miles east of Manistique, a road leads you down a point to the 1895 **Seul Choix Point Light** (672 North West Gulliver Lake Rd., 906/283-3183, www.exploringthenorth.com/seulchoix/ seul.html, Memorial Day through mid-Oct., 10 A.M.–6 P.M. daily), a worthwhile detour. Pronounced "sul-SHWA"—French for "Only Choice"—it sits at the end of a finger of land that offers boaters the only choice for hiding from storms along this stretch of Lake Michigan shoreline. The township of Gulliver has done a splendid job restoring the light and creating a maritime museum in the fog signal building. (It includes an admirable scale model of the lighthouse, made by hand with thousands of miniature bricks.) Climb the tower (small fee/donation) for great views of much of northern Lake Michigan. You'll have a good chance of seeing ship traffic, since Port Inland, just to the east, is an important commercial port. From U.S. 2 at Gulliver, go southeast on County Road 431 (a gravel road) and travel another four miles to the light. The **Manistique East Breakwater**

Lighthouse is located on the east side of Manistique, at the end of the east breakwater arm. The concrete breakwaters were built in the early 1900s as a means of creating safe harbor for large ships. You'll be able to see the red lighthouse, which first shined in 1916, from throughout Lakeview Park; access to the pier and lighthouse can be had on the west side of the park. You won't be able to go inside, but you can get close enough for a good view.

ENTERTAINMENT
Kewadin Manistique Casino

Here at Kewadin Manistique (U.S. 2 E., Manistique, 1-800-539-2346, www.kewadin manistique.com), one of Kewadin's five Upper Peninsula casinos, gamers can try Lady Luck at the slots or hit the tables for blackjack, Let it Ride stud poker and three-card poker. Bingo

THE LAKE MICHIGAN SHORE

MINING AND THE CIVIL WAR

In addition to the soldiers who fought to preserve the Union (including men who fought as part of the Iron Brigade, famous for suffering the highest casualty rate during the war), much of Michigan's contribution to the war effort came from the iron mines of the Upper Peninsula.

There are three iron ranges in the Upper Peninsula, and during the better years in the U.P.'s mining heyday, during and well after the Civil War, they provided several million tons. The wartime demand for high-quality iron was met by the mines of the Menominee, Marquette, and Gogebic ranges, and the Upper Peninsula prospered – railroad lines were built, shipping ports thrived, and business was booming.

But like the lucrative fur and lumber trades, mining couldn't last forever. When supplies began to run thin and demand decreased, the industry collapsed, taking with it towns like Fayette, which was famously left behind as an empty shell of the community it once was.

games are played every Monday and Thursday morning at 10 A.M. in the **Team Spirits Bar.** The bar hosts comedy night on Fridays, and live local entertainment the last Friday and Saturday of each month—during the rest of the week, catch the game on the bar's big screens. If the bar menu isn't enough, visit Mariner's Cove, Kewadin Manistique's 60-seat restaurant, for breakfast, lunch, or dinner at surprisingly good prices.

The casino is located on the north side of U.S. 2 in Manistique—simply take U.S. 2 into town; you can't miss it.

Mackinaw Trail Winery

The small, simply decorated Mackinaw Trail Winery (103 West Lakeshore Dr., 906/341-2303, www.mackinawtrailwinery.com, 10 A.M.–8 P.M. Mon.–Sat. and noon–5 P.M. Sun. May–Sept., shorter hours Oct.–Apr.) tasting room is a testimony to Michigan's growing wine industry. With more than 14,000 acres of vineyards, Michigan is one of the most prolific grape-growing states, producing more than 375,000 cases of wine each year. Mackinaw Trail Winery uses grapes harvested from across the state to make award-winning wines.

SUMMER SPORTS AND RECREATION
Seney National Wildlife Refuge

Several miles north of U.S. 2 (M-77 will take you there), the Seney National Wildlife Refuge (1674 Refuge Entrance Rd., Seney, 906/586-9851, www.fws.gov) has more than 95,000 acres in the area known as the Great Manistique Swamp. Established for resident wildlife, the area provides protection for endangered and threatened species and a habitat for migratory birds. The refuge is one of the U.P.'s prime wildlife-viewing areas. Come here for plenty of hiking, biking, paddling, and fishing in the summer and cross-country skiing and snowshoeing in the winter. Stop at the visitors center for an orientation slide show and information about the refuge's self-guided audio tour. Seasonal nature programs and special events are offered year-round,

provided there are enough visitor services staff members on hand.

◖ Indian Lake State Park

The Upper Peninsula's fourth-largest lake, Indian Lake is well known among anglers and RV campers. (Be warned that Jet Skiers have discovered it, too.) The anglers come for the perch, walleye, and muskie that thrive in the lake's warm and quite shallow waters. The RVers come for its convenient location—just north of U.S. 2 and the Garden Peninsula, with plenty of campsites and sand beaches.

The best known campsites are found at Indian Lake State Park (8970 W. County Road 442, 906/341-2355) with two units, one on the south shore and a second one three miles away on the west shore. Each offers a modern campground and a boat launch. (The lake is the focus here, so hiking is limited.) The western unit sites, while not on the water, tend to be less busy. If you're aiming for a waterfront site in the southern unit, plan to come midweek or off season, and keep your fingers crossed. You'll want to visit the state park for hunting and fishing, boating, beaches, and picnics. To reach Indian Lake State Park, take U.S. 2 to Thompson, then go north on M-149 and east on County Road 442. To reach the west unit, stay on M-149.

Hiking and Biking

A lovely trail hugs the Lake Michigan shoreline several miles directly south of U.S. 2. Take Gould City Road south from Gould City until you hit **Gould City Township Park,** which will drop you off in the middle of the pathway. Head east along a moderately difficult off-trail route that extends about 3.5 miles before doubling back to your car; you can keep going west for another 2.5 miles or so. The trail here is a little difficult to find, and the footing can get hairy at times, but the solitude and the views of the lake make it worth the trouble.

With only two miles of hiking trails, Indian Lake State Park itself probably won't top your list of hiking destinations. However, the **Indian Lake Pathway** has 8.5 miles of trails that are perfect for hikers and bikers. The three loops provide flat-to-rolling terrain and lengths that vary from 1 to 4.5 miles. Don't confuse Indian Lake Pathway with the state park, though, or you're bound to get disappointed. The pathway is located west of the park; the easiest way to reach the trailhead is to take M-149 about 12 miles north of Thompson.

There is an undemanding three-mile trail at **Camp Seven Lake Recreation Area,** some 24 miles north of Manistique in the Hiawatha National Forest, which will occupy two hours. While here, take some time at the picnic grounds and swimming area. The **Rainey Wildlife Area,** on the north side of Indian Lake, has a hiking trail and boardwalks that lead to a wildlife observation platform, where you've got a decent chance of seeing bald eagles in spring and early summer. Head north from Manistique on M-94 for about 5 miles, then take a left on Dawson Road. After 1.5 miles, take an access road north to the parking lot.

Canoeing and Kayaking

You'll find some of the area's best canoeing in and around Curtis. You can paddle Big Manistique Lake, South Manistique Lake, and the smaller North Manistique Lake, but one of the area's most popular trips will take you down the **Manistique River,** which begins at the west end of Big Manistique Lake and empties into Lake Michigan some 70 miles downstream. There are a few access points just west of Big Manistique Lake and then a long stretch of 27 miles between easy take-outs at Mead Creek and Merwin Creek campgrounds. Coming from the other direction, put in to the **Indian River** a good distance north, near Steuben, or farther west, where the river passes beneath County Road H-13. From here, take the river about 30 miles west and south to Indian Lake.

Fishing

The abundance of rivers, streams, and large lakes in the area gives this stretch of the Upper Peninsula tons of fishing options. You can't camp or build fires in the **Seney National Wildlife Refuge** (1674 Refuge Entrance Rd., Seney, 906/586-9851, www.fws.gov), so you'll have to leave for the night, but you can cast a line at Walsh Creek and the Ditch, Creighton, Driggs, and Manistique Rivers, as well as a number of fishing pools. The water (more than 20,000 acres of it!) of the **Manistique Lakes** is, for the most part, less than 30 feet deep. Fishing here includes muskie, northern pike, walleye, bass (largemouth and smallmouth), perch, bluegill, and more. Be warned, though—these waters are accessible to Jet Skis and water-skiers. Try **Camp Seven Lake** (906/341-5666) in Hiawatha National Forest for smaller waters. For more information on popular fishing spots, contact the **Manistique Tourism Council** (800/342-4282, www.visit manistique.com), the **U.S. Forest Service** (2727 North Lincoln Rd., Escanaba, 906/786-4062, www.fs.fed.us), or the **Michigan DNR** (906/452-6227, www.michigan.gov/dnr).

Open-water fishing trips can be chartered through **Delta Dawn Charters** (906/428-9093), which docks at Manistique for salmon fishing. Morning, afternoon, and evening charters are available. Half-day charters are $375 for up to four people, $50 each for additional persons, up to six total. Full-day charters cost $475 for up to four people, $50 each for additional persons, up to six total.

Golf

If you've come to the U.P. to golf, you can find 18 holes at **Indian Lake Golf and Country Club** (1305 North Birch St., Manistique, 906/341-5600, www.indianlakegolfclub.net), on the northeast shore of Indian Lake. The course has a pro shop, cart and club rentals, a full bar and restaurant, and all bent grass greens and fairways. There were only nine holes here for more than seventy years, but the club added an additional nine in 2000. Travel north on M-94 from downtown Manistique for 2.5 miles, turn left at the school, and travel a mile to the golf course.

Stony Point Golf Course (8102 West U.S. 2, Manistique, 906/341-3419, www.stony pointgolf.com, $11–27, mid-Apr.–mid-Nov.)

is a nine-hole course located just two miles west of Manistique. The par-35 family-owned course has bent grass greens and fairways and is nestled among the Upper Peninsula's renowned scenery.

Off-Road Vehicles

Unlike Michigan's Lower Peninsula, the Upper allows off-road vehicles to operate on any state forest road, so long as it isn't specifically posted as off-limits. Even with much of the U.P. accessible via these roads, a designated trail system is also set aside specifically for ORV use. Plenty of multi-use trails thread through the U.P. along and north of U.S. 2—try the 36-mile **Sandtown Trail** just east of the Manistique Lakes. Take M-117 north to Sandtown Road and turn right on Hayes Road to the parking area. The **Brevort/Trout Lake Trail** starts north of Brevort Lake, a short way out from St. Ignace; from there, connect to the Newberry-Rexton Trail and a system of trails that makes its way west. Additionally, all Schoolcraft County roads are open to ORVs, provided you keep to the shoulder at a speed below 25 mph. Detailed off-road vehicle maps

are available from Michigan DNR Service Centers (the closest ones are in Newberry and Marquette), or you can contact the **Manistique Area Tourism Council** (800/342-4282, www .visitmanistique.com).

WINTER SPORTS AND RECREATION
Ski and Snowshoe Trails

The **Indian Lake Pathway** provides some of the area's finest groomed ski trails, with 8.5 miles of flat-to-rolling terrain. There are more than nine miles of trails at the **Seney National Wildlife Refuge,** where skiers are likely to see some winter wildlife. Failing that, the wooded surroundings and views of the frozen Manistique River make the trek worthwhile.

Snowmobiling

The area near U.S. 2 and north of Lake Michigan can be traversed by snowmobile on Trail 2, which starts in St. Ignace and makes its way west to Escanaba and beyond. A number of smaller trails (too many to list here) branch off and provide access to much of the U.P.,

© VITO PALMISANO / TRAVEL MICHIGAN

There are more than 3,000 miles of groomed snowmobile trails that crisscross the Upper Peninsula.

including state and national forests and the Manistique Lakes. Nearing Manistique, Trail 2 skirts the Seney National Wildlife Refuge before dropping south into town. Take Trail 41 or Trail 7 northwest into Hiawatha National Forest.

Ice Fishing

Some people enjoy fishing in sub-zero temperatures on a frozen lake; these people will like the Manistique Lakes near Curtis. The ice tends to form in early December, giving ice-fishers plenty of time for some of the U.P.'s best seasonal fishing for northern pike, walleye, and perch.

ACCOMMODATIONS

Several nice mom-and-pop motels are managing to hang on along U.S. 2, though they're getting more and more competition from chains. Let's hope places like **Star Motel** (1142 E. Lakeshore Dr., 906/341-5363, www .exploringthenorth.com/star/motel.html, $35–65) continue to fend off the big boys. Located a mile or two east of Manistique on U.S. 2, this tidy, vintage 1950s motel has large rooms, rates in the $50 range, meticulous owners, and a nice setting on the lake. It allows well-behaved dogs, too. What more could you ask? Another good non-chain option is the **Beachcomber Motel** (751 East Lake Shore Drive, Manistique, 906/341-2567, $35–80, open year-round), across from the lake, one mile east of Manistique on U.S. 2.

There are only four rooms at the **Royal Rose Bed and Breakfast** (230 Arbutus Ave., 906/341-4886, www.manistique.com, May–Dec., $75–110) in Manistique, but the restored Dutch Colonial offers a quiet, relaxing stay. There are no children allowed, which is good if you're traveling in ones or twos, but families will have to look elsewhere. There's an elegant dining room, a comfortable morning room, and a wraparound deck. Located across from Lake Michigan and within walking distance of the boardwalk, the Royal Rose is a great place to stay while exploring Manistique.

Elk Street Lodge (906 West Elk St., 906/341-1122) is another excellent option for a comfortable room in a historic building.

Visitors get breakfast and a bedtime snack, and you'll find access to the U.P.'s snowmobile trails in wintertime. If you want to do a little gaming while in Manistique, Elk Street Lodge has shuttle service to and from the Kewadin Casino. Lots of **chain motels** are represented along U.S. 2, especially near Manistique.

For Indian Lake lodging, try **Mountain Ash Resort** (3 North County Road 441, Manistique, 906/341-5658, $55–85 daily during off season, $375–575 weekly July and Aug.). Proprietors Rick and Becky Bayer have 12 log cabins and a three-bedroom lodge (you'll pay considerably more for the lodge) that are open year-round and easily accessible to all sorts of recreation—fishing and hiking in the summertime, snowmobiling and cross-country skiing in the winter. The cabins are stocked with dishes, cooking utensils, appliances, and bed linens. Just bring your own towels and some food, and you'll be good to go. Pets are allowed with a deposit. Take County Road 149 north of U.S. 2 at Thompson, turn right on County Road 442 and left on County Road 441; the lodge is located on the east side of Indian Lake.

Camping

The **Log Cabin Resort and Campground** (W18042 County Road County Road H-42, Curtis, 888/879-6448 or 906/586-9732, www .uplogcabin.com, $20–32 campsites, $45–109 cabins) has some 600 feet of Big Manistique Lake frontage on more than 23 acres of property. Here you'll find boat slips, a game room, a sandy beach, and 50 campsites, 34 of which are full-service RV sites.

Some 20 miles north of Manistique, just off M-94, the **Indian River Campground** (Hiawatha National Forest, 906/341-5666) sits on a bluff overlooking the Indian River. The five private, wooded sites provide plenty of seclusion and the feeling of solitude despite the camp's close proximity to the highway. This is a decent stop for paddlers making their way down the Indian River Canoe Trail, with clean drinking water, picnic tables, and grills. **Camp Seven Lake Campground** (906/341-5666) has considerably more campsites—41 of them, each with a table and a fire ring. Camp Seven Lake is perfect for boating, fishing, swimming, and hoofing it along a three-mile hiking trail. Take County Road 442 eight miles east of Forest Highway 13, 24 miles northwest of Manistique.

FOOD

It seems everyone who drives along U.S. 2 stops for a bite at the **Sunny Shores Restaurant** (906/341-5582, open Apr.–Nov.), on U.S. 2 in Manistique. It's known for breakfast, but serves all day long. Also in Manistique, the **Harbor Inn** (238 Cedar St., 906/341-8393) has good whitefish dinners, a bountiful salad bar, and a neat old tavern perfect for a beer after a day of mountain biking or beach-combing.

If you didn't stop at Clyde's Drive-In No. 3 outside St. Ignace, make a point of going to ℂ **Clyde's Drive-In No. 2** (201 Chippewa Ave., 906/341-6021) in Manistique. You'll find the same old-school service, malts, and Big C burgers as at Clyde's other well-known U.P. drive-ins.

Teddy's Pub (100 South Second St., 906/341-8212, 11:30 A.M.–2 P.M. and 4:30–10 P.M. daily Memorial Day–Labor Day, $8–16 dinner) is well known for its pizza, but you can get a steak or pan-fried walleye if you're looking for something a little less casual. The prices are modest, the Victorian atmosphere is family-friendly, and the wine list isn't half bad. **Elkhorn Station Restaurant and Sports Bar** (6055 West U.S. 2, 906/341-2244) is located a mile from Kewadin Casino. It's among Manistique's finer dining spots, with hand-cut steaks and freshwater fish, but the casual atmosphere, full bar, and summer patio dining will tempt you to kick back in your chair and put your boots up. You can get burgers, salads, and sandwiches here, too, at respectable family rates.

INFORMATION AND SERVICES

The Manistique Area Tourist Council (800/342-4282, www.visitmanistique.com) is your source for visitor information in Manistique. You can also contact the **Schoolcraft County Chamber of Commerce** (1000 West Lakeshore Dr., Manistique, 888/819-7420 or 906/341-5010, www.schoolcraftcountychamber.com) and the Michigan DNR (906/228-6561, www.michigan .gov/dnr).

Manistique's hospital is the Schoolcraft Memorial Hospital (500 Main St., Manistique, 906/341-3200, www.scmh.org), 0.25 miles east of M-94. For banking and an ATM, stop at Wells Fargo (266 South Cedar St., 906/341-1900, www.wellsfargo.com) or one of Manistique's many other banks.

GETTING THERE AND AROUND
Car

U.S. 2 unwinds from St. Ignace, just north of the Bridge, for about 90 miles before it runs into Manistique. It keeps going, of course, into Escanaba and on toward Wisconsin, but the long, easy stretch between St. Ignace and Manistique parallels the lakeshore for much of the drive. You'll want to detour on highways north and south of U.S. 2 along the way. Coming from Wisconsin, take U.S. 41 north from Green Bay, cross into Michigan at the twin cities of Marinette (WI) and Menominee (MI), then take M-35 north to U.S. 2 and Manistique. From Munising on the Lake Superior shore, simply drive south on M-94.

Boat

There's a small marina in Manistique, where the river flows into Lake Michigan, that offers a small selection of seasonal and transient slips. The **Manistique Marina** (906/341-6841, www.michigan.gov/dnr) has a harbormaster on duty from mid-June through early August, and can be reached on channel 9 or 68. Marina coordinates are 45° 57.08 N, 86° 14.08 W.

Public Transportation

Regular bus service is provided to Manistique (as well as several small towns along U.S. 2) from St. Ignace and Escanaba, which can be reached from a network of cities throughout Michigan, as well as Green Bay and Milwaukee. Contact Indian Trails (800/292-3831, www.indiantrails .com) for current schedules and rates.

Garden Peninsula

The Garden Peninsula is a quiet, peaceful point of land, filled with little-used blacktop roads perfect for cycling and a handful of sleepy farms and orchards. Garden, the largest city in the Garden Peninsula, is really only worth driving through on the way to Fayette, the Upper Peninsula's most famous ghost town. A bit of history, a moderate climate, and scenic beauty make the peninsula one of the U.P.'s more tranquil destinations.

SIGHTS

If you're curious about the town of Garden and its history, stop at the **Garden Peninsula Historical Museum** (State St., 906/644-2398, June–Labor Day). There isn't much here aside from genealogy and community history (logging, fishing, and the like), but the quaint museum, located in a one-room schoolhouse, will likely appeal to regional history buffs. If you're looking for an in-and-out tour of the Garden Peninsula, keep going to Fayette State Park.

🏰 Fayette Historic State Park

By far the peninsula's most notable attraction—and rightly so—is Fayette Historic State Park (13700 13.25 La., 906/644-2603, www.michigan.gov/dnr). If you make time for just one stop in this part of the U.P., make it this outstanding state park. Once the site of a large smelting operation, Fayette's limestone furnaces converted raw iron ore from U.P. mines into pig iron that was loaded onto barges bound for Escanaba. In the 1880s, stinky and industrial Fayette boasted a population of 500, and its loud, hot blast furnaces cranked away seven days a week. By 1891, nearby forests that fueled the furnaces were all but depleted, and more efficient steelmaking methods came into vogue. The furnaces shut down, and the town died with them.

THE LAKE MICHIGAN SHORE

© JOSH BISHOP

A Lake Michigan bluff is seen through the ruins at Fayette Historic State Park.

THE FURNACES OF FAYETTE

© JOSH BISHOP

Visitors can see remnants of another time at Fayette Historic State Park.

Once the site of a large smelting operation, Fayette's limestone furnaces converted raw iron ore from U.P. mines into pig iron that was loaded onto barges bound for Escanaba. In the 1880s, stinky and industrial Fayette boasted a population of 500, and its loud, hot blast furnaces cranked away seven days a week. By 1891, nearby forests that fueled the furnace were all but depleted, and more efficient steel-making methods came into vogue. The furnace shut down, and the town died with it.

The town was rescued from its untimely demise as a restored historic village, with some 20 historic buildings and scenic overlooks, a visitors center, a dock, and the old furnace complex.

Nearly a century later, Fayette was reborn as a wonderfully restored historic site and state park. Today, Fayette is surely one of the nation's most scenic ghost towns, its dozen limestone buildings tucked alongside the sheer white bluffs and deep clear waters of Snail Shell Harbor. Start at the visitors center, which gives a good historical overview and features a helpful scale model of the village. You can wander in and out of the hotel, opera house, homes, and other buildings, some intact, some more decayed. Horse-drawn carriage rides around the grounds and boat tours are available from Memorial Day to Labor Day. You're welcome to explore the grounds any time. In fact, a very early morning or off-season visit can add to the ghostly appeal of the place.

With the historic townsite acting like a magnet for visitors, the rest of the 750-acre park is often overlooked. It includes a semimodern campground (electricity but no modern restrooms or showers) and several miles of hiking trails, including one that swings north along the bluffs above Snail Shell Harbor.

Marygrove Retreat Center

Although it's clearly a Catholic retreat center (shrines and other Christian icons make this readily apparent), Marygrove (906/644-2771, www.marygrove.org, $105/weekend single, $175/weekend couple) welcomes people of any faith (or none) for retreats that provide tranquility, renewal, and rest. It's taken a lot of continuing work to keep the 1920s building—originally a cancer hospital—in tip-top shape, and it's paying off; the 36 guest rooms are clean and well kept. Located on Garden Bay, the center has 40 acres of wooded property, gardens, a library, a conference center, and an intriguing labyrinth patterned out of stone. Specialized retreats are offered to guests with specific interests or needs. Take M-139 south of U.S. 2 for nine miles.

Fairport

If commercial fishing interests you, continue down County Road 513 to Fairport, near the tip of the peninsula, where a commercial fleet still operates. There's not much else in this simple town, but it's fun to watch the comings and goings of the fishing boats, especially in midafternoon, when they usually return with the day's catch.

Fayette Heritage Days

For more than 20 years, Fayette Historic Townsite has come to life during the annual Fayette Heritage Days festival, celebrating the town's history. The second Saturday in August brings visitors to the state park for period music, food, and displays that channel the ghost town's once busy iron-smelting days.

SUMMER SPORTS AND RECREATION
◖ Bays de Noc

With the exception, perhaps, of Green Bay, Lake Michigan's best-known inlets are the Bays de Noc. The Big and Little Bays are positioned at the northwest end of the lake and are known primarily for their world-class walleye fishing. Equally popular, though, are the vast acres of water themselves—more than

120,000 acres between the two bays make them one of the U.P.'s top summer destinations for water lovers. Come here to fish, boat, paddle, or swim.

Hiking and Biking

There's more to **Fayette State Park** than the historic townsite. A five-mile footpath affords views of the ghost town from the area's limestone bluffs, and some 17 miles of trails wind their way through the forests surrounding the town. **Portage Bay State Forest Campground** (906/452-6227, www.michigan.gov/dnr) has just over two miles of nice trails on the Ninga Aki Pathway. Take County Road 483 10 miles south of Garden.

Canoeing and Kayaking

If you're into kayaking—and sea kayaking in particular—you won't want to miss the opportunity to put in to Lake Michigan at **Fayette State Park.** From here, head north to Snake Island and Garden Bay or south to Sac Bay. The waters close to shore are suitable for all but the least experienced kayakers, offering views of towering limestone cliffs and sandy beaches. Experienced kayakers can head south from the southern point to nose around the offshore islands, but there's plenty of open water involved—steer clear unless you know what you're doing.

Fishing

Although you'll be able to find some fishing at **Fayette State Park** and **Portage Bay State Forest** campground (906/452-6227, www.michigan.gov/dnr), get ahold of **Bay de Noc Charters** (7989 U.S. 2, 906/474-6918, www.baydenoccharters.com) to arrange a fishing trip in legendary walleye waters. Bay de Noc Charters is located in Rapid River, on the extreme north end of Little Bay de Noc, but fishing excursions are available in Big Bay, too.

Boating

There are somewhere around 90,000 acres of water in **Big Bay de Noc.** The larger of

THE LAKE MICHIGAN SHORE

Delta County's two bays fills the gap between the Garden Peninsula and Stonington Peninsula to the west, and its open waters provide some of the area's best boating. There are boat landings at the Fayette Historic Townsite and Garden Bay, as well as at Little Fishdam River to the north and Nahma, a few miles south of U.S. 2 on County Road 497. The Fayette Historic Townsite's Snail Shell Harbor has 300 feet of dock available for overnight or day use, and the waters here are deep enough for larger crafts. Boaters in search of larger marinas will have to dock at Gladstone or Escanaba on Little Bay de Noc or Manistique to the east, on the opposite side of the Garden Peninsula.

Beaches

Located on Lake Michigan's Big Bay de Noc, **Sac Bay Park** (906/786-4902 or 906/786-1020, www.deltacountymi.org) is a 65-acre county park and beach. There isn't much here beyond the sandy lakeshore, a small play area, and some picnic tables, but it serves as a decent enough rest stop for travelers making their way through the Garden Peninsula. **Fayette State Park** has a small swimming beach just south of the town.

Golf

There are two passable golf courses in or near the Garden Peninsula, though more serious golfers may wish to head west for the Bays de Noc golf trail near Escanaba. If you want to stay in the Garden Peninsula (you really can't beat the scenery), you can find some good greens at the **Garden Golf and Supper Club** (15701 18th Rd., 906/644-2693, $16–25 9 holes, $22–35 18 holes), which also has a clubhouse bar and restaurant. Call ahead for all-day golf specials or multi-day specials that include lodging and meals. To get to the Garden Golf Club, take M-183 about eight miles south of U.S. 2. The smaller **Nahma Golf Course** (8588 LL Rd., 906/644-2648, $19) has nine holes on a pretty flat public course. Take County Road 494 south of U.S. 2.

WINTER SPORTS AND RECREATION
Ski and Snowshoe Trails

The same Garden Peninsula trails that make for popular summertime hiking become pathways through the Upper Peninsula's winter wonderland. The five miles of trail that overlook the **Fayette Historic Townsite** (13700 13.25 La., 906/644-2603, www.michigan .gov/dnr) are regularly groomed for skiing every winter. Although the path is suitable for beginners, more advanced skiers will enjoy the views of Big Bay de Noc and the town, even if they do miss the challenge of a more difficult trail. Strap on some snowshoes for a trek through the townsite itself—although it's cold, you'll bypass the summer tourist crowds.

Snowmobiling

Connect to the U.P. snowmobile trail system via Trail 415 (the only designated snowmobile trail in the Garden Peninsula), which starts in the city of Garden and makes its way north to Trail 2. From there, the U.P. is yours.

ACCOMMODATIONS

On the north end of Big Bay de Noc and the Garden Peninsula, where U.S. 2 and M-183 meet, **Tylene's Motel** (16086 U.S. 2, Cooks, 906/450-6010, open Apr.–Dec., $45) has 12 modestly priced rooms, as well as a three-bedroom apartment that's only available as a weeklong or weekend rental. The motel is open year-round and offers clean rooms, lake access, beach views, and—best of all—a diner-style restaurant next door.

Although lodging tends to be a little sparse in the Garden Peninsula, there are a couple of bed-and-breakfasts in the city of Garden itself. Garden's **【 Valentine's Bay Lodge Bed and Breakfast** (8191 M-183, 866/233-0737 or 906/644-5012, $79–125) is a large log home on the Big Bay de Noc waterfront. It has the look of an A-frame cabin, but what it lacks in old-time charm it makes up for with gorgeous views, well-kept rooms, and a casual atmosphere. Book the Whirlpool Room for—you guessed it—a private whirlpool bath; other rooms have deck walkouts or cathedral ceilings and private baths. During breakfast, take the opportunity to chat with Nicole Young, the innkeeper and author whose Patricia Amble mystery series was inspired by the Garden Peninsula setting.

Camping

Camping is readily available at dozens of rustic campgrounds within Hiawatha National Forest, and a particularly nice one is the very secluded—and difficult to reach—**Portage Bay State Forest Campground** on the Garden Peninsula's eastern shore. It's southeast of Garden, at the end of Portage Bay Road. For modern campsites, your best bets are often state parks like **Indian Lake** or **Fayette**. For camping reservations at any Michigan state park, call 800/447-2757 or visit www.michigan.gov/dnr.

FOOD

Rosie's at Tylene's (U.S. 2, Garden Corners, 906/644-7155, open daily 7 A.M.–9 P.M. Memorial Day–Labor Day, 8 A.M.–9 P.M. off season) is a must for guests of Tylene's Motel, if only because it's right next door. The unassuming restaurant is a worthwhile stop for everyone else, too, with its good food and convenient location, just west of the intersection of U.S. 2 and M-183. In Garden, you'll want to visit the **Garden House Bar and Grill** (M-183, downtown Garden, 906/644-2844, 11 A.M.–10 P.M.). Dinners are a little on the expensive side for the U.P.—you can spend upwards of $20—but the fresh fish (locally caught, of course) and prime rib are worth the stop. As its name implies, **Sherry's Port Bar** (4424 M-123, 906/644-2545), south of Garden, is primarily a drinking establishment, but it's managed to become

a catch-all family restaurant with cheap food and a good breakfast. Its proximity to Fayette State Park makes it a popular stop.

INFORMATION

For visitor information and assistance for the Garden Peninsula, contact the **Bays de Noc Convention & Visitors Bureau** (230 Ludington St., 800/533-4386, 906/789-7862, www.travelbaysdenoc.com) and the **Delta County Chamber of Commerce** (230 Ludington St., 888-335-8264, 906/786-8830, www.deltami.org).

Bank choices are limited in Garden, but you can do some banking at First Bank Upper Peninsula (6322 State St., Garden, 906/644-3535, 8:30 A.M.–4 P.M., www.first-bank.com), but there's no ATM on site.

Your best bets for medical attention will be to head to Manistique for the Schoolcraft Memorial Hospital (500 Main St., Manistique, 906/341-3200, www.scmh.org). Take U.S. 2 east, turn left on M-94 north, then turn right on Main Street—the hospital is 0.25 miles up the road.

GETTING THERE AND AROUND
Car

This is really your only viable option for getting to (and around) the Garden Peninsula. There isn't any sort of regular public transportation that makes its way south of U.S. 2, there certainly aren't any airports, and although there are boat landings and docks at Fayette State Park, Garden Bay, and Portage Bay, there are no big marinas like you'll find in Escanaba, St. Ignace, or even Manistique. Besides, even if you managed to get here by some other means, there's nowhere to rent a car—you'll have to drive your own in or rent a vehicle in one of the U.P.'s bigger cities.

THE LAKE MICHIGAN SHORE

Escanaba and Vicinity

A metropolis for these parts, Escanaba and neighboring Gladstone (just a few miles north) are home to some 20,000 people, serving as the industrial and commercial center for the south-central Upper Peninsula. The natural deepwater port gave Escanaba its start back in the Civil War days, when a hastily built rail line linked the iron mines in Negaunee with the port, bringing coveted raw materials to the weapons-makers and railroad builders of the Union Army. Today Escanaba's modern ore port still ships iron, now in the form of iron/clay taconite pellets, to steelmakers in Indiana and Ohio.

Unlike M-35 north of Gladstone, the stretch of highway between Gladstone and Menominee runs close to the coast, and it has been designated the **U.P. Hidden Coast Recreation Heritage Route.** Follow it south from Gladstone into Escanaba.

SIGHTS
Downtown

Downtown Escanaba focuses on Ludington Street, an east–west route that runs from M-35 to the waterfront. Here's where you'll find most of the town's restaurants and shops and a growing local arts presence. The town's landmark is the **House of Ludington** (223 Ludington St., 906/786-6300, www.house ofludington.com), a grand old Queen Anne resort hotel built in 1865. After enjoying a second heyday in the 1940s and '50s, the old hotel has stuttered and stumbled with some shoddy interior remodeling and mismanagement. The most recent owners have reopened the hotel's restaurant with an upscale menu, and the building's imposing facade continues to anchor the downtown.

At the foot of Ludington Street, lovely **Ludington Park** offers paved pathways along the water and to a small island (in-line skates permitted), interpretive signs explaining local history, a band shell that hosts concerts on Wednesday and Sunday evenings in summer, a playground, a beach, tennis courts, and a boat launch.

Escanaba's art scene can perhaps be best witnessed during a visit to the **William Bonifas Art Center** (700 1st Avenue South, 906/786-3833, www.bonifasarts.org, 10 A.M.–5:30 P.M.

ESCANABA IN DA MOONLIGHT

Travelers who haven't been to the Upper Peninsula and don't quite know what to expect could certainly do worse than to track down a copy of *Escanaba in da Moonlight*, an off-color love song to the beautiful, quirky, often misunderstood Yooper culture.

The movie (starring, written, directed, and produced by Michigan native Jeff Daniels) tells the story of the "buckless Yooper," Reuben Soady, a 42-year-old Escanaba man in the humiliating position of never having shot a buck. This is a big deal in Soady's Escanaba. Most of the film takes place at the Soady deer camp, and at the core of it, it's about hunting and family and expectations and the spirit of the Upper Peninsula itself. It's really quite good.

That said, it's quite odd, too. Things get a bit off (and the movie gets a bit weird) when talk turns to UFOs, but the rest of the flick is, at least to an outsider's eyes, pretty well spot on: the accent (Yoobetcha!), the conviction that euchre is the only card game worth playing, the flannel shirts, the hunting camp. This is the Upper Peninsula seen through a sometimes-stereotypical point of view, told by someone who understands and appreciates the land and its people.

Granted, the movie isn't for everyone – film's website says it's rated PG-13 for "uncultured humor," and it hasn't exactly been well-received by critics – but it's worth putting in your rental queue.

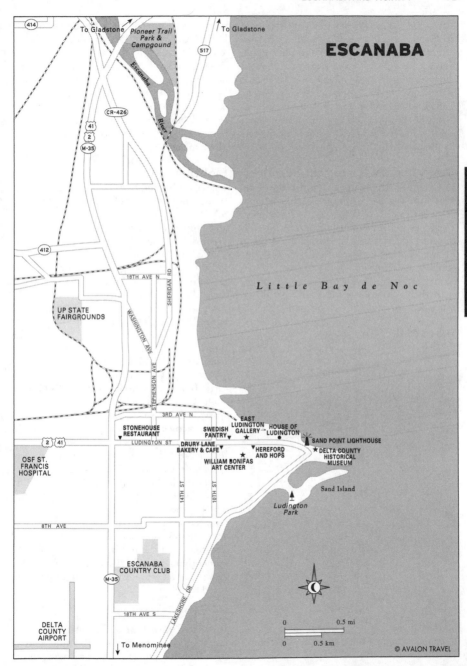

ESCANABA

To Gladstone

414

To Gladstone

Pioneer Trail Park & Campground

517

Escanaba River

CR-426

41
2
M-35

412

18TH AVE N

SHERIDAN RD

WASHINGTON AVE

STEPHENSON AVE

UP STATE FAIRGROUNDS

Little Bay de Noc

3RD AVE N

STONEHOUSE RESTAURANT

2 41

LUDINGTON ST

OSF ST. FRANCIS HOSPITAL

SWEDISH PANTRY

EAST LUDINGTON GALLERY

HOUSE OF LUDINGTON

SAND POINT LIGHTHOUSE

DELTA COUNTY HISTORICAL MUSEUM

DRURY LANE BAKERY & CAFE

HEREFORD AND HOPS

WILLIAM BONIFAS ART CENTER

14TH ST

10TH ST

Sand Island

Ludington Park

8TH AVE

ESCANABA COUNTRY CLUB

M-35

18TH AVE S

LAKESHORE DR

DELTA COUNTY AIRPORT

To Menominee

0   0.5 mi

0   0.5 km

© AVALON TRAVEL

Tues.–Fri., 10 A.M.–3 P.M. Sat.), a community art facility housed in a 1938 building that had originally been a gymnasium and auditorium. Today, the center is open for visitors to tour the changing free gallery exhibits, watch theatrical productions, and attend classes. The **East Ludington Gallery** (619 Ludington St., 906/786-0300, www.eastludingtongallery .com) displays and sells works by more than 35 regional artists.

Delta County Historical Society

Just to the south, the **Delta County Historical Museum** (16 Water Plant Rd., Escanaba, 906/786-3428, www.deltahistorical.org, Memorial Day–Labor Day, $2 adults, $1 children) has interesting and informative displays on local logging, native cultures, military history, and maritime history. The four-room museum has been collecting historical artifacts for more than 50 years, and the result is an important documentation of regional heritage.

Gladstone

Gladstone's most unique attraction certainly

Escanaba's Sand Point Lighthouse is a fine example of a historic light.

© JOSH BISHOP

must be the **Hoegh Pet Casket Company** (317 Delta Ave., 906/428-2151, www.hoeghpetcaskets .com, Mon.–Fri., 8 A.M.–4 P.M.). "You've read about it, you've seen it on television," proclaims one advertisement. "Now tour the only model pet cemetery in the world and see the world's largest pet casket manufacturing operation." Indeed, Hoegh offers tours of the pet casket manufacturing line and explains the pet burial phenomenon.

Lighthouses

One of Ludington Park's most popular attractions is the **Sand Point Lighthouse** (906/786-3763), an 1868 brick light that was restored and reopened in 1990 by the Delta County Historical Society. It was a big job: In the 1940s, the Coast Guard remodeled the obsolete light for staff housing, removing the lantern room and lopping off the top ten feet of the tower. For a couple of bucks, you can climb the tower and take a look at the restored keeper's house. The light's first keeper, by the way, was Mary Terry, one of the nation's first woman lightkeepers. The Delta County Historical Museum is located nearby.

At the tip of the Stonington Peninsula, across Little Bay de Noc from Escanaba, **Peninsula Point Lighthouse Park** is the perfect place to sprawl out on a sunny day: an open meadow, a grassy picnic area, a great shoreline for beachcombing, and—the main attraction—an 1865 lighthouse. Climb the spiral stairway for one of the most expansive views around: a 270-degree survey of the long and leggy Green Bay, and even Wisconsin's Door County on a clear day. The lighthouse was abandoned in the 1930s, replaced by a more effective shoal light several miles offshore. Local volunteers restored and reopened the old light, which was subsequently ravaged by fire in 1959. While the keeper's home was destroyed, the tower withstood the blaze.

ENTERTAINMENT
Island Resort and Casino

Harris, a small town some 13 miles west of Escanaba, has one of the U.P.'s finest gaming resorts. Island Resort and Casino (W399 U.S. 2/U.S. 41, 906/466-2941, 800/682-6040, www.chipincasino.com) is a 24/7 casino with more than 1,400 slot machines and plenty of table games—craps, blackjack, roulette, poker, Texas Hold 'Em, and more. When you get hungry, stop at the Firekeeper's Restaurant for cheap breakfast and lunch or daily all-you-can-eat dinner specials. Other on-site dining can be found at the Beachcomber Restaurant and Bar, Coral Reef Grille, and Bingo Snack Bar. The Island Showroom seats more than 1,300 for headliner shows; for lesser-known acts, visit Club Four One for weekly live bands and comedy nights every Sunday. A golf course, a 113-room hotel with indoor pool, a salon, and an RV park round out the experience and cement Island Resort's reputation as one of the Midwest's premier resort destinations.

FESTIVALS AND EVENTS
Upper Peninsula State Fair
On M-35, between Escanaba and Gladstone, you'll pass the U.P. State Fair Grounds. As further evidence that the U.P. often feels little affinity with its Lower Peninsula counterpart, Michigan hosts two state fairs. The U.P. fair is held the third week of August. For event information, contact the Delta County Chamber of Commerce (230 Ludington St., 906/786-2192, 888/335-8264, www.deltami.org).

Balloons on the Bay and Pioneer Days
The combination is interesting, to say the least—hot air balloons and pioneer heritage. Every year in late June, the U.P. State Fair Grounds become the staging ground for hot air balloons that fill the air above Lake Michigan. Jump in the basket for a tethered balloon ride or experience a bit of the old days while watching lumberjack exhibitions, old-fashioned craft demonstrations, and a barbecue cook-off. Again, for more information, get ahold of the **Delta County Chamber of Commerce** (230 Ludington St., 906/786-2192, 888/335-8264, www.deltami.org).

Monarch Migration
There really isn't anything official about the annual monarch butterfly migration, aside from volunteers, organized by the U.S. Forest Service, who count the populations and help tag the insects for tracking. But when it comes to monarch viewing, you can join the throng of enthusiasts who make the trek to the Stonington Peninsula every August. The peninsula, which extends south into Lake Michigan between the Bays de Noc, is an annual gathering point in the butterflies' great migration south to Mexico—they stop in and around Peninsula Point Lighthouse Park before the long flight across Green Bay and the open waters of the lake. The brilliant orange and black monarchs are best seen in August, although the migration continues into September, often overlapping with the autumn colors Michigan is known for.

SUMMER SPORTS AND RECREATION
Hiawatha National Forest
The 860,000-acre Hiawatha National Forest spans much of the central U.P., with its western unit stretching all the way from the Lake Michigan shoreline of the Stonington Peninsula to the Lake Superior shore near Munising. For information on hiking trails, campgrounds, canoe routes, and other attractions, stop at the **Hiawatha National Forest Visitor Information Station** (906/474-6442) just east of Rapid River on U.S. 2. You can talk with rangers and pick up a wide selection of maps and handouts. The station also includes interpretive displays and a small bookshop.

Hiking and Biking
Hiawatha National Forest's 40-mile **Bay de Noc/Grand Island Trail** follows an old Ojibwa portage route, used to carry canoes and supplies between Lakes Michigan and Superior. Today it ends just short of both lakes, beginning just northeast of Rapid River and ending 10 miles shy of Lake Superior at Ackerman Lake. The trail parallels the Whitefish River, about half a mile to two miles away, tracing its

eastern bluff and often affording high, sweeping views of the forested river valley. It hopscotches over several streams and passes several lakes. Because of the preponderance of hardwoods, the route is particularly beautiful in the fall color season.

Horses and mountain bikes are allowed on the Bay de Noc/Grand Island Trail, but no motorized vehicles. Primitive camping is permitted throughout the national forest (no permit required). To find the trailhead, follow U.S. 2 east from Rapid River two miles, then turn left on County Road 509 and drive another 1.5 miles. You'll see a parking area on the west side of the road.

A few miles east of the Hiawatha National Forest Visitor Information Station, turn north off U.S. 2 onto County Road H-13 to reach the great hiking and mountain biking trails of **Pine Marten Run.** The trail network lies between the Indian River to the north, County Road 440 to the south, Forest Road 2258 to the west, and County Road 437 to the east. This newly signed area includes 26 miles of rolling single-track and overgrown double-track. Various loops wind through huge hemlocks and white pines, around a dozen lakes, and along the pretty Indian River. From County Road H-13, turn right on County Road 440, and watch for the Forest Service sign directing you to Iron Jaw Lake. Alternatively, head north from County Road 440 on Forest Road 2258, where you'll find another trailhead just before the road crosses the Indian River. Get maps and more information from the Hiawatha National Forest Visitor Information Station.

Just three miles north of Gladstone, the Escanaba River State Forest maintains the **Days River Pathway,** a fine nine-mile hiking trail that loops through forest and along the scenic Days River, which cuts a deep gorge near the trailhead. This is a good stream for brook trout, so bring a fly rod. Toss in binoculars, too, since the area is thick with warblers and other songbirds. To reach the trailhead, follow U.S. 2 east of Gladstone three miles, then turn left onto Days River Road. For more information, contact the **Escanaba Forest Area Office** (906/293-3293, www.michigan .gov/dnr).

On the opposite side of Little Bay de Noc, the Stonington Peninsula is largely ignored by tourists, lacking accessible sand beaches or commercial attractions. It is a soft and peaceful place, with smooth slabs of bedrock shoreline and sunny meadows that have reclaimed abandoned farmland. The Hiawatha National Forest manages a nice stretch of shoreline along the peninsula's west side, with a couple of campgrounds and hiking trails. Watch for Forest Service signs south of Garth Point. The peninsula preserves several stands of old-growth hemlocks, hardwoods, and pines. One of the most notable examples is now protected as the **Squaw Creek Old Growth Area,** part of the Hiawatha National Forest. Though these woods are not virgin timber, 19th-century loggers practiced selective cutting (quite unusual in those days) and left behind several large trees, now huge. Trails are few—just a couple of abandoned logging roads open only to foot traffic. Walking is easy, however, since the high shade canopy created by the trees crowds out the underbrush usually found in the woods. (Do take a compass.)

The southern part of the 65-acre tract is particularly scenic, with the clear, tea-colored waters of Squaw Creek slaloming between the fat trunks. You'll find the largest hemlocks south of the creek and huge hardwoods just to the north. Squaw Creek is not marked by a sign and shows up on few maps. To find it, drive south nine miles on County Road 513; just before and after the road crosses the creek, you'll see pull-offs on the east side of the road and old roads leading inland.

Canoeing and Kayaking

Just north of Pine Marten Run and the Indian River, the **Big Island Lake Canoeing Area** offers paddlers a quiet chain of nine lakes. Since there are few launches for powerboats, the lakes usually remain peaceful and pristine even in the height of summer. Again, obtain information and maps from the Visitor Information Station.

You'll find good paddling on the **Escanaba River,** too. Put in northwest of Gladstone and take the river all the way to Green Bay. There are more than 40 miles of good paddling between Gwinn and Gladstone, with periodic access points; most of the river is suitable for intermediate paddlers, though it does get more difficult during a few sections. You can paddle a few miles along the **Ford River,** southwest of Gladstone. Beginners can take the river between County Road 414 and U.S. 2, but there's some whitewater as you get closer to Green Bay (there's an access point at U.S. 2 if you're nervous about continuing on). Of course, openwater kayakers can paddle Little Bay de Noc and Green Bay. Rent a canoe or kayak (or a number of other boats) from **Splash Rentals** (2311 9th Ave. North, 906/789-1009) in Escanaba.

Fishing

Although it's the smaller of the two bays, **Little Bay de Noc's** more than 30,000 acres of water are nothing to laugh at. The bay is known for its fishing, particularly for its walleye in the fall. Captain Dick Stafford of **Take Five Charter Fishing** (7262 U.S. 2, 906/789-0110, www.takefivecharters.com) in Gladstone pilots half- and full-day fishing charters in Little Bay de Noc and Green Bay. Rapid River's **Bay de Noc Charters** (7989 U.S. 2, 906/474-6918, www.baydenoccharters.com), on the northern tip of the bay, can take you on a fishing trip in Little Bay de Noc, and charters into Big Bay de Noc are available as well. Gladstone is chock-full of fishing charters—contact the **Bays de Noc Convention & Visitors Bureau** (230 Ludington St., Escanaba, 906/789-7862, 800/533-4386, www.travelbaysdenoc.com).

If you'd rather set off on your own, get ahold of **U.P. Michigan Boat Rentals** (434 East Prospect St., Marquette, 877/228-5447, www.upmichiganboatrentals.com). Marquette is some 60 miles north of Gladstone, but U.P. Michigan Boat Rentals can deliver fishing or pontoon boats to Little Bay de Noc (plan on spending at least $1/mile for delivery and pickup). Local tackle shops and outfitters include

Bayview Bait and Tackle Shop (7110 U.S. 2, 906/786-1488), between Gladstone and Escanaba, and **Walleye's Choice** (10132 M-35, 906/428-1488, www.walleyeschoice.com). Walleye's Choice also offers fishing charters. Cast a line into the **Whitefish River,** which flows into Little Bay de Noc at Rapid River, for trout and smallmouth bass.

Beaches

In Gladstone, visit **Van Cleve Park** (906/428-2916) on Lake Shore Drive. There's a sandy beach for swimming in the waters of Little Bay de Noc, and a number of other activities make this one of the area's best beaches for family fun—a fitness course, sand volleyball courts, horseshoes, basketball, softball, a gazebo, a playground, and more. The Gladstone Harbor is here, too.

Golf

Golfing in the Upper Peninsula is like most U.P. activities—casual and unpretentious, without the pomp and circumstance found at more expensive destinations. In fact, one of the U.P.'s finest golf trails, right in Delta County, consists of four top-notch courses, each within 20 minutes of the others. You'll spend somewhere around $25 for 18 holes at each of them. The **Escanaba Country Club** (1800 11th Ave. South, 906/786-1701, www.escanabacc.com) is the oldest country club in Delta County (it was founded in 1915). The par-71 18-hole course has a PGA professional on staff and one of the hardest-finishing holes around. Nearby **Gladstone Golf Club** (6514 Days River Rd., 906/428-9646, www.gladstoneschools.com/GGC/ggc.html) is smack-dab in the middle of thousands of acres of forests, and the Days River runs through 5 of the 18 holes. Take U.S. 2 about three miles north of Gladstone and turn left on County Road 446 for two miles. Rated one of the best courses in the area, the 18-hole **Terrace Bluff Golf Club** (7146 P Rd., Gladstone, 906/428-2343, www.terracebay.com) features views of the bay and is suitable for golfers of every skill level. The amenities of Terrace Bay Resort and Convention Center are close at hand. Finally, seven miles west of Escanaba on U.S. 2, the **Highland Golf Club** (906/466-7457, www.highlandgolfclub.net) was Delta County's first 18-hole course.

Off-Road Vehicles

The Forest Islands Trail begins about 10 miles south of Escanaba, west of M-35 (take 4.25 Road to H Road and turn right, then turn left on F Road to parking). The 33-mile trail ends in Cedar River, and is broken into the Limpert Road Loop, the Seven Mile Marsh Loop, and the Westman Road Loop near Cedar River at the south end of the trail.

Waterfalls

They're pleasant enough, and certainly pretty, but with a drop of about five feet spread out over a number of tiers, the **Rapid River Falls** aren't as powerful or impressive as some of the U.P.'s other waterfalls. Still, they're peaceful and relaxing, and a park on the river has picnic tables and grills, as well as a playground. Take U.S. 41 seven miles north of Rapid River and follow the signs to the left.

WINTER SPORTS AND RECREATION
Downhill Skiing

The Escanaba area is only a short distance east of Iron Mountain and the Upper Peninsula's best-known skiing runs, but beginning and intermediate skiers can try **Gladstone Sports Park** (900 North Bluff Dr., 906/428-9130, $8/day ski, $7/day tube), just east of the city. It's a relatively low-key resort (you won't find any chairlifts), but its combination of easy hills and tubing runs makes it ideal for families who want to avoid the crowds and prices of the bigger resorts to the west. There are a few rope tows and a T-bar, three tube runs, and a snowboard terrain park that includes a half-pipe for riders. Concessions are sold in the Ski Chalet.

Ski and Snowshoe Trails

The nine miles of **Days Rivers Pathway** (906/293-3293, www.michigan.gov/dnr), three miles south of Rapid River, are among the most popular groomed ski trails in the area. Choose from loops of between one and eight miles, suitable for beginners as well as experts. Six miles north of Rapid River, the **Rapid River Ski Trails** (906/786-4062, www .fs.fed.us) provide an especially beautiful excursion through varied terrain. Pay attention to the signs, and stay off the 10-mile loop unless you're an expert skier—the other loops are suitable for less-experienced cross-country enthusiasts. Snowshoers can make tracks alongside both trails. Both trails have donation boxes to help support trail maintenance and upkeep, so if you've got a couple bucks, it wouldn't hurt to help out. A surprisingly secluded **Escanaba Cross Country Pathway** is located inside the Escanaba city limits, but it's so quiet you wouldn't know it.

Dog Sledding

In the winter, the Bay de Noc/Grand Island Trail area is the stomping grounds for the sled dogs of **Triple Creek Sled Dog Kennels** (800/364-7533). Owner Bob Johnson, one of the U.P.'s most experienced mushers, offers a variety of two-hour to five-day dogsled trips in the region. Package tours include a stay at **Johnson's Buck Sporting Lodge,** his solar-powered wilderness lodge north of Rapid River.

Snowmobiling

Gain access to the Michigan's seemingly endless 6,100 miles of interconnected snowmobile trails via the **Nahma Grade Snowmobile Trail**; the trailhead is a couple miles east of Rapid River. After following a natural gas pipeline for 11 miles, the trail heads north. From Escanaba, Trail 2 takes you west toward Iron Mountain.

ACCOMMODATIONS

The typical sprawl of chain motels runs along M-35 between Escanaba and Gladstone, but some nice family-owned operations are still holding their own along the waterfront, with rates in the $50–100 range. The **Terrace Bay Resort** (7146 P Road, 906/786-7554, www.terracebay.com, $69–99), on Little Bay de Noc between Escanaba and Gladstone, has nice, clean motel rooms with great bay views. The 200-acre golf resort complex includes an 18-hole golf course, indoor and outdoor pools, tennis courts, a game room, and more. To find Terrace Bay, watch for signs on U.S. 41 south of Gladstone. About six miles south of Escanaba on M-35, **Fishery Pointe Beach Cottages** (E5043 M-35, 616/361-1386, www.fisherypointe .com, Memorial Day–Labor Day, $550–660 per week) and **Sandy Shores Resort** (4717 M-35, 906/786-3625, $55, $550–695 per week for cabins, May–early Oct.) offer housekeeping cottages on a nice stretch of sand beach.

Downtown Escanaba's **(House of Ludington** (223 Ludington St., 906/786-6300, www.houseofludington.com, $55–85) hasn't exactly been restored to its former glory, but the current owners, Ed and Suzell Eisenberger, have made an honest (and respectable) attempt. The hotel's 25 rooms are decorated with different themes, each with an eye to highlighting the hotel's historic past: House of

Ludington was conceived in 1865, renamed in 1871, and torn down and rebuilt in 1883, and it has passed through numerous hands since. It was most recently closed for a few years in the 1990s. Now there is a bar where there had been an inner courtyard, two dining rooms, and modern amenities in the guest rooms.

A few miles south of Escanaba, travelers can find some of the remote peace and quiet that the U.P. is known for at **St. Michael's in Cedar Dells** (2726 M-35, Bark River, 906/786-4541, www.escanabacottages.com, $55–150), a resort tucked away in a cedar grove overlooking Lake Michigan. The rustic but clean one- to three-bedroom cottages are perfect for families. Pets are welcome, too.

Camping
Haymeadow Creek Campground (Rapid River Ranger District, 499 East Lake Shore Dr., Manistique, 906/474-6442, www.fs.fed .us) is about 10 miles north of U.S. 2 on County Road 509 in Hiawatha National Forest. Each of the 15 campsites has a fire ring and a picnic

THE LAKE MICHIGAN SHORE

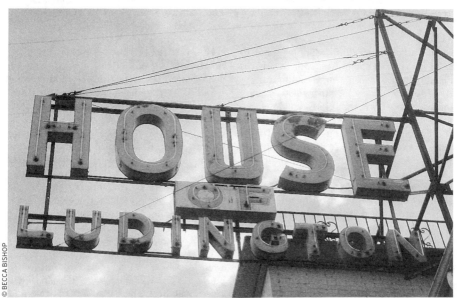

© BECCA BISHOP

The House of Ludington, built in 1865, has been restored into a fine, historic hotel.

table, and drinking water is available on site. You'll be able to connect to the Bay de Noc–Grand Island trail from here, too.

Closer to town, you'll find both tent and RV camping at the **Pioneer Trail Park and Campground** (906/786-4902, www.delta countymi.org, $13–15 tents, $18.50–22 RVs), a few miles north of Escanaba. Of the 75 sites, only 17 are for tenting, but these include fire pits and picnic tables. The rest of the campsites have electric hookups for RVs, and most of them have water. Pioneer Trail is ideal for families: Amenities include a playground and a playing field, a picnic area, showers, and optional cable TV. The campground is on U.S. 2/M-35 between Gladstone and Manistique. There are 25 additional campsites at the **O. B. Fuller Park and Campground** (906/786-4902, www.delta countymi.org, $18–21), a county park on Lake Michigan, 15 miles south of Escanaba. The campground features more than 80 wooded acres, Lake Michigan shoreline, fishing on the Bark River, and electricity and water at each campsite. Follow M-35 south from Escanaba to the Bark River crossing.

FOOD

You'll find your best dining options in downtown Escanaba. The hottest spot in town is (**Hereford and Hops** (614 Ludington St., 906/786-1945), a cook-your-own-steak place and microbrewery in the 1914 Delta Hotel. For homemade soups, sandwiches, and wonderful Finnish baked goods, don't miss the **Drury Lane Bakery and Cafe** (906 Ludington St., 906/786-0808). You can get traditional American meals at the (**Swedish Pantry** (819 Ludington St., 906/786-9606, www.swedish pantry.com), but you'll also find that—true to its name—the cute little restaurant serves up traditional Swedish food the way Momma used to make it. No one will stop you from ordering the meatloaf or roast beef, but you really should try the Swedish meatballs, potato sausage, and rutabaga. The Swedish Pantry is open for breakfast, lunch, and dinner. Grab a massive fresh-baked cookie from the bakery,

and browse the traditional Scandinavian merchandise at the gift shop.

The **Stonehouse Restaurant** (2223 Ludington St., 906/786-5003, www.stone houseescanaba.com, 11 A.M.–2 P.M. and 5–9:30 P.M. Mon.–Thurs. and 5–10 P.M. Fri. and Sat.) doesn't look like much on the outside, but it's got some fine food and a casual atmosphere. Lunch runs around $10 for sandwiches, salads, and entrées (look for the daily plate special), but plan on spending $18–28 for a dinner entrée—steak, lobster, scallops, duck, and more. The Carport Lounge serves mixed drinks and a passable list of wines by the glass.

Of course, you can always make reservations at an Escanaba landmark. The historic **House of Ludington** (223 Ludington St., 906/786-6300, www.houseofludington.com, 11:30 A.M.–2 P.M. lunch Tues.–Fri., 5–8 P.M. dinner Mon.–Thurs., and 5–9 P.M. dinner Fri. and Sat.) has two dining rooms: the King George Dining Room is an elegant choice (you'll dine with antique silver here), while the Emerald Dining Room is slightly more casual. The restored hotel serves gourmet meals for both lunch and dinner.

INFORMATION AND SERVICES

Visitor information for Escanaba and the surrounding area can be obtained from the **Bays de Noc Convention & Visitors Bureau** (230 Ludington St., 906/789-7862, 800/533-4386, www.travelbaysdenoc.com) and the Delta County Chamber of Commerce (230 Ludington St., 906/786-8830, 888-335-8264, www.deltami.org). For recreation information, contact the Michigan DNR (6833 U.S. 2, Gladstone, 906/786-2351, www.michigan .gov/dnr) or the U.S. Forest Service/Hiawatha National Forest (2727 North Lincoln Rd., Escanaba, 906/786-4062, www.fs.fed.us).

Dial 911 for emergencies, and seek medical attention at OSF St. Francis Hospital (3401 Ludington St., Escanaba, 906/786-5707, www .osfstfrancis.org). There are plenty of banks and ATMs in downtown Escanaba and in Gladstone, including Wells Fargo (1205 Ludington St., 906/789-5236, www.wellsfargo.com) and a number of smaller local and regional banks.

GETTING THERE AND AROUND
Car

If you're coming from the Mackinac Bridge or south on I-75 from Sault Ste. Marie and Ontario, you really couldn't have an easier time of driving to Escanaba—you simply take U.S. 2 east from St. Ignace until you hit the city. Since Escanaba is far closer to Wisconsin than it is to the Lower Peninsula, many drivers will want to drive along Green Bay (the bay) from Green Bay (the city) on U.S. 41 to M-35 and take it into Escanaba from the south.

Boat

There are two quality marinas in the vicinity of Escanaba, one in Escanaba itself and the other in Gladstone, a few miles north. The **Escanaba Municipal Marina** (906/786-9614, www.michigan.gov/dnr) has 37 transient and 128 seasonal slips. The marina is open seasonally from May 14 to October 12, and the harbormaster can be reached on channel 9 from 7 A.M.–4 P.M. The marina offers showers, gas and diesel fuel, day-use dockage, and bicycle

rentals. Its location is 45° 44.34 N, 87° 02.05 W. The **Gladstone Marina** (906/428-2916, www.michigan.gov/dnr) is located at 45° 50.15 N, 87° 01.00 W, and the harbormaster is on duty from May 15 to September 1. Gladstone Marina monitors radio channels 9 and 68.

Air

Northwest Airlines services **Delta County Airport** (ESC, 3300 Airport Rd., 906/786-4902, www.deltacountymi.org), a small, two-runway airport located just southwest of Escanaba. You can rent a car from Alamo Car Rental (3300 Airport Rd., 906/786-0603, www.alamo.com) that'll take you where you want to go (and you really will need a car while you're here). Though not as close to the airport, rentals are also available at Delta Economy Car Rental (2920 Ludington St., 906/786-1947) or Enterprise Rent-A-Car (2201 6th Ave., 906/786-6730, www.enterprise.com).

Public Transportation

Regular bus service to Escanaba is provided from Green Bay, Ironwood, Marquette, and St. Ignace by **Indian Trails** (800/292-3831, www.indiantrails.com). You can reach Escanaba from Chicago and Detroit, too, on a combination of Indian Trails and Greyhound buses.

Menominee and Vicinity

Spiking like a canine tooth between Wisconsin and the waters of Green Bay, the triangle of land comprising Menominee County and southern Delta County has been dubbed the peninsula's "banana belt." Well, it does have the U.P.'s most temperate climate, thanks to the warm (okay, relatively warm) waters of protected Green Bay, and the lightest snowfall in the Upper Peninsula—just 50 inches a year on average, a quarter of what typically falls on the rest of the U.P.

Locals take advantage of this quirk of nature not for growing bananas, but for raising dairy cattle and crops like corn and soybeans. Farms

dot the countryside here, many on land long ago clear-cut by loggers. The longtime logging industry still echoes through the region, too, in the historic waterfront district of Menominee and the mammoth Mead Paper plant near Escanaba—a key factor in the area's stable economy. Many visitors, though, have a tough time getting past the big lake always looming on the eastern horizon. The lapping waters of Green Bay are infinitely enticing and easily accessible here.

Don't forget that Menominee is located in the Central Time Zone, an hour behind Escanaba and the majority of the Upper Peninsula.

THE LAKE MICHIGAN SHORE

THE LAKE MICHIGAN SHORE

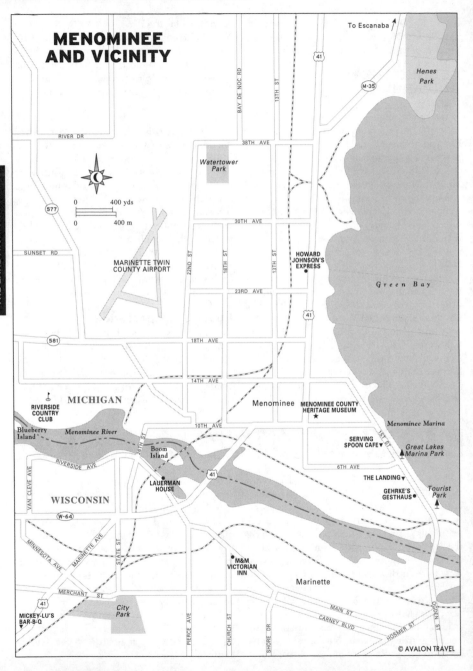

MENOMINEE AND VICINITY

To Escanaba

Henes Park

41

M-35

BAY DE NOC RD

13TH ST

RIVER DR

38TH AVE

Watertower Park

0   400 yds

0   400 m

30TH AVE

577

MARINETTE TWIN COUNTY AIRPORT

SUNSET RD

22ND ST

18TH ST

13TH ST

HOWARD JOHNSON'S EXPRESS

23RD AVE

Green Bay

41

581

18TH AVE

14TH AVE

MICHIGAN

Menominee

MENOMINEE COUNTY HERITAGE MUSEUM ★

Menominee Marina

RIVERSIDE COUNTRY CLUB

10TH AVE

SERVING SPOON CAFE ▼

1ST ST

Blueberry Island

Menominee River

6TH ST

Boom Island

Great Lakes Marina Park

RIVERSIDE AVE

41

6TH AVE

THE LANDING ▼

VAN CLEVE AVE

LAUERMAN HOUSE

GEHRKE'S GESTHAUS ●

Tourist Park

WISCONSIN

W-64

MINNESOTA AVE

MARINETTE AVE

STATE ST

M&M VICTORIAN INN

OGDEN ST

Marinette

MERCHANT ST

41

City Park

PIERCE AVE

CHURCH ST

SHORE DR

MAIN ST

CARNEY BLVD

HOSMER ST

MICKEY-LU'S BAR-B-Q ▼

© AVALON TRAVEL

SIGHTS

The Menominee River spills into Green Bay between the twin cities of Marinette, Wisconsin, and Menominee, Michigan, once the region's richest lumber port. Menominee's bustling business district is centered on 1st Street, along the waterfront. Happily, most of the 19th-century brick and sandstone buildings have survived intact, and renovation and restoration is underway on many of them. You can explore the **historic district** guided by a walking tour brochure available at **Spies Public Library** (940 1st St.). Its 1905 Beaux Arts facade happens to be one of the tour's most handsome buildings. A growing number of shops and restaurants along 1st Street are adding new life to this pleasant area.

The Menominee County Historical Society maintains the **Menominee County Heritage Museum** (904 11th Ave., 906/863-9000, www .menomineehistoricalsociety.org, 10 A.M.– 4 P.M. Mon.–Sat. Memorial Day–Labor Day) in an old Catholic church. Like many of the Upper Peninsula's local history museums, there isn't much here that most people can't live without seeing, but it does outline the county's history since its beginnings, and has displays about logging, Native American artifacts, and other aspects of Menominee's heritage, making it worth the stop for local history buffs.

Bayside Parks

The waterfront district is also home to bayside parks, easily accessible on foot. **Great Lakes Marina Park** stretches along the water between 6th and 10th Avenues, flanked by a new marina and a band shell that hosts summer concerts on Tuesday and Thursday evenings. For a longer walk or bike ride, head south along the water to the **Tourist Park** swimming beach. Continue farther south to the **North Pier Light,** which marks the entrance to Menominee Harbor with a beacon at the end of a rocky breakwater. Although the light is attractive, it isn't open to the public.

MENOMINEE WATERFRONT FESTIVAL

Pay a visit to Menominee's Historic Waterfront district for the **Waterfront Festival,** a popular

THE LAKE MICHIGAN SHORE

© JOSH BISHOP

Pastoral scenes, such as this secluded river, are a staple of the Upper Peninsula.

four-day celebration that offers plenty of traditional activities and events, including live music at the band shell, parades, boat races, and food vendors. Be sure not to miss the amateur lumberjack competition or the stunning fireworks display. The Waterfront Festival is held every year in early August.

SUMMER SPORTS AND RECREATION
Hiking and Biking
Menominee's most popular park is a bit farther afield. Located at the north end of town off M-35, **Henes Park** (906/863-2656) occupies a 50-acre point that juts out into Green Bay. Designed by noted landscape architect Ossian Simonds, this unusual park combines tracts of virgin hemlock and pine with the more-expected park amenities, like walking trails, swimming beaches, and playgrounds.

At the Cedar River, the **Escanaba River State Forest** (906/786-2351) offers a network of hiking and mountain biking trails, with four loops (ranging from two to seven miles) that travel over hilly terrain sculpted by Ice Age glaciers. The Cedar River Trail and Timber Trail in **J. W. Wells State Park** (906/863-9747) both follow the Green Bay shoreline.

Canoeing and Kayaking
The 100-mile stretch of the Menominee River from above Iron Mountain all the way through Menominee separates the Upper Peninsula from Wisconsin—and gives paddlers an intense, high-current ride. You'll have to portage around several dams and reservoirs, but the wildlife viewing and rugged scenery make the effort worthwhile. The upper reaches of the river shouldn't be tried by amateurs, though. The Class IV and V white water is some of the U.P.'s fastest. If you're an inexperienced or timid paddler, put in at an access point closer to Menominee, where the flow is gentler and the rapids (much slower here) are more easily navigated.

Beaches
In the 55 miles between Menominee and Escanaba, several parks and beaches lure you

Lake Michigan is an incredibly popular sailing spot. The marina at Menominee is packed.

© JOSH BISHOP

off the highway. About 13 miles north of Menominee, **Bailey Park** is a favorite swimming beach of the locals, with fine sand and low dunes on a point that stretches away from the highway. Just to the north, **Kleinke Park** is more exposed to M-35, but offers campsites overlooking the bay, as well as a sand beach. There are small swimming beaches at **Tourist Park,** near the Menominee Harbor and the North Pier Light, and at **Henes Park,** on M-35 just north of town.

Fishing

There's some fishing available at Cedar River, north of Menominee, as well as at the Menominee River and several smaller, local lakes and rivers—try Hayward Lake or Walton River. In town, anglers can cast a line off the Menominee Municipal Pier (the same pier that leads to the North Pier Light), but some of the best fishing is in Green Bay and Lake Michigan. Contact **Fish Tales Guide Service** (W4565 9.5 Rd., 906/863-2267, http://user .cybrzn.com/fishtales) for open-water charters lasting five to eight hours. Inland and river fishing is also available.

Boating

Green Bay, Little and Big Bays de Noc, and northern Lake Michigan are among the Midwest's most beautiful, temperate, and sailable waters. Along with sites in Escanaba and Gladstone to the north, boaters can put in at the **Menominee Marina** (906/863-8498, www .michigan.gov/dnr). Although primarily a fishing charter service, **Fish Tales Guide Service** (W4565 9.5 Rd., 906/863-2267, http://user .cybrzn.com/fishtales) can be hired for scenic or lighthouse tours.

Golf

In Stephenson, several miles north of Menominee on U.S. 41, golfers can enjoy a relaxing game at the rural **Indian Hills Golf Course** (N8881 Walnut Rd., 906/753-4781, http://nuttall.net/ihills/index.htm, $12–$18). It may be in the middle of nowhere, surrounded by fields of grain and corn, but there's a certain quaint attraction to the nine-hole course. Closer to Menominee, golfers can visit the **North Shore Golf Club** (2315 M-35, 906/863-3026, $35 greens fees) a few miles north of town on M-35. The club's 18 holes are well maintained, and (one of the most compelling reasons to swing a club here) a few holes provide views of Green Bay. You'll find many of the amenities you'd expect at a higher-level course: a PGA professional, a restaurant, a banquet hall, a pro shop, a driving range, and more.

WINTER SPORTS AND RECREATION
Ski and Snowshoe Trails

One of the best places for non-groomed ski trails is **J. W. Wells State Park** (906/863-9747), on M-35 some 25 miles north of Menominee. The park, open year-round, has almost 700 acres of land available for public use, crossed by eight miles of ski and snowshoe trails, some of which usher skiers along the Green Bay shoreline. You'll find the groomed trails of **Cedar River Pathway** (906/786-2354, www.michigan.gov/dnr) several miles north of J. W. Wells State Park, where M-35 and County Road 551 meet. The pathway has several loops (ranging from two to nine miles) that are perfect for beginning skiers.

Snowmobiling

The expansive Michigan DNR trail system doesn't extend south into Menominee County—your best bet for snowmobiling is to head north on U.S. 41 to Powers, where the trailhead for Trail 331 connects to Trail 2 a few miles north. Take 2 west toward Iron Mountain or east to Escanaba.

Many of Menominee County's unpaved roads and the shoulders of paved roads are accessible by snowmobile; double-check local ordinances for exceptions. Always use extreme caution when riding on public roads. More information about state-wide snowmobile regulations is available from the **Michigan DNR** website (www.michigan.gov/dnr).

ACCOMMODATIONS

Lodging choices are pretty much limited to a few franchise motels in both Menominee and neighboring Marinette, Wisconsin. Two of the best values are **Howard Johnson's Express** (2516 10th St., Menominee, 906/863-4431), which has rooms overlooking the bay, and, in Wisconsin, **Best Western Riverfront Inn** (1821 Riverside Ave., Marinette, 715/732-1000), just west of U.S. 41 at the river.

Cross the river into Wisconsin for comfortable lodging at one of the area's nicest historic inns, the **M&M Victorian Inn** (1393 Main St., Marinette, 715/732-9531, www .lauermanhouse.com, $90–150). Named after the twin cities (not the candy), the M&M is a stunning, restored 1893 Queen Anne–style home with elegant, original woodwork, stained glass, and five rooms. Travelers can also stay at Marinette's **Lauerman House Inn** (1975 Riverside Ave., 715/732-7800, www.lauerman house.com, $90–170). Back in Michigan, **Gehrke's Gasthaus** (320 1st St., Menominee, 906/863-2295) is another fine B&B option.

Camping

J. W. Wells State Park (906/863-9747, 800/447-2757, www.michigan.gov/dnr), about 25 miles north of Menominee on M-35, is the most extensive park along the highway. Flanking both sides of M-35, the 800-acre park is known for its three-mile stretch of rocky beach and large modern campground. The campground doesn't offer much privacy, but all 178 sites are near the beach and 30 back up right to the water. All sites often fill on summer weekends. If you've planned well ahead, you might be able to score one of the park's six rustic cabins, stone and log buildings built as a Civilian Conservation Corps (CCC) project in the 1930s and tucked in secluded woods near the water. They sleep 8–16 and feature barrel stoves for warmth and cooking.

The **Cedar River North State Forest Campground** (906/786-2354, $15, no reservations) in Escanaba River State Forest is a quiet, rustic campground right on the banks of the river, just a few miles upstream from the mouth. The 18 sites are for tent and small trailer use, and 4 of them are walk-in tent-only sites. You'll find vault water and potable water from a rustic hand pump. From M-35 at the village of Cedar River, follow County Road 551 west for eight miles.

Fox Park (906/753-4582), seven miles north of Cedar River, has a 25-site primitive campground that rarely fills and a nice sand beach. The more popular **Fuller Park** (906/786-1020), nine miles north, has 25 modern sites, a sand beach, a bathhouse, a boat launch, and access to the Bark River.

The biggest problem with **River Park Campground** (502 5th Ave., 906/863-5101, www.cityofmenominee.org) is that it's located behind a Kmart. Otherwise, the modern campground's 58 sites are clean, with paved parking pads and a playground. If convenience is your thing, you're within walking distance of a coin laundry—but remember, this is Michigan's Upper Peninsula, and most people come here to find a campsite within walking distance of absolutely nothing at all.

FOOD

Dining in Menominee runs along classic supper-club fare, with an emphasis on fish from the local waters. The **Landing** (450 1st St., 906/863-8034) offers terrific views of Green Bay and good, reliable steaks, seafood, and chicken dishes. Locals will likely point you to **Schloegel's Bayview Restaurant** (2720 10th St., 906/863-7888, http://tastefullydifferent .com), right on U.S. 41, for pies (homemade daily), generous sandwiches, and ethnic items like Swedish pancakes. There's a good view of Green Bay, too.

In addition to the traditional café offerings—coffee, espresso, soups—the **Serving Spoon Cafe** (821 First St., 906/863-7770, 7 A.M.–3 P.M. Mon., 7 A.M.–8 P.M. Tues.–Fri., 8 A.M.–8 P.M. Sat., and 8 A.M.–3 P.M. Sun.) has earned a bit of a reputation for its almost Mediterranean foods. Think pita, light salads, and vegetarian sandwiches. Across the river on the Wisconsin side, **Mickey-Lu's Bar-B-Q** (1710 Marinette Ave., 715/735-7721) looks like

© JOSH BISHOP

THE LAKE MICHIGAN SHO

sandwich shop in downtown Menominee

a hole in the wall, but it's the place to go for cheap food—authentic, old-fashioned butter burgers, malts, and ice cream sundaes.

INFORMATION AND SERVICES

Perhaps the most important piece of information (or at least the one plenty of tourists forget) is that Menominee County is in the Central Time Zone with Wisconsin. Most of the Upper Peninsula, like the entire Lower Peninsula, is set firmly in the Eastern Time Zone, but the counties that share a border with the Badger State share a common time, too. When traveling between Menominee and Escanaba, set your clock forward an hour when heading north to Escanaba and back an hour when driving south.

For visitor information, get ahold of the **Marinette/Menominee Area Chamber of Commerce** (601 Marinette Ave., Marinette, WI, 906/863-2679, www.marinettechamber.com).

Menominee banks include two Wells Fargo locations (M&M Plaza, 906/863-5523, and 962 1st St., 906/863-5515, www.wellsfargo.com)

with ATMs, Stephenson National Bank and Trust (1111 10th St., 906/863-2526, www.snbt.com), and River Valley Bank (3805 10th St., 906/863-7861, www.rivervalleybank.com).

In case of emergency, call 911. The closest hospital is Marinette's Bay Area Medical Center (3100 Shore Dr., 715/735-4200, 888/788-2070, www.bayareamedical.com) in Wisconsin. Take U.S. 41 south to Main Street and turn left, then go right on Shore Drive for a mile and a half.

GETTING THERE AND AROUND
Car

Menominee is located on the border of Michigan and Wisconsin, across the river from Marinette. You'll get to town by taking U.S. 41 from the north or south, or driving along the Green Bay coast south from Escanaba on M-35.

Boat

The **Menominee Marina** (906/863-8498, www.michigan.gov/dnr) has 20 transient slips and a whopping 243 seasonal slips. Open from mid-May through mid-October, the marina has restrooms and showers, gasoline, laundry, and a picnic area with tables and grills. Contact the harbormaster on channel 22 or 16. Menominee Marina is located at 45° 06.21 N, 87° 35.58 W.

Air

The airport most accessible to Menominee is the Delta County Airport in Escanaba, north of Menominee on M-35. You can rent a car in Escanaba.

Public Transportation

Like most of the U.P.'s larger cities, Menominee is accessible on regular bus routes serviced by Indian Trails (800/292-3831, www.indian trails.com). Contact Indian Trails for current schedules and fares.

THE LAKE MICHIGAN SHORE

THE SUPERIOR UPLAND

The western Upper Peninsula is defined by its land. As part of the Superior Upland geographic formation, the western third of the peninsula is filled with rocky crags, rugged landscape, and old-growth forest. In short, it's the wildest region of an already remote destination. The eastern U.P. seems flat and tame compared to the Porcupine Mountains and the other ranges found here.

Gogebic County and the region surrounding Ironwood are known as the Big Snow Country and are the U.P.'s top destinations for downhill skiing. Though Michigan's mountains don't reach even 2,000 feet (not quite world-class skiing for those used to the Rockies or the Alps), the resorts at Bessemer and Wakefield make for some of the best skiing in the Midwest. Visitors in the summer can enjoy the region's numerous waterfalls.

The Porcupine Mountains, or the Porkies, as they're affectionately known, are among the oldest mountain ranges in the United States. Bring your hiking boots. Much of the Porkies—particularly the 85 miles of hiking trails in Porcupine Mountains Wilderness State Park—are only accessible by foot. If you're looking for old-growth hemlock, rustic cabins and remote backpacking, fishing, canoeing, or camping, this is the place for you.

PLANNING YOUR TIME

The western U.P. is made for rugged isolation in the summers and, in the winters, it's where you'll find the best of Michigan's downhill skiing. Plan on two or three days to explore—longer for ski trips or backcountry hiking. No matter why you came, or in what season, you'll

© JOSH BISHOP

HIGHLIGHTS

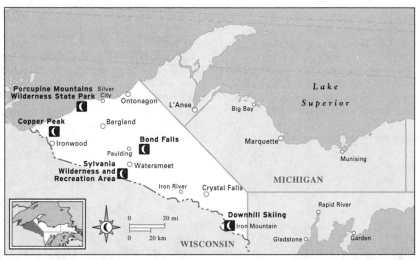

◖ Sylvania Wilderness and Recreation Area: Between the wilderness and recreation areas, Sylvania's more than 20,000 acres are among the U.P.'s finest spots for, well, wilderness and recreation (page 103).

◖ Bond Falls: With a reputation as one of the Upper Peninsula's most beautiful waterfalls, this one should appear near the top of anyone's list. Right behind Tahquamenon Falls, of course, but give this one the number two spot (page 106).

◖ Copper Peak: Sure, there isn't much ski-

ing going on at the ski hill these days, but the view from the top can't be beat (page 111).

◖ Downhill Skiing: World-class skiing in the Midwest? Yoobetcha. The Superior Upland has some of the best runs and deepest snows in the Great Lakes region (page 112).

◖ Porcupine Mountains Wilderness State Park: Virgin forest, Lake Superior shoreline, and miles of trails make the Porkies a rugged, secluded paradise that's perfect for getting away from the crowd (page 117).

LOOK FOR ◖ TO FIND RECOMMENDED SIGHTS, ACTIVITIES, DINING, AND LODGING.

want to set some time aside for the Porkies. Speaking of time, don't forget the time change in the counties bordering Wisconsin—set your clocks back an hour.

HISTORY

Much of the Upper Peninsula traces its heritage to iron. You can read it in the town names—Iron Mountain, Iron River, Ironwood, National

Mine, Mineral Hills—and see it on the faces of the residents, a diverse mix descended from the melting pot of immigrant mine workers.

Federal surveyors first discovered iron ore here in 1844, near present-day Iron River. As workers systematically surveyed this strange landmass recently acquired by Michigan, their compasses swung wildly near Negaunee, where iron ore was so plentiful that it was visible on the surface, intertwined in the roots of a fallen tree. The tree is the official symbol of the city of Negaunee, which itself became completely intertwined with the rise and fall of the iron industry.

Aside from a handful of small mining operations, the unfathomable wealth of the Upper Peninsula's iron remained largely untapped for several decades, until the ever-expanding web of railroad lines reached the area. In the 1870s, the arrival of the railroad prompted the development of the first major mines. World War II and its insatiable demand for iron drove area mines to peak production, eventually depleting some of them. By the 1960s and 1970s, the western U.P. iron ranges grew quiet, after having shipped out nearly two billion tons of ore. All underground iron mines in the U.P. closed by 1978, hurt by foreign steelmakers and the use of more and more plastics in manufacturing.

Iron Mountain and Vicinity

Iron Mountain isn't, on the face of it, a popular tourist destination. You have to look a little harder here. Still, the surrounding forest is beautiful, and the long past of logging and later mining make for some interesting historical sites.

Iron Mountain was first settled in about 1880 and reached its heyday soon after, when vast deposits of iron were discovered underfoot. The Chapin Mine—located near present-day U.S. 2 and Kent Avenue on the north end of downtown—helped boost the town's population to almost 8,000 by 1890. Italian immigrants led the melting-pot mix working at the Chapin Mine, and Italian neighborhoods still thrive around the old mine on Iron Mountain's north side—as evidenced by a mouthwatering supply of Italian restaurants and corner markets.

THE SUPERIOR UPLAND

© JOSH BISHOP

The Iron Mountain Iron Mine, in Vulcan, offers underground mine tours as a means of experiencing the Upper Peninsula's past.

The city's long-abandoned mines still serve an important role, this time as a magnet for brown bats. An estimated two million bats winter in the Millie Mine shaft, protected from predators yet able to enter and exit freely, thanks to bat-friendly grates installed at the mine entrance. As the weather turns cool (usually sometime in September), the bats congregate all around Iron Mountain—an amazing sight—before retreating to the mine.

While iron mining seems to dominate the city's psyche, Henry Ford added to the economic mix in the 1920s, when he bought up huge tracts of nearby forest and built his first company sawmill on land southwest of town, which he dubbed Kingsford (for Iron Mountain's Ford dealer, Edward Kingsford). Soon Ford's Kingsford empire included the main plant for making floorboards for the Model T, residential developments for workers, an airport, a refinery, and even a plant to make newfangled charcoal briquettes. All of it eventually closed or was sold off, including the briquette plant, which relocated to Oakland, California, and still manufactures the ever-popular Kingsford charcoal briquettes.

SIGHTS
Iron Mountain Iron Mine

If you're going to spend any amount of time in Iron Mountain and the rest of the Superior Uplands, you might as well get a firsthand look at the mining industry that made it what it is today. You can't miss the Iron Mountain Iron Mine (906/563-8077, www.ironmountainironmine.com, June 1–Oct. 15) in Vulcan, nine miles east of Iron Mountain, due to the presence of Big John, a towering two-dimensional miner with a pickax in his hands and a smile on his face. The mine tour takes visitors 400 feet below the surface on a half-mile journey. With rain slickers and hard hats in tow, tourists board an underground train to learn about the history and process of mining, including equipment demonstrations. You'll get outfitted for the tour in the gift shop, where you can browse rock and mineral samples.

© AVALON TRAVEL

IXL Museum

A lot of museums bill themselves as a "step back in time," but you truly feel it at the IXL Museum (906/498-2498, www.hermansville.com/IXLMuseum, Memorial Day–Labor Day) in downtown Hermansville, 28 miles east of Iron Mountain. For more than a century, this wood-frame building served as the northern office of the Wisconsin Land & Lumber Company, which got its start in the 1860s, building doors and window sashes in central Wisconsin. After the Great Chicago Fire of 1871, founder C. J. L. Meyer moved north to

THE SUPERIOR UPLAND

THE SUPERIOR UPLAND

tap into the vast pine reserves of the Upper Peninsula. He built the Hermansville office and adjacent sawmill in 1881. "IXL" stands for "I excel," and was used as a logo on all the company's products.

Today, the perfectly preserved IXL building is a time warp, one of the most fascinating museums in the Upper Peninsula. The Dictaphones, the mimeograph machines, the payroll records…they're all still here, in place, as if you popped into the office on a weekend when everyone was off duty. The second floor, originally used as apartments for Meyer

and his family, now displays a variety of machinery from logging days. When Meyer expanded the business north, he came up with a clever little innovation: tongue-and-groove flooring, precision-milled in one operation. The Hermansville operation quickly became the largest flooring plant in the country, crafting the floors for the Mormon temple in Salt Lake City and Yellowstone National Park's main lodge, among other notable clients. At its peak, it held 30 million board-feet of lumber in its yards and operated three railroads to keep the supply coming.

MINING

With the exception of the Keweenaw Peninsula and its copper mines, most of the Superior Upland has its roots in iron mining. The U.P.'s iron industry stretched from the peninsula's western border east some 150 miles, to the Lake Superior port of Marquette and the Lake Michigan port of Escanaba. It comprised three major ranges: the Gogebic Range, with operations centered around Ironwood; the Menominee Range, based largely around the Iron River and Iron Mountain areas; and the Marquette Range, encompassing Marquette and the Ishpeming/Negaunee area.

From the discovery of iron in the 1840s to the arrival of the railway nearly 30 years later, iron mining stayed a fairly small-time operation. The Menominee Range saw the first major mines, and a few years later, the Gogebic Range opened. Many of the early mines were open-pit affairs, but soon the need for iron ore drove miners deeper and deeper underground. Today communities like Ishpeming sit atop a Swiss-cheese patch of earth riddled with mine shafts and adits; occasionally, tracts of land sink, leaving behind tilted and abandoned houses. Near Iron Mountain, the entire town of Norway was moved – twice – when the streets wouldn't stop caving in.

Mining wouldn't last forever, though. Supplies were depleted, and a lack of demand closed the mines by the late 1970s. Only a few open-pit mines remain in operation; you can see one in Republic, where a small viewing platform (free) overlooks a gargantuan crater in the earth. Republic is located just off M-95, about six miles south of U.S. 41 in Marquette County.

After being ravaged by the successive industries of trapping, logging, and mining, the U.P.'s next big money-maker is tourism. The western U.P.'s surprising terrain matches its surprising variety. It is a land of popular downhill ski resorts and private Old World enclaves of the super-wealthy.

Cornish Pump and Mining Museum

Iron Mountain's Chapin Mine once led Menominee Range mining production, but it was also one of the wettest mines ever worked. In 1893, an immense steam-operated pump—a 54-foot-high, 725-ton behemoth—the largest in the world at the time, was put to work. Though electric pumps replaced it just 20 years later, the pump survives intact at the Menominee Range Historical Foundation's Cornish Pump and Mining Museum (906/774-1086, mid-May–mid-Oct. Mon.–Sat. 9 A.M.–5 P.M., Sun. noon–4 P.M.), one block east of U.S. 2 in downtown Iron Mountain. Along with the impressive pump, this comprehensive museum includes a good-size collection of mining equipment, photos, and clothing; a small theater; and, arguably the most compelling display of all, the story of the World War II gliders built by Henry Ford's nearby Kingsford plant, used to quietly deploy troops behind enemy lines.

Menominee Range Historical Museum

The Menominee Range Historical Foundation's other museum, the Menominee Range Historical Museum (300 East Ludington St., 906/774-4276, www.menomineemuseum .com, mid-May–mid-Oct.), provides a overview of the area's history from the 1800s on. More than 100 exhibits are housed in the town's former Carnegie Library, most of them focusing on the everyday life of those who lived in the Menominee Iron Range. You can visit a Victorian parlor, a livery stable, an interactive general store, and much, much more. There are historical archives available for research, too.

Badwater Ski-ters Water Ski Show

Sure, this one is technically in Wisconsin, but it's worth a trip into America's Dairyland to catch the Badwater Ski-ters Water Ski Show (skiters@ charter.net, www.exploringthenorth.com/ski/ ski.html) at Vagabond Park on the Menominee

River, five miles west of Iron Mountain. The world-class, nationally renowned water-ski team performs jumps, trick and barefoot skiing, and the pyramid. Best of all, the shows are free. Catch the Ski-ters every Wednesday and Sunday throughout the summer, from early June through mid-August. Take U.S. 2/141 west from Iron Mountain and look for signs.

Millie Mine Bat Cave

Sure, bats can be a little creepy, but there's something impressive about the million or so bats that spend winters in the abandoned mine shaft. Bats have free access into the mine through a grate, which was constructed to prevent people from falling several hundred feet to the floor of the mine shaft—a good idea all around. The mine's constant 40°F temperature makes it ideal for the bats, which can be viewed entering or leaving the mine each spring (late April to early May) and autumn (August and September). The best viewing time is at dusk. Take Park Street north from U.S. 2 East until you reach the marked viewing area.

PINE MOUNTAIN MUSIC FESTIVAL

The annual Pine Mountain Music Festival (906/482-1542, www.pmmf.org), now in its 18th year, has a lineup of musical performances that take place all across the region, from Marquette and Houghton to Munising and, yes, even Iron Mountain. The annual festival features opera, symphonies, and chamber music, proving that there's not much substance to the myth of the uncultured Yooper.

SUMMER SPORTS AND RECREATION
Hiking and Biking

Where the U.P. isn't bordered by lakes, it's bordered by rivers: the grand Menominee rambles from near Iron Mountain all the way to Lake Michigan's Green Bay, forming nearly half the boundary between Wisconsin and the Upper Peninsula. Just south of Norway, it narrows through **Piers Gorge,** a pretty run of frothing white water and waterfalls. In the mid-1800s, loggers relied on the Menominee to float logs

THE SUPERIOR UPLAND

© JOSH BISHOP

The Western Upper Peninsula is a land of low mountains, pine forests, and wild spaces.

to the river's mouth; they cursed this stretch of river for the logjams it caused, and they built a series of wooden piers here in an attempt to slow the current and channel the flow—hence the name. To view the gorge, follow U.S. 8 south from Norway and turn right on Piers Gorge Road just before you cross the river into Wisconsin. Follow the road about half a mile until it ends at a trail. Along the mile-long trail, you'll be treated to several views of the gorge (from as high as 70 feet above) and several side trails of varying safety, some of which wind down to the river itself. This is not a good choice for those with small children, since steep drop-offs abound.

The trails that encircle the large lake of **Fumee Lake Natural Area** give hikers the chance to see plenty of natural beauty, still untouched by motorized vehicles and development. There are five miles of shoreline and more than 500 acres of water in Fumee Lake and Little Fumee Lake. Choose between loops of one, two, and seven miles, each of which affords views of the lakes and wildlife—bring binoculars or, at the very least, your camera. Fumee Lake Natural Area is located east of Iron Mountain, near Norway. Take Upper Pine Creek Road north of U.S. 2.

Canoeing and Kayaking

Only experienced white-water kayakers who can handle Class III and IV rapids should consider running the **Menominee River**. The narrow canyon walls of Piers Gorge produce some of the Midwest's most thrilling (and difficult) white water. For an easy paddle on the nearby Brule or Pine Rivers, though, contact **Northwoods Wilderness Outfitters** (N4088 Pine Mountain Rd., 906/774-9009, www.north woodsoutfitters.com) in Iron Mountain. This excellent shop will set you up for an afternoon or an extended trip, with canoe and kayak rentals as well as drop-off/pickup service.

Fishing

Even though Lakes Michigan and Superior don't border the Iron Mountain region, there's still plenty of good fishing to be had here. Try

Bass Lake near the Wisconsin border, north of Iron Mountain and two miles west of U.S. 2, or larger **Lake Antoine**, four miles north of Iron Mountain (take U.S. 2 to Lake Antoine Rd.). **Carney Lake** is a little farther away, 16 miles northeast of Iron Mountain on M-95 and Merriman Truck Trail, but its more than 100 acres, boat launch, and rustic campgrounds make it worth the drive. For more fishing sites and advice on fishing the area's rivers, contact the Dickinson Area Partnership (800/236-2447, www.ironmountain.org).

Off-Road Vehicles

When the mining and logging industries waned, they left behind unpaved roads—hundreds of miles of them—making the backcountry around Iron Mountain perfect for off-road vehicle riders. There are also nearly 30 miles of ORV routes on the **Norway Trail**. Take County Road 573 east of Norway to Norway Truck Trail, then go north to parking, or take Foster City Road several miles north of U.S. 2 in Waucedah.

Golf

The **Pine Grove Country Club** (1520 W. Hughitt St., Iron Mountain, 906/774-3493, http://pinegrovecc.org) has been around for more than 100 years, but the semi-private course's elegant new country club is less than a decade old. As nice as it is, though, there is limited open play time for nonmembers: Monday, Thursday, and Friday before noon, and Saturday and Sunday after 1:00 P.M. You'll have a better choice of tee times at **Oak Crest Golf Course** (N1475 U.S. 8, 906/563-5891, $16–24 9 holes, $30–42 18 holes) in Norway. The 18 holes are smack in the middle of oak trees, giving the course both a naturally stately feel and its name. You can also play at **TimberStone Golf Club** (N3332 Pine Mountain Rd., 906/776-0111, www .pinemountainresort.com, $40–45 for 9 holes, $69–79 for 18 holes), part of Pine Mountain Resort. The course's 18 holes are set on 240 wooded acres. Look for package deals on lodging and golf.

Waterfalls

You'll find a couple of waterfalls in the area, but they unfortunately aren't the Upper Peninsula's best. The pretty but small **Fumee Falls** make up for their fairly unimpressive water flow with how easy they are to get to. A trail and viewing platform just off U.S. 2 allow you to see the more than 20-foot total drop without too much trouble. The **Sturgeon Falls Dam** (not to be confused with Sturgeon Falls) isn't quite as easy to get to, but is worth your while. The falls are 3.5 miles south of Loretto on the Menominee River.

WINTER SPORTS AND RECREATION

Ski and Snowshoe Trails

One of the more appealing things about **Fumee Lake Natural Area** (in addition to its natural, undeveloped state) is that it's accessible year-round. The summer hiking trails transition nicely into cross-country ski and snowshoe pathways when the snows fall, which, in the Upper Peninsula, seems to be more often than not. There are loops of varying distance and difficulty, all isolated from the nearby towns. Take Upper Pine Creek Road north of U.S. 2, a few miles west of Norway and east of Iron Mountain. **Merriman East Pathway,** some 13 miles northeast of Iron Mountain on M-95 and Merriman Road, has nearly 10 miles of trails that make for nice Nordic skiing.

Downhill Skiing

You're not far enough west for Michigan's biggest and best ski resorts (head to Ironwood for those), but the Iron Mountain region holds its own with two downhill ski resorts—plus a little something extra. **Norway Mountain** (N2090 Briar Mountain Rd., 906/563-9700, 800/272-5445, www.norway mountain.com, $33–36 adults, $27–30 ages 10–18, children free) has three lifts and runs from beginner slopes to black diamond terrain. There are two terrain parks open to both skiers and boarders, too, with a quarter-pipe, large jumps, and plenty of rails

and boxes—as well as a less-intense area for beginners. Not to be outdone, **◖ Pine Mountain Resort** (N3332 Pine Mountain Rd., 906/774-2747, www.pinemountain resort.com, $50–100, $130–300 condos), in Iron Mountain, has multilevel skiing and lighted nighttime runs, two terrain parks, and a half-pipe. But that's nothing compared to the **Pine Mountain Ski Jump** (N3330 Pine Mountain Rd., 800/236-2447, www.kiwanis skiclub.com), a towering scaffold that tops out at more than 175 feet tall, with a run of 380 feet. There's an international competition here that draws some 20,000 people each year to what was once the world's largest artificial ski jump; the current Pine Mountain record is a 468-foot jump by Austria's Stefan Kaiser.

Snowmobiling

More than 120 miles of snowmobile trails cross Dickinson County, connecting to trails throughout the rest of the U.P. and northern Wisconsin. Iron Mountain and Norway are connected by a trail that skirts Fumee Lake (you can take it east to Escanaba), while Trail 5 will take you north toward Marquette and Lake Superior.

ACCOMMODATIONS

The **Pine Mountain Resort** (N3332 Pine Mountain Rd., 877/553-7463, www.pine mountainresort.com, $50–100 rooms, $50–100 condos) anchors a full-service ski and golf resort on the northwest side of town, complete with dining room, indoor pool, outdoor pool, sauna, tennis courts, hiking and mountain biking trails, and more. Choose from standard lodge rooms or condominiums. Just off U.S. 2, the **Edgewater Resort** (4128 North U.S. 2, 800/236-6244, www.edgewaterresort.com, $430–680 per week) makes the most of its fine setting overlooking the Menominee River, with 10 log cabins scattered across its grounds, along with a picnic area, a playground, a volleyball court, canoes and fishing boats for rent, and more. Two- and three-bedroom cabins with kitchens rent by the week (daily if available at the last minute). Pets are permitted. Two miles north of Iron River, the mom-and-pop **Woodlands Motel** (N3957 U.S. 2, 906/774-6106, $50–75) offers standard motel rooms with small kitchenettes. Look for standard chain motels in downtown Iron Mountain.

Camping

At **Carney Lake State Forest Campground** (906/875-6622, www.michigan.gov/dnr, $15), campers will find 16 rustic sites suitable for tents and trailers. You won't find showers or laundry here, but there are vaulted toilets and clean water from the campground's hand pump. You'll have the best luck during the off season, since there are no reservations and the first-come, first-served sites can get snatched up pretty quickly. The fishing is worth it, though. Take M-95 north of Iron Mountain and head east on Merriman Truck Trail. **Summer Breeze Campground** (W8576 Twin Falls Rd., 906/774-7701, May 1–Oct. 15, $18 tent, $24–28 hookup) is pretty much the opposite—amenity rich, busy, and plenty of room for even the largest RVs. Amenities go beyond heated showers and a camp store (they do have those, of course) to a heated swimming pool, DVD rentals, Wi-Fi, and a book exchange. There are fire rings and tables at every site. Speaking of sites, the 70 campsites here are grassy and shaded, 28 with full hookups and 42 with water and electricity. M-95 North will take you to Twin Falls Road, then turn left. You can find campsites at **Lake Antoine Park** (N3393 Lake Antoine, 906/774-2573) and **Rivers Bend Campground** (N3905 Pine Mountain Rd., 906/779-1171) as well.

FOOD

Italian is the way to go if you're eating out in Iron Mountain. Homemade ravioli, slow-roasted pork, Italian sausage, Roma red sauce…you'll find it all in Iron Mountain's unassuming Italian eateries. For authentic pizza pie, try **Bruttomessos Pizzeria** (305 North Stephenson Ave./U.S. 2, 906/774-0801). **Bimbo's Wine Press** (314 East Main St., 906/774-8420) dishes out mouthwatering

Italian sandwiches like porketta for incredibly reasonable prices ($5 on average). More upscale is **Fontana's Supper Club** (115 South Stephenson Ave./U.S. 2, 906/774-0044) for steaks and, yes, Italian specialties. Save room for cheesecake. Dinner entrées average $15. The food at **Romagnoli's Restaurant** (North Stephenson Ave./U.S. 2, 906/774-7300, closed Sun.) is made from original family Italian recipes. Known for their ribs as much as for their gnocchi, Romagnoli's also serves steaks, fish, and, perhaps as a nod to Midwest America, fries on the side. With the exception of the thin-crust pizzas, **Famers** (N3332 Pine Mountain Rd., 906/774-2747, www.pinemountainresort.com) is the place to go when you're looking for something a little less Italian. The restaurant, which is part of Pine Mountain Resort, is a sports bar, complete with good appetizers, five televisions, cocktails, and big steaks.

In Norway, you'll want to stop by the appropriately named **Norway Deli** (1028 Main St., 906/563-8180, 10 A.M.–7 P.M. Mon.–Fri., 7 A.M.–2 P.M. Sat.), a casual breakfast, lunch, and dinner restaurant that opened in 2006. Stop by on Friday for the fish fry if you like, but you'll definitely want to stop by for the breakfast, which is good and cheap. For slightly heartier fare (try the half-pound burger), head to the **Thirsty Whale Bar and Grill** (825 Murray Road/U.S. 2, Norway, 906/563-5466, open daily for lunch and dinner) west of town.

INFORMATION AND SERVICES

For information on Iron Mountain and the surrounding area, contact the **Tourism Association of the Dickinson County Area** (600 South Stephenson Ave., 800/236-2447, www.ironmountain.org). Also remember that Iron Mountain is on Central Time, an hour behind most of the Upper Peninsula.

If medical attention is necessary, the Dickinson County Hospital (1721 South Stephenson Ave., Iron Mountain, 906/774-1313, www.dchs.org) is located on U.S. 2/141 heading southeast out of town. In addition to a few local banks, Wells Fargo (www.wellsfargo.com) has locations both in Iron Mountain (1805 South Stephenson Ave., 906/774-0930) and north in Crystal Falls (1352 U.S. 2, 906/875-6651).

GETTING THERE AND AROUND
Car
Iron Mountain is located on Michigan's border with Wisconsin, at the intersection of two major highways. Driving into town from the east, take U.S. 2 (it's U.S. 2/141 when you come from the west). North from Wisconsin or south from other parts of the U.P., U.S. 141 will take you right into town. Take U.S. 2/141 north to Crystal Falls, U.S. 2 east to Norway, and U.S. 2 west to Iron River.

Air
There are a few nearby options for people flying into Iron Mountain, including Delta County Airport (ESC, 3300 Airport Rd., 906/786-4902, www.deltacountymi.org), a small airport just southwest of Escanaba. You can rent a car from Alamo Car Rental (3300 Airport Rd., 906/786-0603, www.alamo.com) that'll take you where you want to go (and you really will need a car while you're here). You can fly into Sawyer International Airport (MQT, 125 G Ave., Gwinn, 906/346-3308, www.sawyerairport.com), too. Mesaba Airlines and American Eagle offer daily scheduled flights to and from large cities such as Detroit, Chicago, Milwaukee, Green Bay, and Minneapolis–St. Paul. There are plenty of car rental agencies, too: Avis (906/346-6398), Budget (906/372-9240), Alamo/National (906/346-6378), and Thrifty (906/346-4355). Sawyer is just south of Marquette and a good distance from Iron Mountain (the drive is about two hours, maybe less), but its regular service makes it one of the most attractive options.

Public Transportation
Indian Trails bus service (800/292-3831, www.indiantrails.com) makes regularly scheduled stops at Iron Mountain on the St. Ignace–Escanaba–Ironwood route. You can get here from the metropolises of Chicago and Detroit on a combination of Indian Trails and Greyhound buses. For taxi service, call Tri-City Cab (906/774-7878).

Iron River and Ottawa National Forest

Iron County's population centers around Iron River, an iron mining center, and Crystal Falls, the picturesque county seat 15 miles to the east. Both retain their small-town charm. Like Iron Mountain, Iron River isn't a whole lot more than a small pass-through town on the way to some great skiing or backwoods campsites. Still, it makes for a quaint visit and a convenient stop.

The real draw to the region is the Ottawa National Forest. Sprawling across nearly 100,000 acres, the Ottawa National Forest blankets much of the western peninsula from the Wisconsin border to U.S. 141, which runs north from Iron River. Unlike a national park with a contiguous boundary, the Ottawa National Forest is a patchwork of protected lands, pieced together around towns, private property, and various state parks and forests.

Named for the Ottawa Indians who lived and traded in this region (though they actually populated the eastern half of the U.P. in greater numbers), the Ottawa National Forest encompasses more than 400 lakes, seven major river systems, some of the U.P.'s most outstanding waterfalls, 27 campgrounds, and three wilderness areas: Sylvania, the Sturgeon River gorge, and the McCormick Tract.

SIGHTS
Iron County Heritage Trail
There are 12 total stops along the Iron County Heritage Trail, a trail of destinations of historic interest throughout the county. You won't find

THE SUPERIOR UPLAND

a lot of dramatic lighting and fancy display cases at the **Iron County Historical Museum** (906/265-2617, www.ironcountymuseum.com, daily mid-May–Oct.), two miles south of U.S. 2 off M-189 in Caspian. What you will find is an interesting, appealing, and eclectic blend of local history and culture at this rambling, funky, and homegrown museum. Located on the site of the productive Caspian iron mine—the mine's rusting headframe still looms over the complex—it runs largely on donated money and donated time. In the main museum building, displays cover everything from Native American history to logging, mining, and sporting equipment and kitchenware from the early 1900s. The perennial favorite display is the mechanized iron mine and railroad model: for five cents, a miniature ore skip hauls rocks to the surface and loads them on the railroad.

Other displays not to miss: the Mining Memorial, with a computer database of area mines and miners and a video of life in the mines; a 3-D acrylic mine diagram that shows the depths of the mine, where ore has been mined, and where it remains; a 50-foot-long diorama of a logging camp, complete with hundreds of folk-art figures by local artist William Monogal; newspaper clippings on Iron River's 1920 "rum rebellion," when federal agents from Chicago stormed the house of the priest (discovering eight barrels of rum), only to be defied by the state's attorney; and a history of the local labor movement, which helped boost miners' earnings from $365 per year in 1931 to $1,886 per year a decade later.

Outside, several relocated buildings occupy the grounds, including a streetcar barn, as well as the streetcar that once traveled between the mines in Caspian and Iron River. A small admission fee is charged.

Head to Crystal Falls for a look at the small-town life of miners at the turn of the century. Tour the **Harbor House Museum** (906/875-4341, www.ironheritage.org, June 1–Sept. 1, Tues.–Sat., 11 A.M.–4 P.M.), a restored Queen Anne Colonial Revival home that houses a two-story museum, complete with authentic furnishings and decorations and several exhibits displaying regional artifacts. Pay a visit to **Mile Post Zero and Treaty Tree,** too. There isn't really a whole lot to see here (you guessed it: a mile post and a tree), but the historically important site marks the location of the survey point that set the boundary between Michigan and Wisconsin in 1840.

Other sites on the trail include the **Amasa Museum,** the **Iron County Courthouse,** and **Mansfield Location and Pioneer Church.** Contact **Friends of the Heritage Trail** (906/875-6642, www.ironheritage.org) for maps and additional information.

Triangle Ranch

Much of the U.P. is dotted with ghost towns, but Triangle Ranch may be its only ghost farm. In the 1920s, one developer had grand plans for some of Iron County's clear-cut logging land. He purchased nearly 10,000 acres, building pens, corrals, barns, and a rancher's home, intent on raising beef cattle. The idea went bust after just one year—it proved too costly to care for the animals over the long U.P. winter. Most of the land was sold back to a pulp/paper company (and has since been reforested), but the skeletons of the operation remain. Triangle Ranch remains on the Michigan state map; from Crystal Falls, take U.S. 141 north about 15 miles to the marked Triangle Ranch Road (a few miles north of Amasa). Follow the road east about a mile to the remains of the ranch.

Paulding Mystery Light

If inexplicable, supernatural happenings give you the heebie-jeebies (or if you don't believe in them and would like a little convincing), it wouldn't hurt to track down the Paulding Mystery Light in Watersmeet. Believe it or not, the mysterious light reportedly appears in the distance every night. According to the sign at the site, "Legend explains its presence as a railroad brakeman's ghost, destined to remain forever at the sight [sic] of his untimely death. He continually waves his signal lantern as a warning to all who come to visit." To get here, take U.S. 2 east of Iron River, then follow U.S. 45 about five miles north of Watersmeet to Robbins Pond Road—brown signs will help you find the way from there.

◖ Sylvania Wilderness and Recreation Area

Sylvania protects its assets well—36 crystalline glacial lakes hidden among thick stands of massive, old-growth trees. For anglers who dream of landing (and then releasing) that once-in-a-lifetime smallmouth bass; for paddlers who yearn to glide across deep, quiet waters and along untrammeled shoreline; for hikers who wish to travel under a towering canopy of trees and hear nothing more than the haunting whistle of a loon, Sylvania can be a truly magical place.

One of three wilderness areas within the national forest, Sylvania stretches across 18,000 acres near Watersmeet, an area roughly bordered by U.S. 2 to the north, U.S. 45 to the east, and the Wisconsin border to the south. The adjacent Sylvania Recreation Area acts as a buffer, an additional 3,000 acres of lakes and woodlands with a few developed services, like a drive-in campground, a nice beach, flush toilets, and running water.

Once viewed as just another tract of good timber, Sylvania's fate turned in the late 1890s, when a lumberman who purchased 80 acres near the south end of Clark Lake decided it was too lovely to cut, and instead kept it as his personal fishing retreat. He invited his wealthy buddies—some of them executives of U.S. Steel—who also were captivated by the land. Together, they purchased several thousand additional acres and formed the private Sylvania Club.

Like other upscale U.P. "great camps," the Sylvania Club soon had grand log lodges along its shores, guards to keep trespassing anglers away from its bountiful lakes, and caretakers to squelch forest fires as they cropped up. Ownership changed a few times over the decades, eventually ending up in the hands of Lawrence Fisher of auto company Fisher Body. When he died, his heirs sold the property to the federal government for $5.7 million. It was operated as a recreation area from the late 1960s to 1987, when the bulk of it was converted to wilderness status.

We can partly thank Old Money for the condition of the land today. With the public previously barred from fishing here, Sylvania's lakes now provide some epic fishing, especially for bass. Its waters remain pristine, thanks to the lack of development and powerboat access, as well as the area's topography—Sylvania lies on the divide between Lake Superior and the Mississippi, so it doesn't suffer from runoff of nearby lands. And whatever your thoughts on fire management, Sylvania's decades of fire protection mean that visitors today can marvel at a virgin forest of white pine and hardwoods—hemlocks, maples, and basswood trees more than 200 years old.

Begin a trip to Sylvania with a call or visit to the **Watersmeet Visitors Center** (906/358-4724) at the intersection of U.S. 2 and U.S. 45. The staff can help you with maps, regulations, campsite reservations, and other information. Sylvania's rules can be quite unique—especially the fishing regulations—so take time to ask questions and read through the materials rangers provide. To reach Sylvania itself, follow U.S. 2 west about four miles from the visitors center and turn south on Thousand Island Lake Road. Travel about four miles, following signs to reach the entrance building. All visitors are required to register upon arrival.

The entrance sits in the recreation area, near the drive-in campground on Clark Lake. If you intend to travel into the wilderness area, plan on treating your own water; you'll find water pumps only in the recreation area. Cookstoves are highly encouraged, too, to lessen the number of feet tramping through the forest in search of dead wood. During summer months, make sure you also have ample bug dope or, better yet, a head net to combat mosquitoes and black flies.

ENTERTAINMENT

If you're looking for local U.P. gaming, you can find it at **Lac Vieux Desert Resort Casino**

THE SUPERIOR UPLAND

(N5384 U.S. 45, Watersmeet, 906/358-4226, 800/583-3599, www.lvdcasino.com) in Watersmeet. It's a bit of a drive west on U.S. 2 and then north on U.S. 45, but it's worth the trip from Iron River. The 24/7 gaming room has more than 700 video and reel slots, roulette, blackjack, craps, bingo, a poker room, and plenty more gaming fun. Stop by the Thunderbird Sports Lounge for food, drinks, and free live entertainment every Friday and Saturday night. There's a snack bar for light fare and a restaurant with several buffets in addition to a full menu.

RODEO
One of the biggest events to hit Iron County is the annual **U.P. Championship Rodeo** (Iron County Chamber of Commerce, 888/879-4766, www.upprorodeo.com), which has been hosting professional rodeo events since 1968. Popular favorites like steer wrestling, bull riding, and bareback riding (as well as others) continue to draw crowds each year for Western fun in an unlikely Midwestern location.

SUMMER SPORTS AND RECREATION
Biking and Hiking
In the far south of the Ottawa National Forest, a few miles south of Iron River, the **Lake Ottawa Recreation Area** (Lake Ottawa Rd., 906/265-9259, www.fs.fed.us) has about nine miles of trails. One of the more popular is the primitive but nice Ge-Che Trail, which follows a 2.5-mile loop from the boat landing area. Try the two-mile Brennan Lake Loop, too. The Lake Ottawa Recreation Area is listed as part of the Iron County Heritage Route. Hikers in search of a short, easy trail will find it at **Bewabic State Park** (1933 U.S. 2 West, Crystal Falls, 906/875-3324, www.michigan.gov/dnr), located just off U.S. 2 between Iron River and Crystal Mountain, closer to the Crystal Mountain side of things. The two-mile nature trail ushers visitors from the campground to the day-use area and back—expect to spend about an hour on the trail.

Sylvania Wilderness Area and Recreation Area maintains 15 miles of trails, including a seven-mile trail (marked with blue blazes) around Clark Lake. It provides access to campsites and trails to other lakes. Most of Sylvania's trails are old roads left over from its fishing-camp days; though not always well-marked, they are quite easy to follow. These same roads become a great **cross-country ski** network in winter months. The national forest grooms 15 miles of trails within Sylvania.

The marked and mapped **Pines and Mines** trail system gives a glimpse of the tantalizing mountain biking opportunities in the western Upper Peninsula. A joint effort of local tourism and economic development groups, the Ottawa National Forest, and TRALE-UP (a local trail-access organization), it comprises some 200 miles of trails in three networks. Routes range from tame gravel roads to single-track trails deep in the woods. As a bonus, many showcase waterfalls, remote lakes, and historical features.

Near Marenisco in Gogebic County, the **Pomeroy/Henry Lake network** offers 100 miles of gentle biking on wide gravel roads around a national forest area peppered with small lakes. It's a good choice for families. The **Ehlco network**, just south of the Porcupine Mountains Wilderness State Park, includes more single-track deep in the forest, on grass or dirt paths. (This area can be wet, thanks to some lowlands and the work of local beavers, so avoid it after a rain.) Arguably the best of the three networks is the one located outside the national forest: the Iron County (Wisconsin) system. Trails radiating out of Hurley, Wisconsin, lead you past waterfalls, large flowages, and old mining relics like the Plummer headframe near Pence, Wisconsin. Good interpretive signs help make sense of historic sites. Routes in this system range from gravel roads to terrific single-track, though it's not clear from the map which is which. (Single-track trails 6 and 13 are recommended.)

While the Pines and Mines trails are great, the map is mediocre; it's best to bring your own topographical map, and before you set out, get a little local advice from national forest rangers, local bike shops (Trek and Trail in Ironwood, 906/932-5858), or the Pines and Mines organizers. Pick up a map at the Wisconsin or Michigan state information centers (both on U.S. 2 near the border), local bike shops, or the Ottawa National Forest office in Ironwood.

Canoeing and Kayaking

Seven major river systems flow within the forest, a staggering 1,000 miles of navigable waters for paddlers. Congress has designated more than 300 of those miles as "wild and scenic" or "recreational" rivers, leaving them largely in a pristine state. In general, rivers like the Ontonagon and Presque Isle offer quiet water in their southern reaches, winding through relatively flat woodlands. North of M-28, they begin a more rugged descent through hills and bluffs, requiring more advanced skills and boats appropriate for white water. For strong paddlers with good white water skills, these rivers offer some of the finest paddling in the Midwest.

Of course, all of this can change depending on rainfall and the time of year. Rivers that normally flow gently can be torrents in the spring. Always check with Forest Service officials before setting out. Also, the Forest Service publishes an extensive *River Digest* (free) that outlines navigable rivers, launch areas, liveries, and high flow and low flow times. Pick one up at a district ranger office.

The three branches of the mighty Ontonagon spread across the western U.P. like a spiderweb; at times it seems every road you travel crosses one branch or another. While many parts of the river system are worth exploring, one spot gets particular attention: the upper reaches of the middle branch of the Ontonagon, where **Bond Falls** cascades down a series of black boulders.

Paddling is the best way to explore the Sylvania Wilderness. Most of the lakes are linked by water or by relatively easy portages (though there are a couple "grunt portages" of two miles or more). Many campsites are accessible only by water. Motors and other "mechanized equipment" are forbidden—that even includes sailboats. The one exception is

Crooked Lake, which allows electric motors of 4 horsepower or less.

From the entrance road, you can park your vehicle and put in at Clark Lake or Crooked Lake. According to a ranger, Clark (the largest lake), Crooked, and Loon Lakes are the three busiest lakes. Some of the smaller lakes—like Mountain and High Lakes, both accessible from Crooked Lake—see less traffic and are just a short portage away. One ranger recommends bringing snorkel gear—the crystal-clear waters provide great visibility for viewing monster fish. Rent canoes and kayaks from **Sylvania Outfitters** (23423 U.S. 2, 906/358-4766, www.sylvaniaoutfitters.com) in Watersmeet. You can outfit your entire trip— boat, food, fishing gear, maps—at this helpful spot, and even arrange to have the stuff delivered and picked up from the water's edge.

A small but pleasant chain of lakes is the highlight of **Bewabic State Park** (1933 U.S. 2, 906/875-3324, www.michigan.gov/dnr), located five miles west of Crystal Falls. Boaters can put in at the first of the Fortune Lakes and make their way to Fourth Lake, an easy day's paddling adventure. Though First Lake can be somewhat frenetic on summer weekends, the waters get quieter and downright pristine as you proceed down the chain. Paddlers can escape fishing boats by darting under the low U.S. 2 bridge to Mud Lake. The park itself has a modern 144-site campground with good privacy, a small stretch of sandy beach, tennis courts, and other amenities. For camping reservations (though they're rarely needed), use the state park reservation system (800/447-2757, www.michigan.gov/dnr).

Fishing

Bewabic State Park (1933 U.S. 2, 906/875-3324, www.michigan.gov/dnr) has some fine fishing, too. Fishing for perch and bass is best on First Lake, the park's largest (192 acres) and deepest (72 feet). There are more than 300 lakes here, and miles of rivers and streams for fishing. Of the Upper Peninsula's 13 blue-ribbon trout streams—the state's best, managed by the DNR—five are in Iron County. Try the

12-mile stretch of **Iron River** extending upstream from the city, wade into **Brule River** between M-73 and M-189 south of town, or head to **Cooks Run,** south of U.S. 2. For more information on fishing in Iron County, contact the Chamber of Commerce (50 East Genesee St., 906/265-3822, 800/879-4766, www.iron .org/chamber).

Golf

For 18 holes in the Iron River region, you'll have to (you'll *want* to, really) stop by the **George Young Recreational Complex** (159 Young's La., 906/265-3401, www.georgeyoung .com, $40/day). Not only is it the area's only 18-hole course, but with a professional course measuring 7,030 yards, it's also the U.P.'s longest 18 holes (you can play the standard course at just shy of 5,400 yards if you prefer). The elegant complex is a nonprofit corporation dedicated to recreation and preservation; its lands include miles of trails for biking, hiking, and Nordic skiing. The **Crystal View Golf Course** (602 Wagner St., 906/875-3029, www.crystal falls.org) in Crystal Falls is a nine-hole course owned by the city, located on the banks of Paint River. Another nine-hole course, **Iron River Country Club** (110 Hiawatha Rd., 906/265-3161) is located nearby in Iron River.

Off-Road Vehicles

Off-road enthusiasts can find a designated ORV route stretching some 67 miles from Iron River northwest to Marenisco. There are miles of additional trails that network throughout Ottawa National Forest, but be careful to stay on designated, marked roads and trails. Contact the **U.S. Forest Service** (E6248 U.S. 2, Ironwood, 906/932-1330, www.fs.fed.us) for maps and more information.

Waterfalls

Just off the Black River Road National Scenic Byway, the Black River rolls and tumbles over seven magnificent waterfalls north of Bessemer before rushing into Lake Superior. The site is believed to be the largest concentration of waterfalls in the state. The first two, **Chippewa Falls** and **Algonquin Falls,** 9.5 and 9 miles north of Bessemer, are a little tough to find without a topo map, since they don't lie along well-marked trails. The next five are a different story. The national forest has marked and mapped a good trail network, beginning from a parking lot off M-513, about 13 miles north of Bessemer. From this lot you can hike, from south to north, to **Great Conglomerate, Potawatomi, Gorge, Sandstone,** and **Rainbow Falls.** Only strong hikers and waterfall junkies should try to cover them all in one 10-mile outing—it's a lot of steps and a lot of waterfalls.

Like babies and sunsets, each waterfall is beautiful in a different way, and it's impossible to name the "best." Potawatomi is the closest—just a few minutes' walk from the lot—and accessible by wheelchair. And it is lovely, a delicate fretwork of foam cascading over remnants of an ancient lava flow. The last falls, Rainbow, is the largest of the group, cascading 40 feet. The resulting spray sometimes creates a rainbow effect, hence the name. The best view of Rainbow Falls is from the east side of the river, which you can access from a suspended foot bridge near the river's mouth at **Black River Harbor.**

◖ BOND FALLS

Some consider Bond Falls one of the most spectacular falls in the Upper Peninsula—a mighty big claim—while others feel the setting is far too developed with walkways and viewing platforms. To decide for yourself, head for Paulding on U.S. 45 in Ontonagon County. Bond Falls is three miles east on Bond Falls Road, well marked by signs. Though virtually surrounded by national forest land, the falls themselves sit on power company property, just below a power company dam that forms the adjacent **Bond Falls Flowage,** a popular area for fishing, swimming, and camping. To view the falls, follow the trail down the west side of the river, ignoring the spillway, cement retaining wall, and other power company additions. Once you begin descending the stairs, the falls come into your view to the right, close enough to touch.

© JOSH BISHOP

Bond Falls is one of the Upper Peninsula's most beautiful and well-known waterfalls.

Continue down the path to a footbridge that spans the base of the falls for an in-your-face view. Water gushes down a 50-foot face of chiseled rocks, so perfectly dramatic that it almost looks like a Disney creation. A few miles north of Bond Falls, **Agate Falls** is another striking waterfall, this one with a bridge for easy viewing. Take U.S. 45 north from Watersmeet, then M-28 east from Bruce Crossing.

WINTER SPORTS AND RECREATION
Downhill Skiing
Without the benefit of the "Big Snow Country" marketing muscle that serves the ski resorts of Gogebic County, **Ski Brule** (397 Brule Mountain Rd., 906/265-4957, 800/362-7853, www.skibrule.com) is left to its own devices to sell this appealing ski area six miles south of Iron River. Its gimmick is that it's "first to open, last to close," which translates to about six months of skiing. Brule is reliably open for downhill skiing by mid-November and continues through April. The terrain is nice, too, with 500 feet of vertical, eight chairs and T-bars, and a decent half-pipe for snowboarders. Contact Ski Brule for information on lift rates, rentals, and resort lodging.

Ski and Snowshoe Trails
Ski Brule (397 Brule Mountain Rd., 906/265-4957, 800/362-7853, www.skibrule.com) is also an ideal place for cross-country skiing. Nordic skiers can check out 14.2 miles of groomed and tracked trails, some of which wind along the Brule River. (Because they aren't covered by the resort's snowmaking, the Nordic trails don't always open as soon as the downhill area.) There are some 8.5 miles of groomed trails at **The Listening Inn** (339 Clark Rd., Crystal Falls, 906/822-7738, www.thelisteninginn.com, trail use $6/day), a splendid log lodge and B&B located nine miles north of Crystal Falls. Two beginner loops, separate snowshoe trails, and ski rentals make the inn an ideal ski destination. As with hiking, one of the finest trails for Nordic skiing in the **Lake Ottawa Recreation Area** (Lake Ottawa Rd., 906/265-9259, www.fs.fed.us) is the groomed and marked Ge-Che Trail.

Also, the national forest grooms 15 miles of trails within the Sylvania Wilderness Area and Recreation Area which provide a great cross-country ski network in winter months.

Snowmobiling
As with ORV trails, a network of snowmobile trails leaves Iron River and scatters through Ottawa National Forest. Snowmobile Trail 2 heads west into the forest, eventually reaching Ironwood, while plenty of routes branch off to the north and south to Wisconsin. Trails 2 and 16 head east for Escanaba.

ACCOMMODATIONS
The **Lakeshore Motel** (1257 Lalley Rd., 906/265-3611, www.lakeshoremotelicelake.com, $40–80) sits on the edge of spring-fed Ice Lake in Iron River (just east of downtown on U.S. 2), with tidy motel rooms, some with kitchenette units, and cabins from $50 a night. It's a great find, complete with sand beach and boat launch. Iron River also has an **AmericInn** (40 East Adams St., Iron River, 906/265-9100, www.americinn.com, $100–150) on U.S. 2 just east of downtown, with a nice indoor pool, whirlpool, and sauna. Suites are available. You'll

THE SUPERIOR UPLAND

© BECCA BISHOP

Near Iron River, the Chicaugon Lake Inn is one of the area's finest independent hotels.

THE SUPERIOR UPLAND

find great lodging at 🄲 **Chicaugon Lake Inn** (1700 County Road 424, 906/265-9244), predictably located near Chicaugon Lake in Iron River. The year-round hotel has sparsely decorated but well-kept rooms, whirlpool suites, and free wireless Internet. **Lac O' Seasons Resort** (176 Stanley Lake Dr., 800/797-5226, 906/265-4881, www.lacoseasons.com, $110–240) rents 14 cabins and cottages on the shores of Stanley Lake; in Crystal Falls, **Michi-Aho Resort** (2181 M-69, 906/875-3514, 800/875-0904) has rooms and cottages on the banks of the Michigamme River.

Camping

The 🄲 **Ottawa National Forest** maintains 27 auto-accessible campgrounds, all with tent pads, fire grates, and some sort of toilet facilities. Many are located along rivers and lakes. Most tend to be quite rustic and secluded, with the exception of Black River Harbor, Sylvania, and Bobcat Lake. A few, like Black River Harbor, require a fee and allow reservations through a central reservation system, 800/280-2267 or 800/283-2267. For more

information on a specific campground, contact a district ranger station or the Ottawa National Forest Headquarters (2100 East Cloverland Dr., 906/932-1330, 800/562-1201) in Ironwood.

FOOD

The namesake of **Alice's** (402 West Adams St., 906/265-4764) produces Italian specialties just as her immigrant mother did in Iron River before her, with homemade ravioli and other pasta dishes, gnocchi (Italian dumplings), and soups. Entrées run about $10. For picnics, pick up supplies at **Angeli's Foods,** in Riverside Plaza on U.S. 2 East (906/265-5107). An ordinary-looking modern supermarket from the outside, inside it surprises with a superb bakery, produce department, and deli. The family-run operation also has a store in Menominee. For something a little out of the ordinary, try eating in a train car at 🄲 **The Depot Restaurant & Bakery** (50 4th Ave., 906/265-6341), which serves more than 50 types of sandwiches at the site of the St. Paul Railroad Depot. Although it's a casual atmosphere (it is a train car, after all), fine dining selections include steak and seafood.

INFORMATION AND SERVICES

For more information on the Iron River area and Iron County, contact the **Iron County Chamber of Commerce** (50 East Genesee St., 906/265-3822, www.iron.org) in Iron River. All of Iron County is in the Central Time Zone.

Iron County Community Hospital (1400 West Ice Lake Rd., Iron River, 906/265-6121, www.icch.org) can see to your medical needs (dial 911 for emergencies). For financial needs, including ATMs and branch locations, try Wells Fargo (234 West Genesee St., 906/265-5144, www.wellsfargo.com) or Miners State Bank (312 West Genesee St., 906/265-5131, www.msbir.com).

To make sense of what the Ottawa National Forest has to offer, start with a map. You can pick up a small brochure (free) or large topo map ($4) at **National Forest Headquarters** in Ironwood (2100 East Cloverland Dr., 906/932-1330) or at the **Watersmeet Ranger District** office at the intersection of U.S. 2 and U.S. 45 in Watersmeet (906/358-4551). Other district offices, in Bessemer, Bergland, and Ontonagon, may have maps and brochures, but budget cuts have forced them to curtail other visitor services.

GETTING THERE AND AROUND
Car

Like many of the larger cities in the U.P.'s western reaches, Iron River is located where Michigan and Wisconsin meet. If you're coming up from Wisconsin, take Wisconsin Highway 139 (WIS 139) across the border. U.S. 2 arrives in town from Ironwood to the west and Iron Mountain to the east. If you're coming in from (or going to) the Keweenaw Peninsula, U.S. 141 is the way to go.

Air

If it seems as if the farther west you go in the Upper Peninsula, the farther away you get from convenient airports, it's because it's true. One of the downsides to all this rugged isolation is that no matter where you fly, you'll have a bit of driving to do. Thankfully, both Delta County Airport (ESC, 3300 Airport Rd., 906/786-4902, www.delta countymi.org) near Escanaba and Sawyer International Airport (MQT, 125 G Ave., Gwinn, 906/346-3308, www.sawyerairport .com) near Marquette have plenty of options for car rentals. Wisconsin's Rhinelander–Oneida County Airport (RHI, 3375 Airport Rd., 715/365-3416, www.rhinelandercity hall.org/airport.cfm) is a bit closer, and has daily service to and from Minneapolis–St. Paul and vehicle rentals through Avis and National/Alamo.

Public Transportation

Getting to Iron River can be done easily enough on Indian Trails motorcoaches (800/292-3831, www.indiantrails.com), which run regular trips from Escanaba to Ironwood. Call for schedules and rates.

© TRAVEL MICHIGAN

dogsled racing near Iron River

THE SUPERIOR UPLAND

Ironwood

With mammoth Lake Superior providing the requisite moisture, the northwestern corner of the U.P. isn't exaggerating when it markets itself as "Big Snow Country." Cool air moving across the warmer waters of Lake Superior create lake effect snow when it hits land, generating an average of 200 inches per season. This combines nicely with the area's rugged hills and Midwestern mountains, home to many of the Midwest's largest downhill ski resorts. As a result, the western U.P., especially around Ironwood, is one of the Upper Peninsula's more heavily marketed tourism areas, luring sizable crowds of skiers up I-39/U.S. 51 every weekend from Wisconsin and the Chicago area.

Ironwood hugs the border and merges with its sister city of Hurley, Wisconsin, once the center of civilization for the iron miners of the Gogebic Range. Ironwood had the stores and services; Hurley had the bars and brothels. (Strip joints remain prominent.) At the peak of iron mining—from the early 1900s to about 1930—the population topped 15,000. But mining grew less economically viable and, unlike the riches generated by copper in the Keweenaw, the millions made from iron left the region, without leaving behind opulent mansions or other monuments of wealth.

Consequently, Ironwood today is a tattered town that hardly hints at its past. Still, locals are friendly, and they would probably agree that Ironwood isn't the tourist attraction—the natural beauty of the surrounding area is.

SIGHTS
Downtown Ironwood
There are a few interesting diversions in Ironwood's downtown, not least of which is the **Ironwood Memorial Building,** a beautiful building that serves as a memorial for area residents killed in combat. World War I scenes are portrayed in stained glass, a statue of a soldier stands in the lobby, and displays outline the history of the region. Stop by the **Old**

Depot Park Museum and **Historic Ironwood Theater** for more of the town's history.

Hiawatha
After encountering Big John, the absurdly tall miner at Iron Mountain Iron Mine, you'd be forgiven for thinking the that Upper Peninsula has a thing for really, really big figures. Case in point: Hiawatha, the 50-foot fiberglass Native American that serves as a kitschy roadside tourist attraction. You won't be able to get to Hiawatha without heading through town, and it isn't necessarily worth the trip except for its oddity.

Little Girl's Point
Just minutes from the strip-mall world of U.S. 2, the real U.P. awaits. Follow M-505 north from Ironwood to reach Little Girl's Point, an area favorite. Perched high on a bluff over

A 50-foot-tall Hiawatha statue towers over Ironwood.

THE SUPERIOR UPLAND

© BECCA BISHOP

Lake Superior, this county park features a sand beach, a boat launch, picnic tables, grills, and fantastic views—the Porcupine Mountains to the east, the Apostle Islands to the west.

Black River Road
National Scenic Byway

Gogebic County tourism folks heavily promote this 15-mile stretch of M-513 from Bessemer north to Lake Superior, and for good reason. The two-lane road itself is pleasant enough, a wooded drive that twists in tandem with the Black River, hidden away in the forest just off the road's eastern shoulder. But even better, it links together several notable attractions.

The end of the road for M-513, Black River Harbor is a popular national forest campground on Lake Superior, with a large day-use area, sand beach, and boat launch. You can also pick up the North Country Scenic Trail here. For campground reservations, call the national forest central reservation system, 800/280-2267 or 800/283-2267.

◖ Copper Peak

You'll see the peak long before you reach it. About nine miles north of Bessemer, the rocky outcrop of Copper Peak rises 364 feet above the surrounding countryside, crowned by the 421-foot **Copper Peak Ski Flying Hill** (906/932-3500, www.copperpeak.org). Ski flying is similar to ski jumping but uses different equipment to launch—believe it or not—*longer* distances. (The current record is 512 feet.) Copper Peak, built in 1970, is the only ski flying hill in the Western Hemisphere and the highest artificial jump in the world.

From Memorial Day to Labor Day (and weekends through mid-October) a chairlift, elevator, and steps (fee) will bring you to the top for a heart-thumping skier's-eye view of the chute. This is not a trip for the faint of heart. But if you can get over a little knee-knocking, you'll be wowed by the panorama of the surrounding countryside, with views stretching across the undulating green of the national forest, the serpentine Black River, and the blue, blue horizon of Lake Superior. The Copper

Peak complex also offers 12 miles of mountain biking trails.

SUMMER SPORTS
AND RECREATION
Hiking and Biking

The lengthy **North Country National Scenic Trail** has been mentioned before, but the footpath really is the area's best hiking. When it's completed, the North Country Trail's 4,600 miles will make it the longest off-road hiking trail in the United States, longer even than the renowned Appalachian Trail. The section that passes through Ontonagon and Gogebic Counties cuts through Ottawa National Forest and Porcupine Mountains Wilderness State Park before bowing out of Michigan and into Wisconsin near Ironwood. Although it's one of the nation's longest trails, it's also one of the least traveled, giving you plenty of solitude for long stretches of the path.

In a land filled with stunning views, you'll find one of the best on the **Gogebic Ridge Hiking Trail,** a spur from the North Country Trail, about 40 miles northeast of Ironwood. The trail is eight miles long, and reaches its pinnacle at an overlook on one of the longest, tallest cliff faces in the state, complete with views of Lake Gogebic and the forested countryside. The south end of the trail skirts Weary Lake. Contact the Forest Service (906/884-2411) for information about both the North Country and Gogebic Ridge trails.

When the snow isn't on the ground, the extreme western U.P. is prime **mountain biking** territory. More than 100 miles of the **Pines and Mines Mountain Bike Trail** cut through Gogebic County alone, while nine miles of trails compose the **Wolverine Mountain Bike Trail.** One of the fat-tire highlights is **Copper Peak,** where bikers can enjoy a ride up the hill that would be a ski lift in the wintertime, then tear through the woods on the way back down.

Canoeing and Kayaking

The best paddling can be found in Ottawa National Forest's 1,000 or so miles of streams

THE SUPERIOR UPLAND

and rivers, so paddlers in the Ironwood region will likely want to make the short trip east to the forest.

Fishing

A couple companies in Ironwood charter fishing trips in Lake Superior, the largest, deepest, and coldest of the Great Lakes. Try **Bud's Charter Service** (128 East Larch St., 906/932-5652, www.westernup.com/budscharters) or **Nomad Lake Superior Fishing Charters** (211 West Lime St., 906/932-1576, www.nomadcharters .com) for full- and half-day charters. Your best bet for stream, river, and inland lake fishing will be to head east to Ottawa National Forest's almost 2,000 miles of waterways and some 500 lakes.

Golf

One of the western U.P.'s finest golf courses can be found in Ironwood itself. The **Gogebic Country Club** (200 Country Club Rd., 906/932-2515) has been a favorite Michigan golf spot since the early 1920s, when the attractive stone clubhouse was constructed. Its 18 holes measure around 6,000 yards. Take U.S. 2 a few miles west of Ironwood and turn south on Country Club Road. For a shorter nine-hole course, check out **Indianhead Mountain Resort** (500 Indianhead Rd., Wakefield, 906/229-5181, 800/346-3426, www.indian headmtn.com) or **Boulder Creek Golf Course** (N11868 Heron La., Bessemer, 906/932-9066, www.bouldercreekgolfmi.com).

Contact each golf course for current hours and greens fees.

Off-Road Vehicles

The closest major off-road vehicle trail in Ottawa National Forest is the 67-mile route that runs from Marenisco, 25 miles east of Ironwood on U.S. 2, to Iron River. There are, of course, smaller trails closer to Ironwood, but remember that ORVs are prohibited in the national forest except on designated, marked trails. Maps are available from the **U.S. Forest Service** (E6248 U.S. 2, Ironwood, 906/932-1330, www .fs.fed.us), or you can contact the Department of Natural Resources (906/353-6651).

Waterfalls

From Little Girl's Point, continue west on M-505 to reach **Superior Falls.** The rushing Montreal River puts on its final spectacular show here, plummeting more than 40 feet, then squeezing through a narrow gorge before spilling into Lake Superior a short distance away. You can also reach the falls by taking U.S. 2 about 11 miles west from Ironwood and turning north on Wisconsin Highway 122 (WIS 122), traveling through Wisconsin and back into Michigan in the process. In about 4.8 miles, watch for a small brown sign that directs you west into a small parking area near a Northern States Power substation. From there, it's a short walk to the falls. You also can continue down the path past the falls to Lake Superior, a fine sunset-watching spot.

As you can no doubt guess from its name, **Interstate Falls** is located on the border of—and shared by—Michigan's Upper Peninsula and Wisconsin. Like Superior Falls, Interstate Falls is part of the Montreal River, but this waterfall is less towering (though still more than 20 feet) and wider, with a fairly impressive flow when the water level is high. You'll want to cross into Wisconsin to see it. Take U.S. 2 west across state lines to an unpaved road about 0.25 miles past the border and follow the signs for **Peterson Falls,** which is a short walk upstream.

Heading north from Bessemer on the Black River Road National Scenic Byway will take you to a beautiful (and popular) lineup of five waterfalls on the Black River, which more or less runs parallel to the byway. Within the last few miles before reaching Lake Superior, you'll be able to see the **Great Conglomerate, Potawatomi, Gorge, Sandstone,** and **Rainbow** falls.

WINTER SPORTS AND RECREATION
◖ Downhill Skiing

With the exception of the ski area in the Porcupine Mountains Wilderness State Park, the area's downhill ski resorts line up conveniently along a short stretch of U.S. 2 just east of Ironwood. All welcome downhill skiers and snowboarders. Ticket prices vary with age and season. Package rates that include lodging usually offer the best deals. For those who want to explore all the area's terrain, ask about the interchangeable lift ticket (available at each participating resort), good on weekdays only at the area's four major resorts: Powderhorn, Blackjack, Indianhead, and Whitecap Mountain (located just over the border in Wisconsin).

Heading east from Ironwood, the first resort you'll reach is **Big Powderhorn Mountain** (N11375 Powderhorn Rd., 906/932-4838, www.bigpowderhorn.net) in Bessemer. Powderhorn oozes an early 1970s feel, and the giant fiberglass skier at its entrance—complete with red and blue vintage '70s skiwear—says it all. The resort's 25 downhill runs wrap across two faces, with 700 feet of vertical drop and nine double chairlifts. Perhaps more than the others, Big Powderhorn Mountain caters to families, with affordable lift tickets, mostly tame runs, and plenty of ski-in/ski-out lodging bordering its slopes. The main lodge at the base houses a cafeteria, ski rental and repair, ski school, a bar, and other services. The resort is open daily.

Also in Bessemer, the smaller, family-run **Blackjack Ski Resort** (888/906-9835, www.skiblackjack.com) carves out a niche in the market by making the most of its terrain. Cameron Run and Spillway often are left ungroomed and offer up good bump skiing, and Blackjack is arguably the best resort around for snowboarders, with the area's best halfpipe (served by its own rope tow) and a great terrain park on Broad Ax. Look to Blackjack for a variety of snowboard events, including camps and competitions. It's also a good place to avoid the weekend crowds that can plague Powderhorn and Indianhead. Blackjack offers 16 runs, four double chairlifts, and 465 feet of vertical. A day lodge at the base has food service and rental and repair; some limited condo accommodations line the slopes. The Loggers Lounge upstairs hosts the area's liveliest après-ski scene. Blackjack generally is open daily only during high season, and is closed on Tuesday and Wednesday other times. Call or check the website for a current schedule.

A few more miles down the road brings you to Wakefield and **Indianhead Mountain Resort** (500 Indianhead Rd., 800/346-3426, www.indianheadmtn.com), the area's largest resort, with 638 feet of vertical, five chairlifts, two T-bars, and 22 runs. Indianhead offers some of the region's most challenging (although overly groomed) skiing and pleasant runs that wind for more than a mile through

DOWNHILL SKIING

When people think of downhill skiing, the places that come to mind are more likely to include the Rocky Mountains or the Alps than midwest America – much less the Great Lakes, much less Michigan. And while it'd be more than a little misleading to say that Ironwood has the same caliber of skiing as, say, Breckenridge, it isn't unfair to say that the abundance of ski runs and resorts – combined with an impressive snowfall in the western Upper Peninsula – make it one of the finest destinations for Alpine skiers in the vast, flatish expanse between the Rockies and the Appalachians.

There are plenty of ski resorts within a stone's throw of Ironwood: **Big Powderhorn Mountain, Blackjack Ski Resort, Indianhead Mountain Resort, Whitecap Mountain, Porcupine Mountains, Ski Brule,** and a few other, smaller hills. Whether you like carving a halfpipe or leaving the first tracks on a backcountry slope, you'll find enough variety and deep snow to keep you satisfied, often for a fraction of what you'd pay at one of the big Colorado resorts.

As an added bonus, the U.P. is home to some of the United States' biggest ski jumping and ski flying hills: the **Pine Mountain Ski Jump** and the **Copper Peak Ski Flying Hill.**

the woods. Indianhead's lodging and skier services (sales, rentals, and repairs) sit at the top of the resort and offer more choices than the other area resorts. The day lodge even comes with great views of Ottawa National Forest spilling out across the valley beyond the slopes. Indianhead is open daily.

Ski and Snowshoe Trails

Active Backwoods Retreats (E5299 West Pioneer Rd., Ironwood, 906/932-3502, www .michiweb.com/abrski/), or ABR for short, grooms 25 miles of trails for skiing and striding on hundreds of acres of private land three miles south of Ironwood. The fee is $4. The trails are open daily, as well as some nights for lighted skiing or moonlight skiing. A warming hut, lessons, and rentals are available.

South of Wakefield, **Miljevich Cross Country Ski Trail** (906/229-5267) has 6.8 miles of groomed trails winding through the woods, along with a warming hut, rentals, and more. This is an easygoing kind of place; trails open when Rollie Milijevich can get the parking lot plowed open. There's no fee, but be sure to make a donation so Rollie can buy new snow tires. To find Miljevich's, turn south off U.S. 2 at Sunday Lake Street (the stoplight) and drive about 2.5 miles.

Between Ironwood and Bessemer, take Section 12 Road north from U.S. 2 to reach **Wolverine Nordic Trails.** Situated on private land and maintained by volunteers, the 9.3 miles of groomed trails wind through the hilly country south of the Big Powderhorn ski area. In fact, you can ride one of Powderhorn's chairlifts ($2 per ride) to access the network. Otherwise, begin at the lot with the warming hut on Sunset Road off Section 12 Road. A donation is requested.

If solitude is more important to you than track-set trails, don't overlook the vast terrain available in the 982,895-acre Ottawa National Forest. The **U.S. Forest Service** office (2100 East Cloverland Dr., Ironwood, 906/932-1330) has national forest maps and can suggest trails to try.

Snowmobiling

Of the western U.P.'s snowmobile trails (hundreds of miles of them), plenty are accessible from Ironwood. Trail 2 leaves the city, heading east before fanning out to cross the rest of the U.P.—take Trail 11 north to Porcupine Mountains State Park and Lake Superior. Heading the opposite direction, Trail 11 runs northwest to find Lake Superior where Michigan and Wisconsin meet. Speaking of Wisconsin, plenty of these trails drop south into the neighboring state and connect with the Badger State's network of snowmobile trails.

ACCOMMODATIONS

You'll find a large selection of mom-and-pop motels along U.S. 2, many of which offer great deals and clean, comfortable, if simple, rooms. A couple of good choices are the **Sandpiper Motel** (1200 Cloverland Dr., 906/932-2000) and the **Crestview Cozy Inn** (906/932-4845) at the west end of U.S. 2. Both run $25–75; rates may be higher in peak ski season.

The larger area ski resorts have slopeside (or near-slopeside) accommodations that range from dormitories to simple motel rooms to deluxe condominiums. (This ain't Aspen, so forgive the occasional bad paneling.) Prices range widely enough to fit almost every budget, and they can be a good value in nonskiing months. Try **Indianhead reservations** (800/346-3426) or **Big Powderhorn Mountain and Lodging** (800/222-3131) for plenty of choices. Ask about package deals with lift tickets if you're traveling in winter. The handy Big Snow Country **lodging referral service** (906/932-4850) can fill you in on even more lodging options throughout the region—not just those near downhill ski resorts—from the Wisconsin border to just east of the Porcupine Mountains.

For something a little more intimate, you can't beat the **Bear Track Inn** (N15325 Black River Rd., Ironwood, 906/932-2144). National forest land practically surrounds the inn's three log cabins, which have a great location one mile from Lake Superior's Black River Harbor and near loads of hiking/biking/ski trails. Each cabin has a full kitchen and use of the

The Regal Country Inn in Wakefield has a charming soda fountain inside.

Finnish sauna. From the outside, the **Regal Country Inn** (1602 East U.S. 2, Wakefield, 906/229-5122, www.westernup.com/regalinn) looks nothing like an old Victorian home, but you're in one of its historic or Victorian rooms you'll swear you've booked a B&B. Antique beds and decorations, pieces of local history, quilted bedspreads, and a gourmet breakfast (for an additional charge; continental breakfast is included) add to this inn's charm. Free wireless Internet is an added plus.

Finally, chain motels cluster near the U.S. 2/U.S. 51 interchange, including the **Days Inn** (715/561-3500, $50–100) in Hurley, with an indoor pool; some rooms have microwaves and refrigerators.

Camping

True to Michigan state park form, **Lake Gogebic State Park** (800/447-2757, www.michigan.gov/dnr) offers a fine modern campground, with large (but rather open) sites on the western shore of Lake Gogebic. A boat launch, small sand beach, and nice picnic area are nearby. Lake Gogebic is known for great walleye and perch fishing, so pack a rod even if you don't come with a boat. Though reservations are rarely needed, you can obtain one through the state park central reservation system.

FOOD

Yep, it looks like a classic corner tavern, but **Don & GG's** (906/932-2312) on U.S. 2 in Ironwood might surprise you with its vegetarian dishes and smoked trout salad. Don't worry—you can still get burgers and chicken dinners, too. The **Hoop 'N' Holler Tavern** (115 Hoop 'N' Holler Rd., Merriweather, 906/575-5555) looks like a tavern because it is, and it has some very good tavern grub—burgers, sandwiches, pizza, and plenty of fried food. Located on Lake Gogebic's northwest side, Hoop 'N' Holler has a beach available in the summertime. Unlike Ironwood, the tavern is located in the Eastern Time Zone: add an hour.

Okay, so the **Kimball Inn** (715/561-4095) is actually in Wisconsin. It's worth the extra four-mile drive west on U.S. 2 from the Michigan/Wisconsin border to sample its smoked barbecue, charbroiled steaks, grinders (Italian sandwiches), and more. It's closed Monday. Also in Wisconsin, **Petrusha's Supper Club** (715/561-9888) in downtown Hurley serves up good Italian and supper-club fare, from prime rib to seafood. There are some interesting Austrian dishes, too, like the filet with chicken livers and cognac sauce. Back in Ironwood, the **Royal Bakery** (906/932-1931) at the corner of Cloverland Dr. (U.S. 2) and Douglas Blvd. is a good bet for fresh homemade pasties, as well as basic doughnuts and pastries.

INFORMATION AND SERVICES

For tourism information, assistance, and planning, get ahold of the **Ironwood Area Chamber of Commerce** (150 North Lowell St., 906/932-1122, www.ironwoodmi.org) or the Western Upper Peninsula Convention and Visitor Bureau (906/932-4850, 800/522-5657, www.westernup.info).

Ironwood's hospital is the Grand View Hospital (10561 North Grand View La., 906/932-2525, www.gvhs.org), just north of U.S. 2 between Bessemer and Ironwood. There's no shortage of banks in Ironwood and Bessemer—plenty of them are local and regional banks—or you can go to one of Wells Fargo's two locations.

GETTING THERE AND AROUND

Car

Ironwood is tucked about as far into the U.P.'s western corner as you can get. Take U.S. 2 in from the east or west (you can also drive up Wisconsin Highway 77 from Wisconsin), and U.S. 51 from the south. M-28 serves as the connection from the north and east in the Upper Peninsula.

Air

In addition to the distant Sawyer International Airport (MQT, 125 G Ave., Gwinn, 906/346-3308, www.sawyerairport.com) near Marquette,

MILEAGE FROM WAKEFIELD TO *EAST*

DETROIT	625
ESCANABA	170
IRON MOUNTAIN	120
GREEN BAY	195
MANISTIQUE	225
MARQUETTE	135
MONTREAL	925
NEW YORK	1215
PORT HURON	630
QUEBEC	1100
SOO LOCKS	300
TORONTO	775

© JOSH BISHOP

Wakefield, just east of Ironwood, seems to be a long way from anywhere.

you can find a closer airport in Houghton County, up in the Keweenaw Peninsula. Houghton County Memorial Airport (CMX, 23810 Airpark Blvd., Calumet, 906/482-3970, www.houghton county.org) has regularly scheduled flights from Minneapolis–St. Paul, as well as vehicle rentals. You can also try Wisconsin. The Rhinelander–Oneida County Airport (RHI, 3375 Airport Rd., 715/365-3416, www.rhinelandercityhall.org/airport.cfm) has daily service to and from Minneapolis–St. Paul and vehicle rentals through Avis and National/Alamo.

Public Transportation

Getting to Ironwood via bus is actually pretty easy, even if you're coming from Chicago, Detroit, or other far-off locations. A combination of Greyhound and Indian Trails (800/292-3831, www.indiantrails.com) routes can get you there without too much trouble. Call Indian Trails for current rates and schedules for its St. Ignace–Escanaba–Ironwood line.

Porcupine Mountains and Ontonagon

SIGHTS
◖ Porcupine Mountains Wilderness State Park

Anchored along the Lake Superior shore in the northwest corner of the U.P., Porcupine Mountains Wilderness State Park covers 60,000 acres, making it the largest park in Michigan's excellent state park system. The Porcupine Mountains were considered as a national park site in the 1940s, but were quickly preserved as a state park in 1945 when loggers threatened to get to work on their virgin timber before the federal government took action.

Someone once decided that this rumpled landscape of low mountains and tall pines looked like the silhouette of a porcupine. Hmm. But the name stuck, along with an endearing nickname: "the Porkies." The area is a mecca for casual hikers and hardcore backpackers alike, home to 90-plus miles of well-marked and well-maintained trails—more than you'll find in many national parks, and certainly more than you'll find in most of the Great Lakes region.

And in this case, bigger also means better. The park preserves vast stands of virgin hemlock, pine, and hardwoods—the largest tract of virgin hardwoods between the Rockies and the Adirondacks, in fact—as well as secluded lakes, wild rivers, and some of the Midwest's highest peaks. (Summit Peak tops out at 1,958 feet.) Unlike most state parks, the Porkies are large enough to provide a sense of wilderness and serenity, an escape from the civilized world.

Ontonagon County Historical Museum

The Ontonagon Boulder was pried from its namesake riverbank a few miles upstream from the Lake Superior shoreline community of Ontonagon. Today the two-ton mass of native copper resides at the Smithsonian, and Ontonagon's mining heritage thrives only in museums—especially since

© JOSH BISHOP

THE SUPERIOR UPLAND

Porcupine Mountains Wilderness State Park is Michigan's largest and wildest state park.

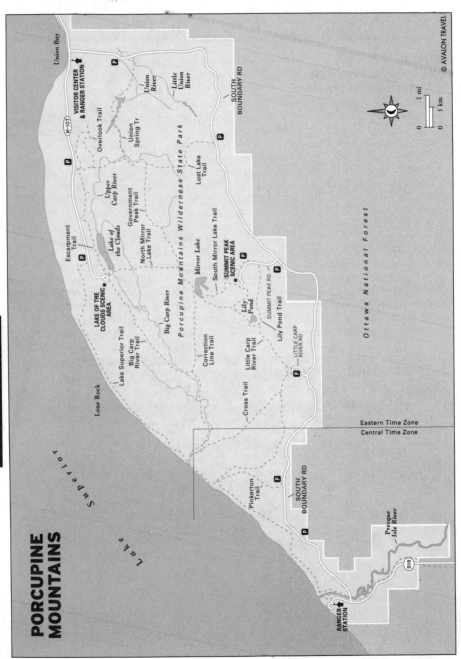

PORCUPINE
MOUNTAINS

© AVALON TRAVEL

Lake   Superior

Union Bay

VISITOR CENTER
& RANGER STATION

M-107

Overlook Trail

Union
River

Little
Union
River

Union Spring Tr

Escarpment
Trail

Upper
Carp River

Government
Peak Trail

North Mirror
Lake Trail

Lake of
the Clouds

P o r c u p i n e   M o u n t a i n s   W i l d e r n e s s   S t a t e   P a r k

SOUTH
BOUNDARY RD

Lost Lake
Trail

Mirror Lake

South Mirror Lake Trail

LAKE OF THE
CLOUDS SCENIC
AREA

SUMMIT PEAK
SCENIC AREA

Lake Superior Trail

Big Carp
River Trail

Big Carp River

Lone Rock

Correction
Line Trail

Little Carp
River Trail

Lily
Pond

Lily Pond Trail

SUMMIT PEAK RD

LITTLE CARP
RIVER RD

Little Carp
River RD

Cross Trail

Ottawa   National   Forest

Eastern Time Zone
Central Time Zone

Pinkerton
Trail

SOUTH
BOUNDARY RD

519

Presque
Isle River

RANGER
STATION

0   1 mi
0   1 km

PORCUPINE MOUNTAINS

Long before Europeans came to the area and began harvesting its abundant natural resources, the Ojibwa people had already (inexplicably) named the peaks and crags along the Lake Superior shore the Porcupine Mountains. The mountains were swept up in the Upper Peninsula's expansive fur trade, and then, in the mid-1800s, copper was discovered. During the last half of the 19th century and into the early 20th, there were 45 copper mines operating inside what is now Porcupine Mountains Wilderness State Park. Loggers began moving in, too.

Logging has had a drastic, often damaging impact on the landscape of the Upper Peninsula, and the threat to the Porcupine Mountains was real. As tree cutting began to encroach on the virgin forests in the early 1920s, people began to talk about preservation. The dream became a reality some 20 years later, when the Michigan state legislature established the park and the Porkies were saved – almost. There were some close calls with copper mining and a scenic roadway, but thanks to constant efforts by state agencies, the park is still in nearly untouched condition.

Today, the Porkies are home to one of the Great Lakes region's largest remaining old-growth forests, hardwoods and eastern hemlock trees. It's an impossibly wonderful park, with plenty of recreational opportunities for the taking.

the nearby copper mine and smelter in White Pine closed in 1995. (White Pine now is little more than a creepy ghost town of 1950s tract housing.) Check out Ontonagon's happier heyday at the worthwhile Ontonagon County Historical Museum (422 River St., 906/884-6165, www.ontonagonmuseum.org), a lavender building on U.S. 41/M-38, downtown's main street.

Adventure Copper Mine

In Greenland, 12 miles southeast of Ontonagon, the Adventure Copper Mine (906/883-3371, www.exploringthenorth.com/mine/venture.html, late May–mid-Oct., 9 A.M.–6 P.M. Mon.–Sat., 11 A.M.–6 P.M. Sun.) operated for 70 years without turning a profit. Today, it's more successful as a tourism destination, offering a number of surface and underground tours that last from 45 minutes to 3 hours. One of the tours recreates the experience of old-time miners by having visitors rappel down a mineshaft in total darkness, explore small areas, and get a little dirty. There are some tamer underground tours, too. To get there, take Adventure Road off of M-38 in Greenland.

Old Victoria

Originally established by copper miners in the

1840s, the tiny town of **Rockland** was nearly leveled by a fire in 1890. It was rebuilt in the popular Victorian style of the day, and several Victorian facades still decorate this small community in the Ontonagon River valley, 14 miles south of Ontonagon on U.S. 45. From downtown Rockland, follow Victoria Dam Road southwest two miles to Old Victoria (906/886-2617), a cluster of miners' log homes huddled around a once-lucrative copper mine shaft. Locals have scratched to save this preservation work-in-progress; its new designation as a Keweenaw National Historic Park cooperating site may funnel new attention and needed funds. The homes are open on most summer afternoons when a guide is on hand to offer tours. Donations are needed and appreciated. You can wander the grounds at any time. Continue past Old Victoria to the **Victoria Dam,** a power company hydroelectric facility and surprisingly pretty spot, popular with local anglers.

Ontonagon Lighthouse

The Ontonagon County Historical Society's biggest project these days is restoring the 1866 Ontonagon Lighthouse, which replaced one of Lake Superior's first lighthouses, built in 1853.

Contact the Historical Society (906/884-6165) to learn more about restoration efforts and public tours.

SUMMER SPORTS AND RECREATION
Hiking and Biking Trails

Many visitors to the Porkies head immediately toward the justly famous **Lake of the Clouds Overlook.** From the parking lot at the end of M-107, it's just a few steps to the overlook, where the placid lake slices a long sliver of blue through a thick mat of jade forest hundreds of feet below. The view is the stuff postcards are made of and is probably the most photographed scene in the U.P.

The overlook also serves as the trailhead for some the park's most rugged and scenic routes. To properly soak in the Lake of the Clouds view, hike the aptly named **Escarpment Trail,** which winds east and skims over Cloud Peak and Cuyahoga Peak. Bordered by a sheer cliff, the four-mile trail is considered by many to be the most beautiful in the park. Allow ample time to stop and enjoy the shimmering lake and valley floor spreading out around you.

At its eastern trailhead, the Escarpment Trail links up with the 7.5-mile **Government Peak Trail.** This secluded route drops south over the Upper Carp River and past Trap Falls, then swings west and scales Government Peak. As quickly as it rises, the trail drops down to quiet Mirror Lake, a perfect spot to soak weary feet after a full day of hiking.

From Mirror Lake, the dull and heavily wooded **Correction Line Trail** heads west, where it meets the **Big Carp River Trail,** another good choice. Running nine miles from Lake Superior to the Lake of the Clouds Overlook, this fine route leads hikers along a shaded river valley of hemlocks and ferns, past the park's highest waterfall (25-foot Shining Cloud Falls), and along a dry ridgetop with more dramatic peeks at Lake of the Clouds.

Several miles south, visitors get another soaring view from the **Summit Peak observation tower.** At 1,958 feet, Summit Peak grows even taller with a 40-foot observation tower at its crest. It's an inspiring panorama, a vast landscape unscarred by humans. In fact, the only sign of civilization is a spindly ski jump 18 miles away, rising above the treeline like a circus clown on stilts. On a clear day, scour the horizon for a glimpse of Lake Superior's Apostle Islands, nearly 40 miles to the west.

One of the park's most spectacular trails is probably its most accessible: the **East and West River Trail** parallels the wild and turbulent Presque Isle River. From the Presque Isle Campground at the park's west end, you can follow the Presque Isle one mile upriver and back down the other bank as it roils and boils through narrow rock walls and tumbles into Lake Superior. Keep a tight hold on children and pets along this trail, and don't think about wading—the current is swift and dangerous. To dangle your toes or let Fido take a swim, there's a wonderfully deep, clear, and placid backwater pool just east of the main channel right near Lake Superior.

Long before the Porcupine Mountains were preserved for their virgin timber and natural beauty, miners harvested the rich minerals buried in their bedrock. At the east end of the park, the **Union Mine Trail** provides a glimpse into the 1840s, when the Porkies pulsed with the excitement of the area's copper rush. Marked with white mine shovels to indicate points of interest, this self-guided interpretive trail forms a mile loop along the spring-fed Union River and the site of an old copper mine, now largely swallowed by nature. In the shadow of lofty hemlocks, you'll see how miners tunneled shafts into the riverbank and learn about their lives in the wilderness—a wilderness still untamed today.

Fishing

Fishing is one of the many recreational benefits in this vast expanse of wilderness. One of the park's more sightly locations, Lake of the Clouds, is accessible to anglers, as are a number of other lakes and streams. Try Mirror Lake and any number of rivers—the Carp River, Presque Isle River, and Union River. Contact the DNR park headquarters (906/885-5275) for regulations and information.

Beaches

Porcupine Mountain State Park is known, in part, for its beaches and long miles (more than 50) of Lake Superior shoreline. The most popular beach in the area is **Union Bay,** in part because of its pleasant-but-chilly swimming and in part because it's easily accessible by car.

Golf

Golfers will have to turn to the nine holes at **Ontonagon Golf Course** (19906 Firesteel Rd., Ontonagon, 906/884-4130, $15 for 9 holes, $25 all day), which isn't a bad thing at all. The clubhouse is nothing to write home about, but the par-35 course makes for a nice round, and the pro shop can provide you with everything you need for an afternoon on the links.

Off-Road Vehicles

The old Copper Range Railroad grade bisects Ontonagon County and the southern Keweenaw from Mass City north to Houghton, a distance of more than 41 miles. Throughout the state, the DNR has purchased many of these old grades and removed the rails, maintaining them as multi-use trails. In the U.P., that usually means snowmobiles and ATVs. Near the intersection of M-26 and M-38 at Lake Mine, the trail spans the Firesteel River on three bridges—65, 75, and 85 feet high. Stop at the DNR office in Barage for a map of the rail trail that shows access points. Where the trail crosses roads, look for a yellow-and-black snowmobile crossing sign on the highway or a DNR ATV wooden trail sign on the trail itself.

Waterfalls

The Porkies' more than 60 waterfalls can seem a bit overwhelming, but despite the overwhelming choices, some falls stand out above the others. Make the brief trek to **Presque Isle Falls** in the western portion of the Porkies. Take South Boundary Road southwest from the visitors center (it's a good drive) to a boardwalk that follows the river to a number of falls, including **Manabezho Falls** and the smaller, less impressive **Manido Falls.**

THE SUPERIOR UPLAND

© JOSH BISHOP

Manabezho Falls can be found in the Presque Isle River Scenic Area.

WINTER SPORTS AND RECREATION
Downhill Skiing

Downhill skiers are surprised to find a state-run downhill ski area within the park, and even more surprised to find it offers a 787-foot vertical and (get this) 42 runs. Runs range in difficulty from bunny to advanced, spanning a north-facing flank and served by two chairlifts, one T-bar, and a rope tow. The ski area recently added more than 100 acres of backcountry terrain when it opened Everest, a half-mile wide section of virgin forest with more than 17 runs and snowcat service. A day lodge at the base has food service, rentals, and a small ski shop. Sure, the lifts are old and creaky, but the terrain is great, the snow is reliable (the annual average tops 175 inches), and the views of Lake Superior from the top are phenomenal. For all its charms, though, this is not a good choice on a day when a strong north wind is blowing—you'll feel the windchill all the way from Canada.

Located just west of the park headquarters on M-107, the ski area is open 9:30 A.M.–5:30 P.M. weekdays, 10 A.M.–5 P.M. weekends. Call the **park headquarters** (906/885-5275) for information on ticket prices and snow conditions.

Ski and Snowshoe Trails

The same chalet and base area serves cross-country skiers, who can access a terrific network of trails. The park service grooms and tracks 14.2 miles of the park's hiking trails, which wind through the eastern end of the park. Some skirt the Lake Superior shoreline, where snow and ice sculptures form. Others scale the hilly terrain in the interior of the park and can be reached via one of the downhill ski area lifts. Skiing is free, but there is a charge for lift service and park admission. Call the park headquarters for more information.

Snowmobiling

In addition to the marked trails in Ottawa National Forest, you can take unplowed M-107 to Lake of the Clouds for a great, groomed snowmobile trail in the Porkies that ends at a spectacularly beautiful location.

ACCOMMODATIONS

You'll find a string of motels along M-64 between Silver City (two miles east of park headquarters) and Ontonagon. Many are plain, somewhat tired mom-and-pop-type places, but they work just fine after a long day outdoors. **Tomlinson's Rainbow Lodging** (2900 M-64, 906/885-5348, $75–150) offers motel rooms and cottages on the shores of Lake Superior, with a private sand beach. Some units have whirlpools and kitchen facilities. Pets are okay. **Mountain View Lodges** (906/885-5256, $100–150) features two-bedroom cottages on Lake Superior with amenities like fireplaces and fully equipped kitchens. The **Best Western Porcupine Mountain Lodge** in Silver City (906/885-5311, $75–150) offers the full array of motel services, including an indoor pool, a sauna, meeting rooms, and a dining room. For other options, contact the Ontonagon Chamber of Commerce (906/884-4735).

Camping

Campers have their choice of two modern campgrounds, both with a number of sites overlooking Lake Superior: **Union Bay** (full hookups) at the east end of the park or **Presque Isle** (no hookups) near the mouth of the Presque Isle River on the park's western edge. Both offer flush toilets and showers. In addition, three rustic campgrounds (called "outposts") with 3 to 11 sites each are located off the South Boundary Road, accessible by car, but with no facilities. They tend to offer more privacy than the modern campgrounds. Reservations for all campsites are recommended in summer (800/447-2757, www.michigan.gov/dnr).

As another option, the park offers 16 hike-in **rustic cabins.** These are great retreats after a day on the trail. They come with two to eight bunks, mattresses, a woodstove, basic utensils, and protection from the elements, but no electricity or running water. Bring your own stove for cooking. Cabins situated on inland lakes even come with a rowboat, so you can finish the day with a lazy drift across the water. Reserve a cabin as much as a year in advance by calling 906/885-5275.

Two more options for backpackers: there are three hike-in **Adirondack shelters** with sleeping platforms (available only on a first-come, first-served basis) and backcountry camping. Trailside camping is permitted throughout the backcountry, as long as you stay a quarter mile or more from cabins, shelters, scenic areas, and roads. All backpackers must register at the visitors center before setting out.

FOOD

Paul's Restaurant (906/885-5311), in Silver City's Porcupine Mountain Lodge, gets high marks for fish and other supper-club fare. In Ontonagon, **Syl's** (713 River St., 906/884-2522) is a classic small-town café, with some of the best pasties around. Fifteen minutes south of Ontonagon on U.S. 45, **Henry's Never Inn** (906/886-9910) in Rockland draws 'em in far and wide for its enormous buffets, with various fish dishes on Friday night and Italian on Saturday. Soups and sandwiches are great, too, but it's really the spirited locals who add flavor to this old mining haunt.

If you're camping in the Porkies, your closest full-service grocery is in Ontonagon, 17 miles east of the park. For last-minute supplies, try the **Silver City General Store** (906/885-5885) on M-107. It has basic camping and fishing supplies, and picnic staples like cheese and bread.

INFORMATION AND SERVICES

Tourism information can be had from the **Porcupine Mountains Convention and Visitor Bureau** (906/884-2047, www.porcupine mountains.com) or the Western Upper Peninsula Convention and Visitor Bureau (906/932-4850, 800/522-5657, www.western up.info) in Ironwood. For maps and information about Porcupine Mountains Wilderness State Park, visit park headquarters (412 South Boundary Rd., Ontonagon, 906/885-5275, www.michigan.gov/dnr).

If you need a hospital, you'll find one in Ontonagon. To get to the Aspirus Ontonagon Hospital (601 South 7th St., 906/884-4134, www.aspirus-ontonagon.org), take Greenland Road (M-38) to 7th Street and turn north. Banking can be done at mBank (601 River St., 906/884.4114, www.bankmbank.com), Citizens State Bank of Ontonagon (501 River St., 906/884-4165, www.csbont.com), or others.

GETTING THERE AND AROUND
Car
M-38, M-64, and U.S. 45 all converge on Ontonagon, which is located on the shores of Lake Superior. From Ironwood, take U.S. 2 to M-28/64 before branching north on M-64. From Ontonagon, take M-64 to M-107 to get to Porcupine Mountains Wilderness State Park—the headquarters are on South Boundary Road, just south of M-107.

Boat
Ontonagon has a small marina that has 29 seasonal slips and 7 transient slips. The **Ontonagon Village Marina** (906/884-4225, www.michigan.gov/dnr) operates from May 1 to October 5 and can be reached on radio channels 16 and 68. Coordinates are 46° 52.57 N, 89° 19.58 W.

Air
Ontonagon's county airport doesn't offer commercial flights, but you'll be able to catch a plane into Houghton County Memorial Airport (CMX, 23810 Airpark Blvd., Calumet, 906/482-3970, www.houghtoncounty.org), which has regularly scheduled flights from Minneapolis–St. Paul. Priceless and National offer vehicle rentals, and taxi and limo service are available. Of course, Marquette's Sawyer International Airport (MQT, 125 G Ave., Gwinn, 906/346-3308, www.sawyerairport .com) is a more distant option.

THE SUPERIOR UPLAND

KEWEENAW PENINSULA AND ISLE ROYALE

If Lake Superior looks like the head of a wolf (and it does), then the Keweenaw Peninsula (KEE-wuh-naw) is seized firmly in its jaw. Parts of the land look like they've been gnawed on, too—remnants of long, hard decades of mining during the 19th-century copper boom. This narrow strip of land isn't called Copper Country for nothing.

Today, the Keweenaw's wealth is measured not in copper but in its incredible natural beauty—a mother lode of wild rivers, hidden waterfalls, and lonely Lake Superior beaches. There's civilization here, too, but the Keweenaw pretty thinly populated even by Upper Peninsula standards. Houghton is the largest city in these parts, with Hancock, just across the river, a close second; together they have a modest population of around 11,000.

The cities are separated by Portage Lake, part of the Keweenaw Waterway that splits the peninsula nicely in half. Some locals even go so far as to call the upper portion—the part containing Hancock and Copper Harbor—Copper Island, which isn't entirely false, though it's a little optimistic.

Copper Harbor, on the shores of Lake Superior at Michigan's extreme north, is the end of the road. Specifically, it's the end of U.S. 41, a long, black, asphalt ribbon that goes all the way south to Miami, Florida. Copper Harbor's reputation as an outdoor destination is high, even in the outdoorsy U.P., and it draws plenty of kayakers, bikers, and snowmobilers. Rugged pleasure-seekers on the way to Isle Royale National Park can catch a ferry here.

© TRAVEL MICHIGAN

HIGHLIGHTS

◖ Quincy Mine: North of Hancock, this historic mine tops the list of stops among the Keweenaw Heritage Sites. The full two-hour tour takes you into the mine (page 130).

◖ Fort Wilkins Historic State Park: Yes, it's another historic fort in the Upper Peninsula, and yes, this one is worth your time, too. Don't miss the costumed interpreters (page 145).

◖ Brockway Mountain Drive: It's only a little bit out of the way, and you won't want to miss this scenic lookout on the way to Copper Harbor – or the view of the city on the way back down (page 145).

◖ Lighthouses: Sand Hills. Eagle Harbor. Copper Harbor. Some of the U.P.'s finest historic lighthouses are here in the Keweenaw – and a handful of them will rent you a room (page 146).

◖ Hiking Isle Royale: It takes a little work to get here, but once you do, you'll have 165 miles of trails beneath your feet and some of America's last true wilderness at your fingertips (page 163).

LOOK FOR ◖ TO FIND RECOMMENDED SIGHTS, ACTIVITIES, DINING, AND LODGING.

Some 48 miles north (and also part of Michigan), Isle Royale National Park lies stranded in Lake Superior, a wild, craggy, roadless archipelago of lakes and forests and moose and hiking trails. It remains the least-visited park in the entire National Park Service system.

The remote Keweenaw has never had the tourist appeal—and subsequent amenities—of say, Marquette. That is just how many people like it, of course. But tourists are beginning to find out anyway. The national park will bring them, more museums and other attractions are opening, and more people every year discover the Keweenaw's unspoiled beauty. Some locals seem almost uneasy about the growing tourism interest. The backcountry is filled with amazing hiking and mountain biking trails, which lead to waterfalls and other gems—but you'll find little guidance in where to go or how to get there.

Yet for those who crave a little adventure and solitude, the Keweenaw Peninsula and Isle Royale offer it up in spades. As it was for those early copper miners, the Keweenaw remains a remarkable land of discovery.

PLANNING YOUR TIME

It's only about a two-hour drive from the base of the Keweenaw to Copper Harbor, but with scenery this stunning and outdoor activities this isolated, you're going to want to plan on spending considerably more time here. Houghton and Hancock make a great home base for outdoor excursions—you can

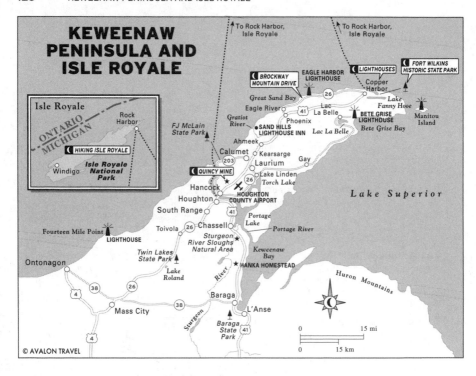

KEWEENAW PENINSULA AND ISLE ROYALE

© AVALON TRAVEL

get pretty much anywhere in the peninsula in a little more than an hour at most. Depending on how many hours you're looking to spend on the trail or in that kayak, visitors often find that a weekend is plenty of time for a good recreation and sightseeing vacation. Of course, if you're going to Isle Royale, you'll want to add several days. The wilderness island is vast—it'll take a while to walk the 165 miles of trails—and ferries run on limited schedules.

HISTORY

Raking off the back of the Upper Peninsula like a ragged dorsal fin, the Keweenaw Peninsula was quickly shunned by early European immigrants to the Michigan Territories: Hopelessly remote. Nearly engulfed by Lake Superior. Smothered in snow half the year. Blanketed by impenetrable forests, which grew out of untillable rock and infertile sand. They dismissed

it as nothing more than a wasteland, even more so than the rest of the Upper Peninsula.

But then in 1840, state geologist Douglass Houghton confirmed the presence of copper. Vast deposits of pure, native copper, much of it right near the surface, there for the taking. The young United States had an insatiable appetite for the metal, first for new industrial machinery, and later for Civil War hardware, electrical wiring, and other innovations. Houghton's find was as good as gold. Actually, it was even better than gold.

The Copper Rush began almost overnight, first with prospectors, then with large mining enterprises flooding the "wasteland" of the Keweenaw. It was the nation's first mineral rush. Copper employed thousands of immigrant laborers, built cities, made millionaires, and prompted extravagant luxuries like opera houses and "copper baron" mansions. Before it was over, King Copper generated more than

$9.6 billion—10 times more money than the California Gold Rush.

The Keweenaw's copper legacy still looms large, but in the form of abandoned mines, ghost towns buried in the forest, and the odd juxtaposition of lavish buildings in almost-forgotten towns. Neglected for most of the 20th century, the Keweenaw's copper heritage finally began to be considered worthy of preservation in the 1970s. The result is the Keweenaw National Historic Park, established in 1992 (and still very much in development). To be sure, a lot of rich history has been demolished, thrown away, or crushed under the weight of winter snows. But an astounding amount remains. While cheesy chain restaurants across the United States line their walls with fake tools and other "junque," here you'll find the real thing: piles and piles of mining artifacts decorating restaurants, front porches, and anywhere else they can think of to put the century-old stuff.

Houghton, Hancock, and Vicinity

When the hip outdoor sporting magazine *Outside* listed Houghton (HOE-ton) among America's "next wave of dream towns," you knew times were a-changin'. Ho-where? Well, turns out *Outside* may have something here. Houghton—and the adjacent city of Hancock—not only offers great sporting diversions, it boasts a quirky ethnic flair, streets lined with beautifully preserved early-1900s buildings, and a university to add a dollop of culture and liveliness. If you find old mining ruins intriguing instead of ugly, then Houghton and Hancock is downright pretty, too.

While the cities provide a refreshing shot of civilization (it's still nowhere near cosmopolitan), there are plenty of outlying towns and destinations that are more than worth your time. They make Houghton and Hancock a great place for hub-and-spoke traveling—find your lodging, spend the evenings in the city, and make your way out on engaging day trips. Let's face it: There's only so much you can do in two cities with a combined population that would fill less than 20 percent of Ford Field in Detroit, where the Lions play football.

The lift bridge that crosses the Portage Waterway is an iconic image of Houghton and Hancock.

© JOSH BISHOP

SOUTH OF HOUGHTON AND HANCOCK

Geographically speaking, the Keweenaw Peninsula merges with the rest of the U.P. at about Ontonagon on its western shore and L'Anse to the east—an imaginary line traced neatly by M-38. Between this highway and the Portage Waterway, the southern Keweenaw is quiet and sparsely populated. It's quite a change from the turn of the century, when the Copper Range Company operated successful mines across this whaleback of a peninsula.

KEWEENAW PENINSULA

Like elsewhere in the Keeweenaw, the tall skeletons of mining shaft houses occasionally lurch skyward out of the pines, dying relics of the Copper Rush.

Here, too, logging came in to fill the void. Today, a sawmill operated by Mead Paper in South Range (south of Houghton on M-26) ranks as one of the area's largest employers, milling the rare and prized bird's-eye maple that grows just north of here. Still, the economy struggles, and the locals have made few attempts—so far, anyway—to fill the void with tourism dollars.

At the foot of Keeweenaw Bay, between Baraga (BARE-a-ga) and L'Anse (LAHNTS), the enormous wooden statue *Shrine of the Snowshoe Priest* looms 35 feet above Red Rock Bluff. It commemorates the life of Bishop Frederic Baraga, a Catholic missionary from Slovenia who gained recognition for his work with local Ojibwa in the mid-1800s, traveling by snowshoe to reach distant communities. Unlike most missionaries in his day, Baraga is believed to have worked in support of the Ojibwa's rights, helping them gain title to their land—a philosophy not too popular with the local European fur traders and government Indian agents. Baraga spoke the native language fluently, and his guide to the Ojibwa vocabulary and grammar is still consulted today.

A few miles south of L'Anse, on U.S. 41, a white clapboard lumber mill marks your arrival in **Alberta.** In 1935, Henry Ford built the mill, dammed nearby Plumbago Creek for the mill's water supply, and added a few streets' worth of homes to house the mill's workers. It's a classic example of a "company town," one that has not changed much since operations shut down in the early 1950s. Today it is operated by Michigan Technological University as a forestry research center. The grounds, including a small museum, are open to the public.

Hanka Homestead

The Finnish Hanka family established this farmstead, hidden away in the creases

of the landscape above Keeweenaw Bay between Baraga and Houghton, in 1896, building a log house, a barn, a milk house (over a spring for natural refrigeration!), and, of course, a sauna. The self-sufficient Hankas raised dairy cows and chickens, grew vegetables and grains, tanned hides, and did pretty much whatever else it took to scrape out a living and get through the harsh winters. What they didn't do much was modernize. Even though the last Hanka, Jalmar, lived here until the mid-1960s, the Hanka Homestead (906/353-7116, Memorial Day–Labor Day Tues., Thurs., and Sat.–Sun. noon–4 P.M., $3 adults, $1 children) remains frozen at about 1920, complete with the Hankas' belongings filling the home and its nine outbuildings. Guides offer comprehensive tours, and the homestead is a cooperating site of the Keeweenaw National Historic Park. It's best to call ahead before you make the drive. To find the homestead, head north about 10 miles on

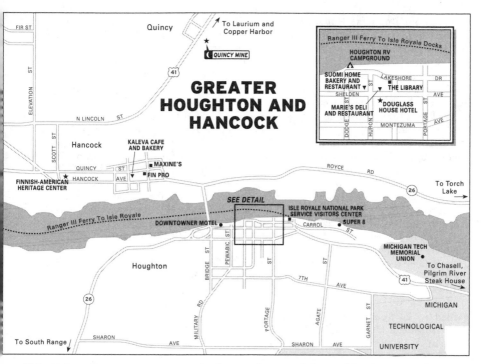

U.S. 41 from Baraga, turn west on Arnheim Road, and follow the small wooden signs (many of which refer to it as the "Finnish Homestead Museum").

HOUGHTON AND HANCOCK

Houghton (population 7,000) and Hancock (population 4,000) face each other across the Portage Waterway, with homes and churches tumbling down steep 500-foot bluffs. (Especially on the Hancock side, streets can be downright unnerving, rivaling those in San Francisco for pitch.) The Portage Waterway effectively slices the Keweenaw in two, a 21-mile passage that saves boaters the 100-mile-trip around the peninsula.

Native Americans had used the route for centuries to cross the peninsula, traveling from Keweenaw Bay across Portage Lake and along the ancient Portage River, then crossing over land the rest of the way to the shores of Lake Superior. In the late 1800s, a dredged canal eliminated the need for the west-end portage. Commercial traffic plied the waterway, largely to serve the smelters, stamping plants, and vibrant cities of the burgeoning copper trade.

A unique lift bridge spans the waterway to link Houghton and Hancock, its huge center section rising like an elevator to let water traffic pass. Today the Portage Waterway largely serves pleasure boaters and the 125-foot *Ranger III*, the ferry that transports hikers to Isle Royale National Park, 70 miles northwest. Houghton and Hancock are considered the gateways to the Keweenaw and to Isle Royale—but visitors just whizzing through will miss an appealing slice of the region.

Downtown Houghton and Hancock

You can conduct your own historic walking tour of Houghton by strolling down Shelden Avenue, the city's main street. Tall facades of red brick and red sandstone line the street, including the **Douglass House Hotel** (517 Shelden Ave.), built in 1860 as a luxury hotel and dining establishment for travelers through the Portage Waterway. An addition in 1899 made it the lavish building you see today. Inside, the **Douglass House Saloon** (906/482-2003) still shows off those genteel days, with original Tiffany chandeliers, leaded glass windows, and frilly trim.

On the east end of town, **Michigan Technological University** stretches out along the Portage Waterway. Nearly 6,300 students attend Michigan Tech, about three-quarters of them in some type of engineering program. Not surprisingly, geology, mining, and interestingly, "industrial archaeology" are some of the school's most notable fields of study. Students interested in mining management get real-life experience here, actually learning hands-on mining practices deep inside the nearby Quincy Mine.

Michigan Tech is home to the highly regarded **A. E. Seaman Mineral Museum** (1400 Townsend Dr., 906/487-2572, 9 A.M.–4:30 P.M. Mon.–Fri., noon–4 P.M. Sat.–Sun. July–Sept., closed Sat.–Sun. Oct.–June, donations welcome, children 12 and under free), the official mineralogical museum of the state of Michigan. The Keweenaw is considered one of the most geologically rich and fascinating regions in the world, and the Seaman Museum holds the premier collection of area minerals and gemstones, including crystallized copper, silver, datolites, greenstones, and agates. Don't miss the nifty exhibit of an iron mine and glowing fluorescent minerals. The museum also houses an impressive collection of minerals from around the world. All in all, its collection numbers more than 30,000 specimens. The museum is on the fifth floor of the Electric Energy Resource Center (EERC) Building, behind the J. R. Van Pelt Library. Obtain a parking pass at the Hamar House, a few buildings to the east of the library.

Michigan Tech isn't the only show in town. Across the waterway sits **Finlandia University,** which began in 1896 as a Finnish academy to serve the area's ever-growing number of immigrant miners' families. Today, enrollment hovers around 550. The institution's **Finnish-American Heritage Center** (601 Quincy St., 906/487-7367, 8 A.M.–4:30 P.M. Mon.–Fri. and until 7 P.M. Wed.) maintains a gallery open to the public that features Finnish artists, as well as archives of the area's Finnish settlement.

Even nonshoppers might be drawn into some of Hancock's stores, with their emphasis on unusual Finnish products. Where else do you shop for sauna supplies but **Fin Pro** (208 Quincy St., 906/482-9202)? The shop owners, who retired here from Helsinki, also carry an excellent selection of Finnish textiles, glassware, books, and music. You'll also find a good array of Finnish glassware and gifts at **Maxine's** (119 Quincy St., 906/482-5101).

◖ Quincy Mine

Just north of Hancock, the mammoth shaft house of the Quincy Mine (906/482-3101, www.quincymine.com, May–Oct., hoist and mine tour $15 adults, $8 children 6–12, under six free; surface tour and tram ride $12 adults, $5 children) dominates the skyline. The

© JOSH BISHOP

North of Hancock, the Quincy Mine preserves a piece of Keweenaw's heritage.

COPPER MINING IN COPPER COUNTRY

The Keweenaw Peninsula isn't known as Copper Country for nothing. After the discovery of Upper Peninsula copper in the mid-1800s, copper mines in the tip of the Keweenaw Peninsula – near Copper Harbor and Eagle Harbor – were among the first to open. The copper business limped along for several years during the Civil War until, several years later, the boom hit and hit hard. In 1860, Copper Country was producing about 12 million pounds of copper per year. Twelve years later, annual production had increased to 25 million pounds. By 1890, Michigan's Copper Country was sending about 100 million pounds of copper per year by ships that traveled through the Great Lakes or by trains headed to Chicago and the rest of the nation. By the 1900s, more than 200 million pounds were produced each year, an average which held from 1905-1912. For 40 years, Michigan produced more copper than any other state in the Union, occasionally accounting for as much as 90 percent of the nation's copper production.

Cornish miners from the south of England flocked to the booming mines, bringing with them their expertise as some of the best miners in the world. At first, they came from other parts of America and Canada, but word soon reached Cornwall that there were fortunes to be made in Copper Country – or at the very least, that there was guaranteed honest paid work – and the Upper Peninsula soon saw an influx of international workers, who brought with them their cultures, their foods, their languages, and their customs. Cornish miners were joined by a large number of Scandinavians, people from Denmark, Norway, Finland, and Sweden, who came to the Upper Peninsula for the same reasons: to work tirelessly in the copper and iron mines and make an honest living. Many of the old mining communities in Keweenaw and other areas of the U.P. are still influenced by their heritage. To this day, Finns are among the most prominent ethnic groups in Michigan's Upper Peninsula.

Cities in Copper Country boomed, springing up overnight from mining camps and small towns to become large cities and industrial centers. Houghton and Hancock became the Keweenaw Peninsula's most prominent cities in the 1800s, a distinction that they hold to this day. In Hancock, the region's mining and immigrant heritage are kept alive through two of the city's most well-known institutions: the Quincy Mine, now a national historic site, and Finlandia University, which was founded in 1896. Other towns in the area born of the copper boom include Calumet, Laurium, Lake Linden, and several other small communities in the peninsula.

Unfortunately, like most things, the prosperity brought about by the copper mines wasn't to last forever. Every boom must, after all, have its bust. Natural resources were limited and mines eventually started petering out; the once-abundant resources dried up by the 1970s.

The effect on the previously booming economies of the area was severe – and lasting. In most U.P. communities, the hole left by the mining industry has yet to be filled with another industry. Tourism is one of the most promising, providing a way to capitalize on the Upper Peninsula's natural resources without exploiting them. If the most you take from the land is a handful of photographs, the industry should last far longer than other, more destructive industries. Fur, lumber, iron, and copper have all passed their heydays – tourism may be the answer.

KEWEENAW PENINSULA

THE COPPER COUNTRY

AN ANCIENT VANISHED RACE MINED NATIVE COPPER HUNDREDS OF YEARS AGO IN COUNTLESS PITS AND TRENCHES SCATTERED AMONG THE HILLS FROM COPPER HARBOR TO ONTONAGON AND ON ISLE ROYALE.

THE EXPLORER, JACQUES CARTIER, REPORTED IN 1536 THAT INDIANS ON THE ST. LAWRENCE RIVER TOLD HIM OF GREAT HILLS OF NATIVE COPPER FAR TO THE WEST.

THE JESUIT, FATHER CLAUDE ALLOUEZ, WAS THE FIRST WHITE MAN TO REPORT SEEING COPPER ALONG THE SOUTH SHORE OF LAKE SUPERIOR. THIS WAS IN 1666.

IN 1771 A COMPANY ORGANIZED IN LONDON ENGLAND WHICH SENT AN UNSUCCESSFUL EXPEDITION TO THESE SHORES TO MINE COPPER A TREATY BETWEEN THE U.S. GOVERNMENT AND THE CHIPPEWA INDIANS ON MARCH 12 TH. 1843 OPENED THE DISTRICT TO MINING.

KEW.CO.ROAD COMM. 08

© JOSH BISHOP

Known as Copper Country, the Keweenaw Peninsula was the center of the Upper Peninsula's copper mining industry.

Quincy ranked as one of the world's richest copper mines in the late 1800s, producing over a billion pounds of copper. Today, a few of its buildings still stand, and the land beneath it remains stitched with the shafts (vertical tunnels) and adits (horizontal tunnels) of the mammoth mine, which stretched more than a mile and a half deep—92 levels!—and two miles wide.

The Quincy Mine is a key site in the Keweenaw National Historic Park, and it offers a fascinating tour that takes you through the historic buildings and deep into the mine itself. Many of the tour guides are mining students at nearby Michigan Tech, so they can handle just about any mining or engineering question you toss at them. The tour begins with a look at the much-ballyhooed steam hoist, the world's largest. A giant spool of sorts, it powered the steel pulleys that hauled the miners and mine cars loaded with copper in and out of the mine. It's nearly twice the size of other steam hoists, since the mine was so much deeper than most.

As interesting as the hoist is the building itself. In an era when miners made $1 a day (considered quite a good wage), the Quincy Mining Company built its hoist house of poured concrete, then decorated it with lovely arched windows, lined the walls with Italian tile, and topped it off with green tiles imported from Spain. Thanks to all that concrete, the immense room remains in pretty good shape. It also houses plenty of artifacts and photos, including bilingual safety instructions posted next to the machinery—an indication of the predominance of Finnish miners.

From the hoist house, the tour continues with a rather dramatic ride in a glass-enclosed tram down the side of a steep hill. Views of Houghton and Hancock are terrific as the tram descends to an entrance to the mine, an adit at Level 7. A tractor carries you a couple thousand feet into the mine, where guides demonstrate mining techniques and give you a feel for what it was like to work deep inside the earth, in a drippy, damp environment with only hand tools and candles. Contact the **Quincy Mine Hoist Association** (49750 U.S. 41, 906/482-3101, www.quincymine .com) for tour times and other information.

Lighthouses

Two of the lighthouses in the Houghton and Hancock area are the **Portage Lake Upper and Lower Entry Lights,** the Upper located at the end of the breakwater at McLain State Park. Built in 1950, the steel tower is one of the Keweenaw's newest lights, but it's really no less attractive for its youth. Take M-203 about 10 miles north of Hancock to F. J. McLain State Park and the light. The Portage Lake Lower Entry Light is on the east side of the Keweenaw Peninsula and the Portage River in the town of Lake Linden. This one was built some 30 years earlier than its companion on the other side of the river; there's a nice long walk along the breakwater pier to get close.

Near the Lower Entry Light, the **Portage River Light** (also called the Jacobsville Light) has been converted into a pleasant, unique bed-and-breakfast in Lake Linden. The Jacobsville Lighthouse Inn (38741 Jacobs St., 906/523-4137, www.jacobsvillelighthouse.com) offers regular tours of the lighthouse and grounds—call ahead for an appointment, or just stop by to see if they're available.

NORTH OF HOUGHTON AND HANCOCK

At the height of the Keweenaw's copper mining glory, the Calumet and Hecla Consolidated Copper Company, operating largely in Calumet, proved the grandest operation of all. At the turn of the 20th century, C&H employed some 11,000 workers, who extracted more than 1.5 billion tons of copper from a web of mines tunneled out under Calumet and adjacent Laurium. A surface plant in town, considered the most efficient in the nation, roared and whistled with the sound of 50 steam engines at work.

C&H generated more than $72 million in revenues. It built low-cost housing for its miners, more than 1,000 dwellings lined up like chess pieces in towns with colorful names like Swedetown and Limerick, reflecting the miners' homelands. Most of all, it spawned the city of Calumet—known then as "Red Jacket," a booming metropolitan area of more than

60,000 residents. Striking red sandstone buildings with false fronts and cornices lined the 12-square-block downtown, filled with elegant shops, soaring churches, some 70 saloons, and even a lavish theater that attracted the nation's leading vaudeville stars. The city buzzed day and night, both above and below ground.

After the mining industry died, no one bothered to "modernize" Calumet—the economy was lousy and the land wasn't worth enough—and those sturdy sandstone buildings survived years of neglect pretty well. As a result, downtown Calumet is a marvel of architecture of the early 1900s, and it was a deciding factor in the area earning national park status. "We are fortunate that this area has been little disturbed since those glory days," said park supporters. "Few modern intrusions have marred the area's scale and the feeling of its mining heritage." Today, Calumet (pop. 800) anchors the new Keweenaw National Historic Park, one of the park's two key units and a designated historic site.

Downtown Calumet

Thanks to the new national park and renewed civic pride, downtown Calumet looks more like a movie set every day. Ugly 1960s facades are coming down off the elegant sandstone and brick buildings, and new money is coming in to further restore and preserve them. To appreciate this architectural bonanza, stop by the **Keweenaw Convention and Visitors Bureau** (56638 Calumet Ave., 906/337-4579, 800/338-7982, www.keweenaw.info) to pick up a walking tour guide. A few stops of particular note: The **Union Building** at 5th Street and Red Jacket Road was home of one of the area's first banks in 1888 and remains in excellent shape, with a decorative metal cornice. **Shute's Bar** (322 6th St.) doesn't look that special on the outside, but inside preserves ornate plaster ceilings and a magnificent back bar with a stained-glass canopy. Across the street, the **Red Jacket Fire Station** typifies the Romanesque style favored for public buildings and churches at the time. At 340 6th Street, the **Red Jacket Town Hall and Opera House,** now called

KEWEENAW PENINSULA

the **Historic Calumet Theatre** (340 6th St., 906/337-2610, www.calumettheatre.com, tours 11 A.M.–2 P.M. Tues.–Sun.) was the pride of the community. The theater portion, added in 1898 and the first municipally owned theater in the country, was a showy extravagance of plaster Rococo in cream, crimson, green, and gilt. It even had electric lights! Referred to as "the greatest social event ever known in copperdom's metropolis" when it opened in 1900, the theater attracted A-list celebrities including John Philip Sousa, Houdini, Douglas Fairbanks Jr., and Sarah Bernhardt.

Keweenaw National Historic Park

The Keweenaw National Historic Park (200 5th St., 906/337-3168, www.nps.gov/kewe) is not so much a place on a map but a place in time. One of the nation's newest national parks, it was established in 1992 "to commemorate the heritage of copper mining on the Keweenaw Peninsula—its mines, its machinery, and its people."

Rather than a park with simply defined boundaries, the Keweenaw National Historic Park consists of historic attractions throughout the Keweenaw. Two units anchor the park—the Quincy Unit at the Quincy Mine in Hancock and the Calumet Unit in historic downtown Calumet—but some of this land remains privately owned. The National Park Service owns outright just a limited amount of land, to preserve key sites and conduct interpretive activities. In addition, the park has designated "cooperating sites" throughout the peninsula, including mine tours and museums, which remain in private ownership, but will benefit from increased visibility and federal funding.

The park will continue to be under development for several years, busy preserving buildings, creating interpretive displays, and developing educational programs. The national park headquarters in Calumet currently operate with just a skeleton administrative staff. For visitor information, contact the Keweenaw Convention and Visitors Bureau (56638 Calumet Ave., 906/337-4579, 800/338-7982, www.keweenaw.info).

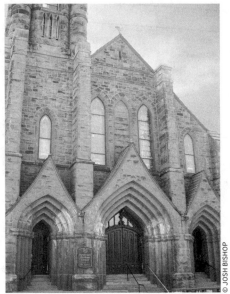

© JOSH BISHOP

The Keweenaw Heritage Center at St. Anne's is part of the Keweenaw National Historic Park in Calumet.

C&H Industrial Core

One of Calumet and Hecla's mines was located right in town, in an area bisected by Red Jacket Road, just west of U.S. 41. Beginning at the Coppertown USA museum, a self-guided "industrial core" walking tour takes you past a drill shop, a powder house, a machine shop, and several other mining buildings in various states of preservation. The park service is adding interpretive signs to guide you along and share mining information, but you'll also want an information sheet that maps the route, available from the Keweenaw Tourism Council, national park headquarters, or the Coppertown USA museum.

Coppertown USA

The mine's pattern shop, where wooden patterns were made as molds for machine parts, now serves as the home of Coppertown USA (25815 Red Jacket Rd., 906/337-4354, noon to 3 P.M., Mon.–Sat., June 1–Sept. 1, $3 adults, $1 12–18 years, free under 12), a privately run museum (and national park cooperating site) that traces the region's copper industry. It includes loads of artifacts, a display of area minerals, a replica of a mining captain's office, a diorama of Native American mining, and more, with all the exhibits close enough to really examine. Don't miss the pattern shop area, which still houses thousands of patterns, lined up on shelves as if they haven't been touched for 50 years. (Some have been relocated to the Smithsonian.) Another interesting exhibit is a 1976 scale model that shows elaborate plans for Calumet, including a cultural center, a festival plaza, and a products exhibit center. The museum is located near the intersection of U.S. 41 and Red Jacket Road.

Downtown Laurium

Just across U.S. 41 from Calumet, Laurium was largely a residential district for the area mines. The west end of town (closest to Calumet) has a few streets of plain company homes remaining, looking rough and dilapidated—like much of Laurium. But a few blocks farther east, around Pewabic Street and 3rd Street, mining management built their homes, and today the area is a quiet and stately neighborhood worth visiting. Pick up a *Laurium Walking Tour* guide from the Keweenaw Convention and Visitors Bureau (56638 Calumet Ave., 906/337-4579, 800/338-7982, www.keweenaw.info) in Calumet. It will direct you to impressive homes like the one at 305 Tamarack Street, where a wise mining investor made enough to create this grand home with seven fireplaces, a third-floor ballroom, and a carriage house.

But the finest home belonged to Captain Thomas Hoatson, founder of the Calumet and Arizona Mining Company, who built his dream mansion at 320 Tamarack Street. Today it operates as the **Laurium Manor Inn** (906/337-2549, www.laurium.info, tours 11 A.M.–5 P.M. daily, $5 adults, $3 children), which means the public can enjoy a glimpse of this remarkable place. Sprawling across 13,000 square feet, the 45-room mansion includes ceilings covered in silver leaf, elephant-hide wallcoverings, a triple staircase of hand-carved oak, and a turntable in

the carriage house so carriages could be rotated to face forward. The inn is open year-round, with most rates $80–140.

Football or cinema fans may want to view the decidedly less dramatic home at 432 Hecla Street. Laurium's most famous citizen was born here—**George Gipp,** the Notre Dame football star. "The Gipper" gave Ronald Reagan his most famous role—until he became president, anyway. A George Gipp Memorial decorates the corner of Tamarack Street and M-26.

Ghost Towns

Ghost towns litter the Keweenaw, faded testament to the boom-and-bust days of copper. The ruins of old mines and stamping plants (facilities that separated copper from rock) line M-26 between Hancock and Calumet. The gray piles of residue are mine tailings or stamping plant leftovers called "stamp sand." Several bona fide ghost towns hide in the woods, too, especially between Calumet and Copper Harbor. At **Central** (watch for the small brown sign on U.S. 41, about 11 miles north of Mohawk), an exceptionally rich mine produced nearly $10 million by 1898; the surrounding town grew to 1,200. Today, nature has all but reclaimed Central, with just a few clapboard houses creaking in the breeze. Turn right near the top of the hill for a look at the mine ruins and rows of house foundations. (Watch where you're walking.)

Just south of Copper Harbor on U.S. 41, another sign announces your "arrival" in **Mandan,** directing you down a dirt road disappearing into birches. Follow it south for about 50 yards and a tidy row of homes suddenly erupts out of the woods. Welcome to Mandan, the last stop on a trolley line from Hancock.

ENTERTAINMENT
Ojibwa Casino and Resort

The Ojibwa Casino (16449 Michigan Ave., 906/353-6333, 800/323-8045, www.ojibwacasino.com) in Baraga (there's another one in Marquette) is tucked away in the southeast corner of the Keweenaw Peninsula, where the long land formation meets the rest of the U.P.

There's enough gaming here to satisfy all but the choosiest players, with more than 300 slot and video poker machines that take denominations as low as a penny and up to five bucks. If you're into table games, the casino offers craps, roulette, blackjack, poker (including 3-5-7 and Texas Hold 'Em), and more. Grab a bite to eat at the Pressbox Sports Bar, which serves up exactly the type of food you'd expect at a sports bar. There are other sports bar staples here, too, like happy hour specials and big-screen televisions, as well as a few things you might not expect—an eight-lane bowling alley and a dance floor. The Pressbox hosts DJs or live bands on weekends. The lodging here is good, too. The Ojibwa Casino hotel went through a series of renovations to their 40 guest rooms, which include double rooms and whirlpool suites at remarkably modest rates ($69 d, $85 suite). To get there from Houghton and Hancock, take U.S. 41 south to M-38, turn right, and go a little more than a mile. From Ontonagon, take M-38 east—if you hit Lake Superior, you've gone too far.

Calumet Theatre

Built more than a century ago, the Calumet Theatre (340 6th St., Calumet, 906/337-2610, www.calumettheatre.com) was Keweenaw's destination for live opera (who said Yoopers aren't civilized?) since 1900. It had a good run while it lasted—John Philip Sousa was here, among other greats—but the live theater began to fade within 30 years, as copper mining started to wane and the advent of movies turned the beautiful hall into a cinema. Summer stock took hold a few times in the '50s and in the '70s, but didn't exactly enjoy a permanent resurgence until the Calumet Theatre Company was incorporated in 1983 and brought year-round entertainment back to the glamorous hall. And it *is* glamorous: the auditorium, with its bowl-shaped proscenium, stunning paintings, and elegant woodwork, was restored in the 1970s with the exterior following suit in the late '80s. Today, it's a National Historic Landmark that regularly hosts theater and opera performances, as well

as any number of other live performing arts (symphony, dance, music). Some 30,000 people come through these doors each year. You can take a guided tour of the historic theater from Tuesday through Sunday during the summer season, while self-guided tours are available year-round at limited times. Take U.S. 41 into town and turn north on 6th Street to get to the theater.

FESTIVALS AND EVENTS

Leave it to those engineering students at Michigan Tech to design and build elaborate snow sculptures at the university's **Winter Carnival** in January. Houghton also hosts the **Bridgefest and Seafood Fest** in June, with food and music on a parking deck overlooking the Portage Lift Bridge. Chassell's **Strawberry Fest** is held the second week in July, just in time for the sweet and juicy harvest.

SUMMER SPORTS AND RECREATION
Hiking and Biking

Mountain bikers new to the area can hardly believe the wealth of terrific trails in the Keweenaw, literally hundreds of miles of old mining and logging roads, overgrown double-track routes, and technical single-track. They loop through towering pines to backwoods waterfalls, to otherwise inaccessible Lake Superior shorelines, even past ghost towns now buried deep in the woods. (Consider this fair warning that many trails also peter out and stop in the middle of nowhere.)

Vast tracts of land in the Keweenaw are privately owned by large corporations—some mining firms, but mostly paper companies. In exchange for a break in state taxes, the companies allow public use of the land for recreation, including hiking, fishing, and mountain biking. Still, for liability reasons, some outfitters and bike shops are loath to hand out maps or endorse these lands for riding. If you ask, though, most bike shops tend to be quite helpful about suggesting trails, especially the **Keweenaw Adventure Company** (145 Gratiot St., 906/289-4303, www .keweenawadventure.com) in Copper Harbor.

If you're going on your own, snowmobile maps make decent trail guides. Cross-reference them with a topo map, though—snowmobile trails often cross frozen lowlands that are impassable in summer months.

And use common sense. Don't venture out without a map and compass and the skill to use them. Stay away from active logging areas, usually marked by signs and the audible presence of buzzing logging equipment. If you hear a logging truck coming, don't just move to the side, get completely off the trail. Logging trucks are wide and heavy, and they can blaze down logging roads at surprising speeds. They aren't expecting to see you and probably couldn't stop in time even if they did.

Old railroad grades threading across the northern Keweenaw have been converted to public multi-use trails, intended for snowmobiles, ATVs, and, perhaps to a lesser extent, mountain bikes. For cyclists not comfortable venturing deep into the woods, they're a nice way to get off the road. The **Jack Stevens Rail-Trail** runs 14 miles from Hancock north to Calumet on the former Soo Line grade. Somewhat less appealing, because it parallels M-26 for a lengthy stretch, is the **Keweenaw Rail-Trail,** an 18-mile route from Hancock along Torch Lake, also ending in Calumet. Note that surfaces can be a rough collection of rock, gravel, wood, and sand—whatever happened to be there when they ripped up the rails—so they're not appropriate for narrow-tire bikes. For more information and a map listing access points, contact the Keweenaw Tourism Council at 800/338-7982.

Like much of the Keweenaw, the forests around Calumet are filled with hundreds of miles of trails for hiking and mountain biking. If you're handy with a map and compass, some fine single-track winds down along the **Gratiot River** about five miles north of town. As a bonus, you can check out the little-visited Upper and Lower Gratiot Falls as the river rolls and tumbles its way to Lake Superior. For other ideas, check in at **Cross Country Sports** (506 Oak St., Calumet, 906/337-4520). Most of the

staff, in fact, are willing to divulge at least a couple of their favorite trails.

For something a little less adventurous, pedal the **Swedetown Trails,** a cross-country trail network on the southwest edge of Calumet. From 6th Street near St. Ann's Church, pick up Oceola Road and follow it south. The trail network has about 25 kilometers of trails over rolling hills and through woods, and all are great for biking except the northernmost loop (the Red Trail), which is too wet. From this small network, you can veer off onto seemingly endless trails beyond, too. In winter, the network obviously offers great Nordic skiing, along with a warming chalet (open noon–5 p.m.). For information, contact the Keweenaw Convention and Visitors Bureau (906/337-4579, 800/338-7982).

Canoeing and Kayaking

Rivers in the Keweenaw tend to be pretty bony, so white water kayaking is limited (though this varies with the year's precipitation). Sea kayaking, on the other hand, is outstanding, the perfect way to access bluffs, caves, sea stacks, and rocky islands all along the Lake Superior shoreline. The Keweenaw Water Trail, still under development, guides small craft around the peninsula and through the Portage Waterway. Canoeing is popular on inland lakes, but open boats are not recommended on Lake Superior.

The **Keweenaw Water Trail** provides a mapped passageway of more than 100 miles through the Portage Waterway and along the Lake Superior shore, indicating accommodations, campgrounds, launches, and more. For more information and to purchase a water trail map, contact the Keweenaw Convention and Visitors Bureau (906/337-4579, 800/338-7982). For white water boaters, Down Wind Sports (308 Shelden Ave., 906/482-2500, www.downwindsports.com) in Houghton is your best source for local information on river conditions.

Fishing

One of the finest fishing rivers in the Houghton and Hancock area is the Salmon

© BECCA BISHOP

The Keeweenaw Peninsula's jagged shoreline juts out into Lake Superior.

Trout River. Flowing for about 12 miles between Lake Superior and the much, much smaller Perrault Lake (the river actually drains into Lake Superior) the Salmon Trout River is a good spot to cast for steelhead and brook trout. Take M-26 a few miles south of Houghton to Old M-26/Erickson Drive in the village of Atlantic Mine. Turn right, then right again on County Highway A-65, which continues as Obenhoff Road to an access point a couple of miles west.

Another popular site for fishing is **McLain State Park** (906/482-0278, 18350 Highway M-203, www.michigan.gov/dnr) seven miles north of Hancock on M-203. You can also try both Portage Lake and Torch Lake for walleye, bass, and northern pike.

Golf

You've only got one choice for 18 holes in the Keweenaw Peninsula, and that's **Portage Lake Golf Course** (906/487-2641, www.portage lakegolfcourse.com, 8 A.M.–7:30 P.M., May–mid-Oct., 18 holes $37, 9 holes $22), a fine

course belonging to Michigan Tech. Don't expect as much as you might from some other courses (including a few in the Upper Peninsula), but it really does offer the best golf in this neck of the woods. Even though it's located off the main drag as you enter town, the well-kept greens are peaceful and the holes have the tree-lined horizons you've no doubt come to expect from U.P. golf. The clubhouse has a pro shop and a bar and grill, which is punningly named the Par and Grill. Its bar is actually a newer addition, since the P&G only received its liquor license and started serving in 2008; now you can get a brew with your sandwich and chips or from one of the beverage carts. There's a putting green, too, and a driving range that closes at dusk.

About 15 miles south of Houghton, in Toivola, the **Wyandotte Hills Golf Club and Resort** (5821 East Poyhonen Rd., 906/288-3720, www.wyandottehills.com, May–Oct., 18 holes $22, 9 holes $17) is a nine-hole course that does double duty as an overnight getaway, with four cabins that can be rented year-round. The wooded and watered course makes for good golfing, while the clubhouse makes good lunch daily. Dinner is offered Tuesday, Thursday, and Friday. Head in the other direction, north of Hancock to Calumet, for the **Calumet Golf Club** (1501 Golf Course Rd., 906/337-3911), another nine holes with club rentals, a restaurant, and more. Contact the Calumet Golf Club for current fees.

Bird-Watching

Birders find good habitat and a variety of northern species, including red- and white-winged crossbills, Canada geese, hawks, peregrine falcons, and bald eagles. An estimated 20 species of warblers are frequently spotted.

Just north of the Hanka Homestead, the Sturgeon River bleeds across the lowlands before emptying into Portage Lake, forming sloughs that attract migrating waterfowl. For the best access, stop at the **Sturgeon River Sloughs Natural Area,** marked by an observation tower along U.S. 41 near Chassell. The 1.5-mile De Vriendt Nature Trail follows a series of dikes and boardwalks back into the slough, with interpretive signs about the herons, osprey, eagles, kestrels, ducks, and dozens of other species that frequent the area.

Off-Road Vehicles
The Michigan DNR's ATV route, Hancock–Calumet Trail, stretches between (believe it or not) Hancock and Calumet. Like all DNR trails, this one is kept lightly groomed. Remember, too, that all state forest roads are open to ORV use, unless specifically marked otherwise. The rail trails and other old railroad grades that can cause headaches for mountain bikers are more suitable for ORV riders; remember, you'll likely be sharing the pathway with nonmotorized travelers, so keep your eyes peeled.

Waterfalls
Far south of Houghton and just north of the imaginary line that forms the base of the Keweenaw Peninsula, the **Wyandotte Falls** drop some 20 feet down in a beautiful display. Take Wyandotte Hills Golf Course Road less than a mile west of M-26 to the parking area, then follow the trail to the falls. The **Hungarian Falls,** north of Hancock, are better still. Take M-26 north to Hubbell, then turn left on 6th Street. Take the left fork two blocks up, then turn left on the second trail road. Both forks lead to the falls—the one on the right goes to the Upper Falls and the one on the left goes to the Lower. At about 25 feet, the Upper Falls drop farther, but the Lower Falls are more beautiful, with a still-impressive 15 feet.

WINTER SPORTS AND RECREATION
Downhill Skiing
If you're into serious skiing, head north to Mt. Bohemia near Copper Harbor, but for novices or skiers who appreciate tamer terrain, **Mont Ripley** (906/487-2340, www.aux.mtu.edu/ski, $35 full day) near Houghton and Hancock (owned and operated by Michigan Tech) also offers some decent downhill runs and is lit for night skiing.

Ski and Snowshoe Trails
A giant snow gauge on U.S. 41 south of Phoenix proudly marks the Keweenaw's record snowfall, a staggering 390.4 inches in the winter of 1977–1978. It wasn't an aberration; the surrounding waters of Lake Superior routinely generate colossal lake effect snows, often averaging over 300 inches per year. That reliable snowfall, combined with the remarkable local terrain, makes the Keweenaw a haven for snowmobilers.

Thankfully, skiers and snowshoers will find there's enough wilderness to go around. Many towns have developed Nordic ski trail systems. For backcountry skiing and snowshoeing, pick up a snowmobile map and steer clear of marked trails. Also note that some accommodations located on signed and groomed trails cater to snowmobilers, and the roar can get pretty deafening. Don't be afraid to ask about the presence of "sleds" before booking lodging in winter months.

Snowshoers should stay off groomed ski trails, but Michigan Tech in Houghton has a series of marked snowshoeing trails. In Calumet, try the marked Swedetown trails.

Snowmobiling
Sure, there are more than 2,000 miles of snowmobile trails in the U.P., but what about Keweenaw? At last count, the peninsula had more than 200 miles of trails, which stretch from south of Houghton all the way into the tip. Most of the trails are clearly identified, well groomed, and between 10 and 16 feet wide. And yes, they do connect to the other 2,000-plus miles up here above the bridge. The Keweenaw Trail (Trail 3) is the main route into and out of Houghton and Hancock, and it connects to plenty of other branches: the North and South Freda trails make for Lake Superior, while Stevens Trail connects to Calumet.

Keweenaw Trail joins the 55-mile Bill Nichols Trail, which ends farther south in Mass City, near Ontonagon. A popular multi-use trail during warmer weather, this converted rail line is one of the most popular scenic snowmobile routes in Keweenaw. For a detailed map, including the locations of gas stations, contact the Keweenaw Convention and Visitors Bureau (56638 Calumet Ave., Calumet, 906/337-4579, 800/338-7982, www.keweenaw.info).

ACCOMMODATIONS

There are a few good options south of Houghton. **Carla's Lake Shore Motel** (906/353-6256, around $50), on U.S. 41 north of Baraga, has clean, inexpensive rooms with a view of Keweenaw Bay, and it gets bonus points for allowing your pooch. Baraga also has a few chain motels, including **Super 8** (790 Michigan Ave., 906/353-6680, www.super8baraga.com) and **Best Western Baraga Lakeside Inn** (900 South U.S. 41, 906/353-7123, www.bestwestern.com). Rates for both run $60–100. After a visit to Hanka Homestead, you can sample a stay at a Finnish farm at **Palosaari's Rolling Acres** (906/523-4947, $50). A tidy dairy farm near Chassell, it offers three simple rooms, a shared bath, a sauna, a nearby swimming beach, and a big country breakfast. Four miles south of Chassell, take North Entry Road east 1.3 miles.

For such a small metropolitan area, Houghton accommodations run a bit on the pricey side. The following all fall in the $50–100 range. Tucked below downtown Houghton along the Portage Waterway, **Super 8** (1200 East Lakeshore Dr., 906/482-2240, www.super8.com) offers one of the best locations in town, on the water and the bike path, with an indoor pool and free continental breakfast. A good mom-and-pop operation is the **Downtowner Motel** (110 Shelden Ave., 906/482-4421, 800/430-0083).

East of town, on the Lake Superior shore in the town of Lake Linden, the comparatively expensive but worthwhile **Jacobsville Lighthouse Inn** (38741 Jacobs St., 906/523-4137, www.jacobsvillelighthouse.com, $150–200) offers five rooms in a well-kept keeper's home with attached lighthouse tower. The 50-foot tower offers stunning panoramic views of Lake Superior and the surrounding land, plus more than 350 feet of lakeshore.

The **AmericInn Motel and Suites** (5101 6th St., 906/337-6463, www.americinn.com, $80–120) in Calumet, north of Hancock, is the area's only full-service motel with an indoor pool and other amenities. The **Wonderland Motel and Cabins** (787 Lake Linden Ave., 906/337-4511), in Laurium, offers good budget accommodations with kitchens in cabins. At the other end of the spectrum, stay in an opulent copper baron mansion at the **Laurium Manor Inn** (320 Tamarack St., 906/337-2549, www.lauriummanorinn.com, $80–140) in Laurium. Across the street, the owners have also restored the 1906 brick **Victorian Hall** (same telephone number). Most rooms have private baths. Another mining executive lived in what is now **Belknap's Garnet Haus** (906/337-5607) on U.S. 41 in Kearsarge. The well-restored home features five rooms with mostly shared baths.

Camping

At Toivola, head 6.2 miles west on Misery Bay Road, then north and west on Agate Beach Road for 4 miles to **Agate Beach Park** (906/288-3644), a rather unknown little spot on Lake Superior. There's no modern plumbing, but an empty curve of sand beach, Lake Superior sunsets, and a $5 tent fee ($7 for sites with electricity) make up for it. The campground at **Baraga State Park** (1300 U.S. 41 South, 906/353-6558, www.michigan.gov/dnr, $14–18) pretty much is the state park. Most come for its modern sites (more than 100, with electricity and showers) with a convenient location: just off U.S. 41, a mile south of the town of Baraga. Reservations are usually not necessary. Across the highway, a day-use area offers a sand beach and a bathhouse. The Bill Nichols Rail-Trail passes through **Twin Lakes State Park** (6204 East Poyhonen Rd., 906/288-3321, www.michigan.gov/dnr, $16–22) in the southern Keweenaw. Though also right along the highway, many of its modern sites sit on the shores of Lake Roland, which someone once determined was the warmest lake in the Upper Peninsula. For campsite reservations at any Michigan state park, call 800/447-2757 or visit www.midnrreservations.com. To rent rustic cabins or walled tents, contact the parks directly.

Sunsets get top billing at **McLain State Park** (18350 M-203, 906/482-0278, www .michigan.gov/dnr, $16–26 campsites, $60 cabins), where the sky often glows in peaches and pinks before the sun melts into Lake Superior. Like most Michigan state parks, the 98 campsites are fine, too, and many come with those waterfront views. Follow M-203 seven miles north of Hancock. The **City of Houghton** maintains an RV-only campground (1100 West Lakeshore Dr., 906/482-8745), with every site near the water. No pets allowed. Tent campers should head instead for the **Hancock Recreation Area** (2000 Jasberg St./M-203, 906/482-7413, www.cityofhancock.com, May 15–Oct. 15) on the Portage Waterway. Follow M-203 a mile from downtown. The primitive sites are situated in a quieter area apart from the 50 RV ones that are so modern they even include—yikes!—cable TV. Showers and laundry are on the premises.

FOOD

Combine a college town with a large ethnic population, and you come up with a good range of eating options in the Houghton and Hancock area. Houghton offers a number of fine places to eat. **(The Library** (62 North Isle Royale St., 906/487-5882, open at 11 A.M. daily) probably ranks as the most popular spot in town, with homemade brews, good salads, pizzas, pastas, and lots of sandwich choices. The **Pilgrim River Steak House** (47409 U.S. 41, 906/482-8595, 11 A.M.–11 P.M. Mon.–Sat., noon–10 P.M. Sun.), on U.S. 41 on the southeast end of Houghton, is *the* place to go for beef of all sorts, especially prime rib. Along with your basic eggs-and-hash-browns fare, **Suomi Home Bakery and Restaurant** (54 North Huron St., 906/482-3220) tosses a few Finnish specialties on the menu. Try the *pannukakku*, billed as a "Finnish pancake" (but more like deep-dish custard pie), topped with raspberry sauce. Most breakfasts come

with *nisu,* a Finnish yeast bread spiced with cardamom. The restaurant is tucked under Houghton's covered walkway, a block down the hill from Shelden.

On Hancock's main street, the **Kaleva Cafe and Bakery** (234 Quincy St., 906/482-1230) draws the locals for its baked goods, including its self-proclaimed "famous" whipped-cream cakes. Kaleva makes a good pasty, a potpie creation of beef, potatoes, onions, and rutabagas—just the kind of hearty, self-contained meal that miners could take with them deep underground. You'll find pasties at coffee shops and grocery-store deli counters throughout the Upper Peninsula.

Though you'll find plenty of traditional grocery stores along M-26 south of town and U.S. 41 north, opt instead for the **Keweenaw Co-op Natural Foods and Groceries** (1035 Ethel Ave., 906/482-2030, 10 A.M.–8 P.M. Mon.–Sat., 10 A.M.–5 P.M. Sun.) in Hancock. A friendly staff, excellent organic produce, and plenty of reasonably priced staples make this a great option for picnic supplies. As you head up the hill on U.S. 41, veer left onto Ethel when the highway swings hard right. (Watch for the colorful wooden sign.) The co-op is a couple blocks ahead on your right.

Head north to downtown Calumet, where **Thurner Bakery** (315 5th St., 906/337-3711) churns out hearty pasties, soups, and baked goods. You can also find similar homemade coffee shop fare—and Finnish bakery items like saffron bread—at **Toni's Country Kitchen** (79 3rd St., 906/337-0611, Laurium). In Ahmeek on U.S. 41, **Streetcar Station** (906/337-0350) serves up sandwiches in, yes, an old streetcar station from the copper glory days. Don't leave without a malt or, in season, a wild blueberry sundae. At the **Lindell Chocolate Shoppe** (300 Calumet St., Lake Linden, 906/296-0793, www.lindellchocolateshoppe.net), visitors come to ooh and aah over this untouched 1920s shop, gleaming with golden oak, stained glass, and marble. Locals, though, come for the food, especially breakfasts and a Friday night fish fry.

KEWEENAW PENINSULA

INFORMATION AND SERVICES

The twin towns of Houghton and Hancock represent the area's largest population center, where you'll find the lion's share of area services, like tourism information and medical care. They also serve as the unofficial gateway to the Keweenaw, even though they sit halfway up the peninsula. With an office in Calumet, the **Keweenaw Convention and Visitors Bureau** (56638 Calumet Ave., 906/337-4579, 800/338-7982, www.keweenaw.info) serves as an excellent one-stop source for attractions and lodging information. If you're interested in Copper Country's historic aspect, direct your inquiries to Keweenaw National Historic Park (200 5th St., 906/337-3168, www.nps.gov/kewe, 9 A.M.–5 P.M. Mon.–Fri.) in Calumet.

If you need medical attention while in Houghton and Hancock, Portage Health (500 Campus Dr., 906/483-1000, 800/573-5001, www.portagehealth.org) in Hancock is the place to go. The hospital is located just west of U.S. 41—take U.S. 41 north or south to Campus Drive, turn west, and follow for 0.5 miles until you reach the Portage Health sign. Farther north, just outside Calumet in Laurium, go to Keweenaw Memorial Medical Center (205 Osceola St., 906/337-6500, www.kmmc .org). Take U.S. 41 into town to M-26/School Street and head east (the only direction you can go) until 2nd Street. Turn right on 2nd, and then left on Osceola, to arrive at the hospital.

There are plenty of banks to choose from on either side of the river. You can find national banks (Wells Fargo, 600 Sheldon Ave., Houghton, 906/482-5500, www.wellsfargo.com), Midwest banks (Citizens Bank, 400 Quincy St., Hancock, 906/482-6002, www.citizensbanking.com), and local banks (Superior National Bank and Trust, 235 Quincy St., 906/482-0404, www.snb-t .com). There's another Superior National Bank (56788 Mine Street Station, 906/337-5983, www.snb-t.com) in Calumet, too.

GETTING THERE AND AROUND

Car

For those traveling by car, U.S. 41 and M-26 are the main routes to the peninsula (U.S. 41 west from Marquette and M-26 north from Mass City), meeting and crossing in Houghton and Hancock and then merging again at Calumet. Many secondary roads in the Keweenaw are dirt or gravel. For old logging roads and other questionable routes, a four-wheel drive vehicle is highly recommended.

Air

Houghton County Memorial Airport (CMX, 23810 Airpark Blvd., Calumet, 906/482-3970, www.houghtoncounty.org) is located a short ways northwest of Hancock. Mesaba Airlines, which runs regional flights as an Airlink for Northwest Airlines (800/225-2525), offers the only commercial airline service, with daily flights. There are a few flights in and out and all of them are from (or to) Minneapolis, so if you're coming from elsewhere, you'll have a layover in Minnesota.

Limos and taxis are available for both local and long-distance trips—call Neil's Taxi at 906/482-5515 or Gregg's Taxi at 906/337-5233. Houghton County Memorial Airport also has a couple of car rental agencies on site: Priceless Rent-A-Car (906/482-5666) and National Car Rental (906/482-6655).

It's not entirely accurate to say that the only air service to and from Houghton is offered by **Northwest–Royale Air Service** (218/721-0405, 877/359-4753) offers daily one-way ($185) or round-trip ($269) seaplane flights to Isle Royale National Park.

Boat

You have a couple of options for boating into Houghton and Hancock, since there's a marina in each city. **The Houghton County Marina** (906/482-6010, www.michigan.gov/dnr) is located, despite its name, in Hancock, and it provides 44 seasonal slips and 10 transient ones. The marina is amenity-rich and provides close-up views of the lift bridge. It's open seasonally from May 1 through October 1, and you can get ahold of the harbormaster on channels 16 and 68. Entry into the Portage Waterway is at 47° 14.08 N, 88° 34.19 W (coming in from the east) or at 46° 57.40 N, 88° 26.00 W (from the west), with the marina itself located at 47° 07.30 N, 88° 34.19 W. Your other option (albeit a limited one) is to put in at Houghton City Marina, which is located just across the Portage Waterway and has 300 feet of broadside dockage but no overnight use. Channel entrances are the same as above; the dock is located at 47° 07.21 N, 88° 34.20 W.

Public Transportation

Bus service is spotty in the U.P. in general, and in the Keweenaw in particular. The city's **Houghton Motor Transit Line** (906/482-6092, www.cityofhoughton.com, $2 adults) runs a regularly scheduled Downtowner Route that runs a one-hour loop from the Michigan Tech campus to the Copper Country Mall. It's nice enough, and pretty convenient, but it honestly doesn't go much farther than you could get on a goodly walk or a bike ride. It does offer on-demand service for locations inside ($5) and outside ($6) city limits, but its scope is limited to the immediate area. Likewise, Hancock Public Transportation (906/482-3450, www.cityofhancock.com, $4 adults) runs a door-to-door demand service within a limited area.

Copper Harbor and Vicinity

Wedged between Lake Superior to the north and long and lovely Lake Fanny Hooe to the south, Copper Harbor has always been an outpost in the wilderness—for the copper prospectors who came in the mid-1880s, for the military who built a fort to keep the miners and the Native Americans at peace, and today, for those who come for its water and its woods.

Copper Harbor marks the end of the road in the Keweenaw Peninsula. Literally. Even U.S. 41 peters out here, circling in a loop some 1,990 miles from its other terminus in Miami. The tip of the peninsula probably draws people precisely because it is the end of the road. And when they get here, they discover one of the Upper Peninsula's most scenic natural areas and one of its most appealing little towns.

The city is a favorite vacation spot for

© JOSH BISHOP

KEWEENAW PENINSULA

Seen from above, Copper Harbor is an idyllic town carved out of the surrounding wilderness at the tip of the Keweenaw Peninsula.

KEWEENAW PENINSULA

kayakers, canoers, and boaters. With its location in the far north of the U.P. and surrounded on three sides by Lake Superior, Copper Harbor feels like the ends of the earth, or, at the very least, the end of Michigan.

SIGHTS
Downtown Copper Harbor

Tiny Copper Harbor, population 75, offers more than you might expect from its size. If shopping is your thing, check out the Finnish pottery at **Sataman Ruukku** (906/289-4636), a shedlike storefront on U.S. 41, and the artwork and gifts at the Laughing Loon (906/289-4813). (No one has—or needs—a street address in a town just a few blocks long.) Rockhounds will like the Keweenaw Agate Shop (906/353-7285) and Swede's Gift Shop (906/289-4596), both with a good selection of local minerals and, as the Keweenaw Agate Shop advertises, "advice and stories."

The **Thunderbird Shop** at the **Minnetonka Resort** (562 Gratiot St., 906/289-4449, www.minnetonkaresort.com) is a terrific source for books on mining, shipwrecks, and other historical subjects. The shop also has a lot of interesting artifacts, like miner's lanterns and clay pipes left behind by miners, for sale at very reasonable prices. The motel's adjacent **Astor House Antique Doll and Indian Artifact Museum** is well worth a visit, too.

You won't find a full-service grocery store in Copper Harbor, so load up in Houghton or Calumet if you're planning a campout or cabin stay. However, the exceptionally friendly **Gas Lite General Store** (906/289-4652) has all the basics, and also happens to be the spot to catch up on local news. (What you don't learn there, you'll hear about at the Pines across the street.) For fresh or smoked fish, head to the ferry dock and **Jamsen's Fish Market** (906/289-4285), run by the last commercial fishing family to pull a living out of the local waters.

Around Town

You can enjoy a couple of nice walks just a few blocks from downtown. From the parking lot of the municipal marina at the west end of town (farther west than the ferry dock), a 3.2-mile round-trip trail winds through the woods and over twisted roots to Hunter's Point. This point helps form the protected waters of the harbor; on the open Lake Superior side, Agate Beach is a good spot to look for the namesake banded rocks. Downtown, a sign will point you south toward **Estivant Pines,** a 377-acre sanctuary of virgin white pines just a few miles south of town. As recently as the 1970s, local conservationists like the late Jim Rooks saved the magnificent trees, some towering nearly 10 stories high and dating back nearly 1,000 years, from loggers' saws. At first the pines seem hidden by the maturing oaks and maples. But just look up, up, up.

(Fort Wilkins Historic State Park

The history of Fort Wilkins (15223 U.S. 41, 906/289-4215, www.michigan.gov/dnr) reads like one of those overblown military spending stories of the 20th century. With miners pouring north during the Copper Rush, the federal government feared fighting would surely erupt between miners and the local Native American tribes, so it ordered the construction of a garrisoned fort. In 1844, the government sent troops of more than 100 men, who built barracks, a mess hall, a hospital, and other buildings behind a tall stockade fence, then hunkered down to fend off the fighting. Only no fighting ever erupted, and the winters proved long, cold, and desolate. By the following year, half the troops were pulled out and sent south, where the

country faced the threat of war with Mexico. By 1846, the rest were gone.

Today, Fort Wilkins stands as one of the only remaining wooden forts east of the Mississippi, with 16 whitewashed buildings wonderfully restored and filled with exhibits of life on the northern frontier. From mid-June to late August, costumed "inhabitants" even re-create military life. Along with the fort, the state park includes rocky and scenic Lake Superior frontage, a few short hiking trails, the 1866 Copper Harbor Lighthouse (accessible only by boat, see below), and an excellent campground on Lake Fanny Hooe. For campsite reservations, call 800/447-2757 or visit www.midnrreservations.com.

(Brockway Mountain Drive

Dubbed "the most beautiful road in Michigan," this 10-mile route traces the spine of a high ridge between Copper Harbor and Eagle Harbor. Rising 735 feet above Lake Superior, it is the highest paved road between the Rockies and the Allegheny Mountains. A

KEWEENAW PENINSULA

© JOSH BISHOP

Fort Wilkins Historic State Park draws tourists with a restored fort and interpretive programs.

parking area midway allows you to stop and soak in the panorama of Lake Superior and the rolling forests of the Keweenaw, an incredible vista no matter how many times you've seen it. Watch for ravens, bald eagles, and peregrine falcons—which sometimes soar below you. Traveling west to east, the end of the drive is marked by a picture-postcard shot of Copper Harbor, tucked between Lake Superior and Lake Fanny Hooe.

Scenic Lakeshore Drive

This stretch of M-26 between Copper Harbor and Eagle River lives up to its name: Lake Superior looms just alongside the road, studded with rocky islands and swelling dunes. Unfortunately, you miss about 10 miles of the route if you take Brockway Mountain Drive. Plan to do both on your trip to Copper Harbor—Brockway is better headed east, this drive better headed west.

About five miles south of Copper Harbor, **Hebard Park** is a good picnic, sunset, or agate-hunting spot. Where M-26 and Brockway Mountain Drive meet, watch for the small sign marking **Silver Falls.** It's a short downhill walk to this pretty little waterfall, splashing and pooling in the forest.

West of Eagle Harbor, the road climbs above **Great Sand Bay** toward Eagle River. From this high vantage point, you can sometimes see huge 1,000-foot lake carriers out in the shipping lanes, which squeeze close to shore to round Keweenaw Point. Inland, beach peas, sand cherries, and wild roses cling to windswept, volatile mounds of sand. Like beach grasses, the plants' spreading root systems help trap sand, stabilizing and building dunes.

The Keweenaw's tilted fault line is particularly pronounced in this part of the peninsula. To the south rises the exposed basalt face of the Cliff Range, while to the north, the fault line drops away so quickly that Great Sand Bay plummets to depths of more than 1,000 feet. In between, deep ridges allow microclimates to thrive. Along the south side of the road, watch for faintly marked **Michigan Nature Association trails** that dip into dark, deep forests, where lichen drapes from the pines and deep cushions of moss cover the rocky path.

◖ Lighthouses

You can't reach the **Copper Harbor Lighthouse** by land because adjacent property owners refuse to grant a right-of-way, so the Park Service has arranged for boat tours of the light and keeper's house, which contains a worthwhile small museum. Originally built in 1849, the stone lighthouse is the oldest operating light on Lake Superior. (An adjacent tall steel tower now does duty, however.) Just wandering around the lovely rocky point is worth the trip. It was on this point, by the way, where Douglass Houghton first spotted a thick green stripe in the rock indicating the presence of copper, a discovery that unleashed the Keweenaw's copper boom. The 90-minute tour leaves from the municipal marina several times daily from Memorial Day to early September. Call 906/289-4966 for specific times and reservations (adults $15, children 12 and under $10). Also ask about sunset cruises. There are a few other lighthouses around Copper Harbor—Gull Rock Lighthouse and Manitou Island Lighthouse, the oldest light on the Great Lakes—but, like the Copper Harbor light, they're only accessible by boat.

One of the Keweenaw's most charming little towns, Eagle Harbor has a sleepy, comfortable feel to it, with a wonderfully protected natural harbor, a perfect crescent of beach, and even a historic lighthouse and observation deck out on the rocky point. In short, a classic summer getaway. "Everybody in Copper Harbor is trying to make money," noted one local. "Everybody in Eagle Harbor has already made it." The red-brick **Eagle Harbor Lighthouse** (906/289-4990, mid-June–mid-Sept., $4), built in 1861, is one of the area's prettiest. Its outbuildings contain a small museum filled with information on shipwrecks, mining, and commercial fishing. The one-room schoolhouse in Eagle Harbor (two blocks west of the harbor on Center Street) was the birthplace of the odd **Knights of Pythias,** a secret fraternal society known for its elaborate rituals and fanciful costumes.

© BECCA BISHOP

Now a bed-and-breakfast on the Lake Superior shore, Sand Hills Lighthouse has been painstakingly restored.

A few miles west of Eagle Harbor, the **Eagle River Lighthouse** is worth a look-see and makes for a nice picture, even if it is closed to the public. The light went out of service in the early 1900s; today it's a private residence. On the other side of the peninsula, in Bete Grise, historic lighthouse aficionados will want to track down **Mendota Lighthouse** for a picture, but it's a private residence, too. If you're looking to get inside a lighthouse—and especially if you'd like to stay the night—try the **Sand Hills Lighthouse Inn** (906/337-1744, www.sandhillslighthouseinn. com) in Ahmeek. The 1917 lighthouse, made for three keepers and their families, underwent a three-year renovation in the early 1990s. Believe it or not, it's just as stunning inside as out.

FESTIVALS AND EVENTS
Copper Harbor hosts the peninsula's best **Fourth of July** fireworks show, and Sam Raymond, owner of Copper Harbor's Keweenaw Adventure Company, puts on a growing **Fat Tire Festival** the day before Labor Day. For more information on all

area festivals and celebrations, contact the Keweenaw Convention and Visitors Bureau (56638 Calumet Ave., 906/337-4579, 800/338-7982, www.keweenaw.info) in Calumet.

SUMMER SPORTS AND RECREATION
Hiking and Biking
You'll need a map to make sense of the area. A snowmobile map (available through local shops and the Keweenaw Convention and Visitors Bureau) is decent for major routes, the *DeLorme Atlas and Gazetteer* includes a few more, and a topo map is best—though no map yet shows even half the trails in the area. Sam Raymond, owner of the **Keweenaw Adventure Company** (145 Gratiot St., 906/289-4303, www.keweenaw adventure.com) in Copper Harbor, has mapped and signed (although the signs keep disappearing) dozens of miles of mountain biking routes. He's also clearing and maintaining the trails with only the help of a few friends. It's a huge undertaking for minimal return, so show Sam

KEWEENAW PENINSULA

A DYNASTY OF PINE

In the mid-1800s, a young and growing United States suddenly had an insatiable appetite for lumber. Settlers were moving west, into the treeless plains, and needed lumber to build their new towns. Burgeoning cities needed lumber to build homes and businesses. Railroads needed lumber as they laid mile after mile of track to connect it all.

Michigan's natural resources proved the perfect mix to fuel a hungry nation. Immense white pines and other conifers grew thick and tall across the Upper Peninsula and across more than half of the Lower Peninsula. Rivers honeycombed these vast forests, providing a route to the Great Lakes, which in turn connected the northern wilderness to Chicago, Detroit, and other railroad centers in the south. Mother Nature had created the perfect delivery system for the logging industry.

Around 1850, logging camps began springing up deep in the woods, from the western U.P. to the shores of Lake Huron. Young men streamed north, some of them farm laborers looking for winter wages, others newly arrived immigrants looking to gain a foothold in their new homeland. It was not easy work. The lumberjacks worked by hand, with ax and saw, tree after tree, acre after acre. With a shout of "timber!" the old pines came down with an earth-shaking thud, some of them as much as 20 feet in circumference and 100 feet tall.

The logging camps operated primarily in the winter months, when it was easier to transport the huge logs. With horses and sleighs, workers hauled the logs from the woods to the river's edge, branded the ends with the lumber company's mark, and stacked them there until spring, when they were floated downriver to waiting sawmills on the Great Lakes.

In the spring, when the ice melted, the colorful and chaotic log drives began. Thousands of logs were shoved into the northwoods rivers, guided downstream by daredevil workers known as "river pigs," who danced across the dangerous mass of moving wood, using hooks, poles, and sometimes dynamite to dislodge log jams. It was the most dangerous job in the trade: With one misstep, river pigs ended up crushed between tons of logs or trapped underwater.

Once at the mills, the jumble of logs was sorted according to the millowner's mark and floated into mill storage ponds. From there, buzzing sawmills sliced the logs into lumber and loaded it onto lumber schooners – and later, barges and steamers – headed primarily to Chicago, the nation's largest lumber market and railroad hub.

your appreciation by giving him your business. Keeweenaw Adventure Company rents and services mountain bikes and sells those helpful maps for a nominal fee.

Not surprisingly, Keeweenaw Adventure Company is your best source for trail suggestions in the area. The **Red Trail** is the region's classic route, a single-track trail with plenty of technical twists and turns. It runs roughly from the gravel **Burma Road Trail,** past the south end of the Keeweenaw Mountain Lodge golf course and the north shore of Lake Manganese, where you can pick up **Paul's Plunge** back to Lake Fanny Hooe. Another good loop is the two-track **Surprise Valley Trail,** which hooks up with the **Kamikaze Trail** that traces the southern side of Lake Fanny Hooe.

In the same general area, the **Clark Mine Trail** drops south out of Copper Harbor at the south end of Lake Fanny Hooe. Just outside town, brown and white signs will direct you to **Manganese Falls,** a pleasant walk down into a ferny oasis; **Manganese Lake,** a popular fishing and swimming hole; and the **Clark Mine,** where the old brick furnace chimney still stands against a backdrop of mine tailings. Where the Clark Mine Trail swings east, make your way south to meet up with the Montreal River if you're interested in a little trout fishing.

In addition to the trails south of Copper Harbor, here are a few other destinations to consider. From the end of U.S. 41, the road continues east as a wide dirt-and-gravel road. Follow it for about a mile to the first main left

In its heyday, the logging industry generated billions of board feet of lumber and billions of dollars, the actual number almost incalculable. Lumber companies made all sorts of proclamations: Michigan's mills claimed they produced enough lumber to lay an inch-thick plank across the state.

Success stories were everywhere. A sawmill in Hermansville, Michigan, came up with the idea of tongue-and-groove flooring and quickly became the largest flooring plant in the country, crafting the floors for the Mormon Temple in Salt Lake City and the main lodge in Yellowstone National Park. Timber baron homes were marvels of hand-carved mahogany, gold-leaf inlay, and cut-crystal chandeliers.

But the era that everyone thought would last forever lasted less than 50 years. By 1900, nearly all the big trees were gone, a scorched, denuded landscape of stump prairies left in their place. When farmers were able to convert some of the southernmost pineries into useful crop land, ambitious entrepreneurs sought to do the same in the north. A newspaper publisher in Menominee extolled the virtues of Upper Peninsula cutover land for farming or ranching. "No matter where the first Garden of Eden was located," he proclaimed, "the present one is in the Upper Peninsula."

Thousands of hard-working folks were lured north by the promise of cheap land in exchange for the back-breaking labor of removing pine stumps and tilling soil. But by the late 1920s, their work proved futile. Nearly half of the U.P. was tax-delinquent cutover land. Ranches had failed. Most farms had failed. The stock market had crashed, and the nation's economy was in shambles.

The federal government took a different approach. In 1911, it established the first national forests in Michigan and Wisconsin, setting aside land and creating tree nurseries as a first step in reestablishing the Midwest's great forests. The Civilian Conservation Corps, established in 1933, continued the reforestation efforts, planting trees, fighting fires, and slowly nursing the remaining great forests back to health.

Although we can never recreate the magnificent old-growth forests of yesteryear, pines once again stretch skyward across Michigan. Logging continues, too, though with sophisticated forest management and reforestation practices that help ensure the livelihood of the state's lumber and paper industries. And a few stands of virgin old-growth timber remain, giving us an awe-inspiring glimpse of a lost Michigan landscape.

branch, which winds north and east to the Lake Superior shore and **Horseshoe Harbor,** a fine place to spend an afternoon scrambling around the rock ledges and beaches. This picturesque sliver of a harbor is owned by the Nature Conservancy, so keep mountain bikes off the property as requested. Backtracking to the main road, continue east about three miles to another left (northeast) turnoff, which skirts **Schlatter Lake** and continues on to **High Rock Bay** at the tip of the peninsula. Don't be surprised to see a camp or two set up here.

Copper Harbor lies at the top of the Keweenaw Peninsula, but it doesn't lie at the end. The tip of the peninsula curves to the east and continues about 10 more miles beyond

town, leaving about a 60-square-mile tract to the east and south of Copper Harbor with no pavement, development, or attractions—unless you like to hike, mountain bike, fish, or just get out alone in the woods.

Probably more than 100 miles of trails crisscross the tip of the peninsula; no one's ever bothered to count. They range from deer trails to tight single-track to wide gravel-and-dirt roads used by logging trucks and snowmobiles. Aside from a few tracts held by the state and the Nature Conservancy, the vast majority of the land is owned by International Paper, which uses it for logging. The paper company has put the land in what is called "Commercial Forest Reserve." CFR lands, common throughout the U.P., give tax breaks to companies that agree to

KEWEENAW PENINSULA

keep the land open to the public for recreation. That means you are free to hike, bike, and otherwise explore this area. Avoid any active logging areas and follow the same guidelines you would anywhere: respect "no trespassing" signs and pack out what you pack in.

Canoeing and Kayaking

Paddling is at its finest in the Keweenaw, where you have plenty of islands, rock formations, and wilderness coastlines to explore. **Keweenaw Adventure Company** (145 Gratiot St., 906/289-4303, www.keweenawadventure.com) rents kayaks, guides trips, and offers lessons. Beginners should try the 2.5-hour introductory paddle, which includes novice dry-land instruction and a fine little trip around the harbor and along the Lake Superior shoreline. Keweenaw Adventure Company also offers some day-long trips around the peninsula—to Horseshoe Harbor, Agate Harbor, and the mouth of the Montreal River—as scheduling permits. Check the website or give them a call for specifics.

If you have your own boat, don't overlook the peninsula's inland lakes. Fanny Hooe, Medora, and other nearby lakes offer classic northwoods peace and scenery, often with the company of bobbing loons or black bears on the shoreline.

Fishing

The Gratiot River, which crosses M-26/U.S. 41 north of Amheek and Mowhawk and continues west to Lake Superior, is a good place to cast a line for brook and rainbow trout, as well as the occasional steelhead. There's an access point on M-26/U.S. 41. To find access where the Gratiot River crosses Cliff Drive, take the turnoff in the village of Amheek and follow Cliff Drive to the water. For another fishing spot, follow Five Mile Point Road from Amheek to Farmer's Road and turn left to the river and its Upper Falls.

You can cast a line at Gratiot River Country Park, too. To get there, take U.S. 41 to Allouez and turn at the BP station onto Bumbetown Road and continue onto Gratiot River Road for just over four miles.

Boat Trips and Tours

The Kilpela family, who run the Isle Royale ferry service, also offer sunset cruises on the *Isle Royale Queen IV* every evening from July 4 to Labor Day. From mid-May through the end of September, the *Queen* earns her keep by ferrying passengers from Copper Harbor to Isle Royale National Park, a 4.5-hour trip. Call 906/289-4437 for reservations and to check the schedule, which varies throughout the summer (one-way cost is $62 adults, $31 children 11 and under; canoes and kayaks an additional $25; fuel surcharge may apply).

Diving

The cold, gin-clear freshwater of Lake Superior offers outstanding visibility for divers. Though there isn't much to look at in the way of plant and animal life—the cold waters make for a pretty sterile environment—the waters provide plenty of entertainment in the form of interesting underwater geologic formations and shipwrecks.

Ships have been running aground for well over a hundred years around the Keweenaw Peninsula, a navigational hazard if there ever was one. Within the 103-square-mile **Keweenaw Underwater Preserve,** divers can explore the *Tioga,* a freighter that ran aground near Eagle River in 1919, and the *City of St. Joseph,* which met its fate north of Eagle Harbor in 1942. Both ships lie in fewer than 40 feet of water, with large sections of their hulls, deck machinery, and other artifacts clearly visible.

One of the Upper Peninsula's oldest shipwrecks, the *John Jacob Astor,* lies just offshore from Copper Harbor, near the Fort Wilkins State Park Lighthouse Overlook. An Underwater Trail marks the location of the rudder, anchor, and other remnants of the *Astor,* which sank in 1844, and another ship. Rumor has it that before the Keweenaw Underwater Preserve was established in 1989, locals learned of a couple salvage divers who were planning on retrieving one of the anchors. Without the legal protection of an underwater preserve, local divers took the matter into their own hands: they hauled up the anchor themselves and hid it in nearby Lake Fanny Hooe, where it remained until a few years ago, when it was safely returned to its original wreck site. Today, disturbing or removing any artifact is a felony under Michigan law.

The U.S. Coast Guard has to be more than a little humiliated about the preserve's most popular dive site, the Coast Guard cutter *Mesquite*. In 1989, the 180-foot *Mesquite* ran aground on a reef off Keweenaw Point while tending to a navigational buoy. Efforts to free her failed and winter winds battered her so badly that the Coast Guard decided to sink her as a dive site rather than pay the costs of retrieving and repairing the aging vessel. The *Mesquite* sits in 110 feet of water in Keystone Bay with virtually all equipment on deck. Experienced divers can explore the *Mesquite's* interior. For dive services, contact **A Superior Diver's Center** (12811 M-26, 906/289-4259) in Eagle Harbor.

Golf

The nine holes of **Keweenaw Mountain Lodge** (906/289-4403, 888/685-6343, www.atthelodge.com, $19 9 holes, $26 18 holes, cart fees $16 for 9 holes and $25 for 18 holes) have as much of a reputation for their beautiful scenery as they do for a good game of golf. The truth is, even if the scenery wasn't quite as eye-catching, this place would be a decent golfing destination—one of the Keweenaw's best. There's a pro shop for all your golfing needs, and meals can be had at The Lodge. If it's nice out and the black flies aren't circling, try dining on the porch. When a full bar, a wine list, and great food are on offer, you'll want to tuck in after a day on the greens.

Off-Road Vehicles

Since there aren't any DNR-designated trail systems this far north in the Keweenaw Peninsula, your best bet for off-roading will be the state forest roads in Copper Country State Forest. All state forest roads are open to ORV use unless they're specifically marked otherwise.

Waterfalls

The Montreal River tumbles over some beautiful waterfalls before joining Lake Superior just to the southeast, but they're difficult to reach. Your best bet is from Bete Grise (bay-duh GREE), Just before you reach Bete Grise Bay, you'll see two dirt routes heading east into the woods. One is signed "This is not the road to Smith Fisheries." Take the other one. It will indeed lead you around Bear Bluff to this old commercial fishing enterprise (now private property). Continue on the smaller trail behind the fishery, a terrific path that traces the steep bluffs of the bay shore. It's about another 1.5 miles to the mouth of the Montreal and its fine waterfalls. West of Bete Grise, the pleasant **Haven Falls** are located at a roadside park. Take Lac La Belle Road south for 4.5 miles, then turn right at the fork and take it to the park.

In Copper Harbor, you won't want to miss the **Manganese Falls,** a thin but inspired flow that drops about 45 feet into a narrow gorge just outside of town. To get there, turn south on Manganese Road for less than a mile; the falls are located a short walk from the roadside. Eagle Harbor has a couple of shorter falls, each of them about seven feet. There are taller, more impressive falls in the Keweenaw Peninsula, but these are pretty easy to get to. **Silver River Falls** is a short walk from M-26, a little more than four miles east of Eagle Harbor. The falls are wide and passably nice, with a picnic area and roadside park nearby. **Copper Falls** is located about three miles south of Eagle Harbor, on the cutoff road between U.S. 41 and town. As you pass Owl Creek on your way south, take the second trail road to the left and park the car. The falls are a very short walk straight off the end of the road.

Eagle River's falls are much more impressive than Eagle Harbor's and still more convenient to get to. Both **Eagle River Falls** and **Jacob's Falls** are more or less on the shoulder of M-26. There's a parking area and pedestrian bridge just off the highway as it enters Eagle River, providing great access to the falls, which have a 60-foot drop. You can see the smaller Jacob's

KEWEENAW PENINSULA

Falls as you drive past on M-26, three miles northeast of Eagle River, but you'll want to stop the car and admire the 40-foot drop.

WINTER SPORTS AND RECREATION
Downhill Skiing

Downhill skiers can check out Michigan's most challenging terrain at **Mt. Bohemia** (100 Lac La Belle Rd., 906/360-7240, 888/937-2411, www.mtbohemia.com, lift tickets $45/day), near Lac La Belle. Mt. Bohemia offers one of the Midwest's highest vertical drops (900 feet), with some steep pitches, rock outcrops, and gladed terrain that may make you think you're somewhere in the Rockies.

Ski and Snowshoe Trails

A few trails stand out from the northern Keweenaw's many miles of Nordic skiing possibilities. First among these is the **Copper Harbor Pathway.** With a number of regularly groomed loops and trails that range from beginner to expert, the miles in and around Copper Harbor provide pleasant skiing and include marked snowshoe trails. The **Fort Wilkins State Park Loop** travels the region between Copper Harbor and the north shore of Lake Fanny Hooe, while the long Kamikaze Trail (not for beginners) hugs the lake's southern shore for more than two miles. Snowshoers will want to make their way into Estivant Pines Nature Sanctuary, 350 acres of virgin pine and towering hardwoods that are purported to be the oldest living trees in the state. You'll be able to choose from three loops of distances between 1 and 2.5 miles, and the ancient woods are worth going out of your way for. It's going to be quiet, too, since no snowmobiles (or any other motor vehicles) are allowed.

Snowmobiling

The Copper Harbor region is no different that the rest of Keweenaw: there are well-groomed snowmobile trails, and plenty of them. The Keweenaw Trail curves north to east as it ascends from Hancock, eventually connecting with the Lac La Belle Trail (steer clear of the Mt. Bohemia skiers), Eagle's Loop, Mandan Trail, Harlow Trail, and other snowmobile routes with trail numbers in the 130s. Take the Brockway Mountain or Powder House Trails into Copper Harbor, and for an end-of-the-road journey to the point of the Keweenaw, take the High Rock Trail to Lake Superior, east of the city. A good trail map is available from the Keweenaw Convention and Visitors Bureau (56638 Calumet Ave., 906/337-4579, 800/338-7982, www.keweenaw.info) in Calumet.

ACCOMMODATIONS

Located high on a ridge above Copper Harbor, the log lodge and cabins of the **Keweenaw Mountain Lodge** (906/289-4403, 888/685-6343, www.atthelodge.com, $95 motel, $129–165 cabin) were built as a public works project in the 1930s. Reservations here can be tough, but shoot for a cabin rather than the uninspired motel rooms (added much later than the other buildings). At the northern boundary of Fort Wilkins State Park and just a short bike ride from town, the **Norland Motel** (15526 U.S. 41, 906/289-4815) is the kind of find you almost hate to share. Mom-and-pop motel rooms are made special with knotty pine paneling, a wonderful setting on Lake Fanny Hooe, extras like canoes and in-room refrigerators (great for picnic lunches), and prices that don't get much higher than $50.

Though not as good a deal, the no-frills rooms at the **King Copper Motel** (906/289-4214, 800/833-2470, www.kingcoppermotel.com, $65–85) come with great views of the harbor and are just a few steps from the ferry dock—perfect for a warm shower and real bed after a week on Isle Royale.

Between Copper Harbor and Eagle Harbor on M-26, **Eagle Lodge** (13051 Lakeshore Dr./M-26, 906/289-4294, 888/558-4441, www.eaglelodge-lakeside.com, $75–130) offers simple housekeeping cabins perched on Lake Superior's shore. In Eagle River, the **Eagle River Inn** (5033 Front St., 906/337-0666, www.eagleriverinn.com, $85–115) offers motel-style accommodations with a similarly outstanding setting, right at the water's edge and flanked by a long sand beach. All rooms come with lake views. In Ahmeek, south of Eagle Harbor, check out the (**Sand Hills Lighthouse Inn** (906/337-1744). It may not be cheap—rooms run $135–200—but with a 90-foot tower to climb and rooms with balconies overlooking Lake Superior, you can justify the cost. Owner Bill Frabotta has restored the 1919 lighthouse, filled it with antiques, and decorated it in lavish Victorian style. There's a great breakfast, too. Take M-26 west out of Ahmeek to Five Mile Point Road.

Camping

Fort Wilkins State Park (15223 U.S. 41, 906/289-4215, www.michigan.gov/dnr) has 165 modern sites in two campgrounds, both on Lake Fanny Hooe. Many sites back up to the water and offer decent privacy. To reserve a spot (but not a specific site), call the Michigan state parks central reservation line, 800/447-2757, or visit www.midnrreservations.com. **Lake Fanny Hooe Resort and Campground** (505 2nd St., 906/289-4451, 800/426-4451, www.fannyhooe.com, $28–38) offers uninteresting sites in an open grassy area, but with a decent location near town and the south shore of Lake Fanny Hooe.

West of Ahmeek on Five Mile Point Road, **Sunset Bay Campground** (2701 Sunset Bay Beach Rd., 906/337-2494, www.sunset-bay .com, late May–mid-Oct.) indeed offers a fine view of the sunset from your tent flap. Several of its 12 primitive sites sit on Lake Superior. There are 18 RV sites available. Many locals simply head out into the woods on weekends and set up camp near a favorite stretch of beach or river. If you choose to do the same, respect "no trespassing" signs and observe all backcountry camping practices (bury waste, hang packs, stay 50 feet from water, etc.)—you'll be sharing the woods with plenty of black bears.

FOOD

The **Pines** (160 Gratiot St., 906/289-4222, www.pinesresort.net), a small café in downtown Copper Harbor, is great for rainy-day breakfasts, with its homemade cinnamon rolls and crackling fireplace. Delicious soups, sandwiches, and local fish specialties keep folks coming all day. The adjacent **Zik's Bar** is the hangout for Copper Harbor locals. The (**Harbor Haus** (77 Brockway Ave., 906/289-4502, www.harborhaus.com, $15–25 dinner entrées) in Copper Harbor offers top-notch dining overlooking the harbor. The staff drop what they're doing to rush outside and perform the cancan when the *Isle Royale Queen IV* passes by. Though the ever-changing menu highlights some excellent German specials, you can't do better than the whitefish or lake trout. Another good choice for whitefish is the **Mariner North** (245 Gratiot St., 906/289-4637, until 2 A.M. daily), featuring steaks and seafood. This Copper Harbor institution lost some of its spirit when the original log building burned to the ground several years ago, but it remains a popular gathering place.

In Eagle Harbor, the **Shoreline Restaurant** (906/289-4441) draws 'em in for homemade pies, but there's plenty of other home-style cooking—like soups, sandwiches, and well-prepared fresh lake trout—to make it worth the stop.

In the Eagle River Inn, **Fitzgerald's Restaurant** (5033 Front St., 906/337-0666, www.eagleriverinn.com, $15–25 dinner entrées) offers upscale dining overlooking Lake Superior. The menu features Black Angus steaks, fresh fish and seafood, inventive vegetarian dishes, and a comprehensive wine list.

INFORMATION

For Copper Harbor tourism information, contact the **Copper Harbor Improvement Association** (P. O. Box 86, 906/289-4212, www.copperharbor.org) or stop by the visitors center in the Grant Township building on the corner of U.S. 41 and 2nd Street. The booth is staffed during the summer months, but not to worry—even if you stop by when the booth isn't manned, you can grab brochures from the lobby at any time. The Keweenaw Convention and Visitors Bureau (56638 Calumet Ave., 906/337-4579, 800/338-7982, www.keweenaw

.info) in Calumet is a great source for information and maps.

Medical emergencies are going to take you south again, though not all the way to Hancock, unless you really want to skirt past the Keweenaw Memorial Medical Center (205 Osceola St., 906/337-6500, www.kmmc .org) in Laurium. Heading into Laurium from Copper Harbor or northern Keweenaw, take U.S. 41 to M-26/School Street and turn left. Take School Street to 2nd Street, turn right on 2nd, then left on Osceola to the hospital.

Just like for the hospitals, you'll have to head south of Copper Harbor to find a bank, but not quite as far this time. Keweenaw's trusty regional bank, Superior National (80 Mohawk St., 906/337-6807, www.snb-t.com) has a branch in Mohawk, about six miles north of Calumet on U.S. 41. You can find an ATM at the Gas Lite General Store on the corner of U.S. 41 and 1st Street.

GETTING THERE AND AROUND
Car
The two main roads that lead north and east to Copper Harbor are the same highways from the base of the Keweenaw to Houghton and Hancock. U.S. 41 and M-6 merge into one highway at Calumet and stay that way for several miles until hitting Phoenix, where they split again. U.S. 41 doubles as the Copper Country Trail Scenic Byway (it actually starts back in Hancock), and it really does make for a peasant drive, striking more or less through the middle of the peninsula. The trail pairs Keweenaw's natural beauty (especially striking during the fall) with a smattering of history—old mines, museums, and other heritage sites. It is beautiful, of course, but drivers should consider jumping on M-26 for the journey between Phoenix and Copper Harbor. Not only does it pass through Eagle Harbor, a pleasant town in its own right, but the highway hugs the Lake Superior shore the whole way through. As

pleasant as the Copper Country Trail is, you'll get a more scenic drive on the detour north. Better still, take one route into Copper Harbor and the other on your way back.

Air
If you're flying in on your way to Copper Harbor, it shouldn't be much of a surprise that the closest airport is south in the comparatively large Houghton and Hancock area. The **Houghton County Memorial Airport** (CMX, 23810 Airpark Blvd., Calumet, 906/482-3970, www.houghtoncounty.org) has daily flights to and from Minneapolis. For car rentals at the airport, get ahold of National Car Rental (906/482-6655) or Priceless Rent-A-Car (906/482-5666).

Boat
The northern part of the Keweenaw is small, but it's got a lot of shoreline and a couple of harbors and marinas to boot. The **Copper Harbor State Dock** (906/289-4966, www.michigan .gov/dnr) is small, with only 10 transient slips available, but there are basic amenities (gas, showers, restrooms, etc.), which is more than can be said for Eagle Harbor. The harbormaster is on duty from 9 A.M.–5 P.M. and can be reached on radio channel 9. Copper Harbor's dock is located at 47° 28.42 N, 87° 51.50 W.

The Eagle Harbor State Dock, about 14 miles west of Copper Harbor, has transient docking, too, and little else. There's an emergency phone number (906/289-4215) and there's a harbormaster on duty. That's about it. You can find the dock at 47° 27.52 N, 88° 09.33 W.

Public Transportation
Sadly, there's no public transportation to speak of—limited taxi and shuttle service (call services in Houghton and Hancock or the airport if you need to, but Copper Harbor isn't exactly close and you can expect to pay accordingly), and bus service is nonexistent.

Isle Royale

Stranded in the vast waters of Lake Superior, Isle Royale is perhaps the model of what a national park is supposed to be—wild, rugged, and remote. No roads touch the 45-mile-long island, and its only contact with the outside world remains ship-to-shore radio. The least-visited park in the National Park Service system, Isle Royale attracts just 18,000 visitors a year—fewer visitors than elbow into Yosemite in a single weekend.

Civilization on Isle Royale (ROY-al, as if there is no "e") is concentrated in two small developments at opposite ends of the island. Windigo, on the southwest end, includes a National Park Service information center, camp store, and marina. Rock Harbor, near the east end, offers the same, plus a no-frills lodge and restaurant across from the ferry dock, and a handful of cabins overlooking finger-like Tobin Harbor. The rest of the island is backcountry, 210 square miles of forested foot trails, rocky bluffs, quiet lakes, and wilderness campsites.

Those who make the trek by boat or sea-plane to Isle Royale come primarily to hike its 165 miles of trails, fish its 46 inland lakes, and paddle its saw-toothed shoreline. Wildlife viewing is popular, too, especially for the moose that swam across from Ontario several decades back, and the eastern timber wolves that later followed their prey across on the pack ice. Though the wolves are notoriously elusive, you can pretty much bet that your wildlife sightings will outnumber your human ones on Isle Royale.

THE LAND
Geography

Backpackers may sense Isle Royale's distinctive topography as they traverse the long, narrow island, which runs southwest to northeast, less than nine miles across at its widest point. A series of ridges and valleys fall away from the park's high interior backbone, the Greenstone Ridge, creating a washboard of forest and rock. Mt. Desor marks the highest point on

Isle Royale is perfect for hikers, paddlers, and backcountry campers.

the island, rising from the Greenstone Ridge to 1,394 feet.

The same Precambrian lava flows that formed the Keweenaw Peninsula more than one billion years ago also formed Isle Royale. After each lava flow, wind and rain carried sand and other sediments into the area, producing slabs of softer rock sandwiched between the hard layers of basalt, and creating the island's characteristic ridge-and-trough pattern. Hikers crossing the width of the island will feel this layout in their quads, as the trail continually rises and falls with each ridge. The topography becomes most obvious on the park's northeastern edge, where it meets Lake Superior: the ridges become long rocky fingers, and the valleys become narrow slivers of water wedged between the rocky points.

When the center of the Superior Basin began to subside, it thrust the layers of rock on Isle

© TRAVEL MICHIGAN

KEWEENAW PENINSULA

Royale upward at an angle, giving the island a northwest side of steep ridges and bluffs, and a southeastern shore that slopes gradually to the water and includes lowlands and bogs. The northern Keweenaw Peninsula is a near mirror image of Isle Royale, with a gradual northern shore and more steeply angled southern side.

The geography of Isle Royale is inseparable from the water that surrounds it. Along with its namesake island—the largest in Lake Superior—Isle Royale National Park actually consists of an archipelago of some 400 islands, all of them remnants of the same landmass. More than 80 percent of the national park lies underwater, beneath shallow ponds, bogs, inland lakes, and the clear, cold water of Lake Superior. And here's some trivia to toss at a backpacker you pass on the trail: Ryan Island, located on Isle Royale's Siskiwit Lake, is the largest island in the largest lake on the largest island in the largest freshwater lake in the world.

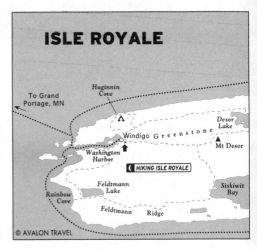

Climate

Isle Royale is the perfect escape from hot, sticky summers. With its water temperature rarely exceeding about 45°F, Lake Superior does a fine job as North America's largest air conditioner. It also has a significant modifying effect on the island: summers are generally a little cooler than on the mainland, with daytime temperatures from mid-May to mid-August ranging from about 65–75°F. Nights are northwoods cool, often dipping into the 40s and even 30s. Clouds obscure the sun more than half the time in summer. And be aware that fog can strike at anytime; more than one disappointed backpacker has returned from Isle Royale without any memories of the island's lovely vistas.

Lake Superior's modifying effect works in winter, too—winters on Isle Royale are a little warmer than on the mainland, though that can be small consolation in this part of the world. Once Lake Superior turns from cobalt to dark gray in late autumn, and its infamous winter storms begin churning, the island becomes shrouded in fog, whipped by wind, and buried under several feet of snow.

Besides, isolation isn't the only reason Isle Royale has low visitor numbers. Come mid-October, it shuts up tight like a summer resort, the only national park to do so. The ferries stop running, the concessionaires in Rock Harbor close down, and the rangers head for Houghton or take seasonal work in warmer climes. Only the wildlife researchers are in their glory, able to track free-roaming wolves and moose by air.

FLORA AND FAUNA

Isolated from the effects of civilization, Isle Royale acts as a living laboratory, a study of how plants and animals interrelate in the ebb and flow of nature's cycles. Because of these unique natural qualities, in fact, the United Nations declared the park an International Biosphere Reserve in 1980.

Flora

Spruce, firs, and jack pines share the island with beech and maple forests. But numerous varieties of wildflowers take center stage in June and July. Forests can be dotted with yellow lady slipper and American starflower; lowlands are brightened by wild iris, calla lilies, and yellow pond lilies. July and August are the months to watch for berries; look for blueberries, thimbleberries, and red raspberries, especially in the sunnier, rockier high areas.

The Island's Most Famous Mammals

The island's **moose** provide the best example. Naturalists believe moose first came to Isle Royale in the early 1900s, several of them swimming the 15 miles from mainland Ontario. With ample vegetation for food and no natural predators, the moose multiplied rapidly, their numbers soaring to somewhere between 1,000 and 3,000 by the late 1920s. But soon they had ravaged their food sources. Starvation, combined with some particularly harsh winters, killed off hundreds of the huge mammals in the 1930s. A fire in 1936 prompted a lush regrowth of vegetation; thanks to revived food sources, the moose population skyrocketed again, followed by another round of starvation.

The seesaw pattern might have continued for decades, but nature intervened in the form of the eastern **timber wolf** (also known as the gray wolf). During the exceptionally cold winter of 1948–1949, the lake iced over between Ontario and Isle Royale, and a small pack of wolves made its way to the island. The wolves found a bountiful food source in the local moose and multiplied, reaching a peak population of about 50 animals in 1970.

Since then, the wolves and moose, fenced in by the waters of Lake Superior, have provided scientists with a fascinating study of the predator-prey relationship. In 2008, the island marked its 50th year of wolf-moose research and study. The study is a joint effort by the National Park Service and Michigan Tech, and it has become the longest predator-prey study in the world. In a large moose herd, wolves cull the sick, the old, and the young, preventing overpopulation. In fact, moose make up around 90 percent of wolves' diet. But a smaller, stronger moose herd means more difficult hunting, which, in turn, reduces wolf breeding.

Populations of both animals have fluctuated rather dramatically over the decades. Today, the moose population hovers around 650. Hikers have an excellent chance of spotting these 1,000-pound mammals, which often feed in ponds and lowlands or along inland lakeshores. Hidden Lake, across Tobin Harbor south of Lookout Louise, is an exceptionally good spot, since moose have a taste for its mineral licks. If you're lucky enough to come upon a moose, give it very, very wide berth. Although they look cartoonish and friendly, moose can be exceptionally dangerous if approached too closely—especially cows with calves or males during the fall rutting season—capable of inflicting lethal blows with their hooves.

KEWEENAW PENINSULA

THE MAMMALS OF ISLE ROYALE

At first glance, this is pretty simple: Moose. Wolf. That's it. There are other mammals, of course – other furry friends include foxes, beavers, squirrels, and hares – but the big ones, in size and notoriety, are the moose and the wolf. They haven't always existed on Isle Royale. Moose arrived around 1900, and wolves about 50 years later – and people have been paying attention ever since. The official study began in 1958 and hasn't stopped, making it the longest predator-prey study in the world.

These two mammals have established a perfect predator-prey relationship within the confines of the 200-square-mile island. It's the island's isolation, lack of human interaction, and limited (not to mention count-able) populations that have made it the ideal place for studying the relationship for the last 50 years. The animals don't readily leave the island, nor is it easy for them to get there. Swimming or crossing the ice is really their only option, so, while the population is by no means stagnant, the ups and downs can be tracked with relative ease and attributed entirely to natural causes: illness, hard winters, and the like. Still, an easy majority of the moose deaths are caused by wolves.

The most important aspect of the wolf-moose relationship that has contributed to the ongoing study is that the two large animals are uniquely interdependent. Wolves are the only natural predator for the moose, and moose make up some 90 percent of the wolves' diets (the rest comes from beaver and snowshoe hare). So the fates of the creatures are tied together. A spike in one population or a drop in the other provides invaluable information to the researchers from Michigan Technological University who study the animals' relationship.

In the summertime, researchers and volunteers head into the wild to study elements of the moose population: examine the carcasses, check the impact of moose ticks, observe the moose as they forage, measure the amount of available food, and collect droppings for dietary analysis. They haven't forgotten about the wolves either – researchers pick up wolf droppings, too. Unlike the moose poo, wolf poo is collected to gather DNA identifications for each of the predators on the island. There's no guarantee that they'll get every wolf, but since they tend to collect a lot of droppings, it's a pretty exhaustive list.

Much of the counting takes place in the winter, after the park is closed to human visitors (with exceptions, of course, for the researchers themselves). In the winter, from mid-January through early March, wolf and moose populations are measured through observation from flyovers in a small aircraft. Researchers also estimate kill rates and perform studies on the carcasses.

In 2008, the wolf population was estimated at 23, while the moose population was somewhere around 650, "a relatively low abundance." The moose population has been below its long-term average for some time now. For the fifth year in a row, 2008 saw the moose afflicted by infestations of moose ticks (a heavily infected moose can carry tens of thousands of the blood-sucking critters), and a series of hotter-than-average summers have negatively impacted the moose, which need to keep cool – not an easy task in the July heat.

For their part, the wolves are split into four packs, with a single lone wolf wandering the island. One of the packs, Paduka Pack, formed in 2007, while the other three packs, East Pack III, Chippewa Harbor Pack, and Middle Pack II, have all existed since at least 2000.

Each year of study brings new information and a few surprises. The only constant, it seems, is that the study will continue – perhaps for another 50 years or more.

For reasons not clearly understood, Isle Royale's wolf population plummeted in the 1990s. By 1998, just 14 wolves roamed the island in three packs, and biologists feared a lack of genetic diversity might mean the demise of the island's wolves. But now they've rebounded again. The winter 2008 count recorded 23 wolves in four packs, the newest of which formed in 2007 (the other three packs have existed since 2000). Whether the wolves will continue to thrive remains one of the most compelling questions this living laboratory has yet to answer.

The wolves tend to hide out largely in the remote southwestern corner of the island, but lately have been migrating east, where moose populations are higher. Only the rare backpacker ever spots one of the shy and stealthy creatures, and many a "wolf howl" heard at night is probably the haunting call of a loon. But the notion that wolves are there, somewhere—perhaps even watching from deep in the forest—is compelling enough for most, especially those lucky enough to spot a pawprint across the trail.

Other Animals

Some of the other large mammals common in the northern Great Lakes region are notably absent from the island. Black bears never made it here, and white-tailed deer introduced for hunting vanished early in the century. Likewise, caribou and lynx, present in the 19th century, also disappeared. Instead, hikers may spot red foxes (which love to scavenge around campsites, so hang your pack), beavers, muskrats, hares, red squirrels, otter, and mink.

Birdwatchers will enjoy scouring the water's surface for the common loon—which is indeed common here—along with the Canada goose, bufflehead, black duck, merganser, and mallard. Smaller birds frequenting the island include warblers, chickadees, thrushes, woodpeckers, and kingfishers.

None of Isle Royale's inland lakes can be reached by car or motorized boat, and many of them require serious effort to reach by foot—a combination that makes for great **fishing.**

While sportfishing boats ply the Lake Superior waters around Isle Royale for lake trout, it is the island's inland waters—nearly all of them!—that offer really top-notch fishing. Northern pike is considered the prime fish in these parts, for its fighting spirit, and can be found in almost any of the local lakes. Hungry hikers will be pleased to know walleye, perch, and trout abound, too. Wise backpackers tote along a pack rod to fish with from shore; many lakes, like Feldtmann, Desor, Siskiwit, Richie, and Chickenbone have foot trails leading directly to them. (Other more remote lakes are open to fishing but require good backcountry skills to reach.) No license is needed to fish Isle Royale's inland lakes, though Michigan regulations apply; if you plan to drop a line in Lake Superior, you'll need a Michigan license, sold at the island's two camp stores.

A discussion of Isle Royale's animal life is not complete with mention of the island's insects. Like much of the Upper Peninsula—and many other wilderness areas—Isle Royale provides a fine home for **mosquitoes** and **black flies,** especially in low-lying areas. From mid-June to mid-August or so, keep insect repellent close at hand. In general, insects are less of a problem on higher trails, which often catch a lake breeze.

THE NATIONAL PARK

While many national parks struggle with their fates as islands of wilderness surrounded by a more developed world, Isle Royale has the advantage of a much larger buffer zone protecting it from outside encroachment and influence. As a result, it is one of the most closely managed holdings in the national park system. That's good or bad depending on your opinion of the Park Service, but it does present some unique opportunities for protecting the wilderness. For starters, it is one of the few parks that already regulates the number of visitors who pass through its gates. Though logistics have done a sufficient job of keeping numbers down thus far, the National Park Service need only cut back on ferry service or campsites to slow the flow.

Limited access also allows the Park Service to enforce rules more effectively. Dogs, for example, are not allowed on the island for fear they might bring rabies and other diseases to the island's wolf pack. Arrive with a poodle on your powerboat—even if it never sets paw on the dock—and you will be quickly waved off the island. Thumbs-down also to wheeled vehicles like mountain bikes or canoe carts. (Exceptions are made for wheelchairs.) The Park Service also takes great pains to preserve the island's backcountry solitude, with a park brochure reminding hikers to "refrain from loud conversation," "avoid songfests," and "select equipment of subtle natural tones rather than conspicuous colorful gear."

Information

For general information on the park, camping, transportation options, and more, contact **Isle Royale National Park** (906/482-0984, www .nps.gov/isro).

Isle Royale was one of the first national parks to charge a "park user fee." Daily fees are $4 per person per day. If you're traveling to the island by ferry or seaplane, the concessionaire will collect your fee. If you're traveling by private boat, you can pay at the ranger station at Windigo or Rock Harbor, or at the Houghton Visitors Center prior to your departure.

The National Park Service had long talked about implementing admission fees to national parks as a way to compensate for shortfalls in federal funding. In the past, the incentive wasn't there, since all gate fees were fed back into the federal government's general treasury. With the new user fee program, however, 80 percent of the monies gathered is spent at the collecting park. (The remaining 20 percent is spent at national parks with priority maintenance projects.) In Isle Royale's case, that means hundreds of thousands of dollars that will be spent maintaining trails and repairing or replacing docks. So hand over your cash willingly.

Getting There

If getting there is half the fun, you'll be positively giddy by the time you arrive at Isle

© BECCA BISHOP

The *Ranger III* takes visitors from Houghton and Hancock to Isle Royale.

Royale. Travel to the island is not particularly convenient or cheap, which probably accounts for the average visitor stays that are considerably longer than most other national park destinations. The average visit to Rocky Mountain National Park is a few hours; to Isle Royale, three days. (And that's counting the day-trippers who flow off the ferry, wander around the harbor for a few hours, and hop back on that afternoon.)

Many, however, come to appreciate even the trip to and from Isle Royale, a mental decompression chamber of sorts that eases the passage between island wilderness and the real world.

Your options for travel to Isle Royale are seaplane, ferry, or personal boat. The National Park Service operates the largest ferry, the 165-foot *Ranger III*, which celebrated its 50 birthday in 2008. It departs from Houghton twice a week (Tuesday and Friday) from the beginning of June through mid-September for the six-hour passage to Rock Harbor. The one-way cost is $60 adults, $20 children 6–12; kids under 6 are free. Canoes and kayaks are an additional $20–50 if they're longer than 20 feet or weigh more than 90 pounds. Make reservations through the national park (906/482-0984, www.nps.gov/isro).

If you'd rather see more of the Keweenaw and spend less time on the ferry, drive another hour up the peninsula to Copper Harbor, where you can catch the *Isle Royale Queen IV* for a three-hour trip to Rock Harbor. It operates from mid-May through the end of September, with a varying schedule (adding additional departures as needed in July and August). The one-way cost is $62 adults, $31 children 11 and under. Canoes and kayaks are an additional $25. The *Queen* is notoriously reliable and has happily surprised weary backpackers by showing up to retrieve them on even the stormiest of days. But it hasn't earned the nickname "the Queasy" for nothing; in heavy seas, its hull can rock and roll at a pretty good pitch. To check the schedule and make reservations, contact the **Royale Line** (906/289-4437, www.isleroyale.com).

A third and fourth ferry run from Grand Portage, Minnesota. The 65-foot *Wenonah* makes the three-hour passage to Windigo, on the island's west end, daily from mid-June to mid-September. The round-trip cost is $49 adults, $27 children under 12. Day trips are essentially just a boat ride, since you'll have less than three hours on the island. Reserve a spot through **Grand Portage-Isle Royale Transportation Line** (651/653-5872, 888/746-2305, Nov.–Apr.; 218/475-0024 or 218/475-0074 May–Oct.; www.isleroyaleboats.com).

A faster but more expensive boat, the 63-foot *Voyageur II*, travels to Windigo from Grand Portage in two hours, then continues on to Rock Harbor. On its way to Rock Harbor, it circumnavigates the island, offering drop-off and pick-up service along the way. (This makes for a slow but interesting trip.) One-way between Grand Portage and Windigo is $59; call for prices to other locations. *Voyageur II* can also carry canoes and kayaks for an additional $56. Again, make arrangements through Grand Portage–Isle Royale Transportation Line.

Seaplane service from Houghton is the most expensive but quickest way to the island—usually. The 35-minute flight is often delayed by wind and fog. The plane flies on demand (except Sunday) and can carry up to five passengers for $269 round-trip per person ($185 one-way). The plane cannot carry stove fuel, but you can purchase it on the island at the park store. Contact **Royale Air Service** (877/359-4753, 218/721-0405, www.royaleairservice.com).

Arriving by private boat is also popular in midsummer—a little too popular for many who resent the whine of powerboats jarring the silence. The Rock Harbor and Windigo marinas offer docking and refueling for powerboats and sailboats; boats also are permitted to drop an anchor in a secluded bay overnight and save the marina fee. Protected harbors are plentiful on the east end of the island (though most remain exposed on an east wind) but are nonexistent on the west end. Every boat arriving at the island must first stop at a ranger station in Windigo or Rock Harbor to obtain a permit and pay the park user fee.

KEWEENAW PENINSULA

Those with boats under 20 feet are strongly urged not to attempt a Lake Superior crossing. Even if you have a larger vessel, consider the passage only if you possess strong navigation skills and a good marine radio. Think ocean, not lake. Remember, these are the waters that sank the 729-foot *Edmund Fitzgerald* like it was a cheap rowboat.

Accommodations and Food

Those just looking for a quiet island stay and some swell day hikes can set up a base in comfort at the **Rock Harbor Lodge** (866/644-2003 or 906/337-4993, www.isleroyaleresort.com). Lodge rooms are pretty much your basic motel-style accommodations, but they sit right at the water's edge with a glorious view of nearby islands and the open waters of Lake Superior. You'll pay for this little slice of civilization in the wilderness: Rates average $360–380 d, including three meals at the lodge dining room, and $230–260 without the meals. (Dinner often features fresh lake trout from the restored Edisen Fishery.) Guests also have use of an adjacent day lodge with a comfy wood-burning fireplace. Nearby housekeeping cottages include small kitchens, one double bed, and two bunk beds. Rates average $220–250 per night, without meals. Reservations are a must.

The Rock Harbor Lodge dining room is open to the public, and its meals taste like a gourmet feast after a week of freeze-dried fare. The Marina Store in Rock Harbor carries a good supply of food, camping supplies, film, fuel . . . pretty much anything important you forgot to pack. Windigo doesn't have any sort of lodging but offers an equally well-equipped camp store. Both stores also offer shower and laundry facilities.

If you want to see more of the island, **(camping** is the way to do it. Rustic campsites are located throughout the island, with three types of sites available: tent sites for one to three tents, group sites for parties of 7–10 campers, and three-sided shelters that hold up to six people. You must obtain a free camping permit outlining your itinerary from the ranger station (groups of 7–10 pay a $25 processing fee), but you can't obtain a reservation. All sites are on a first-come, first-served basis. Should you reach a site at the end of the day and find it full (this can happen, especially in August, especially at sites a day's hike from Rock Harbor), the unwritten rules say double up. No one expects you to hike off into the dwindling light to the next campsite.

Come prepared. The camp stores, though very well supplied, are not the places to outfit your trip. Carry a stove and fuel, since many sites do not permit fires, and dead wood is limited anyway. A water filter is another good idea, unless you plan to boil everything. Potable water is only available in Rock Harbor and Windigo, and chemical purifiers like Halizone tablets will not kill the hydatid tapeworm that can be found in Isle Royale waters.

Boat Tours

The Park Service shuttles visitors to various island attractions on its 25-passenger *Sandy*. For information on destinations, schedules, and fares, contact the **Park Service** (906/482-0984, www.nps.gov/isro). Twice a week, the *Sandy* makes the short trip across the mouth of Moskey Basin to the historic fishery of Peter and Laura Edisen, restored to show what life was like at the commercial fisheries that once thrived on the island. From Edisen Fishery, it's a quarter-mile walk to the stout and simple Rock Harbor Lighthouse, a white edifice built in 1855 to guide ships to Isle Royale's then-busy copper ports.

The *Sandy* also cruises once a week to the Minong Mine, site, in the 1870s, of the island's largest copper mining operation. The boat excursion alone is worth the trip, rounding Blake Point and cruising past Five Finger Bay and Belle Harbor, one of the park's most scenic areas. Once at the mine, you can examine ancient copper mining pits dug by the island's first inhabitants, which probably tipped off the later miners to the area's underground wealth. Relics like ore cars and rails remain visible, too. Hikers can view the remnants of another mine on the Island Mine Trail. A wagon road, an old powder house, and mine tailings are about all that's left of the island's second-largest mining operation. Around all mine areas, watch the ground carefully—shafts and pits remain, but are obscured by undergrowth.

◖ HIKING ISLE ROYALE
Day Hikes from Rock Harbor

Several day hikes are doable if you choose to "motel camp" in Rock Harbor. Don't miss **Scoville Point,** a 4.2-mile loop with interpretive signs that traces a rocky finger of land east of Rock Harbor. Another popular short hike (3.8 miles) is the loop to Suzy's Cave, formed by the wave action of a once much-deeper Lake Superior. **Lookout Louise,** north of Tobin Harbor, offers one of the island's most spectacular views, gazing over its ragged northeastern shoreline. If you've got a canoe, it's a short paddle and a two-mile hike. Without a canoe, it's a fine hike along lovely Tobin Harbor and the eastern end of the Greenstone Ridge, but you'll have to retrace your steps to return to Rock Harbor, about a 20-mile trek in all.

For another all-day hike, follow the Lake Superior shoreline to the Daisy Farm campground and the Ojibway Trail, which heads north and brings you to the **Ojibway Tower,** an air-monitoring station. The tower marks the highest spot on the eastern end of the island, and you can climb its steps (but not enter the tower room) for an unmatched view of the island's interior lakes and bays on both the north and south sides of the island. Travel back via the Greenstone Ridge and along Tobin Harbor for a varied 18-mile hike that will take you through blueberry patches, wildflower meadows, and serene shorelines. For a similar but shorter hike, about 10 miles, turn north at the Three Mile campground to ascend Mt. Franklin, another high point on the Greenstone Ridge.

Day Hikes from Windigo

If you'd prefer not to haul your possessions on your back, it's possible—but a little more difficult—to do day hikes out of Windigo. Because fewer trails exist here, most hikes will be of the out-and-back variety. The best loop option is

to **Huginnin Cove,** a 9.7-mile route that passes through prime moose habitat before emerging onto the Lake Superior shore. (There's a campground here if you choose to make it an overnighter.) The east side of the trail passes an old mine, last active in 1892. Another excellent option is the **Feldtmann Lake Trail,** which winds along Washington Harbor before heading inland to one of the island's least-visited lakes. You can hike the 17-mile route out and back in a day, but you'll be sorry if you don't plan it as an overnight. Set up camp here and you'll likely be treated to moose sightings, dynamite fishing, and maybe, just maybe, the howl of a distant wolf. Plus, if you stay overnight, you'll have the time and energy for the short side trip to Lake Superior's pretty Rainbow Cove.

Longer Hikes

With 165 miles of trail, Isle Royale has far more outstanding hiking options that it's possible to outline here. Consider a comprehensive guide like Jim DuFresne's excellent *Isle Royale National Park: Foot Trails and Water Routes,* published by The Mountaineers. If you prefer to avoid the more bottlenecked areas of Windigo and Rock Harbor, consider arranging for the *Voyageur II* ferry (218/475-0024 or 218/475-0074) or the island's water-taxi service (906/337-4993) to drop you off and pick you up at another location.

In general, the **Greenstone Ridge** is the main route to traverse the island, a 42-mile trail of mostly high and dry terrain. It also is the most popular, though crowds are a relative thing on Isle Royale.

The park's second-longest trail, the 26-mile **Minong Ridge Trail,** easily ranks as its most challenging. Traversing the north end of the island from near Windigo to McCargoe Cove, the rough and lightly used trail hobbyhorses over a rocky ridge and disappears through bogs. If you like primitive and peaceful, and don't get nervous about some poorly marked stretches that may lead you astray, this trail is for you. Wildlife sightings, especially moose, are likely here. Though campgrounds are far apart on this trail, they're worth the effort—Little Todd

KEWEENAW PENINSULA

Harbor and Todd Harbor are some of the nicest on the island.

Finally, the **Feldtmann Ridge Trail** loops along the southwestern shore, a well-marked but also lightly used route of 22 miles. The trail offers outstanding variety, from the shoreline of Washington Harbor, through gentle bogs, up the high Feldtmann Ridge itself, and finally to the open wildflower meadows and waters of Siskiwit Bay.

PADDLING THE ISLAND

For paddlers, Isle Royale is a dream destination, a nook-and-cranny wilderness of rocky islands, secluded coves, and quiet bays interrupted only by the low call of a loon. For first-time visitors, you can't do better than the **Five Fingers,** the collection of fjord-like harbors and rocky promontories on the east end of the island. Not only is it well-protected (except from northeasterlies), it offers some of the finest and most characteristic Isle Royale scenery and solitude. Though Isle Royale is generally better suited to kayaks, open canoes can handle these waters in calm weather.

For kayaks, the entire island offers paddling opportunities, though some areas require long stretches of paddling without good shoreline access. Note that open-water passages on Lake Superior should be attempted by experienced paddlers only, and are not at all recommended in an open boat like a canoe. Capsizing in Lake Superior is not an unfortunate experience, it is a life-threatening one. With water temperatures rarely exceeding the 40s, hypothermia can occur in a matter of minutes.

You can avoid open-water passages and still explore other areas of the island by making use of the *Voyageur II* ferry or the island's water-taxi service, which will transport you and your boat to various docks on the northeastern half of the island. For more information and rates, call the *Voyageur II* (218/475-0024 or 218/475-0074) or the water taxi (906/337-4993).

Ferries can transport your boat, provided it is less than 20 feet long. You also can rent canoes, 14-foot fishing boats, and outboard motors at Windigo and Rock Harbor. For rental information, call 906/337-4993. For Rock Harbor visitors, a wonderful day can be spent exploring Tobin Harbor, where rental canoes await.

Exploring inland lakes is a remarkable experience on Isle Royale. Fishing is often superb, and moose often loiter near the shore, unaware of your presence. Plan your routes carefully, though, to avoid grueling portages. Again, your best bet is to arrange for the water taxi or the *Voyageur II* ferry to drop you and your boat at a mid-island spot like Malone Bay, Chippewa Harbor, or McCargoe Cove. From there you have manageable (and even easy) portages to more than a half dozen lakes, including Siskiwit, Wood, Whittlesey, Intermediate, Richie, LeSage, Livermore, and Chickenbone. And there's nothing quite like drifting across a wilderness lake in the middle of a wilderness island.

MARQUETTE AND THE LAKE SUPERIOR SHORE

As home to the Upper Peninsula's largest, most metropolitan city, the Lake Superior shore is deserving of a good chunk of your time. Marquette is actually pretty hip, especially for a city smack dab in what often feels like the middle of nowhere. It's a college town, which means there's plenty to do, whether you're into bars or live performances or college-level sports or the arts and culture scene. If you're here for the great outdoors, you'll find plenty of it just over Marquette's doorstep: the rugged and undeveloped Huron Mountains lie to the west, while Presque Isle truly is one of the U.P.'s gems.

And while Lake Superior may not have the sandy beaches and swimability of Lakes Michigan and Huron, you'd be hard pressed to find someone who's unmoved by the rough, wild shoreline.

Thanks in part to the rocks, bluffs, and water too cold to swim in, the largest of the Great Lakes is in many ways the most awesome.

Both Munising and Grand Island are located on a picturesque bay that would rival any in the world for sheer beauty. Continue east and it only gets better, as the remarkable colors, cliffs, and rock formations of the Pictured Rocks National Lakeshore stretch out like an artistic masterpiece being unveiled before you (if you've never kayaked before, this would be a good place to start). The national lakeshore is perfectly bookended on the opposite side by Grand Marais.

Don't forget to take a detour inland, where many of the U.P.'s renowned outdoor recreational activities are at your fingertips. Of particular interest is the Seney National Wildlife

© JOSH BISHOP

THE LAKE SUPERIOR SHORE

HIGHLIGHTS

◖ Presque Isle Park: Just a nine-iron away from Northern Michigan University's campus, some of the area's most beautiful scenery is preserved. Take a car through the park or – better still – bike, hike, or ski (page 173).

◖ Hiawatha Water Trail: The 120-mile Hiawatha Water Trail isn't for everyone, but the journey from Big Bay to Grand Marais is a beautiful, adventurous one. There are shorter segments for those short on time or stamina (page 176).

◖ Grand Island: Take a ferry ten minutes off the shore of Munising and spend a day (or a weekend) exploring the island by bike or foot (page 189).

◖ Hiawatha National Forest: Several hundred acres of national forest provide seemingly endless recreational opportunities, no matter what season (page 190).

◖ Pictured Rocks National Lakeshore: These scenic rocks – so named because they look as if someone passed a paintbrush over them – are among the U.P.'s best of the best. Kayaking is the way to go (page 199).

LOOK FOR ◖ TO FIND RECOMMENDED SIGHTS, ACTIVITIES, DINING, AND LODGING.

Refuge, which has 95,000 acres of wetlands, bog, and wilderness. It's home to hundreds of species of birds and other animals, and is ideal for hiking or biking.

PLANNING YOUR TIME

It depends on what you'd like to do, of course, but you'll want to spend at least two or three days in Marquette—there's enough to do that it'll stave off the small-town ennui that can strike unexpectedly up here. Marquette is ideal as a launching pad for hub-and-spoke explorations of the surrounding areas, too. Set aside a day for Munising, Pictured Rocks, and Grand

Marais, longer if you're planning on exploring the lakeshore by foot. Try to get out onto Lake Superior, whether it's by sea kayak, charter boat, or a tour. Four or five days will do you just fine: book a nice hotel, make some dinner reservations, and spend your days exploring.

HISTORY

Marquette and the Lake Superior shore weren't immune to the influence of trade and industry that shaped the rest of the Upper Peninsula. Indeed, its history is remarkably similar, even if it is a little tamer. French missionaries—including the city namesake, Jacques

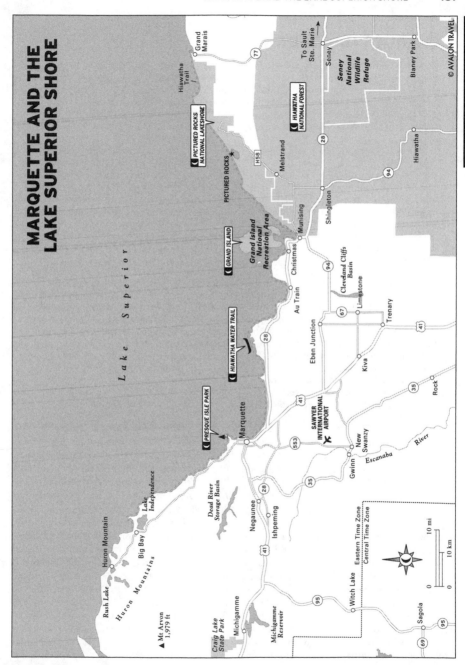

MARQUETTE AND THE LAKE SUPERIOR SHORE

© AVALON TRAVEL

Lake Superior

Grand Marais

Hiawatha Trail

To Sault Ste. Marie

77

Seney National Wildlife Refuge

Blaney Park

PICTURED ROCKS NATIONAL LAKESHORE

HIAWATHA NATIONAL FOREST

H58

Melstrand

PICTURED ROCKS

28

94

Hiawatha

Munising

Shingleton

Christmas

GRAND ISLAND

Grand Island National Recreation Area

Au Train

94

Cleveland Cliffs Basin

Limestone

Trenary

HIAWATHA WATER TRAIL

67

41

28

Eben Junction

Kiva

35

Rock

PRESQUE ISLE PARK

Marquette

41

SAWYER INTERNATIONAL AIRPORT

553

New Swanzy

Escanaba River

Lake Independence

Huron Mountain

Big Bay

35

Gwinn

Rush Lake

Huron Mountains

Dead River Storage Basin

Negaunee

28

Ishpeming

41

95

Witch Lake

Eastern Time Zone
Central Time Zone

▲ Mt Arvon 1,979 ft

Craig Lake State Park

Michigamme

Michigamme Reservoir

95

Sagola

69

0   10 mi
0   10 km

JACQUES MARQUETTE

A Roman Catholic missionary and explorer from France, Jacques Marquette (1637–1675) established a mission among the Ottawa at St. Ignace. He, along with Louis Jolliet, was probably the first European to explore much of the Great Lakes region and the Upper Mississippi.

Born in Laon, France, Marquette joined the Jesuit order in 1656 and spent the next 10 years studying and teaching in France. In 1666, Jesuit priests sent him to New France (present-day Quebec) as a missionary. Like many Jesuits, he lived among the Native Americans and studied their languages. In 1671, he was appointed missionary to the Ottawa tribe, and he established the St. Ignace mission on the north shore of the Straits of Mackinac.

In 1672, French explorer Louis Jolliet arrived at the mission, sent by the governor of New France, Comte de Frontenac, to search for a trade route to the Far East. They had heard from the Native Americans about a great waterway, Missi Sipi ("Big River"), which they thought might flow into the Pacific Ocean. Marquette, with his knowledge of tribal languages, was to accompany Jolliet.

Marquette, Jolliet, and five other Frenchmen set out in canoes across the northern shore of Lake Michigan in May 1673. They traveled down Green Bay and up the Fox River in present-day Wisconsin, where local Native Americans led them to a portage to the Wisconsin River. The team followed the Wisconsin to its confluence with the Mississippi and explored the Mississippi all the way to the Arkansas River. They grew alarmed by both the swiftness of the water and word from the Native Americans about white men downstream. Fearing they would be attacked by Spaniards and deducing that the southerly flow of the river would not lead to the Pacific, the explorers turned back. They paddled the Illinois River to the Chicago River, then followed the western shore of Lake Michigan to Green Bay – a staggering journey of more than 2,900 miles. Along the way, they peaceably traded with dozens of Native American tribes.

An ailing Marquette spent the winter at a mission in Wisconsin, returning to Illinois the following spring to work with the Native Americans he had met along his voyage. In 1675, he died on Lake Michigan, near present-day Ludington, Michigan, en route back to Sault Ste. Marie. Marquette and Jolliet's exploration added greatly to the Europeans' knowledge of North American geography. The Native Americans who treated them so well would later suffer when that new knowledge spurred increasing European settlement.

Marquette—explored the area in the mid-1600s; trappers arrived several decades later, and in the mid-1800s the mines opened up. But it took more than mining to put the city on the map; a combination of industries gave Marquette its prosperity. Iron ore mining, shipping, and wealthy vacationers conspired to make Marquette prosperous by taking advantage of the region's natural resources.

Not all of the Lake Superior shore was exploited, however. The Huron Mountains were largely saved. The preservation wasn't the result of happy accident; beginning around the 1880s, the Huron Mountains became the wilderness retreat of choice for several millionaire industrialists. Cyrus McCormick, head of the lucrative farm implement company that would become International Harvester, amassed a huge wilderness estate around White Deer Lake, now part of the Ottawa National Forest's McCormick Tract Wilderness Area. Frederick Miller of Miller Brewing owned his piece of wilderness at Craig Lake, now a wilderness state park. Dozens of others owned "camps" at the Huron Mountain Club, an organization so exclusive that even Henry Ford was turned down for membership when he first applied. The members easily had enough clout to stop construction of a road that was to link L'Anse with Big Bay—County Road 550 abruptly ends west of Big Bay at a gate and security guardhouse.

Today, the 25,000-acre enclave is shared mostly by the descendants of those original members, who quietly protect and preserve this spectacular landholding. Though locals grumble about the lack of access to the property, no one can argue that the Huron Mountain Club has proved to be an exceptional steward of the land. It kept away the loggers, the miners, and the developers, leaving what some consider the most magnificent wilderness remaining in the state, maybe even all of the Midwest.

The Pictured Rocks National Lakeshore joined the Huron Mountains as an exceptional specimen of nature in 1966, after areas of the Great Lakes shore were scouted for inclusion in the national park system. The 43 miles of scenic shoreline between Munising and Grand Marais became the first national lakeshore in the United States.

Marquette and Vicinity

With just over 20,000 hardy year-round souls, Marquette ranks as the largest city in the Upper Peninsula. Tucked in a well-protected natural harbor almost exactly midway across the U.P.'s northern shore, it grew and thrives largely because of its location—an important Lake Superior port for the iron industry, and a rather central location that has helped it evolve into the U.P.'s center of commerce and government.

Don't be dissuaded by the strip mall blight along U.S. 41. Head toward the water, where you'll discover a thriving downtown rich in architecture, a U.S. Olympic Training Center, Northern Michigan University (home to 9,000 students), and a beautiful setting along the high, rocky Lake Superior shoreline. Marquette has never really billed itself much as a tourist destination, but it's actually a terrific spot to unpack your bags: lodging and good restaurants are plentiful, the downtown and lakefront are ideal for strolling, and the U.P.'s blue-ribbon attractions—rugged hills, waterfalls, wildlife, wild rivers—await you barely outside the city limits.

SIGHTS
Downtown Marquette
Third Street, running north-south, and Washington Street, running east-west, represent Marquette's main cross streets, and where they meet is a good area to begin an exploration of the downtown. This puts you in the heart of the shopping and historic district. Buildings like the 1902 Marquette County Courthouse,

at 3rd and Baraga Avenue, and the 1927 MFC First National Bank, at 101 West Washington Street, showcase the city's affinity for **Beaux Arts architecture.** Step inside the courthouse for a better look, and also to check out a display about Michigan Supreme Court Justice and author John Voelker. Better known by his pen name, Robert Traver, the Ishpeming native wrote *Anatomy of a Murder,* among other works. Scenes from the popular 1959 movie starring Jimmy Stewart were filmed here, as well as in nearby Big Bay, where the actual murder occurred. The **Marquette County Historical Society** (213 North Front St., 906/226-3571, www.marquettecohistory.org, 10 A.M.–5 P.M. Mon.–Fri., open until 9 P.M. on the third Thurs. of the month) offers a walking tour brochure.

Downtown Marquette is home to distinctive shops worth a little browsing time. **Bookworld** (136 West Washington St., 906/228-9490) and **Snowbound Books** (118 North 3rd, 906/228-4448) offer a good selection of local and regional titles. Follow Main down to the waterfront, where **Thill's Fish House** (250 East Main St., 906/226-9851) sells fresh catch and smoked whitefish spread from a little shop at the marina, in the shadow of the old wooden ore dock.

The U.P.'s Scandinavian heritage looms large in Marquette. **Scandinavian Gifts** (1025 North 3rd St., 906/225-1993) showcases the sleek and simple lines of classic Scandinavian design in its selection of glassware and silver (lots of Norwegian sweaters, too). Back on the

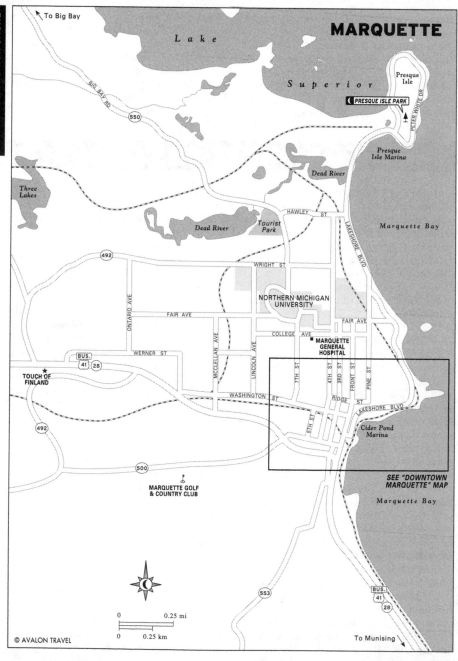

MARQUETTE

To Big Bay

Lake

Superior

Presque Isle

PRESQUE ISLE PARK

PETER WHITE DR

BIG BAY RD

550

Presque Isle Marina

Dead River

Three Lakes

Dead River

Tourist Park

Marquette Bay

HAWLEY ST

LAKESHORE BLVD

WRIGHT ST

492

NORTHERN MICHIGAN UNIVERSITY

FAIR AVE

FAIR AVE

ONTARIO AVE

COLLEGE AVE

MARQUETTE GENERAL HOSPITAL

MCCLELLAN AVE

LINCOLN AVE

WERNER ST

7TH ST

4TH ST

3RD ST

FRONT ST

PINE ST

BUS. 41 28

★ TOUCH OF FINLAND

WASHINGTON ST

RIDGE ST

5TH ST

LAKESHORE BLVD

492

Cider Pond Marina

SEE "DOWNTOWN MARQUETTE" MAP

500

⛳ MARQUETTE GOLF & COUNTRY CLUB

Marquette Bay

553

BUS. 41 28

0   0.25 mi

0   0.25 km

To Munising

© AVALON TRAVEL

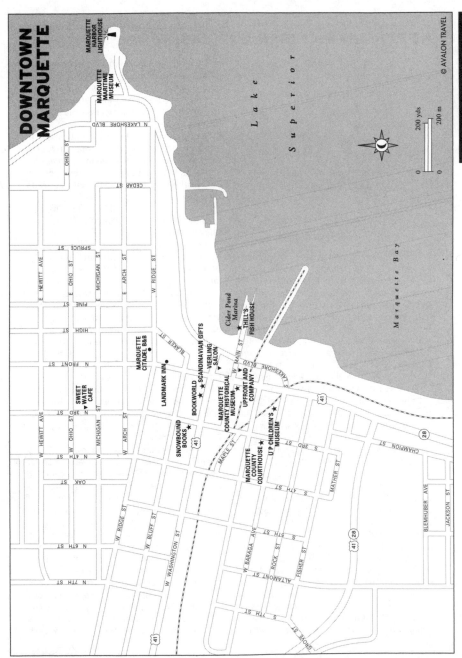

DOWNTOWN MARQUETTE

MARQUETTE HARBOR LIGHTHOUSE

MARQUETTE MARITIME MUSEUM ★

Lake Superior

© AVALON TRAVEL

200 yds

200 m

0

0

Marquette Bay

N LAKESHORE BLVD

E OHIO ST

CEDAR ST

SPRUCE ST

E HEWITT AVE

E OHIO ST

E MICHIGAN ST

E ARCH ST

W RIDGE ST

PINE ST

HIGH ST

N FRONT ST

BLAKER ST

Cider Pond Marina

THILL'S FISH HOUSE

VIERLING SALON ▼

SCANDINAVIAN GIFTS ★

MAIN ST

MARQUETTE CITADEL B&B ●

LANDMARK INN ★

BOOKWORLD ★

MARQUETTE COUNTY HISTORICAL MUSEUM ★

UPFRONT AND COMPANY ★

S LAKESHORE BLVD

SWEET WATER CAFE ▼

N 3RD ST

W HEWITT AVE

W OHIO ST

W MICHIGAN ST

W ARCH ST

SNOWBOUND BOOKS ★

41

MAPLE ST

U.P. CHILDREN'S MUSEUM ★

41

S 3RD ST

MARQUETTE COUNTY COURTHOUSE ★

MATHER ST

28

W 4TH ST

N 4TH ST

OAK ST

W RIDGE ST

W BLUFF ST

W WASHINGTON ST

W BARAGA AVE

ROCK ST

S 4TH ST

FISHER ST

S 5TH ST

ALTAMONT ST

41 28

CHAMPION ST

BLEMHUBER AVE

JACKSON ST

N 6TH ST

N 7TH ST

W 7TH ST

W 6TH ST

S 7TH ST

SHORE ST

41

NORTHERN MICHIGAN UNIVERSITY

*Hail Northern, we thy sons
and daughters*

Now bring thee tribute long deserved

*Thou beacon light –mid
nature's grandeur*

*Through passing decades
well-preserved*

Oh, may we labor with untiring zeal

*That when these golden days
have flown*

We may with honor face the future

And match thy courage with our own.

Students at Northern Michigan University are a rare breed. Not everyone can handle spending their winters in Marquette, on the frozen shores of Lake Superior, where the average temperature drops into the low 10s each January and where, in 1996, the lowest recorded temperature was a shockingly frigid -24°F. It's a place where class is more often cancelled for cold than for snowfall – snowplows and hardy Northerners can handle a little snow, but there's only so much you can do when the weather is cold enough to freeze your eyeballs in your head. And it's not as if Michigan doesn't have any other options – two Big Ten schools, the University of Michigan and Michigan State University, are located in the warmer climate of the Lower Peninsula. No, these students are here, for the most part, because they like it here.

Founded in 1899, NMU is the largest university in Michigan's Upper Peninsula; what started more than 100 years ago with 32 students has grown to an enrollment of slightly more than 9,000 students, quite small compared to some other schools (U of M has 41,000 students and MSU has 46,000). The school offers a fairly traditional liberal arts education with 180 academic majors and 120 academic minors in such subjects as business, technology, education, and sociology. Northern Michigan takes pride in its technology program, which embraces the vision of providing a "learning environment that embraces technology to enhance student access, promote the development of independent learners, and encourage greater student-faculty communication and collaboration." It was this vision that led the school to become the first state university in Michigan to become a laptop campus, providing each of its students with a laptop computer and a standard set of software tools for use during the school year. Students upgrade their computers every two years.

NMU's campus consists of more than 50 facilities located just minutes off the Lake Superior shoreline. The most interesting of these – perhaps the *only* architecturally interesting building – is the Superior Dome, which has the distinction of being the world's largest wooden dome. It really is a sight to see. The dome is 14 stories high, has a diameter of 563 feet, and contains more than five acres, impressively built from Douglas fir (a natural choice considering its location). Containing 781 beams and more than 100 *miles* of fir decking, the dome can withstand up to 60 pounds of snow per square foot. Inside, retractable artificial turf (also the largest of its kind in the world) can host football, soccer, and field hockey, while beneath the turf, when retracted, holds three basketball or volleyball courts, two tennis courts, and a 200-meter track.

But the real action takes place at the Berry Events Center. An Olympic-sized ice sheet (200 by 100 feet) is where the real sporting action takes place. It's no surprise that ice hockey is the sport of choice here, where the long winters and proximity to Canada make the sport popular. While NMU competes in NCAA Division II for most sports – basketball, football, and the like – hockey is a Division I sport, and it is an experience that shouldn't be missed if you're in town for a game.

There are other reasons to visit NMU's campus, too. Check out the theatrical productions staged several times during the year by the school's drama department, or visit the DeVos Art Museum for some of the region's best art.

highway, **Touch of Finland** (2853 U.S. 41, 906/226-2567, www.touchoffinland.com), on U.S. 41 across from Kmart, has a little bit of everything in its 4,000 square feet, including housewares, textiles, and a complete sauna department.

The old red brick waterworks building now houses the **Marquette Maritime Museum** (300 Lakeshore Blvd., 906/226-2006, http:// mqtmaritimemuseum.com, 10 A.M.–5 P.M. daily May 25–Oct. 31, $7 adults, $5 children under 13). This worthwhile stop includes exhibits on everything from Native American birchbark canoes to Great Lakes shipwrecks, lighthouses, an interactive display of a freighter's pilot house, and a working submarine periscope. The **Marquette County Historical Museum** (213 Front St., 906/226-3571, www .marquettecohistory.org, Mon.–Fri. year-round, $3 adults, $1 children over 12) features excellent Native American exhibits, as well as lots of mining and logging photographs and a large collection of old maps. There's a good bookstore, too. If you've got kids in tow, head for the **U.P. Children's Museum** (123 West Baraga Ave., 906/226-3911, www .upcmkids.org, 10 A.M.–6 P.M. Mon.–Wed., 10 A.M.–7:30 P.M. Thurs., 10 A.M.–8 P.M. Fri., 10 A.M.–6 P.M. Fri., noon–5 P.M. Sun., $4 adults, $0.50 children), where they can climb into a tree habitat to learn about its root system, crawl into a replica wasp nest, or explore life in the aquifer under a pond.

Where would you expect to find the world's largest wooden dome? In the heart of logging country, of course, and along Lake Superior, where changing weather regularly foils outdoor sporting events. In 1991, Northern Michigan University completed the 8,000-seat **Superior Dome** (1401 Presque Isle Ave., 906/227-2850), affectionately known as the "Yooper Dome." Enclosing some five acres, the dome is fashioned from a framework of 781 huge fir beams, strong enough to withstand substantial snows. Along with hosting a variety of school sporting events and practices, the dome is open to the public for walking and running on weekday mornings. Call or stop by for specific times.

Presque Isle Park

A thumb of land thrust out into the big lake, Presque Isle Park, about four miles north of downtown, off Lakeshore Boulevard, is a microcosm of the area's beauty: rocky red bluffs, tall pines, and lovely Lake Superior vistas. You can drive through the 323-acre park, but you'd do better to get out and stroll or ski along its many trails. Watch for albino deer (white-tailed deer lacking pigment), which survive in this protected setting. Near the park's entrance, there's a playground, a picnic area, tennis courts, and a marina, and a good spot from which to watch the huge 800-foot freighters arrive at the towering **railroad ore dock.** Trains carrying taconite pellets (an iron/clay mixture) from one of the nearby open-pit iron mines chug out onto the 70-foot-high elevated track, where they empty their loads into the hold below. Chutes transfer the taconite into the bellies of the ore freighters, which transport the shipment to the industrial centers in the southern Great Lakes.

DeVos Art Museum

Although it had its beginnings in the 1975 Lee Hall Gallery, the DeVos Art Museum (1401 Presque Isle Ave., http://art.nmu.edu/ department/museum, 10 A.M.–5 P.M. Mon.– Fri.), part of Northern Michigan University's School of Art and Design, got a facelift with its 2005 reopening, complete with a new building, a grant from the DeVos Foundation of Grand Rapids, Michigan, and a much larger contemporary space. The museum's permanent collection (which represents work from numerous well-known artists, including Salvador Dalí) is displayed on a revolving basis, while other areas of the museum host temporary exhibits. You'll also enjoy the sculpture walk, where an accessible pathway moseys through one of the university's wooded areas.

Lighthouses

The **Marquette Harbor Lighthouse** is one of Lake Superior's most attractive lighthouses. The light—and some of the land surrounding it—was recently acquired by the Marquette

THE LAKE SUPERIOR SHORE

© JOSH BISHOP

The wilderness is only minutes away from downtown Marquette at Presque Isle Park.

Maritime Museum under a lease from the Coast Guard. The lease will expire in 2032, so there's plenty of time to make it to the beautiful red light for a tour (as part of the lease agreement, all tours must be escorted by a member of the museum staff). Built in 1866 and expanded in 1906, the Marquette Harbor Lighthouse serves as an interpretive display and an extension of the museum.

To see another, slightly less scenic lighthouse (and one that's still working, day in and day out), head to Presque Isle Park for a look at the **Presque Isle Upper Harbor Lighthouse.** The light is still guiding ships into the railroad ore docks nearby. Stannard Rock Lighthouse is a little harder to get to, since it's located in Lake Superior, about 50 miles from Marquette's shoreline. Ask around for charters to the light—try **Uncle Ducky Charters** (434 East Prospect St., 877/228-5447, www.uncleducky.com) in Marquette or Shelter Bay Charters (E3394 Old M-28, 906/892-8230, www.shelterbaycharters.com) in Au Train. Similarly, **Granite Island Lighthouse** is located offshore, but only six miles or so. It's a little more than 10 miles northeast of Marquette.

Ishpeming and Negaunee

In many ways, these twin towns 15 miles west of Marquette represent the heart of the iron range. One of the Upper Peninsula's earliest iron mines, the Jackson Mine, opened here in 1847; the nearby Empire and Tilden Mines mark the end of the era, the last operating iron mines in the range.

Ishpeming and Negaunee pretty much faded right along with the glory days of mining. The economy never quite recovered from the closing of the area mines in the 1960s, and the once-vital downtowns were further displaced by the commercial strips along U.S. 41, which passes just north of town. But anyone who enjoys tidbits of history will find these towns intriguing, with their leftover ornate storefronts, ramshackle antique shops, and fenced-off "cave-in" areas—where the land once and for all has succumbed to its mining heritage.

One of the finest museums in the Upper Peninsula, the state-run **Iron Industry Museum** (73 Forge Rd., Negaunee, 906/475-7857, www.michigan.gov/hal, 9:30 A.M.–4:30 P.M. daily Apr. 28–Oct. 31) is well worth the short detour off U.S. 41 to its picturesque location along the Carp River. The spot wasn't chosen for its scenery; it marks the site of one of the area's earliest iron forges, built in 1848. This small facility packs a lot of information and well-done displays into a single exhibit hall. It tells the story of Michigan's $48 billion iron mining and smelting industry, which dwarfed the California Gold Rush ($955 million), Michigan's lucrative logging industry ($4.4 billion), and even Michigan's venerable copper mining empire ($9.6 billion). You'll learn how iron prompted the development of dozens of port towns and the giant 1,000-foot ore freighters that now ply the Great Lakes. The "Technology Timeline" traces the advancements in exploration, working conditions, and mining methods.

Few people think of Ishpeming as the center of the U.S. ski industry, but a lot of those big resorts in the Rockies can trace America's interest in the sport to Michigan. Michigan residents—many of them Scandinavian immigrants—established the Ishpeming Ski Club, one of the oldest continuously operating clubs in the nation, in 1887 and organized the country's first ski jumping competition in 1888. Everett Kircher, visionary founder of Michigan's Boyne Mountain resort, invented the first successful snowmaking machine. As a result, Ishpeming was chosen as the site of the **U.S. National Ski Hall of Fame and Ski Museum** (610 Palms Ave., 906/485-6323, www.skihall.com, 10 A.M.–5 P.M. Mon.–Sat. year-round, free), the sport's official hall of fame, just like the Football Hall of Fame in Canton, Ohio, and the Baseball Hall of Fame in Cooperstown, New York.

The museum, on U.S. 41 between 2nd and 3rd Streets, covers the sport from *way* back, beginning with a replica of a 4,000-year-old ski and pole found in Sweden. Most interesting are the displays of early ski equipment (including early poles, which "often doubled as weapons"), an examination of the evolution of chairlifts, and an account of the skiing soldiers of the 10th Mountain Division, who played an important role in the mountains of Italy during World War II. The Hall of Fame plaques offer insightful short biographies of those who shaped the sport, from racers to resort owners to, ahem, orthopedic surgeons.

Lovers of kitsch absolutely must stop at **Da Yoopers Tourist Trap** (906/485-5595, www .dayoopers.com, 9 A.M.–9 P.M. Mon.–Fri., 9 A.M.–8 P.M. Sat., 10 A.M.–7 P.M. Sun. year-round), a self-mocking gift shop on U.S. 41, just west of Ishpeming. (The world's largest chainsaw draws you in from the highway.) The singing group Da Yoopers from Ishpeming have earned a cult following with their U.P. parodies like "Smelting USA" and "The Second Week of Deer Camp." Some find their humor crude, but others love the inside jokes about beer, bullet-ridden highway signs, and ice fishing and the jabs at the Lower Peninsula. The shop features a goofy array of paraphernalia like beer gut T-shirts and silly bumper stickers, but also surprises with some neat historic photo prints and local crafts and folk art.

ENTERTAINMENT

If you're looking for Marquette gaming, look no further than the **Ojibwa Casino** (105 Acre Trail, 888/560-9905, 906/249-4200, www.ojibwa casino.com) in Marquette. Table games include blackjack, roulette, craps, and poker, while more than 300 reel video and video poker machines play from one cent to $5. There are seven sites available at the Ojibwa Casino RV Park and free shuttle service to and from a number of chain hotels in the area (think Days Inn, Ramada, and Super 8). The Snack Bar serves up all sorts of food right on the casino floor, from soup, pizza, and burgers to shrimp and fish dinners—be sure to check with the casino for Snack Bar specials.

FESTIVALS AND EVENTS

The **U.P. 200** (www.up200.org) is a sled-dog race held in mid-February that begins and ends in Marquette and loops all the way down to Escanaba on the Lake Michigan shore. An estimated 30,000 people watch the annual race, which has quickly grown into one of the U.P.'s most beloved spectator events. The start and finish are the big draws, but the race has prompted a weeklong calendar of activities, from broomball tournaments (hockey with boots instead of skates, balls instead of pucks, and brooms instead of sticks) to fireworks. For information and upcoming dates, visit www .up200.org, or contact the Marquette Country Convention and Visitors Bureau (337 West Washington St., 906/228-7749, 800/544-4321, www.marquettecountry.org).

Summertime brings the **Hiawatha Traditional Music Festival** during the second-to-last full weekend each July. Featuring traditional music such as bluegrass, acoustic blues, folk, old-time, and more, the Hiawatha is the only festival of its type and size in da U.P. Contact the Hiawatha Music Co-op (906/226-8575, www.hiawathamusic.org) for tickets and more information. June brings music of a different type to the Marquette area as part of the **Pine Mountain Music Festival** (906/482-1542, www.pmmf.org), a celebration of opera, symphony, and chamber music that takes place in locations around the Upper Peninsula.

Head to Presque Isle Park for the annual **Art on the Rocks** festival, featuring a juried exhibition and sales. Check out the **International Food Festival,** too. For information and dates for these and other events, contact the Marquette Country Convention and Visitors Bureau (337 West Washington St., 906/228-7749, 800/544-4321, www.marquette country.org).

SUMMER SPORTS AND RECREATION
Hiking and Biking
As County Road 550 heads north out of Marquette toward Big Bay, you'll travel just six miles before the sign and parking area before **Sugar Loaf Mountain** lures you to pull over. Heed your instincts; for a relatively easy 15-minute hike (a stairway makes for a gradual ascent up the rock), you'll be rewarded with a sweeping view of Lake Superior to the north, the city of Marquette to the east, and the rumpled-blanket landscape of the wild Huron

Mountains stretching all the way to the western horizon.

There's great hiking and mountain biking in the surrounding terrain, much of it part of the **Little Presque Isle State Forest Recreation Area.** Several miles of trails wind around nearby Harlow Lake, up Hogsback Mountain, and along the Lake Superior shore. Park in the unmarked lot on the west side of County Road 550, near an old gravel pit, about a mile north of the Sugar Loaf Mountain lot. The South Marquette Trails are part of the Noquemanon Trail Network (906/228-6182, www.noquet rails.org) and provide miles of hiking and biking. The Mount Marquette Loop is a five-mile trail, while the Carp River and Pioneer loops have a combined total of nine miles. The Noquemanon Trail Network was ranked among *Bike* magazine's top 10 trails in 2005.

First, though, pick up the free *Marquette Region Hike and Bike Trail Guide* from the Marquette Country Convention and Visitors Bureau (337 West Washington St., 906/228-7749, 800/544-4321, www.marquettecountry .org) or local shops.

The entire Ishpeming/Negaunee area is part of the comprehensive **Range Mountain Bike Trail System,** with more than 25 miles of trails stretching from Teal Lake to Lake Sally, south of Suicide Bowl. Routes are covered in the *Marquette Region Hike and Bike Trail Guide.*

🄲 Hiawatha Water Trail
One of Lake Superior's greatest kayaking destinations, the Hiawatha Water Trail (www.hiawatha watertrail.org) passes along the shores of Marquette on the way from Big Bay to Grand Marais, 120 miles in all. The most beautiful portion of the trail lies to the east, along Pictured Rocks National Lakeshore between Munising and Grand Marais, but it'll take some hard paddling to get there. Access points and campgrounds are available along the way; get ahold of the official Hiawatha Water Trail Map at **Down Wind Sports** (514 North 3rd St., 906/226-7112, www.downwindsports.com).

Presque Isle is one of Marquette's most

© JOSH BISHOP

Unlike Lake Michigan and Huron, the Lake Superior shoreline is dominated by rough, wild scenery.

beautiful destinations, and the sorry visitors who only manage to see it from land are missing out. This is *the* kayak trip to take. The jagged shoreline—more than two miles of it—is dotted with rugged crags, towering sandstone cliffs, rocks, and an undeveloped shore. Put in and take out at the Presque Isle Marina. For guided tours, contact **Uncle Ducky Outfitters** (434 East Prospect St., 906/228-5447, 877/228-5447, www.paddlingmichigan.com, $85 per person, $65 ages 16 and under). Uncle Ducky also offers guided tours of Marquette harbors, Presque Isle to Little Presque Isle, Huron Island, and Big Bay.

Golf

Marquette holds a few surprises for visitors searching out a round of golf. Try a visit to the new Greywalls course at the **Marquette Golf Club** (1075 Grove St., 866/678-7171, www.marquettegolfclub.com, $125 guest from June 1–Sept. 30, discounted rates spring and fall, fees include cart). Greywalls opened in 2005 to wide acclaim, earning it high marks in *Golf*

Digest and other golf magazines. The course's 18 holes are complemented by Marquette's natural terrain, featuring views of Lake Superior, rocky crags, and evergreen forests. Another 18 holes at the Heritage Course make the semi-private Marquette Golf Club the only 36-hole club in the Upper Peninsula. Of course, golfers will want to try the **Chocolay Golf Club** (125 Chocolay Downs Dr., 906/249-3111, www.chocolaydownsgolfcourse.com, $37 with cart), where the 18-hole public course features the world's longest golf hole—a stunning 1,007-yard par 6.

Beaches

Lake Superior isn't exactly made for swimming; it's cold, the shoreline too often rocky, and the water too deep. Even if you find a few Lake Superior beaches (and in Marquette you can), not many people actually want to dive in. That said, you're more than welcome to go for a dip if you're willing to put up with the goose pimples. Besides, there's more to do at beaches than swim: grill, sunbathe, play a game of volleyball, toss a Frisbee, or whatnot. South Beach, just off Lake Street in Marquette, and McCarty's Cove, on Lakeshore Drive, are two of the city's most popular beaches, and with reason. Both are equipped with playground equipment and restrooms, and each offers pleasing views and sandy beaches perfect for an afternoon by the lake.

Off-Road Vehicles

For an off-road trail that's part of the state system, head south toward Gwinn. About five miles west of Gwinn, the Bass Lake Motorcycle Trail is open to vehicles less than 50 inches wide. The long loop, just under 25 miles, circles several lakes, including Bass, Crooked, Spring, and Pike. Take M-35 to Crooked Lake Road and head southwest to parking, which is near Pike Lake Campground and Bass Lake Campground. The Porterfield Lake Motorcycle Trail is on the border of Marquette and Dickinson Counties, where more than 20 miles of trail are split into several loops. Porterfield Lake Trail is eight miles southwest of Gwinn. Additionally, ORVs are allowed on all trails and forest roads on state land. Contact the **Department of Natural Resources** (DNR, www.michigan.gov/dnr) for more information.

Waterfalls

Among the most scenic of the Marquette region's waterfalls is Warner Falls, a 20-foot drop into the relatively still waters of the Warner Creek (it seems to be more of a pond at this point). Warner Falls is pretty easy to get to, too: about eight miles west of Marquette, take M-35 south past Palmer and pull off less than a mile past the M-35/County Road 565 intersection. The falls are on the right and can easily be seen from the road. The Dead River Falls, just west of Marquette, are pretty but difficult to find and even harder to get to. Take U.S. 41 west of town to Wright Street and head north. Turn left at Forestville Road and drive to a powerhouse about 2.5 miles up, park, and take the gravel road to a clear trail on your left. Follow it down a steep hill, then turn right;

stay on the path until you reach the falls. For a map of additional falls in the area and detailed instructions on how to get to them, contact the Marquette Country Convention and Visitors Bureau (337 West Washington St., 906/228-7749, 800/544-4321, www.marquette country.org).

WINTER SPORTS AND RECREATION

Downhill Skiing

Among skiers and snowboarders, **Marquette Mountain** (4501 County Road 553, 906/225-1155, www.marquettemountain.com, lift rates $17–40) gets the thumbs-up for its 600-foot vertical drop, one of the highest in the state. The 23 trails may not be exceptionally long, but they offer good variety—including bumps and tree runs—and the half-pipe and terrain park grow and improve every year. Located just three miles south of town on County Road 553, it's popular all week long among local residents and college students. Night skiing is offered Tuesday through Sunday in season, which usually runs from about mid-November to early April. Rental equipment is available.

You'd hardly guess that the 300-acre **Al Quaal Recreation Area** (501 Poplar St., 906/486-8301), on the north shore of Ishpeming's Teal Lake, is a city park. To get there, take Deer Lake Road north from U.S. 41. You can make a winter day of it, with a few downhill runs served by a rope tow, a 1.9 mile cross-country loop, an outdoor ice rink, and especially the 1,200-foot iced toboggan run where a small hourly fee includes a rental toboggan. The park is open daily, except for the downhill runs, which are open on weekend afternoons only. Call for specific fees and hours.

Ski and Snowshoe Trails

For Nordic skiing, continue heading south on County Road 553 to the **Blueberry Ridge Ski Trails.** Fifteen miles of groomed and tracked trails loop through the Escanaba River State Forest, including one lighted 1.7-mile circuit (free). Another option is the **Anderson Lake Pathway,** five miles south of Gwinn on County

Road 557, with four hilly loops ranging from 2 to 4.3 miles in length. Both networks are open to mountain bikes in summer months.

Nordic skiers looking for a challenge should head for the ominous-sounding **Suicide Bowl** trail network between Ishpeming and Negaunee. Groomed for skating and diagonal stride, it offers more than 18 miles of trails and a map dotted with phrases like "hairpin curve," "bad downhill," and "very difficult trail." The parking area is south of Business M-28 (follow it past downtown Ishpeming) on Cliff Drive. This area is also the site of **Suicide Hill,** a ski jump used in international competitions.

Luge
Ski jumping not wild enough? How about luge? Just south of Negaunee on M-35, **Lucy Hill** meets International Luge Federation standards as an official luge track, dropping 300 feet with 29 turns. It's open to the public most weekend afternoons, with instruction and equipment available. For information, call 906/475-5843.

Dogsledding
If you arrive in winter, try your hand at mushing. **Triple Creek Sled Dog Kennels** (E5372 M-94, 877/275-7533) offers trips ranging from two hours to five days, powered by a team of eager huskies. Owner Bob Johnson was instrumental in bringing dogsled racing to the Upper Peninsula and is one of the most experienced mushers around. Package tours include a stay at Johnson's Buck Sporting Lodge, a solar-powered wilderness lodge north of Rapid River.

Snowmobiling
Marquette County has more land than any other county in Michigan, which means it has a lot of snowmobile trails, too. The main trail in and out of Marquette is Trail 8, pressing west toward Baraga along U.S. 41/M-28 and south to Gwinn. To get to Au Train or Munising, take Trail 417, which more or less follows M-28 east before dipping south a bit and rejoining with 8. If you're heading up to

Big Bay, take Trail 310 out of town. For a detailed snowmobile trail map, get ahold of the Marquette Country Convention and Visitors Bureau (337 West Washington St., 906/228-7749, 800/544-4321, www.marquettecountry .org). Additionally, snowmobiles are allowed to travel with the flow of traffic on the right-hand side of all plowed roads in Marquette County—provided that they stay single-file and travel at a reasonable speed. For safety (yours and others') be careful, stop at intersections, and keep your eyes peeled for traffic. All snowmobiles are required to be registered and have a state trail permit, available through the DNR (www.michigan.gov/dnr) and at snowmobile shops throughout the state.

ACCOMMODATIONS
The best spot in Marquette is easily the ◖ **Landmark Inn** (230 North Front St., 888/752-6362, www.thelandmarkinn .com, $100–200). Built in the 1930s as the Northland Hotel, it hosted such luminaries as Amelia Earhart and Abbott and Costello. After falling into disrepair and eventually closing in the 1980s, it has been beautifully remodeled and reopened as the Landmark. For not much more than you'd pay for a basic franchise motel room, you get a taste of history, a touch of elegance, and a primo location: Lake Superior on one side, downtown Marquette on the other. For another elegant lodging option, try the **Marquette Citadel Bed and Breakfast** (124 East Ridge St., 906/225-6760, www.marquettecitadel.com), which was the gathering place of the First Church of Christ, Scientist, until 2004. The building was constructed in 1926, and it retains an elegant Greek Revival exterior today. Inside, the suites are well appointed, the ballroom stunning, and the stays comfortable.

For a pet-friendly spot overlooking Lake Superior and rooms with mini-kitchens (some with balconies), try the **Birchmont Motel** (2090 U.S. 41, 906/228-7494, www.birchmont motel.com, $40–75, $110 suites). The **Nordic Bay Lodge** (1880 U.S. 41, 906/226-7516, $50–75) offers tidy Austrian-style buildings on spacious, landscaped grounds overlooking Lake Superior. Small pets are permitted. South of Marquette, check into **Blueberry Ridge Bed and Breakfast** (18 Oakridge Dr., 906/249-9246, http://members.aol.com/blueberr18/) for a quiet stay in the northwoods. Many of the major hotel and motel franchises are represented in Marquette, especially along the U.S. 41/M-28 strip.

Camping

Okay, so you can't pitch a tent at the **Little Presque Isle State Forest and Campgrounds** (906/228-6561, www.michigan.gov/dnr, $65), but the rustic cabins—no electricity, no running water, no roads all the way in—make for great camping and they're available year-round. A half-mile hike from the parking area will get you to your cabin, and once you're there, it's all hand-pumped water, wood-burning stoves, and those "toilets" that you see at the state's roadside parks. There are 18 miles of hiking trails here, along with miles of Lake Superior beach, fishing, and other recreational opportunities. Cabins sleep up to six people, and reservations are required.

More traditional camping (either in a tent or at an RV site) can be had at **Marquette Tourist Park** (2145 Sugarloaf Rd., 906/228-0465, www.mqtcty.org/parks.html). The 40-acre in-town park has 10 rustic or tent-only campsites and 15 sites with full hookups. The rest of the more than 100 sites are electric only. You'll find fire rings, picnic tables, bathrooms, and hot showers, as well as a ball field and a playground. There are another 100 or so campsites at **Gitchee Gumee RV Park** (2048 M-28 East, 866/447-8727, www.gg-rv.com), which also features such amenities as more than 70 cable channels, a movie theater, and a fudge factory.

There are four state forest campgrounds in nearby Gwinn: Anderson Lake West (19 sites), Bass Lake (22 sites), North Horseshoe Lake (11 sites), and Pike Lake (10 sites), each accommodating tents and a few small trailers. There are no reservations and a few rustic amenities, including vault toilets and drinking water from a hand pump. For more information, contact the Michigan DNR's Gwinn Field Office (410 West M-35, 906/346-9201, www.michigan.gov/dnr).

FOOD

For a city its size, Marquette has a very good selection of high-quality, locally owned restaurants. The ◖ **Vierling Saloon** (119 South Front St., 906/228-3533, http://thevierling.com, closed Sun.) stands out for its consistently good food, century-old decor, and interesting views of Marquette Harbor ore docks. (Ask for a table near the large windows in back.) The menu offers lot of variety, including vegetarian dishes and whitefish served five ways. Excellent breakfasts, soups, and sandwiches are available, too. Dinner entrées start at $9. A couple years ago, the owners added a microbrewery downstairs, featuring British-style ales and stouts.

One of Marquette's newer dining additions is ◖ **Upfront and Company** (102 East Main St., 906/228-5200, www.upfrontandcompany.com). Renovated with wood from the city's old ore dock, it's not only beautiful to look at, it features great wood-fired pizza. Frequent live music is turning Upfront into Marquette's most popular nightspot, too. For organic, natural food dishes, you can't do better than the **Sweet Water Cafe** (517 North 3rd St., 906/226-7009, www.marquettedining.addr.com/Sweet_Water.html, breakfast and lunch daily, dinner Wed.–Sat.). Locals give its tofu scramble and pancakes with whipped maple butter extra-high marks. There are good smoothies, too. Locals will also point you to the **Panini Grill** (1125 North 3rd St., 906/226-9000) for good sandwiches, wraps, and soups and to the no-frills **Border Grill** (180 South McClellan Ave., 906/228-5228) for yummy Tex-Mex with fresh salsa.

A bit farther afield, the aptly named **Northwoods Supper Club** (906/228-4343) offers exactly what its name implies: great supper-club fare (read: steaks and seafood, with a salad bar) in a rustic, woodsy log building. The prime rib and lake trout are particularly good. Entrées start at about $10. Follow U.S. 41 three miles west of Marquette and turn south on Northwoods Drive (watch for signs).

INFORMATION AND SERVICES

You'll be able to get tourism information from the friendly folks at the **Marquette Country Convention and Visitors Bureau** (337 West Washington St., 906/228-7749, 800/544-4321, www.marquettecountry.org).

In an emergency, dial 911. For local medical attention, you'll want to go to Marquette General Hospital (580 West College Ave., 906/228-9440, www.mgh.org), a high-quality hospital, emergency room, and trauma care center located in the neighborhood of Northern Michigan University.

Marquette has plenty of banks and ATMs, too, so you won't have to go too far for easy access to your accounts or your cash. Try Wells Fargo (2025 U.S. 41 West, 800/869-3557, www.wellsfargo.com), River Valley State Bank (1101 North 3rd St., 906/226-0300, www.rivervalleybank.com), or Northern Michigan Bank and Trust (1502 West Washington St., 906/228-7300, www.nmbank.com).

Important to note: Marquette and its surrounding areas are in the Eastern Time Zone.

GETTING THERE AND AROUND
Car

Getting to Marquette by car is pretty easy: just remember U.S. 41. If you're coming in from the south near Escanaba, take U.S. 41. From the west, take U.S. 41. From the east, you'll want to take either M-28 or U.S. 2 before hooking up with (you guessed it) U.S. 41. There are a few smaller roads coming in, of course—M-553 is one of them—but you'll want to take the highways. Oh, and U.S. 41 runs through Ishpeming and Negaunee a little west of Marquette. The three cities are beginning to blend into one long stretch of shops and services—it's not quite there yet, but give it another decade or so.

Air

If you're flying into town, head for Sawyer International Airport (MQT, 125 G Ave., Gwinn, 906/346-3308, www.sawyerairport.com), which offers regularly scheduled flights to and from Detroit, Chicago, Green Bay, Minneapolis, and Milwaukee. Service is offered by Mesaba Airlines (906/346-6471, www.mesaba.com), which operates as an affiliate of Northwest Airlines, and American Eagle (800/433-7300, www.aa.com), an affiliate of American Airlines. You'll likely want to rent a car, and Sawyer has rental services aplenty: try Alamo (800/462-5266, www.alamo.com), Avis (800/831-2847, www.avis.com), Budget (800/527-7000, www.budget.com), National (800/227-7368, www.nationalcar.com), or Thrifty (800/847-4389, www.thrifty.com). Bus service is provided into Marquette (or Gwinn, if you prefer) by Marq-Tran (906/225-1112, www.marq-tran.com).

Boat

Marquette has two marinas: the Cinder Pond Marina and Presque Isle Marina. **Cinder Pond Marina** (906/228-0469, www.michigan.gov/dnr) is located near Marquette's distinctive ore dock. There are 91 seasonal slips and 10 transient slips, as well as full amenities like electricity, showers, pump-out, gasoline, and day-use dockage. Cinder Pond Marina is open from early May through late October, can be reached on radio channel 71, and is located at 46° 31.56 N, 87° 22.26 W. The Ellwood Matson Lower Harbor Park stretches out to the west, a 22-acre open space with park benches, picnic tables, and a playground. The Presque Isle Marina (906/228-0464, www.michigan.gov/dnr) has 87 seasonal and 10 transient slips and is located (no surprises here) at Presque Isle Park. Like Cinder Pond Marina, there are plenty of amenities here. The marina is located at 46° 34.20 N, 87° 22.25 W. It's open from early May through late October and can be reached on channel 9.

Public Transportation

Bus service to Marquette is available through Indian Trails (989/725-5105, 800/292-3831, www.indiantrails.com), on a route that stretches from Chicago to Calumet, passing through Marquette (and Escanaba, Houghton, and Hancock) along the way. Contact Indian Trails for current schedules and rates.

The same public bus that shuttles visitors from Sawyer International Airport to Marquette scoots around the area with regular daily stops at a number of communities: Marquette, Negaunee, Ishpeming, and Gwinn.

Marq-Tran (906/225-1112, www.marq-tran.com) also offers door-to-door service for a small fee that increases with distance (though it won't jump over $5.60). Contact Marq-Tran for regular schedules and fees. For taxi service, call Taxi Tycoon (906/249-4428) or Checker Cab (906/226-7777).

Huron Mountains

Ask 10 people where the Huron Mountains begin and end, and you're likely to get 10 different answers. But everyone will agree that they fall within the fuzzy boundaries of Lake Superior to the north and east and U.S. 41 to the south and west. That's a swath of land some 50 miles wide by 25 miles long, where the terrain rises into rugged hills and, yes, even mountains. Mt. Arvon, about 15 miles due east of L'Anse, tops out at 1,979 feet, the highest point in the state.

Look at a map, and you'll see it's an intriguing parcel of land, virtually devoid of towns and roads. What the Huron Mountains do have, however, is washboard peaks and valleys, white pine forests, hundreds of lakes, the headwaters of a half dozen classic wilderness rivers, dazzling waterfalls, far more wildlife than people, and utter silence. Even by U.P. standards, it's a rugged, remarkable place. Within its boundaries lie towering virgin pines, blue-ribbon trout streams, pristine lakes, and waterfalls that don't even appear on maps. If the Huron Mountain Club should ever come up for sale, government officials admit (albeit off the record) that they would clamor to turn to it into a state or national park.

In the meantime, the rest of us have to be content simply knowing that such wonderful natural beauty is there, and lovingly protected. Besides, there's plenty of Huron Mountain wilderness open to the public—more than enough to go around for those who are fortunate and smart enough to explore this special place.

BIG BAY AREA
Many people approach the Huron Mountains from the east, where County Road 550 climbs 30 miles out of Marquette to the tiny town of **Big Bay,** population 260. Sited above Lake Independence and within minutes of Lake Superior, Big Bay is a scrappy little place, where residents take pride in their simple life on the fringes of wilderness. The town has swung from prosperity to near-ghost-town status more than once, first as a bustling logging outpost, then as one of Henry Ford's company towns, home to busy sawmills. More recently, residents joke about how the local bank, well aware of the town's volatile economy, was loath to loan money to Big Bay businesses; while the town's 20 businesses were thriving, the bank closed down. Folks now frequent Big Bay for its Huron Mountains access, Lake Superior harbor, Lake Independence fishing, and unique lodgings.

From Big Bay, your best bets for venturing into the backcountry are County Road 510, which branches off County Road 550 on the southeast edge of town (and continues south all the way to U.S. 41 west of Marquette), and the Triple A Truck Trail, which branches off of County Road 510. Both are usually well-maintained dirt/gravel roads, though wet or snowy weather can quickly render them impassable. Dozens of old logging roads and single-tracks branch off of these main routes. To find your way around, you'll want a topo map or a very good local map (sometimes called the "waterfall map") available free from the Marquette Country Convention and Visitors Bureau.

SIGHTS
Craig Lake State Park
Craig Lake is probably unlike any state park

you've ever visited. For starters, the entrance is nearly seven miles down a rugged truck trail that often requires four-wheel drive and is periodically "improved" with sharp old mining rock that can inflict lethal wounds on your tires. Once you arrive at the Craig Lake parking area, you access the 7,000-acre park on foot or, with a short portage, by canoe or kayak. No wheeled vehicles or boat motors are permitted anywhere within the park.

McCormick Wilderness

Once the private wilderness retreat of Cyrus McCormick, whose father invented the reaping machine, this 27-square-mile tract of wilderness was willed to the U.S. Forest Service by the McCormick family in 1967. Today it remains in pristine wilderness condition—remote, undeveloped, and largely unused. In other words, perfect for backcountry hiking and camping. No-trace camping is permitted throughout the wilderness area. For more information, contact the Ottawa National Forest Ranger District (4810 East M-28, Kenton, 906/852-3500, www.fs.fed.us).

To access the McCormick Tract, follow U.S. 41/M-28 west from Marquette about 50 miles to Champion. Just after you cross the Peshekee River, follow the first paved road north. This is County Road 607, also called the Peshekee Grade or the Huron Bay Grade. In about 10 miles, you'll see a sign for Arfelin Lake; take the next road to your right and watch for a sign and a small parking area.

Once you've arrived, you'll be pretty much on your own to explore this rugged terrain of high hills, rivers, muskeg, and bedrock outcroppings. Don't expect marked and maintained hiking trails. This tract is wild, so with the exception of a well-worn path to White Deer Lake (where the McCormicks' lodge once stood), you'll mostly be traveling cross-country. A compass and topo map are absolute necessities. Wildlife sightings can be excellent—the state's largest moose herd roams here, which in turn has attracted predators like the elusive gray wolf. You're not likely to see a wolf, but you may be treated to one's hollow wail at your camp some evening.

Moose

Van Riper State Park is perhaps best known for its Moose Information Center, a kiosk that tells the story of the U.P.'s successful **moose reintroduction program.** Though moose were once common in the U.P., hunting and disease devastated the herd in past decades. Two "moose lifts" in the 1980s transported 59 of the giant mammals from Algonquin Provincial Park in Ontario to the lightly traveled wilderness along the Peshekee Grade, near the McCormick Tract. It was quite a project: wildlife biologists captured each moose, then airlifted them one by one in a sling, dangling beneath a helicopter, to a base camp where they were trucked 600 miles to the Huron Mountains.

Today, the region's moose population has climbed to 200 or 300. You may see them anywhere in this region, but your chances are best at dawn or dusk, and in wet, swampy areas. The Marquette Country Convention and Visitors Bureau publishes a *Moose Locator Guide,* detailing six backroad tours through areas frequented by moose, including the Peshekee Grade and Wolf Lake Road, east of Champion. For more information, contact Van Riper State Park (906/339-4461, www.michigan.gov/dnr).

Mt. Arvon

It's a pretty tough drive to get to Michigan's highest peak, about 12 miles east of L'Anse—and it isn't really worth the trip if you're not particularly interested in these types of things. For one, it's hard to see the mountain from a distance; for two, you aren't rewarded with any views at all (unless you count the trunks and branches of the forest). The roads in are rough condition, too, and make the 27-mile journey too long for the casual tourist. For a map and directions, contact the Baraga County Convention and Visitors Bureau (755 East Broad St., L'Anse, 906/524-7444, 800/743-4908, www.baragacountytourism.org).

Lighthouses

The **Big Bay Point Lighthouse** is one good-looking light. Located on a cliff at Big Bay Point, the two-story brick building and attached 60-foot-high light have been converted into a charming bed-and-breakfast—good news for lighthouse fans interested in booking one of the rooms.

The 1868 **Huron Island Lighthouse,** located northwest of Big Bay and some three miles off the shore, is only accessible by private boat; the island, which is part of the Huron National Wildlife Refuge, is open to the public during the day. You can charter a sightseeing trip to the Huron Islands at Marquette's **Uncle Ducky Charters** (434 East Prospect St., 877/228-5447, www.uncleducky.com).

SUMMER SPORTS AND RECREATION
Hiking and Biking

Though it's situated right on busy U.S. 41, **Van Riper State Park** is worthy of mention for several reasons. For one, it offers a good, rarely full modern campground on the eastern shore of Lake Michigamme, where you'll find a boat launch, good walleye fishing, and a fine swimming beach with unusually warm water and a sand bottom. Two, many campers overlook the park property on the north side of the road, its largest and most appealing acreage. It includes a rustic campground on the Peshekee River and four miles of hiking trails. Climb the Overlook Trail, a loop that ascends a rocky outcrop, for a great view of the rolling forest land and Lake Michigamme. What's more, Van Riper is less than a dozen miles from the gated entrance of the McCormick Tract—so you can take advantage of modern comforts (hot showers!) while spending your days in the rugged backcountry that begins just across the highway.

Visitors that make their way into **Craig Lake State Park** will be rewarded with the seclusion and backcountry hiking of Michigan's most remote state park. If you're going to make the journey into the park, you should take a vehicle with a high ground clearance for the seven-mile trek off paved roads—especially after a rainfall, when it would be best to have four-wheel drive as well. The park has nearly 7,000 acres and two main trails that total more than 15 miles, half of which is part of the North Country Trail. Trails are rugged, often steep, and frequently blocked by streams or other obstacles. There are six full lakes, several smaller ponds, and plenty of wildlife, including black bears, moose, and the more-common deer. Backcountry practices should be followed; make sure you go in well prepared. Craig Lake State Park is located just north of U.S. 41/M-28 a few miles west of Michigamme. For more information, including backcountry preparation tips, maps, and directions, contact the Michigan DNR (906/339-4461, www.michigan.gov/dnr).

In the town of Big Bay itself, take the Big Bay Pathway, part of the Noquemanon Trail Network. Only one of the loops is good for hiking and biking—the four-mile, relatively flat Hidden Grin Loop. The other three loops, totaling nearly six miles, are more appropriate for cross-county skiing in the winter. Take County Road 550 into Big Bay, then turn left on Dump Road and take it less than a mile to the trailhead, which will be on your right.

The Commercial Forest Reserve Act gives property owners a tax break in exchange for allowing others access to their property, so trespassing isn't really an issue as you explore the Huron Mountains. As a result, you have nearly limitless possibilities for hiking and mountain biking on old logging roads and various foot trails. Two spots worth exploring are **Gobbler's Knob,** a rock outcrop off County Road 510 that overlooks Lake Independence and Lake Superior and the **Elliott Donnelley Wilderness Area,** off County Road 550, where a four-mile trail winds along the Little Garlic River and past Little Garlic Falls.

Keep in mind that the Huron Mountains can be a confusing place. You can drive yourself crazy heading down one dead-end logging road after another, or worse, get hopelessly lost on one of hundreds of unmapped, unmarked trails. Before you head off into the woods, make sure you're comfortable and competent with a map and compass. Otherwise, you're best off hooking up with a local guide who can show you around on foot, mountain bike, or snowshoe.

Canoeing and Kayaking

In addition to its backcountry hiking trails, much of **Craig Lake State Park** is accessible by nonmotorized watercraft. There's a quarter-mile portage from the parking lot to one of several boat landings on the lakes, though Crooked Lake is perhaps the most appealing, with lots of interesting bays and inlets. To reach it, paddle across the southeastern corner of Craig Lake and follow the half-mile portage east. Be aware that many of the lakes are large enough to cause problems during windy or stormy weather. You'll need a state park pass and a vehicle suitable for rough, unpaved roads. Contact the Michigan DNR (906/339-4461, www.michigan.gov/dnr) for more information.

Other large lakes in the area are suitable for canoeing or kayaking. Check out Lake Independence in Big Bay (try taking the Iron River from the lake to Lake Superior). Closer to Marquette, the Dead River Storage Basin offers some nice paddling opportunities on the long, narrow surface. There are plenty of smaller lakes scattered throughout the Huron mountains—ask an outfitter for more information and advice. If you're looking for a good river, put in the Yellow Dog River at County Road 510 and take out five miles downriver at County Road 550 for an easy-to-middling white water trip (the section is rated Class II–V).

Of course, experienced kayakers will want to spend some time paddling along the Lake Superior shoreline. Big Bay is the westernmost end of the **Hiawatha Water Trail** (www.hiawatha watertrail.org), more than 120 miles of Lake Superior shoreline that take paddlers all the way to Grand Marais to the east. There are at least 20 public access points and 23 water-accessible campsites along the way. Trail maps for the Hiawatha Water Trail are available for a fee at **Big Bay Outfitters and Anatomy of a Canoe** (308 Bensinger St., 906/345-9399, 906/250-2457 in winter, www.bigbayoutfitters .com). Big Bay and the shoreline between L'Anse and Marquette aren't as spectacular as Pictured Rocks to the east, but not many places are—and like most of the Great Lakes shoreline, you'd be hard pressed to find a stretch that doesn't make a good place to get your paddle wet. Pay particular attention to the shore on either side of Big Bay Point, and be sure to check the weather reports, as Lake Superior has the tendency to get nasty fast.

Fishing

Big Bay's Lake Independence has the reputation of being a good fishing hole. Anglers can visit the lake for walleye, yellow perch, and smallmouth bass; put in at the boat launch at Perkins Park Campground, just off Big Bay Road/County Road 550. For a more remote, secluded experience, head to Craig Lake, located a little north of U.S. 41/M-28 and a few miles west of Michigamme, where you'll find northern pike, smallmouth bass, and muskie.

As far as rivers go, you could pretty much cast a line blindfolded and hit water. There are plenty of suitable rivers and streams in the area, but you'll want to give the Yellow Dog River a shot for some decent trout. Head to the Little Garlic River, about 10 miles northwest of Marquette on Big Bay Road/County Road 550, for steelhead.

Charters on Lake Superior—as well as inland lakes and rivers—can be arranged through a number of area companies, most of them in Marquette. **Uncle Ducky Charters** (434 East Prospect St., 877/228-5447, www .uncleducky.com) is one of the best all-around charters, while **Rivers North Guide Service** (906/458-8125, www.riversnorth.net) specializes in fly-fishing.

Beaches

Perkins Park Campground on the west side of Lake Independence has a nice, family-friendly beach—and the water will be more comfortable than chilly Lake Superior, too. Lake Michigamme, just off U.S. 41, has a pleasant swimming beach along the half-mile frontage of Van Riper State Park. If it's late enough in the season and you don't mind Superior's nip, there's a small beach by the Big Bay Harbor of Refuge.

Off-Road Vehicles

For such a wide expanse of undeveloped land, there are disappointingly few trails marked for off-road vehicles. In fact, one of the only DNR trails for ATVs near the Huron Mountains is the Champion Trail, which ribbons south from Champion on U.S. 41/M-28 to Republic, a seven or eight mile ride.

Waterfalls

The waterfall map—ask for it from the Marquette Country Convention and Visitors Bureau (337 West Washington St., 906/228-7749, 800/544-4321, www.marquettecountry .org)—will indeed point you toward many of the region's wealth of falls. Some of the finest and most accessible include **Little Garlic Falls, Hills Falls,** and **Big Pup Falls.** The latter two are part of the Yellow Dog River, a beautiful river that splashes and tumbles over cliffs and through canyons from the Yellow Dog Plains north to Lake Independence. Pack a fly rod if you enjoy casting for trout—fishing can be great here. As you might have expected, Little Garlic Falls is located on the Little Garlic River, 11 miles northwest of Marquette. Check the waterfall map for more detailed directions.

WINTER SPORTS AND RECREATION
Ski and Snowshoe Trails

The same loops on the Big Bay Pathway that are less suitable for summertime hiking are great for Nordic skiing once the snow is on the ground. Meditation Loop is two miles long and suitable for beginners, while the Hidden Grin Loop, at four miles, is a longer, intermediate loop. The two other loops are difficult—the three-mile Bear Mountain Loop and its mile-long Ridgeline Extension Loop.

The Saux Head Trails, which, like Big Bay Pathway, are part of the Noquemanon Trail Network, have about 7.5 miles of two-way groomed trails. The loops range from intermediate to advanced. Saux Head Trails are about 11 miles southeast of Big Bay on County Road 550. Take County Road 550 from Marquette, turn right on Saux Head Lake Road, then turn left about a mile later. Parking areas will be on your left. You'll need a trail pass from the **Noquemanon Trail Network** (906/235-6861, www.noquetrails.org) to ski or snowshoe here.

Snowmobiling

Trail 310 winds some 54 miles from Marquette west and north to Big Bay; from the other direction, Trail 14 connects L'Anse and Big Bay over a distance of 56 miles. The two trails connect south of Big Bay via Alternate Trail 310, otherwise they meet up in Big Bay. The Clowry–Big Bay trail (Trail 5) heads north into the Huron Mountains from Clowry, near Champion on U.S. 41/M-23 and joins Trail 14.

Snowmobiles can be ridden on the plowed surface of any of Marquette County's roads, provided you stay on the right-hand side, moving with the flow of traffic and at a reasonable speed. And it goes without saying, but it'll be said anyway: be careful, stop at all intersections, and watch for traffic. Stay off state highways, and double check the laws for riding on paved roads within individual towns and cities.

ACCOMMODATIONS

There's a surprisingly good and varied choice of lodgings in tiny Big Bay. Probably the best known is the **Big Bay Point Lighthouse Bed and Breakfast** (3 Lighthouse Rd., 906/345-9957, www.bigbaylighthouse.com, $125–200). Being a lighthouse, it naturally occupies a dramatic position on a rocky point just a few miles from the town of Big Bay. The red-brick lighthouse keeper's home, attached to the 1896 light, has been restored and retrofitted with seven very comfortable guest rooms, all with private baths. Five have Lake Superior views. The inn has extensive grounds, more than 43 acres and a half mile of shoreline, set far back from busy roads and hustle and bustle. Guests are welcome to use the sauna, climb the light tower, or relax in the living room, where owners Linda and Jeff Gamble have collected loads of lighthouse lore and history. Reserve well in advance.

There are two choices with good locations in Big Bay and rates on the lower end. The **Big Bay Depot** (906/345-9350) occupies an old train depot overlooking Lake Independence. The five refurbished suites include full kitchens, two double beds, and lake views. Pets are welcome. The mom-and-pop **Picture Bay Motel** (906/345-9820) is neat as a pin. Two units have basic cooking facilitles.

A number of houses, cabins, and cottages on Lake Independence are available for rent by the week or day (usually with a minimum stay of at least two nights). Try Henry's Cabin, Mark's Place, or the Dickerson House—make arrangements with Clarence and Yvonne Stortz at **Alder Bay Lodging** (906/345-9914, www .alderbaylodging.com).

Camping

Backcountry campers will find nearly unlimited options in the **Huron Mountains** and **McCormick Wilderness.** Respect private property rights, observe backcountry camping principles, and travel with a map, compass, and other essentials. If you're not experienced in the backcountry, it might be wise to plan your first trip with the company of a local guide like Huron Mountain Outfitters (906/345-9265).

Straddling the highway, **Van Riper State Park** (851 County Road AKE, 906/339-4461, www.michigan.gov/dnr) offers easily accessible modern and rustic campsites, although within earshot of U.S. 41. The park also rents out three rustic cabins, two near the modern campground ($32) and one north of the highway on the Peshekee River ($45). Reserve well in advance.

At 7,000-acre **Craig Lake State Park,** you essentially get an organized campsite tucked in the backcountry wilderness. A rough seven-mile drive and a one- or two-mile hike will bring you to lovely—and often empty—sites. Choose from sites that sit on beds of pine needles above the east shore of Craig Lake, or follow the portage trail east to sites on a small peninsula sticking out into Crooked Lake. No reservations; pay the $6 nightly fee at the parking area. If you were smart, you called

in January and booked one of the rustic cabins on the northwestern shore of Craig Lake. Originally built by Frederick Miller of Miller Brewing fame, these bare-bones cabins offer bunks for your sleeping bag, some utilitarian furniture, and protection from bugs and cold. The larger of the two boasts a huge gathering room with a stone fireplace and sleeps 14 ($45). The other sleeps six ($35). Both have a water pump, firewood, and a rowboat. For maps and information, contact Van Riper State Park.

FOOD

When Thunder Bay Inn closed its doors in early 2008—citing the declining economy— the community lost more than the iconic hotel where *Anatomy of a Murder* was filmed in the late 1950s; it lost a business that was key to the town. Things aren't going so well in Big Bay nowadays, and the slim pickings for restaurant choices are a reflection on the sliding economy. Lunch and breakfast are served at **Hungry Hollow Café** (County Road 550, 906/345-0075, 7 A.M.–2 P.M. Mon.–Thurs., until 4 P.M. Fri. and Sat., 8 A.M.–4 P.M. Sun.), part of Cram's General Store. Try the homemade pasties and soups. For dinner, you can go to the **Lumberjack Tavern** (202 Bensinger St., 906/345-9912), where you'll find earnest, friendly people, great service, and, well, not the best food. But people don't come here for the food; they come for the folks and for the story. It's here, in 1952, that Mike Chenowith was murdered, providing the inspiration for Judge John Voelker's best-selling novel (and later movie) *Anatomy of a Murder.* But if you're looking for more than a good story and a smiling face, it's back to Marquette for dinner.

INFORMATION AND SERVICES

For information about Big Bay and the Huron Mountains, contact the **Marquette Country Convention and Visitors Bureau** (337 West Washington St., 906/228-7749, 800/544-4321, www.marquettecountry.org). They'll have plenty of advice, trail maps for hiking and cross-country skiing, and other information.

See Big Bay Outfitters and Anatomy of a Canoe (308 Bensinger St., 906/345-9399, 906/250-2457 in winter, www.bigbayoutfitters.com) for tour and guide services (waterfall, mountain biking, walking, and kayak or canoeing), rentals, and outdoor retail needs.

Although there are no hospitals in Big Bay, there are two located within 30 miles of the city. Marquette General Hospital (580 West College Ave., 906/228-9440, www.mgh.org) has a hospital, emergency room, and trauma care center located in Marquette, or you can go to Ishpeming's Bell Memorial Hospital (101 South 4th St., 906/486-4431, www.bellmemorial.org), just north of M-28. A third hospital can be found farther away in L'Anse. To get to the Baraga County Memorial Hospital (770 North Main St., 906/524-3300, www.bcmh.org), take Broad Street from U.S. 41 to Main Street and turn right to the hospital.

Likewise, you'll want to do your banking in the bigger cities outside of Big Bay and the Huron Mountains.

GETTING THERE AND AROUND
Car

The Huron Mountains aren't quite as easily accessible as many of the U.P.'s other areas. In fact, there are only two real roads in. The best of these is Big Bay Road/County Road 550, which makes a beeline northwest from Marquette toward Big Bay, while County Road 510 gets there in a less direct fashion. If you're planning on getting off the main road,

be warned that some of these smaller byways are little more than old logging roads—you'll want to have a vehicle with four-wheel drive or, at the very least, high clearance.

Air

The closest airport is Sawyer International Airport (MQT, 125 G Ave., Gwinn, 906/346-3308, www.sawyerairport.com), west of Marquette on U.S. 41/M-28. There are regular flights to and from a number of Midwest cities, including Chicago, Detroit, Milwaukee, and Green Bay, from a couple of carriers: Mesaba Airlines (906/346-6471, www.mesaba.com), which operates as an affiliate of Northwest Airlines, and American Eagle (800/433-7300, www.aa.com), an affiliate of American Airlines. You won't have trouble renting a car at the airport (Alamo, Avis, Budget, National, and Thrifty are all here), and you can grab a bus into Marquette from Marq-Tran (906/225-1112, www.marq-tran.com), though you'll have trouble getting to Big Bay from there without your own set of wheels.

Boat

If you're boating to Big Bay, you can put in at the **Big Bay Harbor of Refuge** (906/345-9353, www.michigan.gov/dnr). With only six transient and four seasonal slips, space is pretty limited, especially for day-use dockage. The Big Bay Harbor has the usual amenities: water, electricity, and gas, as well as bathrooms, showers, and a picnic area. The harbor location is 46° 49.45 N, 87° 43.27 W.

Munising and Grand Island

When it comes to enticing visitors, nature dealt Munising a royal flush. The town of 2,700 curves around the belly of protected Munising Bay. The Grand Island National Recreation Area looms just offshore. Pictured Rocks National Lakeshore begins at the edge of town and stretches for 40-plus miles. The Hiawatha National Forest encompasses the forests to the south and west. If you're looking for outdoor activities, Munising's got all the right cards.

M-28 leads you right to the heart of town, where you'll find most restaurants, mom-and-pop motels, and the ferry dock for cruises to Pictured Rocks.

SIGHTS
◖ Grand Island

Though it's just a 10-minute ferry ride from Munising, the surrounding Lake Superior waters effectively isolate Grand Island. Owned since 1901 by the Cleveland Cliffs Iron Company, the 13,000-acre, largely wooded island was maintained for decades as a private hunting playground for the firm's executives and stockholders. In 1989, Hiawatha National Forest purchased all but 40 acres of Grand Island and proclaimed it a national recreation area. Except for those few patches of private property, you have the entire island—roughly the size of Manhattan—for hiking, beachcombing, mountain biking, and camping.

Don't miss the **historic cemetery** near Murray Bay, where you can pick up a little history and examine the gravestones of various shipwreck victims and the island's first white settlers. Grand Island had long been a summering ground for the Ojibwa when Abraham Williams arrived in the 1840s to establish a trading post. He raised a family, and died on the island in 1873 at the rather amazing age of 81. Today, only the descendants of Williams and their spouses can be buried here.

Autos are not allowed on the island except with special permission or those rare few

owned by island landholders. Van tours now operate under special permit, bumping along a few dirt roads on the island's southern half. ATVs are allowed from October 1 to April 15; mountain bikes are permitted anytime on all public-land trails. Pets on-leash are allowed. Note that drinking water is not available anywhere on the island. The $2 daily user fee for visiting the island is collected by the ferry service. For more information, contact the

Hiawatha National Forest, Munising Ranger District (400 East Munising Ave., 906/387-3700, www.fs.fed.us).

Altran Bus Service offers two- to three-hour van tours of Grand Island, from June through early October. The tour makes six stops on the southern end of the island, including Echo Lake, the Trout Bay Overlook, and Mather Beach, an excellent swimming beach where Echo Creek empties into Lake Superior. Unless you have limited mobility, though, outdoor types likely will grow frustrated with the amount of time spent inside a vehicle. Tours cost $16 for adults, $8 for children, including the ferry fee (but not the $2 recreation area user fee). For schedule information, contact Altran Bus Service (906/387-4845).

☾ Hiawatha National Forest
A huge swath of the massive 860,000-acre Hiawatha National Forest sprawls out to the south of Munising, stretching all the way to Lake Michigan. It offers almost endless opportunities for hiking, mountain biking, and camping. Your best bet for gathering information is the **Hiawatha National Forest Visitors Center** (400 East Munising Ave., 906/387-3700), which shares a building and staff with the Pictured Rocks National Lakeshore.

Alger County Heritage Center
In Munising, a short way east of downtown on Washington Street, the Alger County Heritage Center (1496 Washington St., 906/387-4308, www.hsmichigan.org, 9 A.M.–10 P.M., Mon.–Fri.) keeps a fine collection of local historic artifacts that document the region's past. Visitors can peek at personal objects, Grand Island artifacts (there's even a log cabin from John Jacob Astor's American Fur Company), and Munising Woodenware.

Bayshore Park
At Munising's waterfront, the pleasant Bayshore Park provides a place for travelers to

Hiawatha National Forest has 100 miles of Great Lakes shoreline and 860,000 acres of land.

HIAWATHA

There he sang of Hiawatha,
Sang the Song of Hiawatha,
Sang his wondrous birth and being,
How he prayed and how he fasted,
How he lived, and toiled, and suffered,
That the tribes of men might prosper,
That he might advance his people!

Henry Wadsworth Longfellow,
"The Song of Hiawatha"

There isn't much known about the historical figure of Hiawatha, immortalized in the English-speaking world by Longfellow's popular poem. So little is known, in fact, that some people have questioned whether or not Hiawatha actually existed. The Native American chief is an Ojibwan deity who went by the name of Manabozho, though Longfellow chose his Iroquois name for the simple reason, it would seem, that it sounded better. Some scholars insist, however, that the Iroquoian figure of Hiawatha was real and was added to the Iroquois pantheon after his death. According to the tale, this historical Hiawatha lived in the second half of the 16th century.

There are several different ideas for the meaning of Hiawatha's name, as well. One scholar asserts that the name means "the man who combs" – a reference to a traditional myth about the figure – while others claim that it means "a person of very great wisdom" or "he makes rivers."

Whether Hiawatha was real or not, the accomplishment attributed to him – the banding together of five separate tribes into the Iroquois Confederacy – was real. Interestingly enough, there is almost no similarity between the historical figure who united the tribes and the mythological deity of Longfellow's poem. According to Henry Rowe Schoolcraft, a 19th-century Native American scholar who translated much of the tribes' oral history, the real Hiawatha's rousing speech went something like this:

Friends and brothers: You are members of many tribes. You have come from a great distance. The voice of war has roused you. You are afraid for your homes, your wives, and your children. You tremble for your safety. Believe me, I am one with you. We have one common object. To oppose these hordes of northern tribes singly and alone would prove certain destruction. We must unite ourselves into one band of brothers. We must have but one voice, one fire, one pipe, and one war club ... If we unite in this bond, the Great Spirit will smile upon us and we shall be free, prosperous, and happy; but if we remain as we are, we shall be subject to his frown. We shall be enslaved, ruined, perhaps annihilated forever.

Hiawatha's speech pulled no punches. And it worked. The five tribes – the Mohawks, Oneidas, Onondagas, Senecas, and Cayugas – untied into this "one band of brothers" known as the Iroquois Confederacy. Later, in the 1720s, the Tuscarora would join them as a sixth tribe. All of the tribes were located in upstate New York. The Confederacy worked so well, in fact, that it has been cited as an influence in the founding documents of the United States, including the Articles of Confederation and the United States Constitution. A Smithsonian Institution specialist on American Indian history says that Benjamin Franklin submitted the constitution of the Iroquois Confederacy as an example of how the burgeoning American nation should be governed. Among the similarities between the Iroquois constitution, known as the Great Law of Peace, and the U.S. Constitution are the freedoms of religion and expression and other guaranteed rights.

And to think, all this because of one charismatic man: Hiawatha, the founder of the Iroquois Confederacy.

© JOSH BISHOP

A statue at the Alger County Veterans Memorial Park in Munising honors American soldiers.

stretch their legs, enjoy a relaxing picnic, and admire the marina. In addition to the views of Grand Island just offshore and plenty of picnic tables, you really should pay a visit to the surprisingly lovely Alger County Veterans Memorial Park, where the walkway bricks are engraved with names and messages honoring American soldiers, and you can see artillery, a statue, and a monument.

Christmas

If you're driving into Munising from the west, you'll pass through Christmas, a small, fairly run-down town that is most notable for, first, its Kewadin Casino and, second, **Santa's Workshop** (E8035 St. Nicholas Ave., 906/387-2929, www.santas-workshop-christmas.com), a rather kitschy gift shop that capitalizes on the town's name by supplying Christmas supplies and decorations throughout the year. On the plus side, it supplies visits with Santa for most of the year, too (2 P.M.–close Sun. Mar.–Nov., Sat. and Sun. in Dec.). You'll be able to see

what's supposedly the world's tallest Santa, the tallest Old Woman in the Shoe, and the largest concrete Frosty the Snowman.

KEWADIN CASINO

Thankfully, there's more in Christmas than a year-round gift shop and a huge Santa. The Kewadin Casino (906/387-5475, www .kewadin.com) is located right on M-28 in Christmas, only a few miles west of Munising. With table games like blackjack, 3- and 4-card poker, and Let It Ride—as well as slots—the Kewadin has some of the best U.P. gaming, just minutes from some of the state's finest natural attractions. Grab a bite to eat at Frosty's Bar and Grill.

Alger Underwater Preserve

When loggers were felling the vast stands of pine across the central Upper Peninsula in the 1800s, Munising grew into a busy port, with schooners carrying loads of timber to the growing cities of the southern Great Lakes and iron ore to an ever-growing number of factories. Yet the narrow and shoaly passage between the mainland and Grand Island and along the Pictured Rocks shoreline was the downfall of many ships; their skeletons litter the lake floor here.

The Alger Underwater Preserve covers 113 square miles, from just west of Grand Island to Au Sable Point near the east end of Pictured Rocks National Lakeshore. Nearly a dozen ships lie here, well preserved in Lake Superior's cold, fresh water. Some wrecks, like the 19th-century *Bermuda* and the 145-foot *Smith Moore*, stand upright and nearly intact. The Alger Underwater Preserve marks many of the dive sites with buoys and helps ensure that they will be protected from poachers—it's a felony to remove or disturb artifacts within any Great Lakes underwater preserve.

Lighthouses

Most of Grand Island's private property is on the thumb, including the unique **East Channel Light,** an 1867 wooden lighthouse made of hand-hewn timbers. Sadly, the light has deteriorated badly from vandalism and neglect. Its piecemeal ownership—some 20 landholders own a piece of the lighthouse—leaves its future uncertain. You cannot visit the lighthouse by land, because it's surrounded by private property. You can view it at a distance from Sand Point on the mainland, near the western end of Pictured Rocks National Lakeshore. On North Point, the **North Light** has just a 25-foot tower, but since it rises up from a 175-foot cliff, it earns the honor of being the highest lighthouse above sea level. The 1867 building is now a well-cared-for summer residence; please respect the owner's privacy and stay off the property. The two **Munising Range Lighthouses** were built in 1908 as a means of helping ships navigate the passage to the east and south of Grand Island; they're still shining today. The front tower is 58 feet high, while the rear light is 33 feet. The lights and station building are closed to the public. The two **Grand Island Harbor Range Lights** serve the same purpose for the west passage.

SUMMER SPORTS AND RECREATION
Hiking and Biking Trails

A favorite spot in Hiawatha National Forest is the **Rock River Canyon Wilderness Area.** In this undisturbed corner of the national forest, about 12 miles west of Munising, the Rock River and Silver Creek have carved deep crevices in the sandstone, forming dark and narrow canyons. Adding to the area's wild beauty is **Rock River Falls,** which pours 20 feet over a sandstone ledge. Though there are few developed hiking trails in the area, you can make your way along old logging roads and railroad grades. The canyons themselves require some scrambling for the adventurous. If you plan to explore the area, be sure to bring a compass and topo map; maps are available from the visitors center. To reach the wilderness area, take M-28 west from Munising. About five miles west of Au Train, watch for Rock River Road on your left (also called County Road H-01). Follow it to Forest Road 2276 and turn right (west). Within four miles, you'll arrive at Forest Road 2293; turn south and travel another three-quarters of a mile to a small parking area. A short trail leads down to the canyon and falls.

About 50 miles of trails crisscross Grand Island, mostly old roadbeds. If you're not visiting for a day, a mountain bike is the only way you'll have time to see the entire island: it's about a 23-mile trip around the perimeter. In fact, it's probably one of the best mountain bike routes in the U.P. for the nontechnical rider, with wide grassy paths cutting through hardwood forests, passing under towering pines, snuggling up against Lake Superior shorelines, and rewarding you with grand views of wilderness bays and the distant Pictured Rocks.

Both hikers and bikers can reach **Murray Bay,** about two miles from the ferry dock at the southern end of the island. Murray Bay has a nice day-use area and a sand beach nestled in a grove of pines. There also are two campsites here, but the location near the ferry dock means you'll have less privacy than elsewhere on the island.

North of Murray Bay, the island sprouts a tombolo off its southeastern corner, known as "the thumb." This landmass wraps north and forms **Trout Bay,** a lovely spot ringed with honey-hued beaches and sandstone cliffs. Watch for the low profile of loons bobbing in calm waters. Trout Bay is home to the island's four other developed campsites, and you could camp a long time before finding another site this pretty.

Farther north, the island's most interesting trails follow the eastern and western shorelines. The **eastern shore** climbs high above lake level, offering occasional outstanding views of Pictured Rocks and the Grand Sable Dunes. The **western shore** provides ample opportunities to reach the fine sand beaches that line much of this side of the island. The island's interior trails are largely wooded and somewhat less interesting, unless you're hoping to glimpse a black bear—they're plentiful here.

Canoeing and Kayaking

Paddlers in particular will enjoy Trout Bay, which features some sea caves along its eastern shore and interesting paddling around the thumb. It's a full two-day paddle around the entire island—a trip you'll long remember. It's an outstanding way to experience an outstanding parcel of the Upper Peninsula.

The **Hiawatha Water Trail** (www.hiawatha watertrail.org) is another outstanding way to experience the Lake Superior shoreline in a sea kayak. Bookended by Big Bay to the west and Grand Marais to the east, the water trail stretches in either direction away from Munising and Grand Island. Get a map from Northern Waters Adventures (129 East Munising Ave., 906/387-2323, www.northern waters.com) in Munising. You can also rent sea or recreational kayaks from Northern Waters, as well as sign up for a guided day or overnight trip.

Fishing

Echo Lake lies near the center of Grand Island. Though it offers great bass and northern pike fishing for anyone with a Michigan fishing license, access can be a little tricky, since it is largely ringed with marshy grasses. The remote northern end of the island is perhaps its most outstanding parcel, with high cliffs, creeks, and untouched beaches. In recent years, peregrine falcons have nested nearby. You can also fish areas of Munising Bay (try Sand Point) and Anna River. Ice fishing is particularly good here, too.

Golf

The **Pictured Rocks Golf and Country Club** (10240 County Road H-58, 906/387-3970, www.picturedrocksgolfclub.com) is an 18-hole, 6,246-yard course in Munising. With the exception of Munising's miniature Eagle Falls Adventure Golf (906/387-4653) on M-28 in Munising, Pictured Rocks is the county's only golf course, and it's a good one. The clubhouse has a restaurant and a well-stocked pro shop. Take M-28 to East Munising Avenue before continuing on Munising-Van Meer-Shingleton Road/County Road H-58 to the golf course.

Off-Road Vehicles

Even though there are no state ORV trails near Munising, there's still plenty of opportunity for off-roading, thanks to the vast stretch of **Hiawatha National Forest** (400 East Munising Ave., 906/387-2512, www.fs.fed.us) that blankets the U.P. all the way down to St. Ignace. You can't just ride on any road you chose, though. Get ahold of the U.S. Forest Service for a Motor Vehicle Usage Map, which details mile after mile of forest roads open to ORVs. There are patches of privately owned land scattered throughout the forest—respect private property and stay on federal forest roads.

Waterfalls

The Munising area is thick with waterfalls, and many are easy to reach. (There also are plenty that are difficult to reach, but well worth it, like Rock River Falls in the Rock River Canyon Wilderness.) The **Munising Visitors Bureau** (422 East Munising Ave., 906/387-2138, www.munising.org) prints a waterfall map that will direct you to most of them. Nearby Pictured Rocks National Lakeshore also has several notable falls.

The Tannery Creek spills over **Memorial Falls** and **Olson Falls**, just on the northeast edge of town. Follow County Road H-58 (Washington Street) northeast out of town, and watch for a small wooden staircase on the right side of the road, across from the road to Sand Point and the National Park Service headquarters. (If you've come by car, note that you can't park alongside the road here.) Climb the stairs and follow the trail through a small canyon to Tannery Falls. To reach Memorial Falls, it's easiest to return to County Road H-58, turn right on Nestor Street, and follow the signs.

Right on the outskirts of town, M-28 East leads to **Horseshoe Falls** (turn east on Prospect Street) and **Alger Falls,** which spills down along the highway. The impressive **Wagner Falls** is right in the same area, just off M-94 near the junction of M-94 and M-28. It's a well-marked spot, operated by the state park system as a scenic site. Though it feels secluded, 20-foot Wagner Falls is just a few minutes' walk from the parking area. Continue up the streamside trail past the main falls to a second cascade. About 20 miles west of Munising, wonderful **Laughing Whitefish Falls** has also been protected as a state park scenic site. Here, water plunges 30 feet over hard dolomite rock ledges, then continues rolling and frothing at least twice that far to the bottom of a gorge. To reach Laughing Whitefish Falls, follow M-94 west from Munising to Sundell, then go north on Dorsey Road for 2.5 miles.

Diving

Several factors combine to make the Alger Underwater Preserve one of the finest sport diving locations in the Midwest: there are several wrecks concentrated in one area; the cold, fresh water keeps them from deteriorating; many wrecks are in very shallow water, as little as 20 feet deep; visibility is excellent, usually a minimum of 25 feet and sometimes twice that; and Grand Island helps moderate the cold water temperatures. "It's one of the best wreck diving sites for beginners that I can imagine," notes Pete Lindquist, who operates a dive charter in Munising.

Just offshore from Munising High School, an **underwater museum** among dock ruins includes underwater signs that interpret large maritime artifacts. The Alger Underwater Preserve also attracts divers for its **sea caves** in about 20 feet of water, where sandstone cliffs have been eroded by wave action.

To arrange a dive charter, contact Lindquist's **Shipwreck Dive Tours** (1204 Commercial St., 906/387-4477, www.exploringthenorth.com/scuba/diving.html).

Shipwreck Tours

If you do just one thing in the Munising area, make it this marvelous two-hour tour. Pete Lindquist, an experienced local who also operates a dive charter, came up with the idea of installing viewing wells in the hulls of a couple of tour boats, so even nondivers can marvel at the area's shallow-water shipwrecks.

The view through the 8- to 10-foot-long windows is truly remarkable. The boat glides directly over shipwrecks, some in as little as 28 feet of water. They fill the viewing windows like historic paintings, perfectly visible in the clear water and looking close enough to touch. On the *Bermuda,* you can easily make out deck lines, hatches, and even piles of iron ore lying on the deck. Weather permitting, the tour visits three shipwrecks, dating from 1860 to 1926. Along the way, Lindquist's knowledgeable crew also shares history and points out features (including the wooden East Channel Light) along the shore of Grand Island. Reservations are recommended. Contact **Grand Island Shipwreck Tours** (1204 Commercial St., 906/387-4477, www.shipwrecktours.com) for up-to-date pricing and schedules.

WINTER SPORTS AND RECREATION
Ski and Snowshoe Trails

Four miles south of Munising, in the Hiawatha National Forest, the **Valley Spur** (E8017 M-94, 906/387-4918, www.valleyspur.org) ski trail system has some 27 miles of groomed trails ranging in difficulty from easy to expert. Loops range in length from one to seven miles. The Valley Spur lodge is open most weekends for warmth and a hot beverage. To get to Valley Spur, take M-94 south.

The Munising Ski Trail begins a few miles east of town and skirts close to the Superior shoreline in Pictured Rocks National Lakeshore. Most of the loops on the nearly 12-mile trail are rated for easy to intermediate skiing; lengths vary from less than 1 mile to 2.5 miles. You'll want to be careful to stay on the trails, too, as many portions are located along the tops of sheer cliffs—beautiful sightseeing, but you don't want to get too close. For more information, contact the **National Park Service** (906/387-3700, www.nps.gov/piro).

Snowmobiling

Trail 417 leaves Marquette and takes you east to Au Train before hooking south to catch Trail 8 (heading west, 8 will take you to Gwinn). Take Trail 8 east to follow the Pictured Rocks National Lakeshore all the way into Paradise and Whitefish Point—to get to Munising, head north on Trail 7 or 419. If you're interested in heading south, Trails 7 and 41 will take you there, connecting you to the miles upon miles of U.P. snowmobile trails. Of course, there are more than 300 miles of trails in Alger County alone, so you won't need to leave the county unless you want to. To get a state trail permit, contact the Michigan DNR (www.michigan .gov/dnr).

Ice Fishing

Many of the locations that provide good summertime fishing do just as well for ice fishing when the water freezes over. Try Anna River and the rest of Munising Bay, where fishermen break through the ice for whitefish, lake trout, northern pike, and more.

Ice Sports

For some winter recreation that's a little less common than skiing or snowmobiling, try **ice climbing** on Grand Island. Ice formations form on the sandstone cliffs on the east side of the island, and once the channel and bay begin to freeze over, ice climbers can tackle the 20- to 90-foot-high ice sheets. The **ice caves** just north of Eben Junction and west of Munising make for tamer recreation, but they're just as impressive in their own way. Take snowmobile Trail 8 out of town to the caves that form when water seeping through the walls of Rock River Gorge freezes over.

ACCOMMODATIONS

The **Sunset Motel on the Bay** (1315 East Bay St., 906/387-4574, www.sunsetmotelonthe bay.com, $55–90) has a great location right on Munising Bay at the east end of town. There are 15 rooms, and the motel's three suites have kitchenettes; each of the rooms faces the bay. It's a great find, with great rates, too. Wireless Internet is free, and pets are welcome. The downtown **Munising Motel** (332 East Onota St., 906/387-3187, 906/387-2160, www.munisingmotel.net) has 12 rooms within walking distance of the city dock and Pictured Rocks Cruises. Another good option is the **Terrace Motel** (420 Prospect St., 906/387-2735, www.terracemotel.net, $36–55).

Unlike most commercial strips, the one along M-28 on Munising's near east side is still within walking distance of downtown and the waterfront. It has some nice and tidy small motels like the **Superior Motel and Suites** (500 East M-28, 906/387-2291, $25–50), as well as chain offerings like the **Days Inn** (906/387-2493, $50–75), the best of the chains with a close-in location and an indoor pool. Two miles east of Munising, the Alger Falls Motel (E9427 M-28, 906/387-3536, $45–70 rooms, $105 cottage) has 16 rooms and a housekeeping cottage.

Camping

There are no reservations, fees, or permits required for camping on Grand Island. The island has two designated campgrounds, at Murray Bay (two sites) and Trout Bay (four sites), offering the relative luxury of pit toilets and fire rings. Backcountry camping is permitted throughout the island as long as you stay off the tombolo, off private property, and at least 100 feet away from lakes, streams, cliffs, trails, roads, and natural research areas. No ground fires are permitted. And remember, there is no drinking water anywhere on the island, so come prepared.

For ultimate convenience, but with a sense of seclusion, the Hiawatha National Forest's **Bay Furnace** is a good choice. Just west of Munising north of M-28, it offers 50 rustic sites with a very nice setting next to Lake Superior and overlooking Grand Island. Some sites almost have their own private stretch of beach, and a short cross-country ski trail at the campground's north end gives campers a little extra breathing room.

Near the day-use area, you can check out the remains of the old charcoal furnace that produced 20 tons of iron a day in the 1870s. In its heyday, as many as eight steamers at a time would line up at docks here, bringing wood to fuel the furnace and hauling away iron. The camping fee is $8, no reservation accepted. Take M-28 west from Munising to Christmas and turn north at the Forest Service campground sign.

The Hiawatha National Forest has several other designated campgrounds nearby. Contact the Hiawatha Visitors Center (400 East Munising Ave., 906/387-3700, www.fs.fed.us) for more information and directions.

Families gravitate to the **Wandering Wheels Campground** (906/387-3315) on M-28, three miles east of Munising, with 89 sites in a nice wooded setting. What you lose in wilderness you gain in kid-friendly amenities like an outdoor pool, basketball courts, and a recreation room.

FOOD

For a town on the edge of a national park that presumably gets a fair amount of tourist traffic, Munising has surprisingly little in the way of dining. Try **Sydney's** (906/387-4067, www.sydneysfamilyrestaurant.com), on M-28 downtown, for fresh whitefish and lake trout, as well as steaks and a Friday seafood buffet, served with an Australian touch. **Muldoon's Pasties** (1246 West M-28, 906/387-5880) is the best spot in town for a fresh, authentic taste of this potpie-type meal, a U.P. classic. If you're willing to take a little drive, one of the better restaurants in the Upper Peninsula is about 15 miles west in Au Train. Along the curve of Lake Superior's Au Train Bay on M-28, the **Brownstone Inn** (906/892-8332) serves up original and ever-changing dishes, including delicious versions of the ubiquitous Lake Superior whitefish. There are good vegetarian options and an excellent Friday night fish fry, too.

INFORMATION AND SERVICES

You can get all of the visitor and tourist information you need by contacting the **Munising Visitors Bureau** (422 East Munising Ave., 906/387-2138, www.munising.org).

Dial 911 for emergencies, and for immediate medical care, make your way to Munising Memorial Hospital (1500 Sand Point Rd., 906/387-4110, www.uphcn.org), a smallish community hospital located a little north and east of town. Take East Munising Avenue where it splits from M-28 and follow it northeast to Washington Street; turn left and follow Washington to the hospital.

There aren't as many banks in Munising as in Marquette, but you shouldn't have trouble finding one if you need some ready cash. There's a Wells Fargo on M-28 (419 East M-28, 906/387-2823, www.wellsfargo.com); more immediately in town, you'll find a Peoples State Bank of Munising (100 East Superior St., 906/387-2006, www.bankatpsb.com) and a Citizens Bank (101 West Munising Ave., 906/387-2610, www.citizensbanking.com).

GETTING THERE AND AROUND
Car

To get to Munising by car, take M-28 from Marquette and the west. You'll pass through Au Train and Christmas along the way, and you'll be rewarded with views of Lake Superior and Munising Bay, one of the more picturesque locations in the U.P. If you're coming from the east, it'll be M-28, too—it merges with M-94, which heads north from Manistique and the Lake Michigan shore. It's more of a back road, but you can take Forest Highway 13 north from Nahma Junction on U.S. 2.

Air

Munising's closest commercial airport is Sawyer International Airport (MQT, 125 G Ave., Gwinn, 906/346-3308, www.sawyer airport.com), just south of Marquette, a little less than an hour away. There's no regularly scheduled public transportation from the airport, so odds are you'll be renting a car. A handful of rental companies would be more than happy to help you; see Marquette's *Getting There and Around* for contact information.

Boat

Consider yourself fortunate if you're arriving in Munising by boat. You'll be able to sail past the Pictured Rocks National Lakeshore, an unbelievably scenic stretch of shoreline with plunging cliffs and, in places, very shallow waters. And then you'll sail past beautiful Grand

Island into Munising Bay on your way to **Munising-Bayshore Marina** (906/387-3445, www.michigan.gov/dnr). The marina's slips (9 seasonal and 10 transient) have access to water, electricity, restrooms, and much more. Nearby, there's a pleasant park with picnic tables and benches and plenty of lawn. Contact the harbormaster on channel 16 or 18 from mid-May through mid-October. The marina is located at 46° 24.52 N, 86° 39.06 W.

A **passenger ferry** travels from Munising to Grand Island daily from Memorial Day to early October. The cost is $15 adults, $10 children, under age six free. There's a $5 additional charge for bicycles. Call 906/387-3503 for a current schedule. The ferry's departure point is about two miles west of downtown near Powell Point. Follow M-28 west and watch for the signs. Even if you're planning just a day trip, you'd be wise to pack some warm clothing and a method for

purifying water. Rough weather can cancel ferry service at any time; similarly, more than one hiker or biker has lost track of time and missed the last ferry. There is a ship-to-shore radio at Williams Landing in the event of an emergency. **Private boats** may be pulled ashore at Williams Landing and Trout Bay, and moored offshore in Murray Bay and Trout Bay.

Public Transportation

Although there isn't a major bus company that provides transportation to Munising, you can find regional transportation between Munising and Marquette from Alger County Transit (Altran, 906/387-4845, www.altranbus.com) for $6 each way. Altran also provides dial-a-ride service for a fee; call at least 24 hours in advance for reservations. You can also catch an Altran bus tour of Grand Island ($20 adults, $10 children, June 15–Labor Day).

Pictured Rocks and Grand Marais

Lake Superior takes center stage at this national park, just 3 miles wide but stretching 40 miles along the magnificent lake from Munising to Grand Marais. Pictured Rocks derives its name from the sandstone bluffs that rise 200 feet directly up from the water's surface, washed in shades of pink, red, and green from the mineral-rich water that seeps from the rock. These famous bluffs stretch for more than 15 miles, in places sculpted into crazy castle-like turrets, caves, and arches. The national lakeshore also features a lesser known, but equally spectacular, stretch of shoreline called the Grand Sable Banks, where 200-foot sand dunes are hemmed by a 12-mile ribbon of sand and pebble beach. If that's not enough, you'll also find lakes, forest trails, waterfalls, a lighthouse, and other historic attractions—enough to put Pictured Rocks at the top of the list for anyone visiting the Upper Peninsula. For general information, contact Pictured Rocks National Lakeshore (906/387-3700, www.nps.gov/piro).

Pictured Rocks' tourist season is short—most

© JOSH BISHOP

This tree, which is growing on the naked rock, is one of many distinctive features of the Pictured Rocks National Lakeshore.

of the park's 300,000 or so annual visitors come in July and August, when they're most likely to enjoy summerlike weather and daytime temperatures in the 70s. Visit in June and you'll share the park with fewer people, but the black flies and mosquitoes often aren't worth the trade-off. May and September may be the park's finest months.

No matter when you go, pack plenty of warm clothing along with the shorts. Even at the height of summer, evenings are almost always cool, dipping into the 50s. And the giant refrigerator of Lake Superior—where the water temperature rarely climbs out of the 40s—can put a chill in the air near the shoreline. In fact, a Lake Superior beach on a sweltering August afternoon may just be the most refreshing place on earth.

SIGHTS
◖ Pictured Rocks National Lakeshore

To really see the namesake bluffs, you need to get out on the water. **Pictured Rocks Boat Cruises** offers three-hour trips up the shoreline from Munising, sidling up practically close enough to touch the rock formations and giving you the perspective you need to appreciate turreted shapes like Miners Castle. Though trips are offered up to seven times a day, plan for a late-afternoon cruise, when the sinking sun shows off the multicolored sandstone in its best light. The boats depart from the Munising City Pier. For more information, contact Pictured Rocks Cruises (906/387-2379, www.picturedrocks.com, Memorial

PICTURED ROCKS NATIONAL LAKESHORE

WOODLAND PARK
Sable Falls
Grand Marais
GRAND SABLE VISITOR CENTER (SUMMER ONLY)
Grand Sable Dunes
Grand Sable Banks
Grand Sable Lake
LOG SLIDE OVERLOOK
AU SABLE LIGHT STATION
Au Sable Point
HURRICANE RIVER
Hurricane River
Lake Superior
TWELVEMILE BEACH
Alger
Underwater
Preserve
Lakeshore Trail
KINGSTON LAKE
State Forest
Twelvemile
Beach
Beaver Lake
Little Beaver Lake
LITTLE BEAVER LAKE
Lake Superior
Spray Falls   Spray Creek
Chapel Beach
Chapel Lake
Grand Portal Point
Chapel Falls
CHAPEL ROAD
Melstrand
Mosquito Falls
Mosquito River
Lake Superior
State Forest
Alger
Underwater
Preserve
Miners Castle
Miners Falls
MINERS CASTLE ROAD
Miners Creek
◖ GRAND ISLAND
Grand Island National Recreation Area
Sand Point
NATIONAL LAKESHORE HEADQUARTERS
Munising
Munising Falls
MUNISING FALLS INTERPRETIVE CENTER
MUNISING INFORMATION CENTER
Bay
Alger Falls
Munising
Hiawatha National Forest
© AVALON TRAVEL
0   4 mi
0   4 km

Day–mid-Oct., $33 adults, $10 children 6–12, under 5 free).

Munising Falls Area

The highlight of this spot used to be the trail that led hikers behind the 50-foot Munising Falls, but erosion problems prompted its closure. It's still worth a stop here, though, for the falls and the adjacent **interpretive center,** which offers a glimpse of the history of this peaceful area, home to a belching pig iron furnace in the 1860s. Munising Falls also marks the west trailhead for the **Lakeshore Trail,** a 43-mile segment of the North Country Trail that spans seven states from New York to North Dakota. The Lakeshore Trail runs the length of the Pictured Rocks National Lakeshore—predictably, never far from the water's edge. The park's eastern trailhead lies near Sable Falls.

Past Munising Falls, the paved access road ends at **Sand Point,** home of the national lakeshore headquarters. While the headquarters primarily houses offices (not visitor services), it displays some interesting Coast Guard and shipwreck artifacts on its grounds. Sand Point has a small beach and a boat ramp, a good spot to launch a small craft for exploring nearby Grand Island.

Miners Castle

For whatever reason, we love to attach manmade descriptions to natural creations. Thus, the sandstone cliffs five miles northeast of Munising Falls are known as Miners Castle, for the turretlike shapes caused by wind and wave erosion. The nine-story-high rock formation is impressive and ranks as one of the park's most popular attractions. Boardwalks and steps lead you to two viewing platforms out on the rock, where you can peer down into the gloriously clear waters of Lake Superior. If that entices you to do a little beach-combing and wading, a nearby trail leads down some steps through the pines to inviting **Miners Beach.**

To reach Miners Castle, follow County Road H-58 east from Munising to the well-marked turnoff for Miners Castle Road. Before you

reach the Miners Castle formation itself, you'll see another sign on Miners Castle Road directing you to Miners Falls. It's a one-mile walk to these pleasant falls, where Miners Creek tumbles 40 feet over a rocky escarpment.

Chapel Basin Area

Continuing northeast on County Road H-58, the next auto-accessible route into the heart of the park is at Melstrand, where the gravel/dirt Chapel Road bumps six miles toward the shore and another park highlight, the Chapel Basin area. Park your car here and you'll find plenty to entertain you during a long day hike or a weekend: three waterfalls, a deep inland lake, Superior beaches, and a good loop hiking trail. Chapel Falls is the key attraction, as evidenced by the wide paved pathway that leads 1.5 miles to the falls.

If you turn left instead of right at Chapel Beach, you can make a 10-mile loop around Chapel Basin. Along the way, you'll pass Grand Portal Point—another significant Pictured Rocks landmark—before returning to the parking area. Don't leave Chapel Basin without a visit to Mosquito Falls, a little farther inland off Chapel Road. The Mosquito River spills over a series of ledges, creating an accessible waterfall calm enough for wading and soaking fatigued hiking feet. A trail leads to various sections of the falls and links up with the Lakeshore Trail.

Beaver Lake

Located near the center of the park, 800-acre Beaver Lake is the largest inland lake in Pictured Rocks. Anglers are drawn to the lake and the tributaries that feed it, especially for trout. Little Beaver Lake, connected by a small channel, has a boat launch. Boats are limited to 10 horsepower or less, making this a pleasant waterway for paddlers. Little Beaver has one of the park's three auto-accessible campgrounds, with eight sites available on a first-come, first-served basis. Be aware that wetlands cover much of the terrain between Beaver Lake and Lake Superior, so bugs can be a problem here especially in June and early July.

Lake Superior State Forest

Traveling east from Beaver Basin, several dirt roads spiral south off County Road H-58 into the woods. These lead into the Lake Superior State Forest, part of the buffer zone protecting Pictured Rocks. They offer plenty of inland lakes, hiking and biking trails, and rustic campgrounds, and are largely ignored by the summer visitors to the national lakeshore. For more information on the state forest, contact the Michigan DNR (www.michigan.gov/dnr). Topo maps ($4) of the area are available at the visitors center in Munising.

Grand Sable Dunes

Just east of Au Sable Point, the **Log Slide Overlook** marks the site of a once-busy logging operation. In the late 1800s, loggers used this high point—some 300 feet above Lake Superior—to send freshly cut logs down to the water's edge, where they were loaded on Great Lakes schooners. Today, you can stand on a platform and simply marvel at the view, with the lighthouse to your left, the great dunes to your right, and the brilliant blue of the big lake filling the horizon.

Grand Marais

Though not part of Pictured Rocks National Lakeshore, sweet little Grand Marais marks the park's western boundary and is an excellent jumping-off point for a visit to the national lakeshore. This sleepy New England village is worth a visit of its own for its simple windswept beauty. With an outstanding natural harbor—rather rare on Lake Superior's southern shore—Grand Marais was originally settled by fishermen. Loggers soon followed, when sawmills were built here in the 1860s and 1870s to handle the logging that went on just south of here.

Today, commercial fishing remains an economic factor (though an increasingly difficult way to make a living), but a little bit of tourism is what keeps the town slowly ticking along. The downtown huddles around the harbor, which, incidentally is a good spot for kayakers to play in the surf on a north to east wind.

The few streets here offer some arts and crafts shops and a handful of clean, inexpensive motels and restaurants.

Follow the bay around to its western point to reach the pier (popular with anglers) and a small volunteer-run **maritime museum** (906/494-2660) in the former Coast Guard Station. Hours vary, so call ahead. The adjacent Lake Superior shoreline offers a nice sand and pebble beach, sometimes closed if endangered piping plovers are nesting. Rockhounds should continue west along the beach, past the Woodland Park city campground, to reach a good spot for **hunting agates.**

Lighthouses

It's a 1.5-mile walk along the Lakeshore Trail from the Hurricane River campground to the **Au Sable Light Station** at Au Sable Point. Built in 1874, the 87-foot brick light and its keepers did yeoman's duty for decades—warning ships away from the rock shoals that extend out for nearly a mile and create shallows of just 6 to 30 feet. Nonetheless, at least 10 steamers were wrecked here. As you walk the trail from the campground, look for parts of the **shipwrecks** just offshore, often poking out of the sand bottom and easily visible in the gin-clear water. The light was automated in 1958.

Several recent restoration projects involved renovating the lightkeeper's quarters, rehabilitating the landscape and installing a photovoltaic (solar power) system to power the site. Tours are offered for a small fee (Wed.–Sun. noon–5:30 P.M. late June–late Aug., $3 for ages six and older), although tours for summer 2009 may be delayed due to road construction on County Road H-58.

SUMMER SPORTS AND RECREATION

Hiking and Biking

Two good hiking trails leave from the campground at Little Beaver Lake. The short and pleasant 0.7-mile **White Pine Trail** is a self-guided nature trail that circles through a 300-year-old pine forest. The five-mile **Beaver Basin Loop Trail** makes a lap around

LAKE SUPERIOR

By the shores of Gitche Gumee,
By the shining Big-Sea-Water . . .

Henry Wadsworth Longfellow,
"The Song of Hiawatha"

Gitche Gumee is Longfellow's misspelled version of the Ojibwa name for Lake Superior, *Gichigami*, which means "big water." The Ojibwa could be accused of understatement: Lake Superior isn't just big water – depending on how you measure it, Lake Superior is the biggest freshwater lake in the world.

Lake Superior is the largest freshwater lake in the world by surface area. As a comparison, the surface area – 31,700 square miles – is about the same size as the state of Maine. The shoreline stretches an amazing 1,826 miles, farther than the drive from Houghton to Miami.

Superior is also the deepest of the Great Lakes (its deepest point drops 1,332 feet), but if you measure by volume there are still two lakes larger: Lake Tanganyika in East Africa and Lake Baikal in Siberia. By no means does that mean it's a small lake. Lake Superior is large enough to hold each of the other Great Lakes, as well as all the water from Lake Erie an additional three times. The lake holds 3 quadrillion gallons of water (write the number 3, then put 15 zeroes behind it), a full 10 percent – that's *10 percent* – of the world's fresh water. More than half of the water from the Great Lakes is contained in Superior, and, if it were poured out of the lake, like a kiddie pool onto the lawn, the water would submerge all of North and South America to a depth of one foot.

And that's not all. Not only is there an incredible amount of water in Lake Superior, but it's also remarkably clean – the cleanest, clearest water in the Great Lakes.

How did such an aquatic treasure get here? Well, exactly the same way the rest of the Great Lakes were formed. To get there, we have to go back to prehistory, about a billion years ago (give or take). The Mid-Continent Rift split open, and, over a period of several million years, spilled volcanic material. This molten basalt eventually formed a thick (up to 10 miles thick), incredibly heavy rock layer that sunk as the rift opened, forming the Superior basin. From there, the ice took over. As the glaciers retreated, they continued to carve the land into the massive basin it is today; as the last of the ice melted, the water was trapped in the lake, which, at the time, was much deeper than today.

With the retreat of the ice came humans. A series of native peoples came to the area over the course of at least 10,000 years, some who hunted with stone-tipped spears, others who developed new fishing techniques, and still others who were the ancestors of today's Chippewa tribes. Eventually the Europeans arrived, drawn by the lucrative fur trade. More recently, the lake has drawn several million tourists each year with its reputation as a wild and rugged place, as well as a sportsman's paradise.

Little Beaver and Big Beaver Lakes, then follows the Lake Superior shore past sea caves cut by the lake's pounding waves. Boardwalks skirt the wetlands before returning you to the trailhead.

If you're in the mood for some exercise, the two-mile stretch of the **North Country Trail** from the Log Slide to the Au Sable Light Station is one of the park's most scenic hikes.

The **Grand Sable Banks and Dunes** (*grand sable* is French for "big sands") stretch for nearly five miles from the overlook, glacial banks of gravel supporting the huge mounds of sand. They are magnificent when viewed from a distance, glowing gold and rising up abruptly from the cobalt waters of Lake Superior. In many areas, especially near the overlook, the dunes are free of grasses and plants, so you can play around on them without fear of damaging fragile plant life or causing erosion. Though park officials discourage it for safety reasons, no one will stop you from flopping on your butt and rocketing down a slope. Be aware, though, that the climb back up takes a lot longer!

Most people, however, choose to explore the dunes from the eastern end. Near the Grand Sable Visitors Center, a trail winds across the top of the dunes, where marram grass, beach pea, and sand cherry cling to the sand for dear life. (Be careful to stay on the trail here.) Interpretive signs discuss the plants' tenuous hold on the environment.

Canoeing and Kayaking

Paddlers can get the best view of Pictured Rock by **sea kayak.** You avoid the somewhat cheesy narration of the Pictured Rocks Cruise and really experience the grandeur of this shoreline. Safety warnings cannot be overemphasized, however. Only experienced paddlers should venture out on their own, and only in a closed cockpit (no canoes) and after scrupulously monitoring weather conditions. Paddlers can get themselves into serious trouble at Pictured Rocks, caught in sudden summer squalls along the 15-mile rock wall with nowhere to hide. Having said that, sea kayaking along Pictured Rocks ranks as one of the finest paddles on all the Great Lakes.

The stretch of Pictured Rocks and Superior shoreline leading into Grand Marais is also the easternmost stretch of the **Hiawatha Water Trail** (www.hiawathawatertrail.org), which ends here, 120 miles from where it began in Big Bay—or, if you're heading in the other direction, it's the beginning of a long and satisfying journey in a sea kayak.

If you're unsure of your abilities, hook up with **Northern Waters** (129 East Munising Ave., Munising, 906/387-2323, www.northern waters.com). The company offers outstanding day-long guided trips ($85 adults, $65 ages 16 and under), ferrying guests and boats to a departure point at Miners Castle. Beginners are welcome, since the day includes some basic instruction and you'll be traveling with an experienced guide. Kayak rentals (and longer trips to Grand Island and Isle Royale) are also available.

Beaches

An icon near the Twelvemile Beach campground says it all: indicating that this is a permitted beach area, it shows a swimmer not in the usual crawl position, but with water lapping at his ankles. In other words, the water here is damn *cold.* Swim if you dare, but wading is really more realistic . . . which is what keeps Twelvemile Beach the pristine, stunning ribbon of sand that it is. After all, if such a perfect beach boasted 75°F water, it would be overrun with boomboxes, jet skis, and zinc oxide. Instead, it's a beach where you can stroll for hours with only the company of peregrine falcons, bald eagles, deer wandering down for a drink, and even the occasional black bear snorting around in the sand.

The **Twelvemile Beach campground** is easy to reach, just a short drive off County Road H-58 through a pretty birch forest. Many of the 37 campsites string out along a bluff over the beach—come midweek (or early on Saturday, often a turnover day) for one of the choice spots. Some are larger than the average house lot and undoubtedly have better views. Well-placed stairs deposit campers and picnickers at lake level. The campground also has a nice **day-use area** at its east end.

Just about five miles farther up the beach (or County Road H-58) lies the auto-accessible **Hurricane River campground,** where the Hurricane River spills into Lake Superior. This is also an exceptionally scenic campground, with 21 sites and a good location near the water and Au Sable Point.

Farther west, across County Road H-58 near the Grand Sable Visitors Center, the sandy shores and often warm waters of **Grand Sable Lake** are a wonderful spot for a swim or picnic.

Fishing

Fishing in the Pictured Rocks National Lakeshore—both in Lake Superior and the inland lakes and rivers—is a bit different from fishing elsewhere in the Upper Peninsula, if only because it's been specifically allowed by Congress for more than 40 years. It's not just an opportunity—it's your right. You'll be able to cast a line for a large selection of game fish, including (but not limited to) walleye, northern pike, whitefish, smelt, smallmouth bass, coho salmon, and brook, rainbow, and lake trout. Try Lake Superior, Grand Sable Lake, Beaver Lake, and Little Beaver Lake for the biggest variety of fish; for rivers, give it a shot at Sable Creek, Hurricane River, Beaver Basin Streams, and Miners River, among others. Get a hold of the staff at Pictured Rocks National Lakeshore (N8391 Sand Point Rd., 906/387-2607, www.nps.gov/piro) for guidelines, regulations, maps, and tips.

For fishing on state land near Grand Marais, try North and South Gemini Lakes for bass, bluegill, perch, and walleye; Ross Lake, two miles east, for bass, bluegill, perch, and pike; and Canoe Lake, two-and-a-half miles south, for perch and pike. Contact the Michigan DNR (906/452-6227, www.michigan.gov/dnr) for more info.

Off-Road Vehicles

East of Grand Marais, near Lake Superior between Blind Sucker Flooding and Muskalonge Lake, the first of two DNR ATV trails has an impressive 46 miles in three large loops. Pine Ridge Trail has parking at the intersection of County Road 416 and County Road 407; there's also access from Holland Lake Campground if you continue west on County Road 416. The Two-Heart Trail actually connects to the Pine Ridge Trail, adding almost 34 miles (that's 80 miles in total, if you haven't put it together already). Use the same trailhead parking as Pine Ridge, or you can get access to Two-Heart from the Mouth of Two-Hearted River Campground (there's gas here, too) or Pike Lake Campground. The DNR (906/452-6227, www.michigan.gov/dnr) has more information and maps.

Waterfalls

Just inside the park's western boundary, a short trail leads to 50-foot **Munising Falls,** which spills into a narrow gorge before emptying into Lake Superior's Munising Bay. Head east to the Chapel Basin Area where, amid a pale birch forest some 1.5 miles from the parking area, frothing water drops like a horsetail 90 feet into a deep gorge and Chapel Lake below. Continue past the falls another 1.75 miles to reach Chapel Beach, where you'll find a backcountry campground. From here, you can turn right to Chapel Rock and follow the Lakeshore Trail 1.5 miles to **Spray Falls,** one of the least visited and loveliest waterfalls in the park, where Spray Creek drops over the sandstone cliffs right into Lake Superior.

The trail to **Sable Falls** leaves from the Grand Sable Visitors Center, a half-mile walk largely composed of steps. As you work your way downhill, you'll be treated to several views of this exceptionally pretty falls, which drops in tiers through a narrow canyon and out to a rocky Lake Superior beach.

WINTER SPORTS AND RECREATION
Ski and Snowshoe Trails

The **Grand Marais Ski Trail** has several loops on the extreme east end of Pictured Rocks National Lakeshore, where County Road H-58/Au Sable Point Trail passes near Sable Falls and the Lake Superior shoreline. In fact, one of the trails (E) loops close to the shore on an intermediate, two-mile journey out and back. All of the loops here range from easy to intermediate, and vary in distance from less than a mile to nearly 2.5 miles, for a total of 10.4 miles altogether. Parking is on either side of County Road H-58, just west of William Hill Road. It goes without saying that you should watch for traffic when crossing the highway; look out, too, for snowmobiles. For trail maps and additional information, the staff at Pictured Rocks National Lakeshore (N8391 Sand Point Rd., 906/387-2607, www.nps.gov/piro) would be more than happy to help. You can jump on the North Country Trail as well.

Snowmobiling

There are more than enough snowmobile trails in the Pictured Rocks/Grand Marais region—the most important one is Trail 8, which cuts east–west from Munising to Sault Ste. Marie. At Pictured Rocks National Lakeshore, Trail

89 bends away from 8 and takes you north to the Superior shoreline; south of town, Trails 443 and 43 connect to the rest of the U.P.'s snowmobile trails—south to St. Ignace, west to Escanaba, Ironwood, and the Keweenaw Peninsula. There's a web of smaller trails woven around the city: Trails 88, 888, 9, and 492 will take you between the main trails and to other places in the region. Contact **Grand Marais Sno-Trails** (800/831-7292, www.sno-trails .net) for more information and a detailed map. And remember: According to the state, snowmobiles are allowed on the shoulders of plowed roads—and on any unplowed road. Follow the speed limits and drive with care.

ACCOMMODATIONS

Formerly the ArborGate Inn, **Beach Park Motel** (21795 Randolph St., 906/494-2681, $65 d) has large rooms, each with a view of the water. A block east of County Road H-77 on Randolph, it's within walking distance to everything in town. Pets are welcome for an additional $10. East of County Road H-77 on Wilson Street, **Voyageur's Motel** (21906 Wilson St., 906/494-2389, $50–100) sits atop a ridge overlooking Grand Marais Harbor. Nice newer rooms with mini-fridge and a sauna/whirlpool facility make this a good choice. Other affordable options include **Dunes Motel** (906/494-2324, www.thedunesmotel.info) on the corner of W. Wilson and M-77, **North Shore Lodge** (22020 Coast Guard Point, 906/494-2361), and **The Superior Hotel** (14245 Lake Ave., 906/494-2539).

Still affordable, **Hilltop Cabins** (14176 Ellen St., 906/494-2331, www.hilltopcabins.net, $65–150) rents one-, two-, and three-bedroom cabins, each one furnished with a full living room, kitchen, and bathroom. Motel rooms with views of the bay are available, but you'll want to spring for one of the cabins. For more information and other lodging options, contact the Grand Marais Chamber of Commerce (906/494-2447, www .grandmaraismichigan.com).

Camping

Pictured Rocks has three auto-accessible campgrounds—Beaver Lake, Twelvemile Beach, and Hurricane River—with water and pit toilets. No reservations are accepted, and fees are $10 per night. **Backcountry camping** is permitted only at designated hike-in sites, mostly along the Lakeshore Trail. A $15 permit, good for one to six campers and for any number of nights, is required. Most sites do not have water or toilets. Camping is also available in Munising, Grand Marais, and Lake Superior State Forest, which borders Pictured Rocks to the south.

With an excellent location just outside the national lakeshore boundary, **Woodland Park** has more than 100 sites; opt for the more secluded ones that require you to hoof it up the beach a bit. It's open May 15–October 15.

FOOD

Grand Marais has a couple of good finds in the food department, both right downtown on County Road H-77. The **Sportsman's Restaurant** (906/494-2671) is more distinctive than its name suggests, with good fish dishes, salads, and homemade soups, as well as plenty of burgers and steaks. Visit for breakfast, too—how many places have "two eggs and pan-fried whitefish" on the menu? Down the street, **⟨ Lake Superior Brewing Company** (N14283 Lake Ave., 906/494-2337) does the microbrewery tradition proud, with homemade brews like Sandstone Pale Ale and Granite Brown, as well as sandwiches, soups, and great homemade pizzas. For a summer treat, stop in the time-warpy **Superior Hotel** on the corner of Lake Avenue and Randolph Street, where a soda fountain still sells phosphates and penny candy. For fresh and smoked fish, head two miles east of town on County Road H-58 to **Bugg's Fish Market.** You can't do better for a Lake Superior beach picnic.

INFORMATION AND SERVICES

You'll find visitors centers at both ends of the national lakeshore—one in Munising, the other inside the park at the Grand Sable Dunes, just a few miles from Grand Marais. Be sure to stop at one of these centers before beginning your visit—they have rangers on duty and very good maps (at least pick up a free general park map), displays, and historical information that will enhance your visit. Both have small but very good bookstores, too. The **Munising Information Center,** serving both the Pictured Rocks National Lakeshore and Hiawatha National Forest (400 East Munising Ave., 906/387-3700, www.nps.gov/piro, 9 A.M. to 4:30 P.M.) is open year-round, daily in "peak season" (which seems to change from year to year), and is closed Sundays and holidays from mid-September through Memorial Day. The **Grand Sable Visitors Center** (E21090 County Road H-58, 906/494-2660, www.nps .gov/piro, 9 A.M.–5 P.M.) is open from late May to Labor Day only.

The two closest hospitals are Helen Newberry Joy Hospital (502 West Harrie St., 906/293-9200, 800/743-3093, www.hnjh.org) in Newberry and Munising Memorial Hospital (1500 Sand Point Rd., 906/387-4110, www .munisingmemorial.org) in Munising. For either hospital, head south on M-77 until you hit M-28. To get to Helen Newberry Joy Hospital, turn left and follow M-28 to M-123; turn left again and travel north on M-123 to Harrie Street, then turn left to the hospital. For Munising Memorial Hospital, turn right onto M-28 from M-77, then turn right on Connors Road. Hang a left at Munising/Shingleton Road, then another right at Washington Street to the hospital.

In Grand Marais, do your banking at the Peoples State Bank of Munising (N14264 Lake St., 906/494-2265, www.bankatpsb .com). There's another branch of the Peoples State Bank on M-28 in Seney (906/499-3306). Otherwise, head into Newberry or Munising for more choices.

GETTING THERE AND AROUND
Car
The easiest route between Munising and Grand Marais will bring you well south of Pictured Rocks—take M-28 east from Munising, then M-77 north to Grand Marais.

County Road H-58 provides access to the park, winding roughly along the park's southern boundary and linking Munising and Grand Marais. A large stretch of the road—from Beaver Lake to the Grand Sable Dunes—is unpaved and can deteriorate into washboard rough enough to jar your dental work. It's a problem that the county is working to fix. For now, leave the '55 T-bird at home and plan your time accordingly—it's about a 90-minute trip from one end of the unpaved road to the other.

Of course, much of the road is paved. From the Grand Marais end of the lakeshore park, you'll be able to get as far as the Kingston Lake Campground; from Munising and the west, you can get to the Little Beaver Lake Campground. County Road H-58 is scheduled to be paved from one end to the other by the end of 2010—until then, be prepared for road closures and other traffic problems.

As a linear park, Pictured Rocks perennially struggles with auto accessibility versus invasiveness. There have been stop-and-start discussions for decades about a "Beaver Basin Rim Road" that would weave through the park nearer Lake Superior, offering easier auto access to park attractions but undeniably changing the spirit and peacefulness of the largely road-free preserve.

Air
The closest commercial airport is Chippewa County International Airport (CIU, 5019 Airport Dr., Kincheloe, 906/495-2522, www .airciu.com), nearly 80 miles away, south of Sault Ste. Marie. Northwest Airlink offers regularly scheduled flights to and from Detroit; car rentals are available from Avis (906/495-5900, www .avis.com) and Hertz (906/495-5190, www.hertz .com). If you're traveling from other major cities, you may need to fly into Sawyer International Airport (MQT, 125 G Ave., Gwinn, 906/346-3308, www.sawyerairport.com) instead, though the drive from Marquette is much longer than that from Sault Ste. Marie.

Boat
The **Burt Township Marina** (906/494-2613, 906/494-2381 off-season, www.michigan.gov/

dnr) in Grand Marais is the only natural harbor of refuge between Munising and Whitefish Point. You'll find a boat launch, fuel, electricity, water hookups, a pump-out station, and transient dockage. The marina is open seasonally from May 1 to October 15 and is located at 46° 41.05 N, 85° 58.15 W.

Public Transportation

For now, consider a superb compromise: the **Altran Shuttle,** a county bus that makes regular runs (three times a week during the high season) to Munising Falls and Grand Marais and will drop off hikers at any point along County Road H-58. It's the perfect way for backpackers to enjoy the park without contributing to the growing vehicle problem. Call Altran (906/387-4845) for updated schedules and rates or to make a reservation (at least one day in advance).

Seney and Vicinity

> The train went up the track and out of sight, around one of the hills of burnt timber. Nick sat down on the bundle of canvas and bedding the baggage man had pitched out of the door of the baggage car. There was no town, nothing but the rails and the burnt-over country. The thirteen saloons that had once lined the one street of Seney had not left a trace.
>
> – Ernest Hemingway,
> *Big Two-Hearted River*

Well, not exactly. Seney still exists, a small dot on the map at the crossroads of M-77 and M-28. But by the time Hemingway—or rather, his Nick Adams character—was tramping through the central U.P., the town of Seney was indeed just a shadow of its former self.

"Helltown in the Pine!" loggers once called it, the new center of a logging trade that had crept northward into the U.P. after depleting the lucrative stands of red and white pine in the northern Lower Peninsula. Seney was the center of the action in the 1880s, both in and out of the woods. Situated along a railroad siding and the shores of the Fox River—used to transport the logs—the city became an important transit point. But in addition to logging, the local economy thrived on drinking, gambling, and womanizing. Seney didn't lack for local color: legendary (and mythical?) characters included P. K. "Snap Jaw"

Small, who entertained barroom crowds by biting the heads off live toads and birds, and "Protestant" Bob McGuire, who sharpened his thumbnails into miniature bowie knives. Seney was sensationalized in the national press, right along with Tombstone and other towns of the Wild West.

Problem was, Seney never had the huge fertile forests so common elsewhere in Michigan. Glaciers scrubbed this swath of the central U.P. flat, creating a patchwork of rivers, wetlands, and rocky, sandy soil. The red and white pines that did grow here were leveled in just a few short years; soon loggers were settling for the less valuable hardwoods and small conifers, burning the scrub as they went. Shortly after the turn of the century they moved on, leaving behind the denuded land and vast "stump prairies."

Optimistic farmers followed the quickly departed loggers. They burned the brush and went to great lengths to drain the wetlands, digging miles of 20-foot ditches. Yet their hopes were quickly buried by the area's poor soils and they, too, departed almost as quickly as they came. But the fires had a more lasting effect, scarring the fragile soil deeply.

These days, humans are finally trying to help instead of harm this beleaguered land. The immense Seney National Wildlife Refuge now manages and protects 150 square miles immediately west of M-77, restoring the wetlands with an intricate series of dikes and control ponds that began as a 1930s Civilian Conservation Corps project. Today the refuge is an important sanctuary and nesting place for a rich variety of waterfowl.

The area's rivers remain a wonderful resource, too—the Fox, the Manistique, and the Driggs all twist through the land, along with countless creeks and lesser branches. Henry Ford, Calvin Coolidge, and Ernest Hemingway fished these legendary trout waters, as anglers continue to do today. Here, too, Hemingway used a little literary license: it was really the Fox that he so eloquently chronicled in his Nick Adams stories—he merely borrowed the more romantic-sounding name of the Big Two-Hearted River, which flows just east of here.

SIGHTS
Iverson Snowshoe Company
Aluminum snowshoes now dominate the sport, but for beauty and tradition, they simply can't match white-ash-and-rawhide snowshoes. In Shingleton, 25 miles west of Seney on M-28, Anita Hulse and her two sons operate this wonderful factory, where workers hand-shape strips of local ash into classic snowshoe frames.

Visitors are welcome to visit Iverson Snowshoe (E12559 Mill St., 906/452-6370, www.iversons-snowshoes.com, 8 A.M.–4 P.M. Mon.–Fri.), one of just two wooden snowshoe manufacturers left in the country. You can watch workers shave and saw strips of ash, steam them, bend them around a form, and send them to a drying kiln overnight. Finished frames are laced with gummy strips of rawhide or newer-style neoprene. All of this happens in a small building, where visitors practically lean over the shoulders of the workers.

Iverson manufactures about 11,000 snowshoes a year, about a third of which go to L.L.Bean. Other customers include REI, the Norwegian army, park rangers, and utility workers. Iverson also makes rustic chairs and tables, by order only. It doesn't hurt to call ahead if you're interested in a tour. (Groups of more than five or six should definitely call.) To find Iverson, turn north on Maple Street (just west of the stoplight) in Shingleton.

Seney National Wildlife Refuge
The Seney National Wildlife Refuge occupies a huge swath of land west of M-77 and south of M-28. It is an intensely managed 95,000-acre parcel, with dikes and control structures used to artificially raise and lower the water levels in 21 major pools, simulating a natural wetlands cycle.

The system impounds more than 7,000 acres of water in these pools, and natural wetlands sprawl beyond that. While humans on foot or bicycle can access much of this preserve via an extensive network of maintenance roads, the refuge offers plenty of seclusion for its inhabitants. More than 200 species of birds and nearly 50 species of mammals have been recorded here, including bald eagles, trumpeter swans, loons, and even the occasional—though infrequently spotted—moose or wolf. Whether you're a dedicated and experienced birder or a casual observer, Seney is a wonderful place to get in among a fascinating array of wildlife.

Start your visit at the excellent **National Wildlife Refuge Visitors Center** (9 A.M.–5 P.M. daily May 15–Oct. 15), five miles south of the town of Seney on M-77. A 15-minute audiovisual program, very good displays, and printed materials give you a good overview of what you can expect to see (or at least look for) in the refuge. Some of the handouts will increase your chances of spotting bird life, pinpointing things like eagle nests and ponds frequented by loons. Sightings are often best in early morning and evening.

The **Pine Ridge Nature Trail** departs from the visitors center and allows for a quick 1.4-mile foray into wetland habitat. The self-guided trail circles a pool, and a stretch of boardwalk spans a marshy area.

The one-way **Marshland Wildlife Drive** also departs from the visitors center and makes a seven-mile driving loop through the refuge, with several interpretive signs placed along the way. The route includes three observation decks equipped with spotting scopes. You can also borrow binoculars from the visitors center. An eagle's nest is visible from the road, as are several pools frequented by herons and swans.

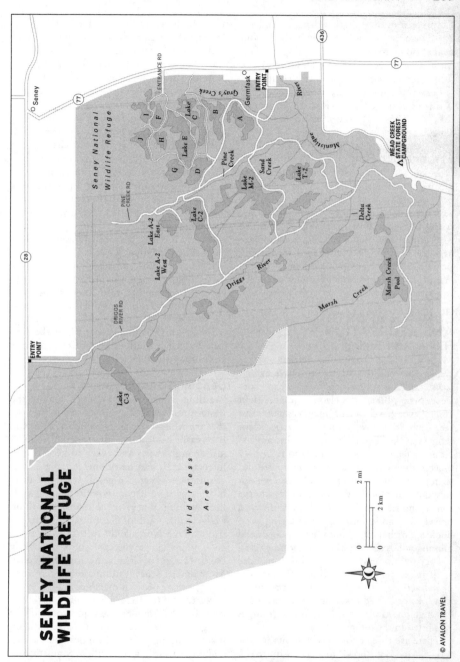

SENEY NATIONAL
WILDLIFE REFUGE

Seney National Wildlife Refuge

Seney

ENTRANCE RD

Gray's Creek

Gray's Creek

Germfask

ENTRY POINT

I
F
J
H
G
D
Lake E
Lake C
B
A
Pine Creek
PINE CREEK RD
Lake A-2 East
Lake C-2
Lake M-2
Sand Creek
Lake T-2
Manistique River
MEAD CREEK
STATE FOREST
CAMPGROUND

DRIGGS RIVER RD

Lake A-2 West

ENTRY POINT

Lake C-3

Driggs River

Delta Creek

Marsh Creek

Marsh Creek Pool

Wilderness Area

0   2 mi
0   2 km

© AVALON TRAVEL

Trumpeter swans were hand-raised and released here, and are now seen regularly. Tundra swans also migrate through in spring and fall. An adjacent three-mile **fishing loop** accesses a fishing platform and is also open to autos.

For information, contact Seney National Wildlife Refuge (1674 Refuge Entrance Rd., 906/586-9851, www.fws.gov/midwest/Seney).

Strangmoor Bog

One of Seney's most unusual features, Strangmoor Bog lies deep in the wetlands near the refuge's western boundary (it's not very accessible to visitors). Strangmoors, or string bogs, are fingerlike bogs alternating with sand ridges that are relics from ancient beaches. They are typically found only in arctic and subarctic regions, and Seney's bog is one of the southernmost examples in North America.

SUMMER SPORTS AND RECREATION

Hiking and Biking

Many visitors to Seney never get out of their cars and beyond the Marshland Drive, which is a shame. A bicycle is really the way to experience Seney. Bikes are welcome on more than 100 miles of gravel and dirt maintenance roads, which are closed to all motorized traffic except refuge vehicles. Though you won't find any exciting or technical rides—the land is *flat*—a bicycle allows you to cover far more ground than you could hiking and is quiet enough not to spook much of the wildlife. Besides, there's something magical about spinning down a gravel road amid chirping, twittering, and honking, with nothing but waving grasses and glinting ponds surrounding you for miles.

Easy terrain, easy access, and well-marked trails make Seney a great choice for families or less-active cyclists. You will want a mountain bike or hybrid bike, since the gravel can be tough on skinny tires. No off-road riding is permitted in the refuge.

There are three main access points for the refuge. One is at the visitors center on M-77,

where trails sprout off the Marshland Drive. Though this area is the most heavily visited, trails here weave between many pools, so riding is interesting, and waterfowl sightings can be particularly good. Note that Loops 1 and 2 are part of the Marshland Drive and are open to motor vehicles.

A second access point is about three miles south of the visitors center, near the Grace Lutheran Church. Turn west at the sign for the Northern Hardwoods cross-country ski area. (This area is called Smith Farm by locals.) You'll soon reach a small parking area and a gate across the road; the trail begins just a few hundred yards west. This is a more lightly visited area of the refuge. From here, Loop 5 makes a 12.2-mile circle, including a stretch paralleling the Driggs River.

If you stay on the trail that follows the Driggs (rather than swinging back east to complete Loop 5), in about nine miles you'll emerge onto M-28, eight miles west of the town of Seney. This is the third access point, called Driggs River Road. (It is indeed a road for the first mile and a half south of M-28, until it arrives at the refuge boundary.)

Canoeing and Kayaking

Paddling is an excellent way to explore the western reaches of the refuge, and it happens that the Manistique is a wonderful canoeing river, easily navigable, with a sand bottom and just enough twists and turns to keep things interesting. It can be popular at the height of summer, though, so go off-season or early in the day if your goal is solitude and wildlife watching. Put in at the roadside park on M-77, a mile south of Germfask, or arrange a trip through Northland Outfitters. If you've got your own boat, you can opt for the lightly traveled Driggs or Creighton Rivers. Both cross M-28 west of Seney. Paddling is not permitted on any refuge pools or marshes.

Northland Outfitters (906/586-9801) is located on M-77 in Germfask, just south of the refuge entrance. The company rents mountain bikes, camping gear, and canoes and kayaks, and offers paddling trips on the Manistique.

Fishing

The refuge allows some fishing within its boundaries; pick up information on its unique regulations at the visitors center. Perch and northern pike are most common. Fishing can be quite good on area rivers, especially for bass, northerns, and walleye. You'll need to head for the upper reaches if you're after trout.

The Fox River

In 1919, Ernest Hemingway stepped off a train in Seney, asked for directions to a good trout stream, and was directed up an old railroad grade to the east branch of the Fox. Where truth meets fiction we'll never know, but Hemingway's U.P. travels resulted in "Big Two-Hearted River," his Nick Adams tale about fishing what was really the Fox. (The more lyrically named Big Two-Hearted actually flows about 25 miles to the northeast.) Consequently, the Fox has always carried a special cachet in the U.P. and among trout fishermen.

Of course, Michigan has dozens of superb **trout fishing** streams, but most anglers seem to agree that the Fox belongs on the A-list. According to Jerry Dennis, author of several Michigan fishing books, it has produced some gargantuan brookies: "The Fox even today has a reputation for brook trout of a size rarely encountered elsewhere in the United States. Fish fifteen to twenty inches long are taken with fair regularity," he writes. The east branch still is considered the river's prime stretch, partly because it's more difficult to reach. (You can hike in from M-77 north of Seney where it flows just west of the road. A state forest campground eight miles up M-77 from Seney offers public access.) Many locals simply cast near the bridge at Seney, where the main river flows under M-28. Because of the Fox's allure, the DNR is considering instituting special fishing regulations; check with authorities before heading out.

The **Fox River Pathway** was no doubt prompted by perennial interest in Hemingway's river. The route stretches 27 miles north from Seney, to just shy of Pictured Rocks National Lakeshore, and by U.P. standards, it's really nothing that special. Its most appealing stretch—especially for anglers looking for fishing access—is the southern end, where the trail parallels the main river for 10 miles. Farther north, it follows the Little Fox and the west branch. Heading north, the trail traverses the Kingston Plains, where loggers left behind "stump prairies." Markers along the route provide information about the area's logging history.

Because it passes through a lot of cutover land, the trail can be extremely hot and dry. If you plan to hike it, be sure to carry a water purification system. You'll find rustic campgrounds at both trailheads, and just one along the route, six miles from the southern end.

For hikers, another option (albeit much shorter) is the trail that heads north from the Fox River Pathway's northern terminus at Kingston Lake Campground. Not considered part of the pathway, this trail winds through pines and hardwoods in the Lake Superior State Forest for four miles before spilling out onto a particularly deserted and delightful stretch of Twelvemile Beach on Lake Superior, part of the Pictured Rocks National Lakeshore.

WINTER SPORTS AND RECREATION
Ski and Snowshoe Trails

It seems that as soon as the snow falls, the wildlife refuge is open for cross-country skiing and snowshoeing. The largely flat trails are groomed from the mid-December through mid-March and make for a pleasant way to pass an afternoon. The trailhead for six different skiing loops is located just off Robinson Road west of M-77. Stop by the visitors center for maps and more information. Half of the trails are easy and suitable for beginners; the others will present a little bit of a challenge, but, given the relatively flat terrain in these parts, they won't give experienced skiers any problems. Loops range from less than one mile to two miles in length. You can snowshoe anywhere in the refuge except on the groomed ski trails.

Snowmobiling

The best part about snowmobiling in Seney is its proximity to the trails that spread across the Grand Marais region north of town. The Seney Trail (Trail 43) cuts diagonally through Seney before connecting to the remaining miles of the Upper Peninsula's trails. Unplowed roads and the shoulders of plowed roads are open to snowmobiles as well.

ACCOMMODATIONS AND FOOD

It wouldn't be true to say that there's no lodging in Seney, but it is true that, with the exception of camping, there's no reason not to find a hotel or motel somewhere else—Newberry, Manistique, Munising, and Grand Marais are all within an easy drive (half an hour or less). If you are going to stay in town, try a room at the affordable **Fox River Motel** (906/499-3332, www.foxrivermotel.com, $40–60 in summer, $50–75 in winter) on the corner of M-77 and M-28 downtown.

If you're hungry, stop at any of the smattering of restaurants that have gathered along M-28 as you approach town from either direction. In short, there's not much here (sort of a recurring theme for Seney).

Camping

Camping is a different story. There are plenty of campgrounds to choose from, even if none of them are in the refuge. (Sorry, there's no overnight camping allowed.) Still, there are a couple of places to go nearby. The **East Branch Fox River State Forest Campground** (906/452-6227, www.michigan .gov/dnr, $15) has 19 sites for tents or small trailers that work on a first-come, first-served, no-reservations system. Take M-77 north of Seney about seven miles. To get to the **Fox River State Forest Campground** (906/452-6227, www.michigan.gov/dnr, $15), take County Road 450 northwest of Seney to the seven rustic campsites for tents and small trailers only. You can't make reservations here, either. For more camping options, ask at the wildlife refuge visitors center.

INFORMATION AND SERVICES

Tourist information for the Seney National Wildlife Refuge can be obtained from the **U.S. Fish and Wildlife Service** (1674 Refuge Entrance Rd., 906/586-9851, www.fws.gov/ midwest/Seney). When you first arrive at the center, stop by the Visitor Center for an orientation slide show, exhibits, and information. The center is located on M-77 a few miles north of Germfask.

For medical care or the hospital, head east along M-28 to Newberry and the Helen Newberry Joy Hospital (502 West Harrie St., 906/293-9200, 800/743-3093, www.hnjh .org). Take M-28 to M-123 and turn left; take another left on Harrie Street to the hospital. Do your banking at the Peoples State Bank of Munising's Seney branch (906/499-3306, www.bankatpsb.com) on M-28. For more banks and other services, drive to one of the larger towns nearby.

GETTING THERE AND AROUND

Car

You couldn't ask for an easier way to get to Seney by car. The town is at the intersection of M-77, the north–south highway that runs between U.S. 2 and Grand Marais, and M-28, the main vehicle artery that cuts east–west through the middle of the peninsula. Seney is 40 miles from Manistique; 35 miles from Munising; and 25 miles from Grand Marais.

Air

Seney is pretty much smack-dab in the middle of an unfortunately long drive from either Chippewa County International Airport (CIU, 5019 Airport Dr., Kincheloe, 906/495-2522, www.airciu.com), south of Sault Ste. Marie, or Sawyer International Airport (MQT, 125 G Ave., Gwinn, 906/346-3308, www.sawyerairport.com), near Marquette. Both airports have plenty of car rental options, and it's easy to get to Seney: just hop on M-28 and drive. It'll be at least an hour and a half from either airport.

Public Transportation

You'd be forgiven for thinking that Seney's central location might afford it a level of public transportation not usually given to small towns. Sure, transportation might not go *to* Seney, but it has to pass through here, right? Wrong. The U.P. workhorse of bus lines, Indian Trails, takes U.S. 2 on its way west, leaving Seney high and dry and—as far as public transportation is concerned—in the middle of nowhere.

WHITEFISH BAY TO THE LAKE HURON SHORE

On the western end of the bay, Whitefish Point boasts the oldest active lighthouse on Lake Superior, but it is probably better known for its proximity to Tahquamenon Falls, the largest waterfall in the U.P. Whitefish Bay is the place to go for some Lake Superior swimming, since the water tends to be warmer here than in, say, Marquette. Paradise is going to be your destination and base of operations for visits to Whitefish Point and Tahquamenon Falls State Park (which really should be a must-see for all visitors to the U.P.).

The quickest way to Sault Ste. Marie is via I-75, but then you'll miss out on the drive along the bottom of Whitefish Bay, where Lake Superior drains into St. Mary's River. Take Lake Shore Drive/Whitefish Bay Scenic Byway instead. You're in Michigan's Upper Peninsula—what's the rush?

You'll want to spend time at Sault Ste. Marie, watching the big ships make their way through the locks or strolling along quaint Portage Avenue. Shoot, some of you will want to cross into Canada and visit the other Sault Ste. Marie, which is okay, too; there's plenty to do with America's friendly northern neighbors.

Les Cheneaux and Drummond Island are perfect for taking things easy. These quiet isles are close to both Sault Ste. Marie and the unimaginably busy Mackinac Island—but you'd never know it. Get out onto the water. Explore the channels and islands. And when you discover how much you love the area, don't go telling too many people.

© 123RF.COM

HIGHLIGHTS

❰ Lake Superior Nature Sanctuary: Located on a remote portion of Lake Superior's shore, the sanctuary is home to several endangered and rare species (page 218).

❰ Tahquamenon Falls State Park: When it comes to determining the Upper Peninsula's most beautiful falls, it's a toss-up, but even money says Tahquamenon comes up on top (page 219).

❰ Soo Locks: Sure, it sounds a little boring to watch giant freighters make their way through a set of locks, but it's an entirely en-

gaging way to spend a couple of hours in Sault Ste. Marie (page 229).

❰ Drummond Island: Snowmobile trails (including a couple across the ice to Canada), hiking paths, and fantastic golf are only a few reasons to head to this relaxing, out-of-the-way destination (page 239).

❰ Les Cheneaux: Although the 36 islands are located only 30 miles from the Bridge, the Les Cheneaux area is often overlooked by tourists and is worth a visit for its sightseeing and seclusion (page 241).

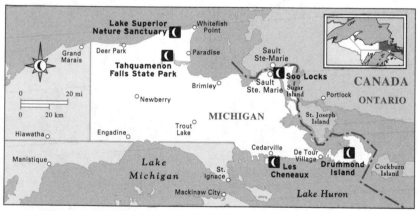

LOOK FOR ❰ TO FIND RECOMMENDED SIGHTS, ACTIVITIES, DINING, AND LODGING.

PLANNING YOUR TIME

Sault Ste. Marie is the biggest city in the eastern U.P., and it's worth a day or two of your time (you could easily spend an entire afternoon at the locks). Throw in a trip to Tahquamenon Falls and a visit to Les Cheneaux, and most visitors will want to be here for about three days. Serious hikers, bikers, or boaters should plan on a longer stay, since there's plenty of reason to stick around—state parks galore, Hiawatha National Forest, and the waters of Lake Huron. Head out to Drummond Island for some fairly secluded hiking if you've got time.

HISTORY

The Ojibwa were the first settlers of the area, migrating here in the 1500s. They discovered a rich supply of whitefish in the area's turbulent waters, and established a permanent settlement at the edge of the rapids, making this one of the oldest continuously settled areas in the Midwest. *Addik-kim-maig,* the Ojibwa name for whitefish, means "deer of the waters," a reference to the fish's importance as a food source. The Ojibwa lived off the river's riches here for more than 300 years. But in a sad and repetitive tale, the white man and progress put an end

THE LAKE HURON SHORE

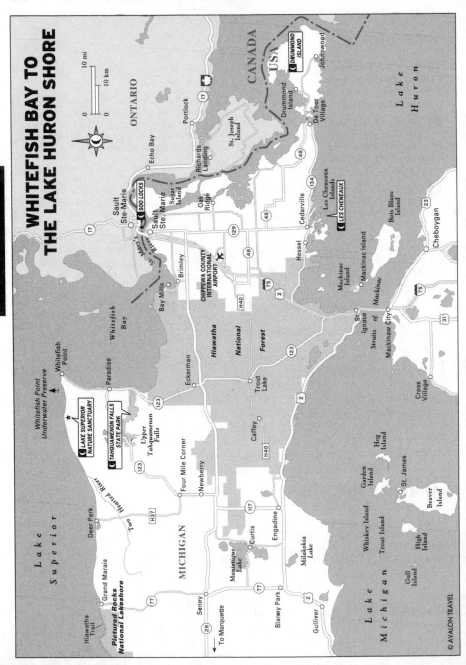

WHITEFISH BAY TO
THE LAKE HURON SHORE

© AVALON TRAVEL

to the Ojibwa way of life and took away this important fishing ground. The combination of warring Iroquois—forced west by European immigrants taking over their homelands—and new European settlement in the Soo eventually drove the Ojibwa out of the region.

The French, too, lived off the area's riches for many years, establishing a major fur trading post here in the mid-1600s, then a Jesuit mission. By the early 1800s, Michigan's northern reaches were increasingly settled, and people were discovering the bounty of natural resources—copper, iron, lumber, grain—ringing the shores of Lake Superior.

The only problem was those rapids. For decades, ship cargo had to be unloaded by hand, portaged around the rapids by horses and mules pulling carts, then reloaded onto another boat. In 1839, the American Fur Company built a short railroad line, which eased the job, but transport remained backbreaking and exceedingly slow. While Great Lakes shipping was booming on the lower Great Lakes, Lake Superior remained largely isolated, its cargo backed up by the rapids.

© TRAVEL MICHIGAN

view of ship in the Soo Locks

Eastern industrialists began lobbying for government-funded locks. The portaging business was the lifeblood of Sault Ste. Marie's economy, though, so the community opposed such a project. Locals managed to stave off the inevitable for more than a decade, until 1852, when President Millard Fillmore signed a bill authorizing the first lock at Sault Ste. Marie.

In 1855, the State Lock opened, a system of two locks, each 350 feet long. They were an instant success. In the first year, nearly 12,000 tons of iron ore passed through the locks; within a decade, that figure grew to more than 120,000 tons per year. By World War I, the nation's hunger for iron and copper, coupled with the opening of vast iron mines in Minnesota's Mesabi Range, made the Soo Locks the busiest shipping canal in the world. Even today, the freight transported across Lake Superior and through the Soo Locks exceeds that of the Panama and Suez Canals put together.

Soon after the completion of the State Lock, the burgeoning commercial traffic made it clear that more locks were needed. The 515-foot Weitzel Lock opened in 1881. Since then, a succession of locks have been built, both to handle the traffic and the growing size of Great Lakes ships. Today, three U.S. locks are in operation (there's a fourth smaller lock on the Canadian side), including the 1,200-foot Poe Lock, built in 1968 to accommodate the huge lakers now common on the Great Lakes.

The oldest city in Michigan, Sault Ste. Marie is inseparable from the locks that shaped its past and continue to define it today. A linchpin of the Great Lakes economy, the city's own economy has been rather stagnant. The Ojibwa-owned Kewadin Casino and a prison complex south of town rank as the area's largest employers. Some state government administrative jobs and the small Lake Superior State University help, too. But tourism remains a staple of the economy—with many of those visitors coming specifically to see the parade of commerce that passes incessantly through town.

THE LAKE HURON SHORE

Paradise and Vicinity

"The searchers all say they'd have made Whitefish Bay if they put 15 more miles behind her . . ." Singer-songwriter Gordon Lightfoot immortalized the ill-fated ore carrier *Edmund Fitzgerald* for the masses, but locals here need no reminders. Less than 20 miles from Whitefish Point and the safety of Whitefish Bay, the huge laker and all 29 hands on board were swallowed up in mere minutes by a fierce November squall in 1975.

On Lake Superior—the largest and fiercest of the Great Lakes—northwest storms can build over 200 miles of cold, open water. They unleash their full fury on the 80-mile stretch of water from Grand Marais to Whitefish Point (hence the nickname "Graveyard of the Great Lakes"). Whitefish Point has long served as a beacon for mariners, a narrow finger of land reaching toward Ontario and forming the protected waters of Whitefish Bay, one of the few safe havens on the big lake.

SIGHTS
◖ Lake Superior Nature Sanctuary

The Lake Superior Nature Sanctuary is wild and undeveloped by even Upper Peninsula standards. The 369-acre plot of land, right on the Lake Superior shoreline, is filled with endangered, threatened, and rare plant species—as well as some of the more expected animals: bears, deer, coyotes. The land is preserved by the Michigan Nature Association (517/655-5655, www.michigannature.org), which recommends guided visits and organizes field trips to the sanctuary. It's pretty tough to get to, and only foot traffic is allowed within the sanctuary; plan on making a day of it if you go. Contact the MNA to inquire about visiting.

Centennial Cranberry Farm

While cranberries are better known as crops from Wisconsin or Massachusetts, when it comes to Michigan, Whitefish Point is cranberry country. Seriously. In 2008, the state House of Representatives passed a resolution making it official. Centennial Cranberry Farm (30957 West Wildcat Rd., Paradise, 906/492-3314, 877/333-1822, www.centennial cranberry.com) was established well over 100 years ago, in 1876. The gift shop sells fine cranberry-related products and, during harvest, fresh cranberries. In fact, the best time to visit the farm is during harvest time, when there's more hustle and bustle in the flooded cranberry fields. Centennial Cranberry Farm is open from Memorial Day through the end of October.

Great Lakes Shipwreck Museum

To commemorate the many ships that failed to round that point of safety, Whitefish Point is now the proper home of the Great Lakes Shipwreck Museum (18335 North Whitefish Point Rd., 888/492-3747, www.shipwreck museum.com, 10 A.M.–6 P.M. daily mid-May– mid-Oct., $12 adults, $8 children, 5 and under free, $32 families). With dim lighting and appropriately haunting music, this fine, compact museum traces the history of Great Lakes commerce and the disasters that sometimes accompanied it. Several shipwrecks are chronicled here, each with a scale model, photos or drawings, artifacts from the wreck, and a description of how and why the ship went down. Most compelling is the *Edmund Fitzgerald* display, complete with a life preserver and the ship's huge bell, recovered in a 1994 expedition led by museum founder Tom Farnquist, an accomplished diver and underwater photographer.

Housed in the former Coast Guard station, the museum also includes the restored lightkeeper's home, a theater showing an excellent short film about the Fitzgerald dive, and an interesting gift shop with nautical charts, prints, books, and more. To reach the museum, take M-123 to Paradise and follow Whitefish Point Road 11 miles north. The museum alone makes this out-of-the-way point a worthy detour.

THE MEMORY AND THE MYSTERY OF THE *EDMUND FITZGERALD*

Superior they said never gives up her dead
When the gales of November come early . . .

Gordon Lightfoot,
"The Wreck of the Edmund Fitzgerald"

In early November 1975, the 729-foot lake carrier *Edmund Fitzgerald* departed Superior, Wisconsin, loaded with 26,000 tons of taconite pellets, bound for the port of Detroit and area steel mills. Launched in 1958, the *Fitzgerald* had a long and profitable record for the Columbia Line, the ship's Milwaukee-based owner. This was to be one of the last trips across Lake Superior before the shipping lanes and Soo Locks shut down for the season.

The *Fitzgerald* had rounded the Keweenaw Peninsula when, at dusk on November 10, one of the worst storms in 30 years screamed across Lake Superior. Winds howled at 90 miles an hour, whipping the immense lake into 30-foot seas. The *Fitzgerald* was prepared for bad weather from the northeast; Superior was notorious for her November gales. Like the captain of the 767-foot *Arthur M. Anderson* traveling nearby, the captain of the *Fitzgerald* had chosen to follow a more protected route across the lake, some 20 to 40 miles farther north than usual.

Just 10 miles apart, the two captains had been in intermittent visual and radio contact, discussing the perilous weather, which had dangerously shifted from northeast to northwest. At 7:10 P.M., the *Fitzgerald* captain radioed, "We are holding our own." Then abruptly at 7:15, radio contact was lost. Turning to his radar, the captain of the *Anderson* stared in disbelief: the *Fitzgerald* had completely disappeared off the screen. A 729-foot lake carrier and all 29 hands simply vanished, without a single distress call, without a trace.

When the storm cleared, the wreck of the *Edmund Fitzgerald* was found in 530 feet of water, just 17 miles from the shelter of Whitefish Bay. She lay at the bottom in two pieces, 170 feet apart, with debris scattered over three acres – evidence of the force with which the massive hull hit bottom. Many believe the *Fitzgerald* torpedoed bow-first, which would have meant nearly 200 feet of the ship was towering over the water's surface at impact.

But even after almost 30 years, an exhaustive Coast Guard investigation, and several dives to the site, no one really knows what happened. Theories abound, of course. The Coast Guard's best deduction is that the ship took on water through leaking hatches, then developed a list and was swamped by the storm's huge waves. Others believe that, outside the normal shipping lane, she scraped bottom on uncharted shoals. Still others believe the warm taconite pellets weakened the structure of the ship, causing it to snap in two when caught between two particularly enormous waves. No doubt books will continue to be written and new theories put forth.

Meanwhile, the *Edmund Fitzgerald* remains in its grave at the bottom of the lake, along with all its victims, whose bodies were never recovered. It ranks as the worst modern-day disaster on the Great Lakes, a constant reminder of the power of these inland seas.

THE LAKE HURON SHORE

Whitefish Point Underwater Preserve

For experienced divers, this preserve offers a fantastic array of wrecks—18 steamers and schooners littered all around the point. (The *Edmund Fitzgerald* is not among them.) Good visibility is a hallmark of this 376-acre preserve. Most wrecks lie in deep water, though—anywhere from 40 to 270 feet—and in an area with few protected harbors. Needless to say, only very experienced divers and boaters should consider this spot. Contact the **Paradise Area Tourism Council** (P.O. Box 64, 906/492-3927, www.paradisemi.org) for information on area dive services.

Tahquamenon Falls State Park

West of Newberry, the headwaters of the

TAHQUAMENON
FALLS STATE PARK

Lake

Superior

123

To M-28

Tahqua Trail

River

Tahquamenon

Camp 10 Lakes

North Country Trail

FARM TRUCK RD

123

Water Tank Lakes

Tahquamenon Falls
State Park

Sheephead Lake

Clark Lake

Lower Falls

Upper Tahquamenon Falls

Portage Trail

Betsy Lake

Natural Area Pathway

North Country Trail

0   1 mi
0   1 km

To Newberry

© AVALON TRAVEL

© CARL TER HARR / TRAVEL MICHIGAN

The Upper Tahquamenon Falls are Michigan's largest waterfalls and among the biggest east of the Mississippi.

Tahquamenon bubble up from underground and begin a gentle roll through stands of pine and vast wetlands. Rambling and twisting northeast through Luce County, the river grows wide and majestic by the time it enters its namesake state park. Then, with the roar of a freight train and the power of a fire hose, it suddenly plummets over a 50-foot drop, creating a golden fountain of water 200 feet wide.

As many as 50,000 gallons of water per second gush over the Upper Tahquamenon, making it the second-largest falls (by volume) east of the Mississippi, outdone only by Niagara. Adding to Tahquamenon's majesty are its distinctive colors—bronze headwaters from the tannic acid of decaying cedars and hemlocks that line its banks, and bright white foam from the water's high salt content.

Accessing Tahquamenon Falls is easy, since both the Upper Falls and Lower Falls lie within Tahquamenon Falls State Park (41382 West M-123, 906/492-3415, www.michigan.gov/dnr), which has provided short, well-marked paths to prime viewing sites. At the Upper

Falls, follow the trail to the right and down the 74 steps to an observation deck, which brings you so close you can feel the fall's thundering power and its cool mist on your face. The view provides a dual glimpse of the placid waters above and the furious frothing below. Four miles downstream, the Lower Falls plunges over a series of cascades. The best vantage point is from a small island mid-river; a state park concessionaire obliges visitors by renting canoes and rowboats to make the short crossing.

Tahquamenon Logging Museum and Nature Study Area

Just north of Newberry, the Tahquamenon Logging Museum and Nature Study Area (906/293-3700) presents an overview of the region's logging history. Antique mining equipment, old logs of impressive size, and photos, maps, and other artifacts are all housed in original, rustic Civilian Conservation Corps buildings. Stop by the Cook Shack Kitchen for an old-time lumberjack meal in an old-time lumberjack setting. The "Nature Study Area" added to the museum's name refers to the trail and boardwalk that can take you into the Tahquamenon Forest and along the Tahquamenon River. Take M-123 north of Newberry to the museum.

Luce County Historical Museum

Another of Newberry's history museums, the Luce County Historical Museum (411 West Harrie St., 906/293-5709, 2 P.M.–4 P.M. Tues.–Thurs. late June–Labor Day or by appointment, free) doesn't just retell area history—it's located in it. The 1894 building is listed on the National Register of Historic Places, and it served as both the jail and the sheriff's home. Today, it houses historic artifacts, an original jail cell, and an old-fashioned schoolroom, courtroom, and other rooms filled with items of interest.

Oswald's Bear Ranch

It's true: There are bears in the Upper Peninsula. Wild black bears. Bumping into them on a camping excursion can be a

THE LAKE HURON SHORE

hair-raising experience; bumping into them at Oswald's Bear Ranch (13814 County Road 407, 906/293-3147, www.oswaldsbearranch .com) is anything but. Thirty live black bears roam the habitats here, safe for visitors to observe in a natural setting. This is one of the United States' largest bear ranches, and it once held the largest captive black bear in the world. Tyson Bear, who passed on to bear heaven in 2000, weighed 880 pounds. You won't see Tyson Bear anymore, but you can observe the rest on a walking tour (no vehicles allowed) from Memorial Day through the end of September. North of Newberry, take M-123 to M-407/County Road H-37 and head west to the ranch.

Lighthouses

Whitefish Point Light first beamed a warning light in 1849, and has done so ever since, making it the oldest operating light station on all of Lake Superior. Marking the bay's entry, the Whitefish Point Light is a utilitarian-looking

© TOM BUCHKOE / TRAVEL MICHIGAN

Visit Whitefish Point Light and, nearby, the Great Lakes Shipwreck Museum.

80-foot steel structure supported by a framework of steel girders. Though it looks relatively modern, the current structure actually dates to 1902. The beefy design was considered an extraordinary engineering experiment at the time, but one deemed necessary to withstand the gales that frequently batter this exposed landscape. The light was automated in 1970 and continues to do yeoman's duty.

If lighthouses are your thing, here's a truly obscure one to add to the list. The 58-foot **Crisp Point Light** sits on a tiny arc of land 14 miles west of Whitefish Point, on an isolated, unbroken stretch of Lake Superior shoreline. Though an automated light took over duty decades ago, the handsome 1904 tower and adjacent home still stand. The buildings definitely need work, but the tower was recently painted, so there's some preservation afoot. You'll need a map or the *DeLorme Gazetteer* to find the light—and a four-wheel drive vehicle wouldn't hurt either. (Don't attempt the last couple of miles if the ground is wet.) The light is about nine miles east of the mouth of the Two-Hearted River. Reach it from the west on County Road 412, or from the east via the Farm Truck Road truck trail off M-123.

SUMMER SPORTS AND RECREATION
Hiking and Biking

Wedged on a quarter-mile strip of land between Lake Superior and Muskallonge Lake, **Muskallonge Lake State Park** (906/658-3338, www.michigan.gov/dnr) occupies the site of the old Deer Park township, once home to a sawmill, a hotel, and no doubt a saloon or two. Today, a couple of fishing resorts represent the only commerce in this remote area, 18 miles east of Grand Marais. The North Country National Scenic Trail passes through here, though, and there are a few feeder trails letting you hook up and hike a section of the historic path.

The trails at **Pretty Lakes Quiet Area** (906/293-3293) connect to the North Country Trail, too. The lakes themselves (five of them, and they are quite pretty) are connected by a short trail. Take M-123 to County Road 407 north of Newberry, then go left on County Road 416 to the campground. There's another short trail (1.25 miles) at nearby **Bodi Lake State Forest Campground** (906/293-3293). M-123 connects with County Road 500 near Tahquamenon Falls State Park; take County Road 550 north to County Road 437 and follow it to Bodi Lake.

With the dramatic centerpiece of Tahquamenon Falls, it's easy to overlook the rest of the 40,000-acre Tahquamenon Falls State Park, Michigan's second largest. In sharp contrast to the often frenzied crowds at the falls (more than half a million people per year, the most of any U.P. state park), the vast majority of the park remains peaceful, etched with 25 miles of little-used **hiking trails.** From the Upper Falls, the Giant Pines Loop passes through a stand of white pines before crossing M-123. Once on the north side of the highway, link up with the Clark Lake Loop, a 5.6-mile hike that traces the southern shoreline of the shallow lake.

Canoeing and Kayaking

The Two-Hearted River is a fine canoeing river, clean and clear and usually quite mellow—except in spring when, depending on snowmelt, it can crank out some pretty serious white water. A state-designated wilderness river, the Two-Hearted winds through pine and hardwood forest; the only signs of civilization you're likely to see are a handful of cottages at the river's mouth. It offers plenty of low banks and sandbars, so picnic spots are easy to find. The Two-Hearted is also a widely regarded blue-ribbon trout stream, so be prepared for plenty of anglers when the season opens in April.

Put in at the High Bridge State Forest Campground on County Road 407 for a 23-mile trip to the mouth. (You'll find two state forest campgrounds and other camping sites along the route.) Alternatively, you can hook up with **Two Hearted Canoe Trips** (32752 County Road 423, 906/658-3357), a livery based out of the Rainbow Lodge at the river's mouth. It operates trips ranging from a couple of hours to three days. A popular half-day trip departs from the Reed and Green Bridge (east of Muskallonge Lake State Park on County Road 410) and takes out at Lake Superior.

It's possible to **paddle** nearly all 94 miles of the Tahquamenon. A popular put-in is off County Road 415 north of McMillan, but you'll start off through several buggy miles of wetlands. A better choice is about 10 miles downstream, off County Road 405 at Dollarville, where you'll also avoid portaging around the Dollarville Dam. Beyond Newberry, you'll be treated to a pristine paddle, since no roads come anywhere near the river. Watch the banks for bears, deer, and other wildlife. Naturally, you'll have to portage around the falls, but then you can follow the river to its mouth without any other interruptions.

Fishing

Water is the draw at **Muskallonge Lake State Park** (30042 County Road 407, 906/658-3338, www.michigan.gov/dnr). The park's two miles of Lake Superior frontage are wonderfully secluded, with low, grass-covered dunes stretching off to the east and west and no visible development in either direction. Muskallonge Lake is stocked by the DNR and produces good fishing opportunities for northern pike, walleye, smallmouth bass, and perch. Because the lake is relatively shallow, it warms up enough for comfortable swimming—a U.P. rarity that accounts for this park's somewhat surprising popularity in summer. A modern campground has several sites overlooking the water. Sites are usually available even in summer, but you can always reserve one by phone or online.

The final 16 miles of the Tahquamenon River wind through the park, spilling into Lake Superior's Whitefish Bay at its eastern end. Fishing for muskie and walleye is usually quite good in the pools below the Lower Falls. Also consider joining the fleet of runabouts and anglers in waders near the mouth of the river, where trout often school.

Bird-Watching

A needed resting spot for birds migrating across

Lake Superior, Whitefish Point is a birdwatcher's dream. Beginning with the hawk migration in April, and continuing through late fall, the point attracts an amazing variety of birds. Eagles, loons (by the *thousands!*), songbirds, waterbirds, owls, unusual arctic species like arctic loons and arctic terns, and more all pass through, some 300 species in all. Even if you're not a birder, plan to spend some time at this lovely point, where you can wander the sand beaches, watch the birds, and keep an eye out for the big lakers that pass quite close to shore as they round the point. Bring along binoculars and an extra jacket. Contact the **Whitefish Point Bird Observatory** (6914 North Whitefish Point Rd., 906/492-3596, www.wpbo.org) with any questions or for more information.

Golf

For golfing in the area, head to **Newberry Country Club** (5073 M-123, 906/293-8422, www.golfnewberry.com, $23 for 9 holes with cart, $39 for 18 holes with cart), a challenging, 18-hole championship course on the corner of M-28 and M-123. The Newberry Country Club has been around for more than 80 years—not as long as some clubs up here, but it's not exactly short in the tooth, either—and provides a driving range, a pro shop, and a refreshment bar. Contact the country club to ask about packages, special rates, and events.

Off-Road Vehicles

There's a sorry choice of off-road vehicle trails in the immediate Whitefish Point area. Some DNR trails aren't too far away, of course, but you'll have to head west or south to find them. That doesn't mean you won't see any off-road vehicles up here, though. Remember, you can ride on any state forest road that hasn't been specifically marked otherwise, which means you'll still be able to get your kicks—try Lake Superior State Park. Also, many of the roads in the Hiawatha National Forest are available for off-road vehicle use. Contact the Sault Ste. Marie Ranger District (4000 I-75 Business Spur, 906/635-5311, www.fs.fed

.us) for more information and motor vehicle usage maps.

Waterfalls

For another look at Tahquamenon River and Falls, you may want to plan a day for the **Toonerville Trolley and Riverboat** (906/876-2311, 888/778-7246, www.exploringthenorth .com/toonerville/trolley.html, mid-June–Labor Day, $42 adults, $26 youth 9–15, $17 children 4–8, 3 and under free). It's much more appealing than its cheesy name suggests and a good way to experience a remote stretch of the river. Departing from Soo Junction near Newberry (watch for a sign on M-28), a narrow-gauge train chugs its way five miles along an old logging route, through roadless spruce and maple forest, tamarack lowlands and peat bogs. In about half an hour, the train sighs to a stop deep in the woods at the Tahquamenon's banks. Here you'll transfer to a large tour boat and cruise downstream nearly two hours toward the falls. Just as the river begins roil and boil, the boat docks on the river's south shore, and guests walk the last half mile to the falls. It's a nifty 6.5-hour trip, one that has been in operation since long before a state park provided easy access to the falls. Originally, the tour operator—the grandfather of present-day owner Kris Stewart—used a Model T truck with train wheels to reach the river. You can also opt for just the train trip to the riverbank and back, a 1.75-hour trip ($15 adults, $9 youth 9–15, $7 children 4–8, 3 and under free). Show up by 10 A.M.; reservations are recommended.

WINTER SPORTS AND RECREATION
Ski and Snowshoe Trails

The exciting thing about Paradise is that it really is a paradise, even when it's buried under several feet of snow. Nordic skiers will find a couple of well-groomed loops just off M-123 about a mile west of town. Paradise Pathway's loops range between 1.5 and 3 miles long; contact the **Paradise Area Tourism Council** (P.O.

Box 64, 906/492-3927, www.paradisemi.org) for more information.

Nearby, **Tahquamenon Falls State Park** (41382 West M-123, 906/492-3415, www.michigan.gov/dnr) has several miles of groomed ski trails, and countless more if you're interested in backcountry skiing. The River Trail leaves the parking area and travels about four miles to the ranger station—this isn't a loop, so you'll have to double back. There's the mile-long Nature Trail, too. The Giant Pines Loop is 3.5 miles and closest to the parking area; farther away are the Wilderness Loop at 7.4 miles and the 5.6-mile Clark Lake Loop. A number of these loops and trails connect to the North Country Trail, so you potentially have an additional 4,400 miles available. Good luck with that.

In Newberry, try the Canada Lake Pathway (906/293-3293) for 14 miles of groomed ski trails near Natalie State Forest Campground, southeast of Newberry.

Snowmobiling

If you want to snowmobile up to the very end of Whitefish Point, it's going to be Trail 453 that eventually gets you there, although there's a network of trails that you'll need to take first. If you're heading east from Grand Marais, Trail 8 will get you to Paradise before it curves south and east to Sault Ste. Marie. Several miles before Paradise, though, Trail 8 intersects with Trails 452 and 451, which head north and hit 453—to the end of Whitefish Point. Heading down to Newberry, take Trail 49.

ACCOMMODATIONS

There are a few decent hotels in and around Paradise and Newberry, but for more selection (including plenty of chains), it's worth the drive into Sault Ste. Marie. One of the nicest hotels up here, though, is the **Paradise Inn** (906/492-3940, www.exploringthenorth.com/paradise inn/motel.html), located at the junction of M-123 and Whitefish Point Road. Two of the 36 rooms at this modest but well-kept motel are Jacuzzi suites; continental breakfast and guest laundry are available as well. And if you simply must stick with what you know, there's a Best

Western (8112 North M-123, 906/492-3770, $100–150, www.bestwestern.com) on M-123.

There are more options in Newberry than up in Paradise. The **Bear Den Motel** (906/293-8023, www.bear-den.us, $50–100) is located several miles west of Newberry on M-28, but Linda Pease has done a fine job with the place. It's clean and affordable, and it's got plenty of amenities, from Wi-Fi to campfire pits. Be warned, though, that the beds are doubles—not the more typical queens. Pets are welcome for an extra $5. At the historic **Falls Hotel** (301 Newberry Ave., 906/293-8621, www.thefalls hotel.com, $60–100), you'll find some of the town's more exceptional lodging, and still at an incredibly affordable rate. The 1915 hotel has plenty of options to choose from (standard rooms, two-bedroom suites, and a corner suite with a sitting area). For another historic stay, try an elegant, intimate bed-and-breakfast, **The MacLeod House** (6211 County Road 441, 906/293-3841, www.superiorsights.com, $75–105). Chain hotels include America's Best Value Inn, Comfort Inn, and Super 8.

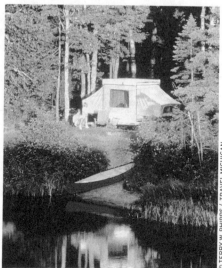

If you're looking to get in touch with Upper Peninsula wilderness, camping is the way to go.

© TERRY W. PHIPPS / TRAVEL MICHIGAN

THE LAKE HURON SHORE

Camping

About 11 miles east of Grand Marais on County Road H-58, you'll reach the **Blind Sucker River** campground, an incredibly horrid name for an appealing place to set up camp. (You'll cross the river once or twice before that.) There are three state forest campgrounds in this area, along the Blind Sucker River, along the Blind Sucker Flooding, and near Lake Superior. (If you choose to camp along Superior, be prepared for cold nights, even in August.)

Even more attractive may be the state forest's **Pretty Lakes Quiet Area,** about eight miles to the southeast. Here you'll find five small and clear lakes, ringed with sand, linked together by short portages. There are canoe campsites on Beaverhouse, Camp Eight, and Long Lakes, along with an 18-unit rustic campground near the approach road at Pretty Lake. No motors are allowed on Pretty, Brush, Beaverhouse, or Long Lakes. This is indeed a pretty, secluded spot where you'll listen to loons and other wildlife rather than the whine of powerboats and automobiles. To reach it, it's easiest to stay on County Road H-58, which becomes County Road H-37/County Road 407 when it swings south at Muskallonge Lake State Park. About five miles south, turn west on County Road 416 and follow it 2.5 miles to the campground. (If you have a good map, you can also follow County Road 416 from the Blind Sucker area.)

There are dozens of other lakes and campsites in the Lake Superior State Forest. Pick up a good topo map and contact the state forest office (906/293-5131) for more information.

FOOD

In addition to being one of Newberry's nicest hotels, the **Falls Hotel** (301 Newberry Ave., 906/293-8621, www.thefallshotel.com) also has a casual, tasty restaurant and lounge. There's nothing fancy here, but the menu's wide selection of appetizers and entrées and the full bar in the lounge make this a great place to stop for a quick bite—or to wind down before turning in for the night. If you want to cut loose, head to **Timber Charlies** (110 Newberry Ave., 906/293-3363, www.timbercharlies.com, 7 A.M.–7 P.M. daily), a family-friendly place that serves your basic restaurant fare and a little something special: the five-pound Ox Burger. That's right. Five pounds of ground beef on a massive bun. It puts that 72-ounce steak place in Texas to shame. And no, you can't eat it by yourself; you'll want to split this one with your friends. For a normal-size meal, try selections of Mexican, Italian, seafood, steak, normal-size burgers, and more. There's also a full bar.

In Paradise, you can't do much better than the (**Tahquamenon Falls Brewery and Pub** (906/492-3300, www.superiorsights.com/tahqfallsbrew/), a microbrewery and restaurant with great food and a relaxed brew pub atmosphere. Selections of steak, fresh fish, hefty burgers, and other sandwiches give way to that Yooper classic, the pasty. If you haven't stopped for one at a roadside dive, get one here.

INFORMATION AND SERVICES

For tourism and visitor information for the area, get ahold of the friendly people at the **Newberry Area Tourism Association** (P.O. Box 308, 906/293-5562, 800/831-7292, www.newberrytourism.com) or the Paradise Area Tourism Council (P.O. Box 64, 906/492-3927, www.paradisemi.org).

Since the stretch of land between Grand Marais and Sault Ste. Marie is relatively secluded, most of the top-end services (airports, hospitals, and the like) are located in the bigger cities west and east of Whitefish Point—but that isn't to say that you'll be on your own, either. Although Newberry is small (there were an estimated 1,550 people living in the small town in 2007), there's a good community hospital here. The Helen Newberry Joy Hospital (502 West Harrie St., 906/293-9200, 800/743-3093, www.hnjh.org) provides health-care services to Newberry and the surrounding communities. To get there, take M-123 into Newberry and head west on Harris Street to the hospital. Helen Newberry Joy Hospital offers weekly clinic services in Paradise, with a physician or nurse practitioner visiting the

Paradise Community Health Center (906/492-3881) on M-123 each Thursday.

Most of the area's easily accessible banks are located in Newberry. The Tahquamenon Area Credit Union (www.tacumi.com) has a branch in Paradise (7960 North M-123, 906/492-3555) as well as in Newberry (7693 M-123, 906/293-5117, 800/575-5117) and a few other locations—Engadine, Rudyard, and Pickford. Other branches in Newberry include mBank (414 Newberry Ave., 906/293-5165, www.bankmbank.com) and First National Bank of St. Ignace (1014 South Newberry Ave., 906/293-5160, www.fnbsi.com).

GETTING THERE AND AROUND
Car

If you're coming from Grand Marais, you've got two choices. The quickest and easiest is to head south on M-77 to M-28 and turn left, then take M-28 east until you reach M-123. Another left onto M-123 and take it through Tahquamenon Falls State Park into Paradise; it'll take 1.5 hours, maybe a little more. The other choice doesn't go quite as quickly, but the first stretch of it stays close to Lake Superior, and the drive is more scenic than M-28's stretches of pavement and flat, uninspired scenery. It's about a two-hour drive if you head east out of Grand Marais on the Grand Marais Truck Trail, which bends south after Muskallonge Lake State Park as M-407. Continue on the road south, follow the leftward bend to the east, then turn left on M-123 and follow it into Paradise. After Paradise, M-123 continues south until it reconnects with M-28 far east of Newberry.

From Sault Ste. Marie, take I-75 south to M-28 and head west until you come to M-123; take it north.

Air

The closest airport to Paradise, Tahquamenon Falls, and the rest of Whitefish Point is **Chippewa County International Airport** (CIU, 5019 Airport Dr., 906/495-5631, 800/225-2525, www.airciu.com), south of Sault Ste. Marie. You'll have to rent a car if you fly in, since there's no regular public transportation to Paradise. The airport has both an Avis (906/495-5900, www.avis.com) and a Hertz (906/495-5190, www.hertz.com). The drive to Paradise will take you a little more than an hour if you follow M-80 toward I-75 (follow the signs), and take the interstate north to M-28. Take M-28 west for 30 miles before you hit M-123, which will take you north to Whitefish Point. Northwest Airlink has regularly scheduled daily flights to and from the airport.

Boat

There's a small state dock located near the tip of Whitefish Point, with only a handful of slips and limited amenities. But **Whitefish Point State Dock** (906/492-3415, www.michigan.gov/dnr) is passable, and it's one of only a couple harbors between Grand Marais and Sault Ste. Marie. The other is **Little Lake State Dock** (906/658-3372, www.michigan.gov/dnr), which pretty much splits the difference between Grand Marais and Paradise. Little Lake has even fewer amenities (read: a vault toilet) than Whitefish Point State Dock. Whitefish Point is located at 46° 45.32 N, 84° 57.52 W; coordinates for Little Lake are 46° 43.06 N, 85° 21.48 W.

Sault Ste. Marie

At the foot of Whitefish Bay, grand Lake Superior narrows to a close at the St. Mary's River, the sole waterway that links it to Lake Huron and the other three Great Lakes. With Superior 21 feet higher than the other lakes, the St. Mary's naturally erupted in a series of falls and rapids near Sault Ste. Marie. "Sault," pronounced SOO (and often spelled that way as a city nickname), means "Falling Water," a name bestowed by early French explorers.

Compared to much of the eastern U.P., Sault Ste. Marie is urban. It's the U.P.'s second-largest city, with a population of 14,000. This historic city is well worth a visit, especially to view the boat traffic through the famous Soo Locks, which link Lakes Superior and Huron. But don't overlook the area to the south and east, where the lovely blue-green waters of Lake

Huron wrap around the end of the peninsula, a scalloped shoreline of quiet bays and a scatter of islands.

SIGHTS
Curtis Lewis Memorial Highway
The twisting, scenic Curtis Lewis Memorial Highway (also called Lake Shore Drive) follows the curve of Lake Superior's Whitefish Bay from M-123 east 20 miles or so to Sault Ste. Marie. It's almost an attraction in itself, passing through the Hiawatha National Forest and offering up plenty of water views and a handful of worthwhile stops.

Mission Hill Overlook is the kind of road where every view is better than the last. As the highway curves south, watch for the turn-off to the west marking this terrific overlook.

THE LAKE HURON SHORE

Drive up the sand and gravel road for grand, sweeping views of the river and bay, Ontario's Laurentian Mountains, the cityscape of Sault Ste. Marie, freighters that look like toy ships, the Point Iroquois light, and, just below, Spectacle Lake.

Four miles west of tiny Dollar Settlement, the federally run **Pendills Creek National Fish Hatchery** (21990 West Trout La., 906/437-5231, www.fws.gov) raises thousands of lake trout that grow up to tempt anglers in Lakes Superior, Michigan, and Huron. Visitors can wander around the tanks to peer down at the hundreds of wriggling trout fry (the raceways are covered to keep birds and other predators from helping themselves to a free lunch) and the breeder trout that weigh in at 15 pounds or more. It's free and open weekdays; call for current hours. Outdoor areas are also accessible on weekends.

Just beyond the Bay View campground, the **Big Pine Picnic Grounds,** a day-use area in the Hiawatha National Forest, is a wonderful spot to take a break. It offers a pleasant shaded area under a canopy of huge white pines, and a pretty sand and pebble beach along Whitefish Bay.

Continuing east, don't miss a chance to climb the tower at the **Point Iroquois Light,** where Whitefish Bay narrows into the St. Mary's River. Since 1855, a beacon here has helped guide ships through this extremely difficult passage, where reefs lurk near the Canadian shore and the rock walls of Point Iroquois threaten on the Michigan side. In 1870, the original wooden light tower was replaced with the present one, a classic white-painted brick structure. A keeper's home was added in 1902.

With fewer and fewer lighthouses open to the public, it's fun to climb the iron spiral staircase for a freighter captain's view of the river, the bay, and the frequent shipping traffic. Stop in the adjacent lightkeeper's home, too, where the local historical society has restored some rooms to illustrate the life of a lightkeeper; other rooms feature displays and old photos. The lighthouse and adjacent beach are now

part of the Hiawatha National Forest, which should help ensure continued protection. The complex is open 10 A.M.–5 P.M. daily, and also from 7 P.M.–9 P.M. Friday–Sunday, Memorial Day–October 15. Call 906/437-5272 for more information.

◖ Soo Locks

Nearly every visitor to the Soo makes a pilgrimage to the locks, right in the heart of downtown at the end of Ashmun Street (Business I-75). The city has smartly dressed up this area, with lovely **Locks Park.** Blue freighter signs mark the **Locks Park Walkway,** which wanders along Water Street and is dotted with interpretive plaques that share the city's history.

In the heart of the rather formal park, the U.S. Army Corps of Engineers manages the locks and a **visitors center** (906/932-1472, www.soolocksvisitorscenter.com, 9 A.M.–9 P.M. mid-May–mid-Oct.) next to a raised **viewing platform** that lets you peer down on the action. Start at the visitors center to make sense

© JOSH BISH

Huge freighters pass through the Soo Locks with only inches to spare.

THE HISTORY OF THE SOO LOCKS

The St. Mary's Rapids have been causing problems for as long as people have lived in the area. Faced with a more-than 20-foot drop on the way from Lake Superior to Lake Huron, the native Ojibwa would take their canoes out of the water and portage around the rapids before continuing on their way. Early European settlers did the same thing, which worked well enough for a while – until the fur trade and an increased European presence demanded larger ships, ships that were too big to portage. So they solved the problem by having two sets of ships, one on the Lake Superior side, and one on the Lake Huron side. It went something like this: Follow the St. Mary's River from Lake Superior until you reach the rapids, then land your watercraft, unload the furs, supplies, and other goods, carry them around the rapids to waiting boats on the other side, reload all of the supplies, and move on your merry way. It's easy to see why this didn't work very efficiently.

Then, in the late 1790s, the Northwest Fur Company built the rapids' first locks, on the Canadian side of the river. The locks were small, only 38 feet long, and could only be used by small boats, but they were effective nonetheless, and they remained effective until they were destroyed in the War of 1812. After the destruction of the locks, shippers again resorted to the old system of portaging their supplies around the rapids to waiting boats on the other side.

The next locks weren't built until 1853-1855, when the Fairbanks Scale Company agreed to construct two locks in exchange for a quarter million acres of public land, which the company hoped to exploit by mining. The two 350-foot locks were turned over to state control upon completion. They stayed under state control for more than 25 years, when national interest demanded new locks that were too expensive for the state. In 1881, they were turned over to the United States Army Corps of Engineers. The Army continues to operate and maintain the locks today.

The Soo Locks are an incredible feat of engineering, requiring regular maintenance and upkeep and an incredible amount of power. To meet the challenge, part of the Soo Locks facility is the U.S. Hydroelectric Power Plant just north of the locks. The plant generates more than 150 million kilowatt-hours of electricity each year, and the locks get first dibs. Any remaining power is rerouted to Sault Ste. Marie, Michigan, and the surrounding communities in the eastern Upper Peninsula.

Of the four locks – the Davis Lock, Sabin Lock, MacArthur Lock, and Poe Lock – the Poe Lock is the largest and is one of the two locks that sees regular use. The other is the MacArthur Lock. Each of these locks is capable of handling large ships (the Poe Lock is 1,200 feet long and can take ships with up to 72,000 tons of cargo) and are capable of quick operation: the MacArthur Lock drains in 7 minutes and fills in 8, while the Poe Lock takes 10 minutes to drain and can be filled in 12. About 10,000 ships pass through the locks each year, despite the locks being closed during the icy winter months, which are, incidentally, a convenient time for the Corps of Engineers to work on maintenance and repairs.

You can watch the daily operations of the Soo Locks from the Soo Locks Visitors Center. The visitors center lets you get up close (but not too close) to the massive freighters as they make their way along the St. Mary's River. The center has several informative displays about the history of the locks and details on their operation. Try a trip through the locks with Soo Locks Boat Tours.

of what's going on. A moving model shows how the locks raise and lower ships by opening and closing the gates of a lock chamber and allowing water to rush in or rush out. No pumps are required; the water simply seeks its own level. Other displays explain the construction of the locks. A knowledgeable staff with a P.A. system, along with video cameras upriver, notify you about approaching vessels. In summer months, you can usually count on a ship coming through every hour or so. You can also call the visitors center to get the day's shipping schedule, but times can change depending on weather conditions and other factors.

It's easy to while away an hour or two watching the ships as they slither into the locks with seemingly just inches to spare. Summer evenings are especially pleasant, when you'll likely have the platform to yourself to watch the illuminated ships. If you're lucky, you might see a "saltie," an ocean-going vessel that's likely hauling grain to foreign ports. Overall, the three most plentiful Great Lakes shipments are iron ore (for steelmaking), limestone (a purifying agent for steelmaking, also used in construction and papermaking), and coal (for power plants).

The locks and viewing platform are open throughout the Great Lakes shipping season, which runs from March 25 to January 15. Those are the official dates when the locks cease operation for maintenance; ice buildup on Superior sometimes affects the length of the shipping season, too.

After viewing the locks, you can "lock through" yourself on an extremely popular **Soo Locks Boat Tour** (800/432-6301, www.soolocks.com, early May–mid-Oct., $21 adults, $10.50 children 5–12). The two-hour trip takes you through both the American and Canadian locks and travels along both cities' waterfronts. At busy times, you'll be in the midst of freighter traffic, dwarfed by their enormous steel hulls. The large passenger boats have both heated and open deck areas. Boats depart as early as 9 A.M., from two docks on Portage Avenue.

Museums

After you've watched the big Great Lakes boats,

the **Museum Ship Valley Camp** (501 Water St., 906/632-3658, 888/744-7867, www.thevalleycamp.com, 10 A.M.–6 P.M. May 10–mid-Oct., longer hours in July and Aug., $10 adults, $5 children 6–16) gives you a chance to see what it was like to live and work aboard a giant steamer. This 550-foot steamship logged more than a million miles on the Great Lakes, hauling ore, coal, and stone from 1907 to the mid-1970s. Now it's permanently docked five blocks east of the Soo Locks. Visitors can tour the pilothouse, engine room, main deck, crew quarters, coal bunker, and more. Throughout, the ship has a number of aquariums and maritime displays, some better than others. The most popular is a display on the sinking of the *Edmund Fitzgerald*, including two tattered lifeboats found empty and drifting on the lake. All in all, it's well worth a couple of hours. Make sure to stop at the museum shop, housed in a separate building next to the parking lot. It has an excellent selection of maritime books and videos.

Like most observation towers, the **Tower of History** (326 Portage Ave., 906/632-3658, www.thevalleycamp.com, 10 A.M.–5 P.M. daily mid-May–mid-Oct., $6 adults, $3 children 6–16), four blocks east of the Soo Locks, is sort of an ugly blight on the landscape—a 21-story stark concrete monolith—but with a wonderful 360-degree view of the twin Soos, the St. Mary's River, Lake Superior, and forests rolling off in the distance. Rather than being stuck behind windows, you get to enjoy the views from an open-air deck. (Bring a jacket!) The tower also includes a few small exhibit areas and a theater showing documentary videos. Yes, there is an elevator to the top. Curiously, the tower was originally built as a bell tower for the neighboring church—a project that went, uh, slightly over budget.

The **River of History Museum** (209 East Portage Ave., 906/632-3658, www.thevalleycamp.com, 10 A.M.–5 P.M. Mon.–Sat., noon–5 P.M. Sun., mid-May–mid-Oct., $5.50 adults, $2.75 children 6–16) uses the St. Mary's River as the framework for telling the story of the region's history. Life-size dioramas depict things like Native Americans spearfishing in the rapids and a French fur trapper's cabin (the French were the first European settlers in the region). The museum incorporates lots of sound in its displays: dripping ice from melting glaciers, roaring rapids, Ojibwa elders passing down legends. One hopes this relatively new museum (founded in 1992) will keep building on this idea.

Lighthouses

Soo Locks Boat Tours (1157 East Portage Ave. and 515 East Portage Ave., 906/632-6301, 800/432-6301, www.soolocks.com, $49, free for children 3 and under) offers the option of extending their popular locks tour with the **St. Mary's River Lighthouse Cruise.** After riding through the Soo Locks, you'll get a short tour of the St. Mary's River and a float-by of a bunch of lighthouses. See the unoccupied but intact keeper's residence at **Cedar Point** and the remains of the original light on **Round Island.** You'll go into Canadian waters (no, you don't need a passport) and see the **Gros Cap Reefs Lighthouse** and the **Point Louise Range Lights.** Morning departures include a continental breakfast and coffee, and box lunches are available with advance reservations. During the trip, you'll be able to see the **Point Iroquois Lighthouse** from the boat, but this one is worth going out of your way to visit as a landlubber.

Sault Ste. Marie, Ontario

Just across the International Bridge lies the Soo's sister city in Ontario, also named Sault Ste. Marie. With a population of 75,000, it's the larger of the two cities, home to a huge steel plant and paper company. But along with these industries, Sault Ste. Marie, Ontario, also

THE OTHER CITY

Sault Ste. Marie, Ontario, is located just across the St. Mary's River from its sister city, Sault Ste. Marie, Michigan. On the Michigan side of the river, the Soo is the state's first city (it's the Midwest's first city, too), founded by Jesuit priests in 1688. The Jesuits were sent to establish a mission at the mouth of Lake Superior, which they called Sault du Gaston before changing it to a more holy name honoring the mother of Christ: Sault Ste. Marie. Although a number of the Jesuits moved on from the mission, the French settlement has stuck around considerably longer, splitting in the late 1700s into two separate cities that share a common name. Translated, the cities' name means "The Saint Mary Rapids."

That isn't all they have in common, either. The cities are bound together by the International Bridge, which stretches nearly two miles and carries as many as 10,000 cars between the countries on a busy day (7,000 is more common). The sister cities are joined by the Soo Locks, too. Essential to the Great Lakes shipping industry, the Soo Locks are one of the most critical portions of the

Great Lakes Waterway and the St. Lawrence Seaway.

But despite all their similarities, the cities have some essential differences that extend beyond their American and Canadian identities. For starters, the Canadian city is larger. While the Michigan side has a population of only 14,000, the Sault Ste. Marie in Ontario boasts more than five times as many residents – around 75,000 people. The economy is largely based on steel and forestry, while Michigan's Soo's is based largely on tourism.

Sault Ste. Marie, Ontario, is no stranger to tourism either. If you've brought your passport, you'll probably find it worthwhile to pop across the river for an evening or a day . . . or a weekend. Popular attractions include the Agawa Canyon Train Tour, the Canadian Bushplane Heritage Centre, the Sault Ste. Marie Museum, the Prince Township Museum, and the Casino Sault Ste. Marie. Its close proximity and easy accessibility – as well as the close ties to Michigan's first city – make Sault Ste. Marie a perfect place to visit America's friendly neighbors to the north.

has a lot to offer visitors. Downtown, a lovely **boardwalk** rambles along the river for a mile or so, beginning at the bridge and extending east past fishing platforms, shops, and the MS *Norgoma,* the last passenger cruise ship built for the Great Lakes, now a museum. On Wednesday and Saturday, there's a farmers market near the tented pavilion.

One of the most advertised and popular visitor attractions is the **Agawa Canyon Train Tour** (129 Bay St., 705/946-7300, 800/242-9287, www.agawacanyontourtrain.com, once daily early June–mid-Oct. and weekends Jan.–Mar., C$65 for adults, C$25 children five and older, C$20 children under five), a seven-hour round-trip through the scenic wooded gorge of the Agawa Canyon. The day-long tour includes a two-hour stopover in the canyon, where you can hike to lookouts, visit waterfalls, wander along the river, or just hang out in the grassy picnic area. The train trip is even more popular (and more expensive) in the fall color season, which usually runs from mid-September to mid-October, and in winter, when it is known as the "Snow Train." (The two-hour layover is eliminated in the winter trip.) Tours depart at 8 A.M. from the station. Reservations are recommended.

As in Alaska, bush planes are an integral part of life in the wilds of the Canadian interior. A small plane with pontoons can get you where no auto can, since almost any remote lake can serve as a landing strip. The **Canadian Bushplane Heritage Centre** (50 Pim St., 705/945-6242, 877/287-4752, www.bushplane.com, open daily year-round, C$10.50 adults, C$2 children), near Pim and Bay Streets on the waterfront, chronicles the history of Canada's bush planes, which began with the Ontario Air Service in the 1920s, established to fight forest fires. Others besides aviation buffs will enjoy this unique museum, housed in the Air Service's old waterfront hangar.

Reach Ontario via the three-mile-long **International Bridge** (934 Bridge Plaza, 906/635-5255 U.S., 705/942-4345 Canada,

THE LAKE HURON SHORE

© VITO PALMISANO / TRAVEL MICHIGAN

Point Iroquois Lighthouse, located near Brimley

$2 toll one-way). You can exchange money and pick up maps and other useful area information at the **Ontario Travel Information Centre** (705/945-6941) at the foot of the bridge. Bring your passport, or you won't be crossing the border.

ENTERTAINMENT AND EVENTS
Bay Mills Resort and Casino

Not only does Bay Mills Casino (11386 West Lakeshore Dr., 888/422-9645, 877/229-6455, www.4baymills.com) in Brimley have the gaming standbys—blackjack, roulette, craps, three-card poker, Texas Hold 'Em, and more—but it's got something that's pretty rare in these parts: free domestic drinks while actively gaming. If that's not enough to bring you to their doors, there are more than 1,000 slot and video poker machines, Royal Ascot video horse racing, and several dining options—Black Bay Grille and Games is located right on the waterfront, Sacy's Restaurant provides a fine dining environment, and there are also two lounges and a café. Bring the clubs for a round of golf (if you've forgotten them, rent some from the pro shop), or stay the night in the hotel with 140-plus rooms.

Brimley's other casino, **Kings Club Casino** (12140 West Lakeshore Dr.), is actually part of the Bay Mills Resort—shuttle service is offered between the two casinos. Kings Club is one story, and it has more than 250 slot and video poker machines. That's a far cry from the casino's beginning, when Kings Club was the first tribally-operated blackjack casino in the States and Michigan's first casino to offer slots and keno.

Events

The **International 500 Snowmobile Race** has been held in Sault Ste. Marie since 1969. Forty years ago, the I-500 was conceived as a snowmobiling version of the other I-500—you know, the big automobile race they put on in Indianapolis every year. The 500 miles are handled by a team of drivers (although someone will occasionally go it alone) on a one-mile iced track, while Sno-Cross races are held at

the same time and venue. Races are usually held in February.

In a nod to self-effacing Yooper humor (and more than a little potty humor), the annual **Big Stinker Classic Outhouse Race** is held on the streets of the Soo. The **International Bridge Walk,** held each summer, is similar to the annual bridge walk at the Mighty Mac, except the 2.8-mile walk is about half as far and you actually get to stroll into Canada (take your passport).

SUMMER SPORTS AND RECREATION
Hiking and Biking

West of town, the **Algonquin Pathway** has more than nine miles of trails for hiking and biking and, in the winter, cross-country skiing (two miles are lighted). Take I-75 to 3 Mile Road and head west, turn right on 20th Street and left on 16th Avenue to the trailhead. Another good spot is the **Pine Bowl Pathway,** 19 miles southwest of Sault Ste. Marie. Pine Bowl has nearly eight miles of trails and rolling terrain. To get there, take I-75 south to the Kinross/Tone Road exit and head east on Tone Road, then turn right onto Wilson Road.

You'll be able to find some good trails at a number of area campgrounds, as well. **Monocle Lake Campground** (Forest Road 3699, Hiawatha National Forest, 906/635-5311), 21 miles west of Sault Ste. Marie, near the Point Iroquois Light, has a nice two-mile loop accessible from its day-use parking lot. A viewing platform overlooks an active beaver pond before the trail heads uphill to another overlook—this one will let you peer out to St. Mary's River and beyond—before coming back down to the parking lot. At **Soldier Lake Campground** (Forest Road 3138, Hiawatha National Forest, 906/635-5311), some 30 miles west of the city, there's a footpath that winds its way around the 15-acre lake and a spur that connects to the North Country Trail. A little farther out, 38 miles west of Sault Ste. Marie and a couple miles south of M-28, **Three Lakes Campground** (Forest Road 3142, Hiawatha National Forest) has an easy one-mile loop around Walker Lake.

Fishing

Sault Ste. Marie is uniquely positioned for some of the Upper Peninsula's finest fishing. With Lake Superior above and Huron below, Sault sits on the wide ribbon of St. Mary's River that connects the two—and gives you the chance to snag some walleye, perch, pike, trout, salmon, and more. And, of course, whitefish. Contact the Sault Ste. Marie Convention and Visitors Bureau (536 Ashmun St., 906/632-3366, 800/647-2858, www.sault stemarie.com) for more detailed information and a peak fishing guide; in the meantime, here's some general info.

For inland lake fishing, try a visit to Monocle Lake, a 172-acre inland lake with walleye, smallmouth bass, pike, and perch. The lake is 40–45 feet deep and has two reefs near Monocle Lake Campground (Forest Road 3699, Hiawatha National Forest, 906/635-5311); there's a boat launch between the campground and the day-use area. Soldier Lake Campground (Forest Road 3138, Hiawatha National Forest, 906/635-5311) is on the shores of a much smaller lake (15 acres) with bass and perch for the catching. Consider **Lake George** and **Munuscong Lake** as well.

As a local fisherman with more than 40 years of experience on St. Mary's River and the surrounding waters, Captain Harold Bailey runs **Blue Heron Fishing Charters** (11589 East Village Rd., 906/635-5134, 906/632-1775, www.blueheronfishingcharters.com, $299 day trip, $50 each additional person) from April through November. Captain Bailey will provide you with all the equipment you need (you can bring your own if you prefer), but you'll be responsible for bringing along a lunch and, more importantly, a Michigan fishing license. A Canadian license wouldn't hurt, either, but it isn't always necessary. **River Cove Fishing Charters** (2841 Riverside Dr., 906/632-7710, www.rivercove.com, $280 half day, $390 full day, $250 night) offers half- and full-day charters, as well as night fishing for walleye. It isn't local, but **Riverquest Charters** (616/837-0440, 866/837-0440, www.riverquestcharters.com), located in the Lower Peninsula, offers seasonal charters for St. Mary's Atlantic salmon.

Boating

In addition to fishing charters, **River Cove** (2841 Riverside Dr., 906/632-7710, www.river cove.com) can take up to five passengers on a scenic boat cruise—choose from Soo Harbor and the north end of Sugar Island ($250), Neebish Island Cut/St. Joseph Island iron bridge ($275), and a sunset Soo Harbor cruise ($225). You can get scenic dinner cruises from **Soo Locks Boat Tours** (1157 East Portage Ave. and 515 E. Portage Ave., 906/632-6301, 800/432-6301, www.soolocks.com, $43 adults, $30 children 3–12). After the dinner buffet and dessert, you'll experience what it's like to travel through the impressive Soo Locks.

Golf

The 18 holes at the **Sault Ste. Marie Country Club** (1520 Riverside Dr., 906/632-7812, www .saultcountryclub.com, $24 for 9 holes with cart, $37 for 18 holes with cart) are among the choicest of the Upper Peninsula, and some of the oldest, too. The course opened more than 100 years ago, and was expanded into an 18-hole course in the 1980s. Visit the pro shop or have an evening dinner at the clubhouse restaurant. Take Portage Avenue east out of the city to the country club. There are another 18 holes at **Tanglewood Marsh** (2600 West 16th Ave., 906/635-0617, 906/635-7651, www.tanglewoodmarsh.com, $19 for 9 holes with cart, $34 for 18 holes with cart). Take I-75 to exit 392 and head west on 3 Mile Road. Turn right on 20th Street and left on Oak Street, then curve right on 16th Avenue to the clubhouse.

Brimley has one of the U.P.'s top-rated golf courses at Brimley's **Wild Bluff Golf Course** (11335 West Lakeshore Dr., 906/248-5860, 888/422-9645, www.wildbluff.com, $29 for 9 holes with cart, $42 for 18 holes with cart), which is part of the Bay Mills Resort. The 18-hole championship course received an impressive 4.5 stars from *Golf Digest*, and it's easy to see why. A fine pro shop and an elegant player's lounge complete the golf experience. And don't forget the casino across the street.

THE LAKE HURON SHORE

THE LAKE HURON SHORE

Bird-Watching

Like Whitefish Point, the Sault Ste. Marie area is a popular spot for bird-watching. Among the best places to scout for our fine feathered friends is **Sugar Island,** the large island east of Sault Ste. Marie between Michigan and Ontario. Fifteen-mile-long Sugar Island and the St. Mary's River both attract migratory birds, particularly snowy and great gray owls. Both the Little Traverse Conservatory and the Osburn Preserve, which is owned by the University of Michigan Biological Station, help conserve and preserve the island's wildlife—and make the southern part of the island a great place for bird-watching. Look for spruce grouse, black terns, sedge wrens, and long-eared owls.

Beaches

One of the finest beaches in the area is on the edge of **Monocle Lake** (906/635-5311, www.fs.fed.us) in Hiawatha National Forest, some 20 miles west of Sault Ste. Marie on Lake Shore Drive. The large lake makes for some great swimming—certainly better than chilly Lake Superior nearby—and you can easily get to the swimming area (there are grills and picnic tables here, as well) from the day-use parking area. To get there, take the Whitefish Bay National Scenic Byway (Lake Shore Drive) as it follows the shoreline west of St. Ignace to Forest Road 3699. If you do want to take a dip in the Big Lake, head over to **Brimley State Park** (9200 West 6 Mile Rd., 906/248-3422, www.michigan.gov/dnr) on the shores of Whitefish Bay. The water here tends to be among Lake Superior's warmest, though it isn't exactly toasty, either.

Off-Road Vehicles

There isn't much here by way of DNR off-road trails. The only one in Chippewa County is the **Kinross Motorcycle Trail,** a nearly 29-mile trail about 20 miles south of Sault Ste. Marie, near Kinross and the Chippewa County International Airport. As its name implies, the trail is open only to motorcycles; three main loops all extend from a central parking area. Take Tone Road east from I-75 to Wilson Road and turn right to parking. Of course, even though there are no other designated trails in the county, all state forest roads are open to off-road vehicles unless specifically marked otherwise. Many forest roads in the Hiawatha National Forest are open to ATV/ORV use—more than 2,000 miles worth, in fact. For motor vehicle usage maps and more information, contact the Sault Ste. Marie Ranger District (4000 I-75 Business Spur, 906/635-5311, www.fs.fed.us).

WINTER SPORTS AND RECREATION
Ski and Snowshoe Trails

On the west side of the city, the trails at **Algonquin Pathway** offer cross-country skiers a series of loops that total some nine miles, with one of the loops—at about two miles—lighted for night skiing. To get there, take I-75 to 3 Mile Road, then head west to 20th Street and turn right. Take 20th Street to the intersection with 16th Avenue. The Pine Bowl Pathway is about 20 miles southwest of the city, and it has nearly eight miles of groomed trails. To get to Pine Bowl from Sault Ste. Marie, head south on I-75 to the Kinross/Tone Road exit (exit 378) and take Tone Road east to Wilson Road; turn right on Wilson to the pathway.

Downhill Skiing

You could go to **Minneapolis Woods Recreation Area** (2601 Minneapolis St., 906/635-6961, www.sault-sainte-marie.mi.us) for some downhill skiing, but don't expect too much. It's fair to say that the big draw here is tubing, with seven downhill runs. If you're looking for better skiing, you'll be better off heading elsewhere in the U.P., or consider crossing the border into Canada for the **Searchmont Resort** (103 Searchmont Resort Rd., Searchmont, 705/781-2340, 800/663-2546, www.searchmont.com) in northern Ontario—but either way, you'll be spending several hours in the car.

Snowmobiling

The main drags into and out of Sault Ste. Marie by snowmobile are Trail 8, which heads west and north to Whitefish Point, Manistique, and Marquette, and Trail 49, which drops south toward Les Cheneaux before connecting to the rest of the Upper Peninsula's network of trails. In the city itself, Trails 8, 49, and others (449 and 497) help navigate the city. After crossing Power Canal near the Soo Locks, you must stay on the trail or risk a fine.

ACCOMMODATIONS

Now part of the Ramada chain, the rather plush **Ojibway Hotel** (240 West Portage Ave., 906/632-4100, 800/654-2929, www.waterviewhotels.com, $125–200) has the nicest accommodations in town, and the best location, too, overlooking the St. Mary's River and the locks. Ask for an upper-level north-facing room. The elegant 1928 building has been well restored, with large rooms, an indoor pool, a whirlpool, and Freighters restaurant. Ask about packages for a better deal.

For the same good location but for less money, try the **ℂ Long Ships Motel** (427 West Portage Ave., 906/632-2422, 888/690-2422, www.longshipsmotel.net, $50–100), a clean and comfortable mom-and-pop-style motel with a fine spot across from Locks Park. A little farther east, but still within walking distance of the river and downtown is the **Mid-City Motel** (304 East Portage Ave., 906/632-6832, $50–100).

Much of the Soo's lodging is sadly giving way to chain motels, which tend to boost the number of available beds (good for tourism), but lose the charm and surprise of the old mom-and-pops. If you're going to find them in the eastern U.P., they're going to be here, in the region's biggest city and most popular tourist draw. Most of them aren't within walking distance of the Locks, either. Still, if you're pressed for a room, you'll probably find one somewhere in Sault Ste. Marie.

Camping

Right in Sault Ste. Marie, there's a modern, 65-site **municipal campground** at Aune-Osborn

Park, on the St. Mary's River near the Suga Island ferry dock. Just east of Brimley, **Brimle State Park** (906/248-3422, www.michigan .gov/dnr) offers about a mile of sandy Lake Superior beach, a large modern campground, and not a whole lot else. Still, it's a good choice for anyone looking for an easy place to set up camp to enjoy the Soo and other nearby attractions. This is a popular park, so consider making reservations if you're aiming for a summer weekend. For a little more seclusion, head farther west to the **Hiawatha National Forest** (906/635-5311, www.fs.fed.us). Within a half-hour drive of the Soo, you can find pretty and private tent sites next to the Lake Superior shore at Bay View, or on a good fishing lake at Monocle Lake. No reservations are taken.

FOOD

Start your day at **Cup of the Day** (406 Ashmun St., 906/635-7272, www.cupoftheday.com) for good coffee drinks, a juice bar, and sandwiches and salads at lunchtime. In the Ojibway Hotel, **ℂ Freighters** (240 Portage Ave., 906/632-4211, www.waterviewhotels.com) offers a wall of glass overlooking the locks and a very nice menu featuring steaks and seafood, especially local fish. This is a great spot for a good breakfast, too. For an old-fashioned service-at-your-car burger joint, cruise on over to **Clyde's Drive In** (1425 Riverside Dr., 906/632-2581), at the Sugar Island ferry dock, for the great grilled hamburgers they've been making since 1949. Inside seating and a menu of other fried items are available, too. **Antler's Family Restaurant** (804 East Portage Ave., 906/632-3571, www.antlersgiftshop.com) serves up burgers, ribs, fresh fish, Mexican-style dishes, and such in a taxidermist-gone-mad setting with more than 300 mounts and who knows how many antlers. Don't go when you have a headache—they have the wacky habit of setting off sirens and whistles for no particular reason. Kids love this place, naturally.

INFORMATION AND SERVICES

For more information on the Sault Ste. Marie area, contact the **Sault Ste. Marie Convention**

and Visitors Bureau (536 Ashmun St., 906/632-3366, 800/647-2858, www.sault stemarie.com). For regional information and maps, stop by the **Michigan Welcome Center** (1001 Eureka St., 906/632-8242) near the International Bridge.

Here's the scoop on **crossing the border:** if you're entering or leaving the United States, you'll need to make sure you have a passport, a passport card, or another travel document that's compatible with the Western Hemisphere Travel Initiative (this can include U.S. military ID with military travel orders, Native American Tribal Photo ID, or a trusted traveler card, such as NEXUS, among others). For a complete list of acceptable documents, visit the U.S. Department of State's travel website (http://travel.state.gov), but for most visitors it's as simple as a passport and, for foreign visitors, a passport and your travel visa. You'll be stopped at the border crossing, you'll show your passport, and you'll have to answer a few questions—that's it. Just make sure you're prepared and truthfully answer all of the questions.

There are a few situations when things get a little more (but not excessively) complicated. Be prepared to declare goods, too, particularly items purchased or left abroad (gifts) and firearms. You'll have to pay duty on larger amounts of certain items: wine and liquor (more than 40 ounces), beer (more than 23 12-ounce cans or bottles), and cigarettes (more than 200). If you're traveling with children and you're not their parent or legal guardian, you need to have a letter from their parents or legal guardians giving them permission to leave the United States and enter Canada; make sure a contact phone number is included. For more information, you can get ahold of the United States Customs Service (906/632-2631) or Canada Customs Service (705/941-3063).

What about medical care in Sault Ste. Marie? In case of emergency, call 911. And for hospitals, Sault Ste. Marie's got one of the best. For more than a century, War Memorial Hospital (500 Osborn Blvd., 906/635-4460, www .warmemorialhospital.org) has been providing the eastern Upper Peninsula with health care.

To get there, take Ashmun Street to Spruce Street and head west to the hospital.

You won't have any trouble finding banks or ATMs here, either. Two of the big ones are located on Ashmun Street, just south of Portage Avenue: Huntington Bank (511 Ashmun St., 906/635-5251, www.huntington.com) and National City Bank (320 Ashmun St., 906/635-4300, www.nationalcity.com). There are several other banks near the Soo's main waterfront drag—try Citizens Bank (501 Court St., 906/632-6888, www.citizensbanking.com) or Central Savings Bank (511 Bingham Ave., 906/635-6250, www.centralsavingsbank.com), among others.

GETTING THERE AND AROUND
Car
If you're coming north over the bridge from the Lower Peninsula, Sault Ste. Marie is a short, easy drive along I-75; it'll take you about 45 minutes or so. If you're going to Portage Avenue and downtown, get off at exit 394 and turn left onto Easterday Avenue. Take the next right, onto Eureka Street, which quickly becomes Portage Avenue and takes you along the riverfront to the locks. There's a very helpful visitor information center as soon as you turn onto Eureka Street—stop here for maps, brochures, and additional information.

Of course, if you decide not to get off at exit 394, you'll soon find yourself at the International Bridge and a border crossing into Canada. Make sure you have your passport. And if you're heading to the American Sault Ste. Marie from across the border, Highway 17 (the Trans-Canada Highway) will get you to the International Bridge.

Finally, those of you coming from elsewhere in the Upper Peninsula will want to get on M-28 anywhere west of I-75 and take it east to the interstate, then north into town.

Air
The closest commercial airport is **Chippewa County International Airport** (CIU, 5019 Airport Dr., 906/495-5631, 800/225-2525

www.airciu.com) in Kinross, about 20 miles south of Sault Ste. Marie. Daily flights are scheduled into and out of Chippewa Airport by the Northwest Airlink, Mesaba Airlines, and car rentals are available from Avis (906/495-5900, www.avis.com) and Hertz (906/495-5190, www.hertz.com).

Boat

There are two marinas in Sault Ste. Marie: the **Charles T. Harvey Marina** (2442 Riverside Dr., 906/632-6741, www.michigan.gov/dnr) and the **George Kemp Marina** (485 East Water St., 906/635-7670, www.michigan.gov/dnr). The Charles T. Harvey Marina is located on the lower St. Mary's River and has more than 30 boat slips and the usual amenities—electricity, water, shower, pump-out, and more. Charles T. Harvey Marina is located at 46° 28.15 N, 84° 18.00 W and can be reached on channel 9. The George Kemp Marina, meanwhile, is in downtown Sault Ste. Marie. It has more than 50 slips with the same basic amenities as the Harvey Marina. Kemp Marina is located at 46° 29.57 N, 84° 20.21 W. Use radio channel 9.

Public Transportation

If you're trying to get to Sault Ste. Marie by public transportation from elsewhere in the United States, your best bet is that old standby of Michigan bus transportation, Indian Trails (989/725-5105, 800/292-3831, www.indiantrails.com). The bus line has regular service to the city—call for current schedules and rates. You can also grab a ride from Mackinaw Shuttle (888/349-8294, www.mackinawshuttle.com) if you're already in northern Michigan.

The Huron Shore

East of I-75, the Upper Peninsula narrows and dribbles off into a series of peninsulas, points, and Lake Huron islands. The area has a simple, pretty feel, the kind of place where casual cycling, beach-combing, and picnicking set the pace for a summer day. While there's plenty to explore for the casual putterer, there are few true "destinations." In fact, the whole area is often overlooked by guidebooks—which is just fine with the locals and summer cottage owners. So don't get too excited about sightseeing. Just pack a lunch, put on a pair of comfortable shoes, and while away the day along a rocky shoreline.

SIGHTS
DeTour Village

DeTour Village marks the end of the road and the end of the Upper Peninsula mainland. This small village has long served an important navigational role for ships heading up and down the St. Mary's River. Many ships squeeze through DeTour Passage here, the narrow waterway between the point and Drummond Island. They make a turn, or detour, to chart a course from the St. Mary's River to the Straits of Mackinac. When Detroit was still a blank spot on the map, DeTour Village was busy guiding ships, with a navigational light as far back as 1848. It remains a pleasant place to watch the ship traffic from public parks and gardens along M-134.

Nearby Lime Island marks the centerpiece of the **Island Explorer Water Trail,** a boater's route that travels from Lime to Mackinac Island along a linked network of islands. For more information, contact the **DeTour Area Chamber of Commerce** (906/297-5987, www.detourvillage.com). You can also stay at cabins and cottages on state forest land on Lime Island. For more information on rates and availability, contact the Sault Ste. Marie Forest Management Unit (906/635-5281, www.michigan.gov/dnr).

(Drummond Island

Here's a trivia question: What's the largest U.S. island in the Great Lakes? Probably few would guess Drummond, a low-key place if there

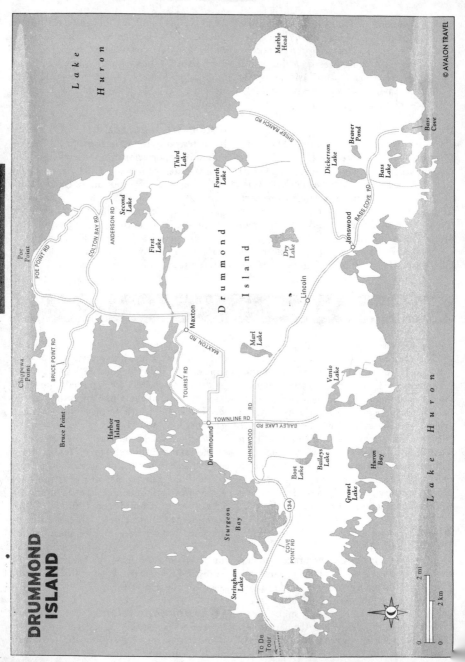

DRUMMOND ISLAND

© AVALON TRAVEL

ever was one. Some 65 percent of Drummond Island is state-owned land; the rest is largely owned by summer residents, who swell the island's population to about 5,000 in July and August. You'd never know it—life in this fishing-oriented place is concentrated along the shorelines, which you can rarely see from the island's few roads.

With rocky shorelines, inland lakes, marshy lowlands, hardwood forests, and open meadows, Drummond Island boasts remarkably diverse animal and plant habitat. More than 24 different kinds of orchids grow wild on the island. Loons, bobcats, moose, and a pack of wolves all roam here, along with more common species.

Drummond and its neighboring islands are humps of limestone, part of the Niagara escarpment that stretches from Door County, Wisconsin, and across northern Lake Michigan. In an area called the Maxton Plains at the island's north end, this slab of limestone bedrock lies right near the surface, covered by just a thin layer of alkaline soil. This unusual combination supports one of the world's foremost examples of alvar grassland, a rare mix of Arctic tundra and Great Plains plants, including Hill's

thistle, false pennyroyal, and prairie dropseed. The Nature Conservancy owns more than 800 acres of the Maxton Plains. The preserve is open to the public, so you can explore this lunar-like landscape where large boulders of conglomerate flecked with red jasper—called "puddingstone"—punctuate the barren expanses of limestone bedrock.

For more information on Drummond Island, call the **Drummond Island Tourism Association** (906/493-5245, 800/737-8666, www.drummondislandchamber.com).

◖ Les Cheneaux

"The Snows," everyone calls them, though the real name for these islands is Les Cheneaux (lay shen-O), French for "The Channels." And there are channels aplenty. Like shards of glass, 36 long and narrow islands lie splintered just off the U.P.'s southeastern shore, forming a maze of calm channels and protected bays in northern Lake Huron, just 35 miles from the Mackinac Bridge. Not surprisingly, it is a delight for boaters. Tall sailboats, small runabouts, classic cabin cruisers, and simple canoes all share these waters, as they have for more than a century.

© RAYMOND J. MALACE / TRAVEL MICHIGAN

The Les Cheneaux islands are a boater's paradise on Lake Huron.

Les Cheneaux first attracted boaters in the 1880s, drawn here from nearby Mackinac Island—already a popular vacation getaway for the wealthy—for the area's renowned fishing. At first, resorters from Mackinac came on daylong excursions. Before long, they were building their own cottages, reveling in the solitude not found in the other established Great Lakes resort areas. Though its summer guests were, by and large, wealthy industrialists from southern Michigan, Indiana, Illinois, and Iowa, Les Cheneaux quickly developed a tactful, understated style. Cottages were elegant, but not ostentatious; boats were sleek, but not showy.

Les Cheneaux still maintains that genteel, yet simple, air. If you're the kind of person who doesn't need (or even like) to "be entertained," then you'll enjoy this charming area, free of in-your-face tourism. Boating remains king here, and in proper Les Cheneaux style, it rarely is expressed in macho powerboat posturing or screaming Jet Skis. No, boating here is best defined by the amazing array of classic wooden craft you'll see puttering and purring through the channels. The nation's first (and now, oldest) Criss Craft franchise was founded in Hessel in 1926. Many of those early boats survive today, thanks to the area's clean freshwater, short boating season, and careful maintenance, which help preserve the somewhat tender wooden hulls.

Les Cheneaux's love affair with classic boats is put on parade each summer at the annual **Les Cheneaux Antique Boat Festival** at the Hessel docks. Held the second Saturday in August, it is believed to be the largest such show in the country, featuring more than a hundred wood-hulled vessels. For information, contact the Les Cheneaux Historical Association (906/484-2821, www.lchistorical.org).

For information on the Les Cheneaux area, contact **Les Cheneaux Islands Area Tourist Association** (670 West M-134, Cedarville, 888/364-7526, www.lescheneaux.org).

Harbor Island National Wildlife Refuge

About 1.5 miles off the shore of Drummond Island, the comparatively small Harbor Island National Wildlife Refuge is far enough to be remote, but still close enough that it isn't tough to get to. You can access the 695-acre island by private boat. Some popular recreational activities include offshore fishing and hunting; there's a swimming beach, too, but it does seem like a little far to go for a stretch of sand. Wildlife includes foxes, snowshoe hares, grouse, and sparrows, and—in the wintertime—the refuge has been known to welcome timber wolves from Ontario's nearby St. Joseph Island. The refuge is managed by Seney National Wildlife Refuge (1674 Refuge Entrance Rd., 906/586-9851, www.fws.gov).

Lighthouses

Lighthouse lovers won't want to miss a tour of **DeTour Reef Light Station,** a more than 80-foot-tall light that's listed on the National Register of Historic Places. Stationed between Drummond Island and the village of DeTour, the 1931 light underwent an extensive restoration project and reopened for tours in 2005. It's a bold, boxy lighthouse, with sharp lines that seem suited to its job of warning ships about a dangerous reef below the surface. The DeTour Reef Light Preservation Society (906/493-5648 June–Aug., 616/874-9458 Jan.–May, www.drlps.com, $95 nonmembers, $75 members) arranges tours of the lighthouse Saturdays and Sundays during the summer. The two-hour tour, which is limited to six people, takes visitors to the light, up a 20-foot ladder, through the house, and to the top of the watch room.

ENTERTAINMENT AND EVENTS

The eastern U.P. seems to be pretty heavy on the casino count—there are casinos in St. Ignace, Sault Ste. Marie, Christmas, Brimley, and more, all within a couple of hours of Les Cheneaux and Drummond Island. But that hasn't stopped Kewadin from opening a small **Kewadin Casino** (3395 North 3 Mile Road, 906/484-2903) in Hessel. Gaming is limited to slots and blackjack, but mainly slots.

There are no hotel rooms here (told you it was small), and a deli is first among the casino's few amenities.

Every August, Hessel is home to the **Les Cheneaux Islands Antique Wooden Boat Show,** the largest show of its kind in the Midwest. Wooden boat owners and aficionados from around the country show up in the small U.P. town to celebrate wooden boats of all types. **The Festival of Arts** goes on at the same time, so even if you're not keen on wooden boats, there's plenty for you to do. Browse the vendor booths in search of handmade crafts and artwork.

SUMMER SPORTS AND RECREATION
Hiking and Biking

A mountain bike is a fun way to explore Drummond Island, since M-134 dissolves into a variety of double-tracks and, eventually, single-track. (Don't expect technical riding—the island is quite flat.) When you go into state land, you'll likely end up sharing some of the designated DNR trails with ATVs, which can be both irritating and potentially dangerous, but with 76 miles of trail, you're sure to find stretches with little or no traffic. For specific trails, ask about **Marble Head View Point,** and **Warners Cove** and **Gravel Lake** on the south shore. Trail information is available from the Drummond Island Tourism Association (906/493-5245, 800/737-8666, www.drummondislandchamber.com).

An eastern Upper Peninsula road biking map is available from the Michigan Department of Transportation or from the **Les Cheneaux Tourist Association** (670 West M-134, Cedarville, 888/364-7526, www.lescheneaux .org). The map highlights major biking roads in the area—including Hessel, Cedarville, DeTour, and other cities—and advises on traffic levels, shoulder width, and other issues of concern to bikers. For mountain bikers, there are plenty of two-tracks, trails, and back roads. You can get detailed information from the visitors center on the island, located at the corner of M-134 and Townline Road.

Canoeing and Kayaking

A canoe or kayak is the best way to explore the waters of Les Cheneaux. The fjord-like bays and 150 miles of ragged shoreline make this a magical place to paddle. One of the best routes to take is the **North Lake Huron Paddle Trail,** which extends for some 75 miles from DeTour nearly to St. Ignace, passing among the islands of Les Cheneaux on the way. It's best to get a guide while paddling the islands, since the ins and outs of the waterways make it easy to lose yourself. For kayak tours, rentals, and advice, pay a visit to **Woods and Waters Ecotours** (20 Pickford Ave., 906/484-4157, www.woods waterecotours.com), an outfitter and guide company in Hessel. Multi-day guided tours of the North Lake Huron Paddle Trail are offered, as well as half- and full-day kayak trips. Custom tours can be arranged.

Fishing

Anglers aren't going to spend much time in Les Cheneaux before the channels start calling. And why not? This is a place unlike any other. Book a fishing charter with specifically and lengthily named **Les Cheneaux Islands Water Tours and Charter Services** (117 North Greenwood Dr., Cedarville, 906/484-3776, 866/322-3776, www.fishingwithnorm .com, $425 half day, $750 full day) for a full- or half-day trip. You can also arrange for a tour with **Dream Seaker Charters and Tours** (888/634-3419, www.dreamseaker.com).

One of the popular spots for inland fishing is **Munuscong River State Forest** (906/635-5281, www.michigan.gov/dnr), where you can cast at the river for walleye, pike, bass, perch, and more, or head a mile east to Lake Munuscong for more fishing. For more fishing spots and information about fishing seasons, get ahold of Les Cheneaux Islands Tourist Association (670 West M-134, Cedarville, 888/364-7526, www.lescheneaux.org).

Boating

The best way to see Les Cheneaux, of course, is to get out on the water. Aside from the pretty wooded islands themselves, part of the fun is

LAKE HURON

When it comes to the Great Lakes that border Michigan's Upper Peninsula, Huron seems to get short shrift. It tends to be overlooked for Lake Superior's rugged shorelines and Lake Michigan's reputation as a pleasure-seeker's destination, but that doesn't mean Lake Huron deserves it. Its shallow sandy shores are immensely popular for summer cottages and vacation homes, particularly in Canada and Michigan's Lower Peninsula. In the Upper Peninsula, the Lake Huron shoreline is marked by the boating paradise of Les Cheneaux and, just offshore, Drummond Island, a secluded recreational paradise.

Lake Huron is the third largest of the Great Lakes by volume, holding some 849 cubic miles of water. Of course, it's the second largest of the lakes by surface area (23,010 square miles), but just try telling any Michigander – Yooper or otherwise – that Lake Michigan isn't quite as good as Lake Huron.

In actuality, the competition is nonsensical, as the two lakes are hydrologically one – a technical way of saying that they have the same surface elevation and are connected by the Straits of Mackinac (which has a depth of 295 feet). Since the flow occasionally reverses direction, the straits can hardly be considered a river. In fact, the United States Army Corps of Engineers considers the two lakes to be one, called Lake Michigan-Huron. (Surprisingly, due to its incredible depth, Lake Superior's water volume is still far larger than the two lakes combined).

That said, there are a few other remarkable factoids about Lake Huron. Manitoulin Island is the largest island in a freshwater lake in the world, with an area of more than 1,000 square miles (the island has more than 100 lakes of its own, including the world's largest lake on an island in a lake). And, if you count the shorelines of Lake Huron's approximately 30,000 islands, it's got the longest shoreline of any of the Great Lakes. Lake Huron was the first of the Great Lakes to be discovered by Europeans – in fact, it was initially called the Freshwater Sea before any of the other lakes were discovered.

Lake Huron is fed by Lake Superior via the St. Mary's River, which runs about 75 miles from Whitefish Bay to Lake Huron. The river itself is vitally important to Great Lakes shipping and commerce, made possible by the Soo Locks in Sault Ste. Marie. The river drops more than 20 feet on its journey into Lake Huron, so the Soo Locks are essential for the ships that pass through the Great Lakes Waterway and the St. Lawrence Seaway all the way to the Atlantic Ocean (ships can – and frequently do – journey from the Great Lakes to the Gulf of Mexico, too).

eyeing the beautiful old boathouses that dot the shorelines, especially on Marquette Island. If you've got your own craft, you'll find launches in Hessel and Cedarville, the only two towns in the area. Though the waters are protected and normally quite safe, be sure to bring a chart, or at least a map provided by local businesses. The various bays and channels and points can get pretty confusing to a newcomer. Many cottages rent boats or include them in their rates.

Golf

For such a mellow place as Drummond Island, you might be surprised to run across **The Rock** (33494 South Maxton Rd., 906/493-1000, 800/999-6343, www.drummondisland.com, $35–59 for 18 holes, depending on season), a spectacular "designer" golf course completed in 1990 by then-owner Tom Monaghan, owner of the Domino's Pizza chain. The first-rate course makes fine use of the natural environment, its holes weaving through woods and limestone outcroppings. In 2008, The Rock earned a four-star rating from *Golf Digest* as part of the magazine's "Best Places to Play." Contact The Rock for specials and packages.

The nine-hole **Les Cheneaux Club Golf Club** (1407 Golf Links Rd., 906/484-3606, www.lescheneauxgolfclub.com, $13 9 holes, $21 18 holes, $12–24 for a cart) in Cedarville is the oldest still-playable and continuously played links in Michigan. It was first played more than 110 years ago, in May 1898, on grounds dictated by the land: forest, sand, water, rock. In Hessel, make for **Hessel Ridge Golf Course** (2061 North Three Mile Rd., 888/660-9166, www.hesselridge.com, $20 9 holes with cart, $36 18 holes with cart, reduced rates after 3 P.M. and on weekdays). The 18-hole, 6,415-yard course is located on a ridge overlooking Hessel (ergo, Hessel Ridge), with tree-lined boundaries, well-manicured greens, and beautiful views.

Off-Road Vehicles

Three off-road trails are maintained within the Les Cheneaux area. The farthest west is Bay City Lake Trail, a short distance north of Hessel. The 50-inch trails here consist of three loops that total nearly eight miles around Bay City Lake. To get there, take 3 Mile Road north of Hessel to Bay City Lake Road, just past Hessel Ridge Golf Course, and turn left to parking. The 8.4 mile Birch Hill Trail is for motorcycle use only, and is located east of Cedarville. Take M-134 to Prentiss Bay Road and take it north to parking. Nearby, the Foreman Lake Trail has several additional miles of trails. Continue north on Prentiss Bay Road, turn right on Traynor Road, and then right again on Springer Road. Closer to DeTour, Cranberry Lake Trail runs for eight miles from M-48 to Caribou Lake. This trail is for vehicles less than 50 inches in width, and there's parking at the trailheads on M-48, just north of M-134, and on M-134 itself, near the turnoff for DeTour Campground.

You might suspect that Drummond Island, with its vast stretches of state-owned land, would be a good place to take your ATVs—and you'd be right. There are more than 65 miles of trails, many of them looped and much of them through old-growth boreal forests. Pay special attention to the island's northern shore, which has plenty of stunning Lake Huron views. What's more, with the exception of M-134 between the ferry and Channel Road, all of Drummond Island's roads (paved and unpaved) are ATV-friendly. Ask for a full-color map from the **Drummond**

Island Tourism Association (906/493-5245, 800/737-8666, www.drummond islandchamber.com) or local businesses. But it doesn't stop there. Drummond Island is also home to **Turtle Ridge Off-Road Terrain Challenge Park** (www.turtleridgeorv.com, $25 per day, multiple day discounts), which has rock crawls, hill climbs, mud, and more.

WINTER SPORTS AND RECREATION
Ski and Snowshoe Trails

On Drummond Island, cross-country ski trails include 4.5 miles at the Rainbow Trail, a groomed, mostly flat trail on Maxton Cross Road. Sorry, there's no snowshoeing at the Rainbow Trail. The Drummond Island Resort and Conference Center has 15 miles of groomed trails for Nordic skiing—rental skis are available to resort guests for free.

Visitors interested in snowshoeing can head to a section of trails specifically set aside by Drummond Island Resort, and there are two

THE LAKE HURON SHORE

© VITO PALMISANO / TRAVEL MICHIGAN

In winter, Drummond Island is a great snowshoeing destination.

miles of snowshoe trails available on the Island Heritage Trail at Drummond Island Township Park. Additionally, all 76 miles of the island's designated DNR trails are accessible by snowshoe. The Drummond Island Tourism Association (906/493-5245, 800/737-8666, www.drummondislandchamber.com) will have more information for you.

Back on the mainland, skiers can try the five groomed miles at the **Peek-A-Boo Hill Cross Country Ski Trail,** maintained by the Les Cheneaux Nordic Ski Club. To get to the trail, take Blindline Road north of M-129, then go west on State Avenue to the Les Cheneaux Community Schools' running track, where you'll find the trailhead. The Search Bay Back Country Ski Trail is a good one, too, five miles west of Hessel. The two 1.5-mile loops make a figure-eight. They're groomed and easy to ski, taking you out onto the small peninsula of St. Martin's Point. The trailhead is accessible south of M-134.

Snowmobiling

Drummond Island Resort and Convention Center is a good place to start when snowmobiling on the island. It's a good place to gain access to Drummond Island's 100 miles of groomed snowmobile trails—that's right, 100 miles. But back to the rentals: Drummond Island Resort rents snowmobiles for $199–225 per day, along with a required $500 damage deposit. Free snowmobile maps are available from local businesses and the tourism association.

But Drummond Island's snowmobiling excitement doesn't end with the 100 miles of trail. It extends across international borders into Canada; more specifically, it extends across international waters, on the International Ice Bridge. The International Ice Bridge to St. Joseph Island is 12 miles long, while the bridge to Thessalon, Ontario, is 18 miles long. Like the ice bridge to Mackinac Island, these bridges are marked by a trail of Christmas trees that stretch out across the ice on the only direct, legal access from the United States to Canada. Make sure you check in with customs on both sides of the border, and have your passport with you, as well as snowmobile registration and trail permits for both Michigan and Canada. You can get a Canadian trail permit from Drummond Island Resort.

The trails in Les Cheneaux don't connect directly to Canada, but they do connect with the hundreds of miles of trails that crisscross the Upper Peninsula. Trail 47 extends from DeTour and will take you to Trail 2 near St. Ignace, making stops in Cedarville and Hessel along the way. Trail 491 splits north from 47, taking you to Pickford, while Trail 49 will take you north to Kinross and Sault Ste. Marie. Additionally, you can operate your snowmobile on all unplowed roads in Mackinac County, as well as on the far right side of paved roads and the unpaved portions of highways. Obey traffic laws and speed limits, and be careful.

ACCOMMODATIONS

On Drummond Island, stay in luxury at **Woodmoor Lodge** (33494 South Maxton Rd., 906/493-1000, 800/999-6343, www .drummondisland.com, $119–155), the grandiose retreat with handsome log lodge rooms dreamed up by pizza magnate Tom Monaghan. Guests have access to all Drummond Island Resort facilities, including an outdoor pool, tennis courts, bowling, and even sporting clays. You can also rent some Frank Lloyd Wright–style cottages, many overlooking Potagannissing Bay, for varying rates. Another good lodging choice is **Drummond Island Yacht Haven** (33185 South Water St., 906/493-5232, www.diyachthaven.com, $100–400 per night, $675–1,900 per week), with large cabins overlooking island-studded Potagannissing Bay. The larger three-bedroom cabins have limestone fireplaces. The property also boasts sand beaches, boat rentals, and other amenities. Contact the Drummond Island Tourism Association (906/493-5245, 800/737-8666, www.drummondisland chamber.com) for more choices.

Along the Lake Huron shore near Cedarville, the **Spring Lodge Cottages** (916 Park Ave., 906/484-2282, 800/480-2282, www.spring lodge.com, $100–150) have a wonderful location in the heart of Les Cheneaux, right on the Snows Channel. Large and well-kept grounds house cottages, most overlooking the water. Boat rentals are available on site. For nicer-than-average motel rooms and an indoor pool, try the **Cedarville Inn** on M-134 in Cedarville (906/484-2266, $100–150). **Islands Inn Motel** (90 East M-134, 906/484-2293, www.islandsinnmotel.com) and **Les Cheneaux Motel** (769 East M-134, 906/484-2581, http://lescheneaux.com) are other good, affordable choices.

Camping

Drummond Island's best camping is at **Township Park,** just north of M-134, not far from the ferry dock. This rustic campground (no showers) has pretty sites tucked in the woods on Potagannissing Bay. There's a sand beach and a boat launch. No reservations; $8 for sites without electricity; $9.25 for sites with electricity.

Camp along the Lake Huron shore and under the pines in a former state park now managed by the Lake Superior State Forest (906/293-5131, www.michigan.gov/dnr). The marked beach/picnic area is on M-134, six miles west of DeTour Village. For more seclusion, boaters should head for **Government Island,** the only publicly owned island in Les Cheneaux. Once a Coast Guard station, it's now part of the Hiawatha National Forest (906/643-7900, www.fs.fed.us). Outhouses and picnic tables are available at a couple of primitive sites on the northeastern and southern ends of the small island; no-trace camping is permitted anywhere on the island.

FOOD

One of the local standbys, where the home-cooked food is always good, is **Hessel Bay Inn** (186 Pickford Ave., 906/484-3203). Open for breakfast, lunch, and dinner, Hessel Bay Inn has a wide selection of menu options, including fish, pasta, corned beef, steaks, and more. Make sure you try the all-you-can-eat whitefish, or stop by for the Sunday buffet. And if the weather's nice, ask for a seat on the deck, which has a view of Hessel Bay and the marina.

For such a small town, Cedarville actually has a decent selection of restaurants. Take **Cattail Cove Restaurant and Lounge** (22 Hodeck St., 906/484-2995), for example. It's no surprise to see fresh, local fish on the menu here (and you really should try a Great Lakes catch while you're in the area), but you can get a good char-grilled prime rib, too. The outdoor deck overlooks Cedarville Bay, making it the perfect place for a fair-weather cocktail or two. If you're in the mood for some Italian, you've got to hit up **Ang-Gio's** (232 West M-134, 906/484-3301) for some pizza.

In DeTour, stop by **Fisher's Restaurant** (168 Ontario St., 906/297-2801, www.fishersrestaurant.net, 9 A.M.–4 P.M. Tues.–Thurs., 9 A.M.–7 P.M. Fri.–Sun., closed Mon.) for good food, great service, and a worthwhile lunch buffet. Another favorite is **Mainsail Restaurant and Saloon** (410 N. Ontario St., 906/297-2141, www.mainsailrestaurant.com), a casual restaurant that serves three hearty meals daily. Think steak, shrimp, fresh fish, salads, and burgers—you know, solid American food with a few burritos tossed on the menu for excitement. Stop by the saloon for draft beer and mixed drinks. As an added bonus, Mainsail is home to the original blueprints for the Edmund Fitzgerald, the tragic freighter made famous by Gordon Lightfoot.

Drummond Island has a fair handful of restaurants, too. The **Port of Call Restaurant** (30420 East Johnswood Rd./M-134, 906/493-5507, www.drummondislandfudge.com) prides itself in offering a selection of international items (Port of call? Get it?) that aren't usually found in U.P. restaurants. Traditional breakfast items like eggs Benedict and bagel sandwiches give way to Belgian waffles, Greek gyro omelets, and European bakehouse breads like Russian pumpernickel and Jewish rye. Lunch and dinner menus feature Oriental vegetable noodle soup, Greek gyros, English fish and chips, pierogi with Polish sausage—and plenty of traditional, Midwestern American food, too. Port of Call features an impressive wine selection. **Bayside Dining** (33494 South Maxton Rd., 906/493-1000, 800/999-6343, www.drummondisland.com) is a higher-end restaurant located at Drummond Island Resort and Conference Center; there aren't many restaurants in the Upper Peninsula where entrees top $30, and this is one of them. Here's where you'll find shrimp- and lobster-crusted whitefish, buffalo strip loin, duck, and braised lamb. For the resort's more humble fare, try **Pins** (33494 South Maxton Rd., 906/493-1000, 800/999-6343, www.drummond island.com), where you'll find burgers, pizza, wings—and bowling.

INFORMATION AND SERVICES

There are a few sources for helpful visitor information. Among the finest are **Les Cheneaux Islands Tourist Association** (670 West M-134, Cedarville, 888/364-7526, www.lescheneaux .org) and the **Drummond Island Tourism Association** (906/493-5245, 800/737-8666, www.drummondislandchamber.com).

The nearest hospital is St. Ignace's Mackinac Straits Hospital (220 Burdette St., 906/643-8585, www.mshosp.org), about a half-hour drive from Cedarville and an hour or so from DeTour. Take M-134 to I-75, then head south until you hit U.S. 2, just before the Bridge; turn left on U.S. 2, then right on Burdette Street to the hospital. Another option is War Memorial Hospital (500 Osborn Blvd., 906/635-4460, www.warmemorialhospital.org) in Sault Ste. Marie, but it's a little farther away. Dial 911 for emergencies.

Most of the area's banks are in Cedarville. Here you'll find a Central Savings Bank (143 West M-134, 906/484-2036, www.centralsavingsbank .com) on M-134 as you pass through town; First National Bank of St. Ignace (192 South Meridian St., 906/484-2262, www.fnbsi.com) has a branch; and the Soo Co-Op Credit Union (90 Beach St., 906/484-2073, www.soocoop.com) is right downtown. In DeTour, go to the Central Savings Bank (109 Elizabeth St., 906/297-3061, www .centralsavingsbank.com) near the Drummond Island Ferry dock. While on the island itself, go to Detour Drummond Community Credit Union (34857 South Townline Rd., 906/493-5721, www.ddccu.com).

GETTING THERE AND AROUND
Car

One of the Huron Shore's draws is its convenient accessibility. If you're taking the Bridge up from the Lower Peninsula, then Cedarville is a short half-hour jog up I-75 and along M-134. It's another half-hour along M-134 to DeTour and Drummond Island. From Sault Ste. Marie, you can drop down on I-75 and catch M-134 or take M-129 straight down. M-129 is a shorter distance, but the interstate is fast and convenient and won't add too much time to your drive.

And you can take your car to Drummond Island, but you won't be able to drive it there. The one-mile crossing is managed by loading the vehicle on the **Drummond Island Ferry** (906/235-3170, $12 car, pickup truck, and driver) for a 10-minute trip across the St. Mary's River. Ferry service is offered year-round; for current schedules and additional pricing for trailers, snowmobiles, camper units, and other details, contact the Drummond Island Tourism Association (906/493-5245, 800/737-8666, www.drummondislandchamber.com).

Air

As with most air passengers to the eastern U.P., you'll likely be flying into **Chippewa County International Airport** (CIU, 5019 Airport Dr., 906/495-5631, 800/225-2525, www.airciu.com). There are daily flights into the airport, and rental cars from two companies: Avis (906/495-5900, www.avis.com) and Hertz (906/495-5190, www.hertz.com). It'll take you about an hour, maybe more, to get to DeTour from Chippewa County Airport. **Pellston Airport** (231/539-8423), south of Mackinaw City in the Lower Peninsula, is about 80 miles away. There's a small airport on Drummond Island, too, but it won't do you much good unless you own or are planning to charter a plane.

Boat

Les Cheneaux's 36 islands, sheltered channels, and bays make it a boater's dream. If you're one of the fortunate ones boating here, you'll want to head to the **Hessel/Clark Township Marina** (906/484-3917 or 906/484-2672, www.michigan.gov/dnr), which has 30 transient slips and a boatload of amenities. Along with the expected water, electricity, pump-out, showers, and the like, Hessel Marina is close to marine repair supplies, a fish cleaning station, laundry, and more. The marina is open from late May through early September and is located at 46° 00.05 N, 84° 25.30 W. Use radio channel 9. Farther east, you can go to **DeTour State Dock** (906/297-5947, www.michigan .gov/dnr). Another marina with basic amenities, DeTour has a harbormaster on duty from mid-May through late September. Use radio channel 16, then switch to 9. It's located at 45° 59.43 N, 83° 53.50 W. For other marinas, consider Cedarville Marine (906/484-2815) in Cedarville or Hessel's E.J. Mertaugh Boat Works (906/484-2434, www.ejmertaughboat works.com). Additionally, there are a number of private marinas on Drummond Island; contact the Drummond Island Tourism Association (906/493-5245, 800/737-8666, www.drummondislandchamber.com) for more information.

Public Transportation

There isn't any regularly scheduled public transportation to take you into Les Cheneaux, so you'll want to make sure you've got your own transportation lined up ahead of time.

BACKGROUND

The Land

GEOLOGY AND GEOGRAPHY

Michigan is easily one of America's most geographically odd states. Split in two, it consists of two enormous peninsulas, each surrounded—for the most part—by Great Lakes. Most people automatically associate the state with the mitten-shaped Lower Peninsula, though the Upper Peninsula looms plenty large—big enough to hold the combined states of New Jersey, Connecticut, Rhode Island, and Delaware within its scalloped borders.

A combination of cataclysmic volcanic eruptions and soupy tropical seas initially formed what we know now as Michigan. In the northern part of the state, around Lake Superior and northern Lake Huron, erupting volcanoes billions of years ago laid down thick layers of basalt, which later tilted and faulted, forming the area's rugged, rocky topography of ancient mountain ranges and steep, saw-toothed shorelines.

Much later, powerful glaciers added their indelible touch to the Michigan landscape, the last one as recently as 12,000 years ago. Four separate ice sheets scraped across the region, scouring out depressions that became lakes, lowlands, and ragged shorelines. When the ice melted and the glaciers retreated, the meltwater filled vast basins and created the modern-day Great Lakes.

© BECCA BISHOP

© JOSH BISHOP

More than 300 named waterfalls can be found across the Upper Peninsula.

Michigan's Upper Peninsula comprises two distinct land regions, the Superior Uplands and the Northern Highlands. The Superior Uplands spans the western two-thirds of the Upper Peninsula, the region formed by that ancient volcanic activity. It is a landscape of dramatic beauty, characterized by rugged basalt cliffs and thick boreal forest of fir, spruce, and birch, all of it part of the vast Canadian Shield that dips down from the Canadian arctic, across portions of the northern Great Lakes region, and back up the west side of Hudson Bay in a giant horseshoe. Much of the region rises more than 1,000 feet above sea level, including the state's highest point, Mt. Arvon, which tops out at 1,979 feet. The Superior Uplands harbors some of the nation's richest sources of minerals, especially copper and iron ore deposits.

South and east of the Superior Uplands lies the Northern Highlands, covering the eastern Upper Peninsula and extending down into the northern half of the Lower Peninsula. Here basalt bedrock gives way to sandstone and limestone, and boreal forests segue into pine and hardwoods. Once heavily logged for its vast, valuable stands of white and red pine, today the Northern Highlands area is prized largely for the recreation provided by its woods, water, and wildlife.

Geographically, no other state is so distinctly cut in two; the Upper Peninsula is largely circled by Lakes Michigan, Superior, and Huron, and is connected to the Lower Peninsula solely by the manmade Mackinac Bridge, which spans five miles across the Straits of Mackinac. Unless they arrive by boat or drive through Wisconsin, everyone traveling between the peninsulas gets there by the same 54 foot-wide roadway.

The Upper Peninsula shares a border with northeastern Wisconsin, then stretches east for 334 miles between Lakes Superior and Michigan. It reaches a third Great Lake, Huron, where it terminates at Drummond Island. Also considered part of the U.P. is 45-mile-long Isle Royale, the largest island in Lake Superior, and several smaller surrounding islands. The entire Isle Royale archipelago

© JOSH BISHOP

The shoreline preserved at Pictured Rocks is filled with remarkable scenery.

is a national park, one of the most remote and least-visited in the national park system.

Altogether, the U.P.'s landmass covers more than 16,000 square miles—but it is water that defines the peninsula. Of Michigan's 3,288 miles of shoreline (second only to Alaska), the U.P. has more than half of them, 1,700 miles on the shores of the three largest Great Lakes. The inland U.P. encompasses more than 4,000 lakes, 12,000 miles of rivers, and more than 300 named waterfalls. It boasts 11 federally designated Wild and Scenic Rivers and is also home to America's first national lakeshore, Pictured Rocks.

The Great Lakes State, Water Wonderland, Land of Hiawatha…many of Michigan's nicknames accurately describe the Upper Peninsula, but up here you'll most often (and perhaps more accurately) hear that you're in God's Country.

CLIMATE

It's difficult to make too many generalities about the Upper Peninsula's weather, since the Great Lakes tend to complicate weather patterns a whole lot. Temperatures in the U.P. are probably more moderate than you think, since the ever-looming Great Lakes cool the hot air of summer and warm the cold winds of winter. There are four distinct seasons. Summers are shorts and T-shirt weather pretty much everywhere (except when you get close to Lake Superior, where you never want a sweatshirt too far away). Average July and August temperatures are in the 70s; come December through February, they drop to the 20s—and they regularly get much, much colder than that. Temperatures listed in the book are in degrees Fahrenheit.

But don't take any of this too seriously. You can enjoy spring-like skiing conditions in the U.P. in February or freeze to death at Thanksgiving. You may swelter on a summer hike through the woods, then grab for your Polarfleece on a Great Lakes beach. Boring it ain't.

The Lake Effect

The Great Lakes act like big insulators—slow to warm up, slow to cool down—and have a dramatic effect on snowfall. Dry winter air travels over the Great Lakes on the prevailing western winds, absorbing moisture. When this air hits land, it dumps its load of precipitation in the form of snow. Weatherpeople and locals alike refer to this phenomenon as **lake effect snow.** These snows can be surprisingly localized, which is why, for example, you'll find most of the U.P.'s successful ski resorts clustered near Iron Mountain along the western edge of the peninsula.

The prevailing western breezes also affect Great Lakes water temperatures, most noticeably on Lake Michigan. In summer, the warm surface waters tend to blow right into those nice, sandy eastern Lake Michigan beaches along the Lower Peninsula. While Lake Michigan is rarely warm enough for much swimming on the Wisconsin side, it can be downright pleasant in the Lower Peninsula and certainly tolerable in the Upper—as evidenced by the hundreds of popular swimming beaches lining the west side of the state.

Lake Superior is another story. Temperatures on this deep, huge, northern lake never climb out of the 40s, save for the occasional shallow bay. "No one's ever drowned in Lake Superior," the saying goes. "They all die of hypothermia first."

Freshwater freezes faster than saltwater, and the Great Lakes will often freeze over from land to several miles out. The ice gets thick enough that brave souls snowmobile to the islands, especially nearby ones like Mackinac, or across the frozen ice bridge from Drummond Island to Canada. The commercial shipping season shuts down from January 15 to March 25, but bad weather often hampers it for much longer. Commercial ships regularly pound through ice up to a foot thick; more than that, and they rely on the Coast Guard's *Mackinaw,* a 240-foot heavily reinforced ship specifically designed for ramming a passage through ice. The *Mackinaw* can "back and ram" its way through walls of ice as high as 10 feet.

A Few Words about Winter

Yes, Michigan's Upper Peninsula has winter—long and cold. You can usually count on snow and cold temperatures from about Thanksgiving to Easter. If you want reliable snow, you've come to the right place. Sure, it snows in the Lower Peninsula (the Detroit area averages less than 40 inches of snow a year), but the U.P. gets blanketed with more than 160 inches annually.

That's an average. U.P. snows are legendary, especially in the Keweenaw Peninsula, where 300-inch winters aren't that unusual. (Sticking far out into Lake Superior, it *really* gets nailed with lake effect snows.) In summer, you'll often notice curious pier-like contraptions sprouting from front doors and leading to sidewalks on Keweenaw homes, usually a couple feet off the ground. They're there to cut down on shoveling—no need to shovel that front walk until there's at least 24 inches on the ground. Ladders nailed to roofs are there for a reason, too. When accumulated snows threaten to collapse the roof, the ladders provide a foothold from which to clear the stuff off.

You should be aware of a dangerous little thing called the **windchill factor,** the threat that comes when cold temperatures are coupled with biting winds. When it's 5°F outside, a 15-mph wind will make it feel like -25°. Not only is this exceedingly uncomfortable, it means you're at an even greater risk for frostbite or hypothermia. Weather forecasts tend to warn you about the windchill factor, but not always; remember to take into consideration both the temperature and the wind speed when dressing for the outdoors.

Having said all this, many people welcome the Upper Peninsula's winter, and it's a huge piece of the state's tourism pie. Few other areas in the Midwest can offer as reliable a season for skiing, snowboarding, snowmobiling, ice fishing, and snowshoeing. Of course, sitting around a fire or soaking in a hot tub is acceptable behavior, too.

When to Go

When to visit Michigan's Upper Peninsula depends on your interests. For traditional warm-weather pursuits, count on summer arriving sometime in early June and lasting until early September. July is the warmest month, but in the U.P., it's also the buggiest. They don't call it black fly season for nothing. Try to time a camping trip before the mosquitoes and black flies hatch—*usually* in mid-June or after mid-August.

Autumn may be the best time to visit, when days are warm, nights are cool, bugs are gone, and Michigan's hardwoods put on a color show to rival Vermont's. September and October are fine months in the U.P., though be aware that late October can become quite winterish. For peak autumn color, figure on the first or second week of September, then figure that this will not be accurate the year you plan to visit.

Winter kicks in pretty reliably in December in the U.P. and sticks around through March most years. For snow sports, February is probably your safest bet to ensure good cover.

If you can, avoid November and April, both characterized by gray skies and rain/snow/sleet mixtures. Ugh. Spring usually doesn't begin showing up until mid-May at the earliest. The shady pine forests of the U.P. can easily hold snow until Memorial Day. Like autumn, spring in Michigan can be wonderful, with moderate temperatures and blossoming trees.

ENVIRONMENTAL ISSUES

The Upper Peninsula's environmental concerns have all revolved around the same core issue: protecting the peninsula's uncommon natural resources. Thankfully, people have always been willing to step in and stand against those who would use and abuse the land. Of course, the culprit puts on a different mask every so often. It started with the fur trade, then moved on to mining and logging; more recently it's been mining regulations, asbestos dumping, nuclear waste, and watershed protection. There's an ongoing fight to keep metallic sulfide mining—and its devastating environmental damage—out of the U.P. Whether or not it succeeds is still up in the air.

In short, just because the Upper Peninsula is a wild peninsula doesn't mean that it will always stay that way. It takes a lot of hard work from the folks at the Upper Peninsula Environmental Coalition and similar organizations to keep it the outdoorsy paradise it is today.

PRESERVATION

Beginning in the 1920s, as the mining and timber industries began their declines, the current value of preserving the land and its resources started taking shape, beginning with the Ottawa and Hiawatha National Forests in the late 1920s. In 1931, Isle Royale became part of the National Park System. The 1940s added both Porcupine Mountain and Tahquamenon Falls State Parks, and more land would follow, including the Pictured Rocks National Lakeshore in 1966. The recent history of the Upper Peninsula tells the story of a region that had once been exploited for its resources slowly but surely becoming a region that recognizes the importance of preservation.

Flora and Fauna

Though it's called the Wolverine State, there's no evidence wolverines ever lived in Michigan, even in the Upper Peninsula—just a lot of highly suspect tall tales about how it acquired the nickname. (Most likely, early fur traders brought wolverine pelts to the numerous trading posts here.) With an estimated 85 percent of the peninsula forested, the U.P. harbors lots of gray and red foxes, skunks, squirrels, beaver, minks, muskrats, and other small **mammals.** All of Michigan has a huge—and often problematic—population of white-tailed deer, and the Upper Peninsula is no different. Of all the large mammals, this is the one you'll see more often than any other—and often not until one of them leaps out in front of your car. The U.P. has some more uncommon mammals, too: a very healthy number of black bears, a couple hundred wolves, some moose, bobcats, and cougars.

Some 300 kinds of **birds** live in the state, including such notable species as bald eagles, peregrine falcons, loons, swans, herons, and dozens of songbirds. Hunting for game birds such as ducks, geese, grouse, and pheasant is popular. Michigan lies on a major migratory pathway, so it offers excellent bird-watching in spring and fall. Of special note is the hawk migration, as thousands fly between the southern Lower Peninsula and Canada.

With so much water, **fish** thrive here, too, of course, in both the Great Lakes and inland waters. Though commercial fishing has decreased dramatically in the last few decades (the result of overfishing and the accidental introduction of the lamprey eel and zebra mussel), sportfishing remains popular on the Great Lakes, for chinook salmon, coho, steelhead, lake trout, and brown trout. On inland waters, the walleye and yellow perch are prized for flavor, while

© CARL TER HARR/TRAVEL MICHIGAN

A successful moose reintroduction program brought the majestic animal back to the Upper Peninsula.

the muskie and northern pike are considered top sport fish. Bass, trout, and panfish can also be found in inland waters. Michigan has several blue-ribbon streams, especially in the eastern U.P.

INSECTS

And yes, Michigan's Upper Peninsula has its share of pesky insects. There's a reason you spot those corny T-shirts proclaiming the **mosquito** the Michigan state bird. The first hatch of mosquitoes usually occurs in early June (depending on local weather conditions), and the little buggers immediately discover their love for humans. Most mosquitoes won't hurt you—much—but their bites will cause a small lump and an itchy reaction. Be aware, too, that some mosquitoes can carry communicable diseases. You won't have to worry about malaria this far north, but other scary infections like the West Nile virus have been making national headlines, so it'd be best to take measures against bites. Mosquitoes can persist all summer, but tend to be less of a problem as

summer wears on, especially if conditions are dry. Mosquitoes are most populous in low-lying wet areas and woods; unfortunately, that's a goodly portion of the U.P. They tend to be most active at dusk. Your best way to avoid them is to stay in a breeze and wear long pants and long sleeves. Many people swear by repellent; the stuff with DEET is most effective, but studies have linked it with various health risks. If you choose to use repellent, be sure to wash your hands carefully before eating, and read the label warnings, especially before applying it to small children. Some people swear that eating a lot of garlic makes one less attractive to mosquitoes. (Probably to your hiking partners, too, but, hey, this is about survival.)

Black flies can be an equally obnoxious travel companion. They pose less of a health risk than mosquitoes but have a far nastier bite—somewhere between a mosquito bite and a bee sting on the pain scale. Black flies look like houseflies on steroids. They tend to be worst in the deep woods and in early summer. U.P. black flies can be the stuff of legend;

MICHIGAN STATE SYMBOLS

- State tree – white pine
- State bird – American robin
- State fish – brook trout
- State flower – apple blossom
- State gem – Isle Royale greenstone
- State stone – Petoskey stone
- State reptile – painted turtle
- State fossil – mastodon
- State soil – Kalkaska Sand
- State wildflower – dwarf lake iris
- State game mammal – white-tailed deer

anyone planning time in the backcountry would be wise to carry the nastiest repellent he or she can find, and pack a head net, too. Even if you're not in the backcountry, odds are you'll run into one or two of the little pests—and several hundred of their friends. Some people have full body nets. "Surely," you say, "it can't be all that bad." But that's before you step out of the car and look down to see that your blue jeans (wear long pants during fly season) aren't so much blue as blue-with-moving-black-spots. Remember: If you come prepared, they're more irritating than problematic.

REINTRODUCTION AND MANAGEMENT PROGRAMS

Two of the Upper Peninsula's mammals are testimonies to the effectiveness of reintroduction and management programs. The **gray wolf** is believed to have been present in every one of Michigan's counties at some point, but by around 1910 they were relegated to the Upper Peninsula. Before their reappearance in the 1990s, Michigan's last wolf pups were born in the mid-1950s, in the area now protected

as Pictured Rocks. Wolves were protected in 1965, and were listed as endangered in 1973. When four of the animals were relocated to the U.P. from Minnesota in 1974, however, all four of them were killed. Today, though, wolves are thriving. In 1991 a pair of wolves produced the first pups born in the state's mainland for more than four decades. That population, which was estimated at about 20 animals in 1992, is believed to have descended from animals that wandered here from Minnesota, Wisconsin, or Ontario. Although the wolf remains on the state's list of threatened species, there was a healthy population of more than 360 wolves in 2004.

In the 1980s, **moose** were reintroduced to a remote area south of the U.P.'s Huron Mountains, with officials releasing a total of 61 moose from Ontario in two separate operations. Most interesting was the method of reintroduction: Wildlife biologists airlifted the moose one by one, in a sling dangling beneath a helicopter, to a base camp, from which they were trucked 600 miles to the Huron Mountains. Van Riper State Park in Michigamme has an interesting display with photos of the famous "moose lifts." The reintroduction worked, though not as well as hoped or expected. The moose population failed to meet the project goal of 1,000 animals by 2000—today, several hundred moose roam the western U.P., and the population continues to grow.

Programs for the management of wolf and moose in the Upper Peninsula don't take into account Isle Royale, where there are healthy, dynamic natural populations of both animals. In fact, a scientific study of the predator-prey relationship between the species has been ongoing for more than 50 years, the longest continuous study of its kind anywhere. Of course, island populations rise and fall from year to year—at last count, the moose population was around 450, while the wolf population hovered around 30.

TREES

There's a reason the **white pine** is the state tree—vast stands of the magnificent trees once covered the northern portions of the state, making Michigan the nation's leading lumber center. Michigan pine largely rebuilt Chicago after the Great Fire and supplied a hungry nation as it expanded westward across the treeless plains.

Today, a few tracts of virgin white pine, red pine, hemlock, and cedar remain in the Upper Peninsula, magnificent species scraping the sky several stories above. Much of the U.P.'s original prime logging land is now second-growth pines, many growing tall again. Today's logging operations still clear-cut, but in much smaller sections, and are increasingly shifting to selective-cutting methods.

History

MICHIGAN'S NATIVE PEOPLES

Buried under layers of glacial ice until about 10,000 years ago, the land that is now Michigan was inhospitable to many of the native cultures that thrived in much of the Midwest, such as the Paleo and Archaic Indians. Some of the first signs of Michigan civilization can be found in the Upper Peninsula's Keweenaw Peninsula, where the Copper Culture Indians of about 5000–500 B.C. left evidence of their skill as prehistoric miners, devising ways to extract copper from bedrock and fashioning it into tools. Archaeologists believe they may be the earliest toolmakers in all the world.

The **Algonquin** people migrated to the Great Lakes region from the banks of the St. Lawrence Seaway later, probably after A.D. 1000. The Algonquins were divided into three tribes: the **Ottawa** (or Odawa), the **Ojibwa** (or Chippewa), and the **Potawatomi.** Together, they called themselves the **Anishinabe,** or "First People." They named their new land "Michi Gami," meaning "Large Lake." In and around that lake they found the state's abundant wildlife—including white-tailed deer, great schools of fish, moose, elk, and black bears—and rich natural resources that nourished the tribes for centuries before the arrival of Europeans.

The three tribes coexisted peacefully, each moving to a different area. The Ottawa settled around the Straits of Mackinac, Sault Ste. Marie, and the Leelanau Peninsula; the Ojibwa moved west, along the shores of Lake Superior; and the Potawatomi headed south, to the southern half of the Lower Peninsula. They communicated regularly, and their peaceable relationship proved valuable when invaders came to their lands. Together, they successfully fought off the warring Iroquois who came from the east in the 1600s, and they presented themselves as a strong, unified people when Europeans arrived.

THE FRENCH

Étienne Brûlé, the first European to arrive on the state's soil (in 1615), was more interested in exploiting the land than worshipping it. Brûlé was sent by Samuel de Champlain, lieutenant governor of New France, who hoped to find copper and a shortcut to the Far East. Brûlé sent back reports recounting the land's untamed beauty and strange new flora and fauna.

Other opportunists soon followed. Some were after Michigan's rich supply of furs, others after the souls of what they saw as a godless land. Among the most famous of these early explorers was Father Jacques Marquette, who established the state's first permanent settlement, at Sault Ste. Marie in 1668, and a second outpost at the straits of Michilimackinac in 1671. The French *coureurs de bois,* a loose term for unlicensed traders, provided a sharp contrast to the priests and nobility. Rugged individualists, they lived among the Native Americans, respected their customs, and hunted and trapped the region's rich stores of game.

Marquette's 17th-century writings brought even more settlers, mostly fur traders, such as John Jacob Astor. In the early 1800s, Astor's American Fur Company, headquartered on

Mackinac Island, made him the richest man in the United States.

THE BRITISH

The area wasn't peaceful for long. As the fur trade became more lucrative, the British wanted an increasingly larger piece of the pie. The late 1600s saw British traders make their way to across Lake Huron from New York to St. Ignace, offering their trade goods for pelts and, from the French point of view, nosing in on the fur trade and threatening the alliances made with local tribes. Before too long, the intensity of the British and French animosity reached its peak, resulting in the French and Indian Wars in the mid-1700s. The war effectively ended the century-and-a-half-long French era and, in 1759, ushered in British rule. Skirmishes between the French, British, and natives continued, though, especially around the Straits of Mackinac. In one of history's more exciting moments, a group of Ojibwa successfully raided the British-run Fort Michilimackinac in 1763 as part of Pontiac's Rebellion. Today, museums and historic state parks in the area chronicle the events.

The British ruled the colony with an iron fist. While the French had treated the Native Americans with a certain amount of respect, the British allied themselves with tribes that were traditional enemies of those native to the area. After Pontiac's Rebellion, the natives negotiated slightly better terms for their relationships with the ruling British, who made peaceable and necessary changes to some of their policies. The British actively discouraged settlement of the state's interior to protect their rich fur empire. In 1783, the Treaty of Paris gave the lands to the newly independent United States.

ON TO STATEHOOD

In 1825, New York's Erie Canal, which connected Albany on the Hudson River to Buffalo on Lake Erie, opened. This new water route enabled more and more people to move westward and settle in the Michigan Territory. From 1820 to 1830, the population more than tripled, to just over 31,000. In 1837, the burgeoning territory was awarded statehood, making Michigan the 26th state in the Union.

Interestingly enough, most of the Upper Peninsula was almost left out of the deal. At the time, due to some sloppy surveying, the state of Ohio and up-and-coming Michigan were feuding over a 468-square-mile section of land known as the Toledo Strip. The Toledo War (a bit of a misnomer, as there was no physical fighting) ensued, and the dispute wasn't resolved until Congress awarded the strip to Ohio and gave to Michigan, as a somewhat disappointing consolation prize, the western three-quarters of the Upper Peninsula, which likely would have gone to Wisconsin otherwise. It seemed like the short end of the stick for Michigan—until the seemingly worthless frontier of the Upper Peninsula began to give up its mother lode of minerals in the ensuing copper and iron booms.

By 1840, more than 200,000 people had moved to Michigan. Early industry revolved around farming and agriculture, with lumber becoming a hugely successful enterprise in the later part of the century. Altogether, more than 160 billion board feet of pine were cut and hauled from Michigan's northwoods by the 1890s—enough to build 10 million six-room houses. While the southern part of the state grew increasingly civilized, the northwoods and the Upper Peninsula were filled with wild and rollicking logging camps.

INDIAN REMOVAL ACT

In one of the saddest chapters in our nation's history, President Andrew Jackson signed the Indian Removal Act in 1830, giving the U.S. government permission to "trade" Native American lands east of the Mississippi for unspecified lands out west. The federal government claimed it was for the tribes' own protection, reporting—and correctly so—that settlers would continue to surge into their homelands in the name of frontier expansion.

The Native Americans, of course, had no interest in leaving areas that had been their homelands for centuries. For unknown reasons, tribes in northern Michigan and Wisconsin were largely ignored by the federal Indian Bureau at first. Most likely, it was only because the government found their lands undesirable at the time; the Potawatomi, who lived on desirable farmland in southern Michigan, were forcibly removed.

Unfortunately, the federal government didn't leave Michigan's Native Americans alone for long. By the mid-1800s, treaties had "legally" taken away much of the tribes' land in both the Upper and Lower Peninsulas and established many of the reservations that exist today.

The new state government, however, did treat the tribes with a modicum of decency. In 1850, Native Americans were given the right to vote and even to run for office in counties where the population was predominantly native—a concession unheard of elsewhere for many years.

THE COPPER RUSH

In 1840, state geologist Douglass Houghton confirmed the presence of copper in the Upper Peninsula's Keweenaw Peninsula—vast deposits of pure, native copper, much of it right near the surface, there for the taking. The U.S. acquired the western half of the U.P.—and its mineral rights—from the Ojibwa in 1842, as prospectors began flooding toward the wild and remote Keweenaw. The young United States had an insatiable appetite for the metal, first for new industrial machinery and later for Civil War hardware, electrical wiring, and other innovations. Houghton's find was nearly as good as gold.

The Copper Rush began almost overnight, first with prospectors, then with large mining enterprises swarming the Keweenaw. Lucky prospectors secured deck space on Great Lakes vessels, sailing up Lakes Huron and Michigan, then along the southern shore of Superior. But

TWO STATES IN ONE

Is it a case of simple sibling rivalry or a marriage of irreconcilable differences? The Upper and Lower Peninsulas of Michigan are a five-mile bridge and a world apart. Lower Peninsula residents – non-outdoorsy ones, anyway – dismiss the Upper Peninsula as a bug-infested backwoods filled with yokels. U.P. residents (who proudly call themselves "Yoopers") find the generalizations insulting, especially when those same Lower Peninsula folks (you can call them "Trolls" if you like, since they live below the Bridge) seem to enjoy the U.P.'s woods and wildlife and beaches while on vacation, thank you very much.

The fact that the two are joined as a single state is a bit of a lark in the first place. The Michigan Territory actually wound up with the Upper Peninsula as a consolation prize, part of a deal struck with Ohio in 1837. Both Michigan and Ohio had fought over the "Toledo Strip," a valuable port on Lake Erie. For Michigan to earn admission to the Union, Congress demanded that the Michigan Territory relinquish all rights to the Toledo Strip in exchange for

the "barren wasteland" of the Upper Peninsula. Michigan got the last laugh, though, when priceless quantities of iron ore and copper were discovered just a few years later.

Much of the rivalry is good natured. Yoopers joke about blowing up the Mackinac Bridge and like to display a bumper sticker portraying a giant U.P. with a tiny Lower Peninsula dangling from its eastern end. Yet there is a kernel of truth to the squabble. Upper Peninsula residents feel they pay state taxes to a distant state capital and receive very little in return – except for some government-protected land or wildlife programs, which they think they have plenty of, anyway. From time to time, residents launch pseudo-serious drives to declare sovereignty from the rest of Michigan and create the state of Superior. As a musical group from Ishpeming, Da Yoopers, sings, "Dear Mr. Governor, you better turn us loose/We asked you for some rest stops, instead you sent us moose/The honeymoon is over, the declaration's written/We'll take what's above the bridge, and you can keep the mitten."

hundreds of others straggled through the roadless wilderness, trudging overland through northern Wisconsin by snowshoe, or following rivers through thick forests to reach the fabled riches. It was the nation's first mineral rush. Copper employed thousands of immigrant laborers, built cities, made millionaires, and prompted extravagant luxuries like opera houses and "copper baron" mansions. Before it was over, King Copper had generated more than $9.6 billion—10 times more than the California Gold Rush.

The entire nation turned to the Keweenaw for its copper. From 1845 to 1895, the Keweenaw Peninsula produced 75 percent of U.S. copper; during the Civil War, it produced 90 percent. More than 400 mining companies operated in the Keweenaw over the course of the 19th century, and the resulting demand for labor drew immigrants from more than 30 countries—most notably, the British Isles and Scandinavia. With multiple cultures sharing the same mine shafts and communities, Copper Country served as one of the nation's first true melting pots.

But virtually all the big mines disappeared one by one in the mid-1900s, sealed up by economic conditions, leaving behind tattered houses and empty streets. They had extracted the easiest-to-reach copper; soon newer mines in the southwestern United States and South America proved more cost-effective.

Economy and Government

ECONOMY

For almost two centuries, Michigan has been a mirror of the country's great industrial transition. As the state's economy has evolved from agriculture and fur trading to metals, logging, and, finally, in the Lower Peninsula, automobile manufacturing, the state has ridden a roller coaster that shows no signs of stopping.

Ironically, the ups and downs that sometimes curse the state's economic fortunes are nothing new. Just as today's auto industry has experienced both wild success and dismal failure, so it was with the mining era in the Upper Peninsula, which left a legacy of fantastic wealth juxtaposed with depressed towns huddled around played-out mines. Unfortunately, the Upper Peninsula seems to be going through one of these downturns—many of today's towns (and some of the cities) seem remarkably depressed. When the mines closed, many Yooper communities were left without a comparable source of jobs and income, leaving them a shell of what they once were. Escanaba, for example, has a vibrant community, a growing arts presence, and fantastically attractive areas—particularly the waterfront—but on a drive through the historic downtown it's impossible not to think that the city is a shadow of what it once was, that its streets are an echo of more prosperous times.

Many of the small ex-mining towns are beginning to show significant wear around the edges, but that's okay. It's part of the unassuming, small-town charm. Besides, Yoopers aren't the sort of people to throw in the towel during tough times, whether it's a particularly bitter winter or a particularly rough economy. In any case, the reason most people come to the U.P. is precisely because it's the opposite of metropolitan. Don't let a few shabby downtowns distract you from the Upper Peninsula's remarkable beauty.

INDUSTRY
Logging and Mining

The Upper Peninsula's economy was long based on logging and mining. Great fortunes were made in logging in the late 1800s, as Michigan's vast stands of virgin timber produced enough wood to lay an inch-thick plank across the state—with enough left over to cover Rhode Island, too. Few can even grasp the riches of Michigan's copper and iron mining industries, which each dwarfed the Gold Rush in California. Michigan produced more than

© TRAVEL MICHIGAN

a freighter at the ore docks in Marquette

$9.6 billion in **copper** and a staggering $48 billion in **iron,** compared with $955 million from the Gold Rush. The riches and the miners disappeared as the most accessible deposits were exhausted and global economics began to play a role. Nearly all the U.P.'s mines shut down by the mid-1900s.

Tourism

As the mines became less and less productive (and more and more expensive), and as the U.P.'s lucrative timber began to thin, those industries gave way to tourism, which continues to be the U.P.'s most important industry—and, in many ways, its saving grace. Mackinac Island already had a reputation as one of America's prime vacation spots, even before the iconic Grand Hotel was built. Today, the entire U.P. is capitalizing on tourism, rightfully marketing its natural resources and recreational opportunities as its most attractive assets. It's working. In 2005, ShermansTravel cited the "majestic wildlife, unspoiled rivers, waterfalls, and dense forests" as just one of the

reasons for putting the Upper Peninsula on its list of the Top 10 Summer Destinations, an honor the U.P. shared with the Hamptons, the Greek Islands, and London.

Shipping

Just as semis rumble down the interstate, commercial ships transport commodities across the Great Lakes. Officially designated as the nation's "Fourth Seacoast" by Congress in 1970, the Great Lakes serve as a vital transportation artery for the nation's commerce. Without the Great Lakes, the auto industry and other Michigan manufacturers probably could not survive.

With its hundreds of miles of Great Lakes shoreline and deepwater ports, Michigan's Upper Peninsula is a key player in the Great Lakes transportation network. What's more, the Soo Locks that link Lakes Superior and Huron at Sault Ste. Marie rank as the largest and busiest lock system in the world.

Iron ore forms the foundation of the Great Lakes trade. In Upper Peninsula ports like

Escanaba and Marquette, huge lake carriers (as long as 1,000 feet) load iron ore from nearby mines, then transport it to steelmaking centers in the southern Great Lakes, where the steel is, in turn, used by heavy manufacturers like Detroit's auto industry. The Great Lakes fleet hauls up to 125 million tons of cargo each year, including more than 58 million tons of iron ore—nearly twice the "float" of any other commodity. Shipping is an economical way to transport heavy and bulky commodities like ore.

Great Lakes shipping does face its share of competition. Much of it comes from overseas, in the form of imported finished products ranging from refrigerators to automobiles. That translates to a decrease in steel production here, which in turn reduces the need for iron ore shipments. Secondly, other transportation networks, like trains and trucks, compete with shipping for certain commodities. But overall, shipping has proved to be a steady industry, and total cargo shipments have remained pretty even over the last decade.

GOVERNMENT

A long time ago, the state was a traditional stronghold of the Republican party. One of the major developments of the post–World War II years in Michigan, however, was the emergence of a competitive two-party political arena. Starting during the Depression, the Democratic Party made major inroads into a state that had traditionally been Republican.

Since then, parts of the state—particularly the Detroit area and most of the Upper Peninsula—have managed to swing the state for the Democrats during presidential elections since 1992 and in an overwhelming majority of the senate elections during the past 40 years. The Upper Peninsula is part of the 1st District, which has put a Democrat in the House of Representatives since 1933.

But all this talk of Republicans and Democrats seems so passé when compared to the Upper Peninsula's relatively recent and occasionally serious talks of seceding from Michigan to form its own autonomous state. It would be called the Superior State, clearly a reference to Lake Superior, even if it does sound suspiciously like the Yoopers are thumbing their noses at the Lower Peninsula. Nothing much has ever come from these efforts, of course, and it's likely that nothing ever will. The Superior State was most popular back in the 1960s and 1970s, and lives on today in half-joking comments and a few bumper stickers.

People and Culture

While the Algonquins were the land's first inhabitants, the residents of Michigan's Upper Peninsula today reflect a more diverse population. The French "empire builders" were the first Europeans to come, and in due time the British replaced the French. Early American settlers included a large group of Yankees from western New York and New England. From Europe came immigrants seeking a better life, particularly Finns, Swedes, Italians, and Cornish people who worked in the Upper Peninsula mines and lumber camps.

Today, Upper Peninsula residents number around 312,000, comprising about three percent of Michigan's more than 10 million citizens (making Michigan the eighth most populous state). According to the U.S. Census Bureau, the U.P.'s five largest cities contain about 20 percent of its people: Marquette's population is 20,780, Sault Ste. Marie's 14,000, Escanaba's 12,300, Menominee's 8,400, and Iron Mountain's 7,800.

NATIVE AMERICANS

In most books of Michigan history, the land's first inhabitants are given little more than a cursory nod, a line or two that identifies the approximately 100,000 early Native

Americans as belonging to the tribes of the "Three Fires," the **Ojibwa, Ottawa,** and **Potawatomi.** The three tribes collectively called themselves the *Anishinabe*, or "First People." Another tribe with a significant presence in the Upper Peninsula during the 1700s was the **Menominee,** who lived in northern Wisconsin and parts of the U.P.

Today, Michigan is home to one of the largest Native American populations in the country, estimated at 50,000, many of them in the Upper Peninsula. Surprisingly, no one can name an exact figure, since the label of "Native American" or "Indian" can be defined in more than one way—by political (tribal membership), ethnic (genealogy), or cultural (were you "raised Indian?") criteria. Depending on how you count, Michigan may have the largest Native American population east of the Mississippi. Whatever the accurate number, only a small percentage live on reservations.

There are a number of reservations in the peninsula, including federally recognized tribes in Brimley, Wilson, Baraga, Watersmeet, Manistee, L'Anse, Ontonagon, and Sault Ste. Marie, home of the Sault Ste. Marie Tribe of Chippewa Indians, the largest federally recognized U.S. tribe in the Great Lakes area. Of these tribes, five are authorized to operate their own tribal courts, which exercise exclusive jurisdiction over certain laws involving Native Americans and events that occur on their reservations. Tribal courts have broad powers in matters involving child welfare and in a variety of civil matters involving tribe members and nonmembers when the activities in question occur on their reservations. In addition, Native American tribal councils throughout the state provide a variety of outreach services, economic development initiatives, and cultural activities.

Many reservations have cultural centers with museums, or at least displays, open to the public. Many tribes also host powwows (native dance ceremonies) and festivals. Check with

local convention and visitors bureaus, or inquire at tribal headquarters, which are prominent and well-marked buildings on most reservations.

THE IMMIGRANTS

Traveling Michigan's numerous rivers as early as the 1600s, the French fur traders, missionaries, and voyageurs were the area's first European settlers, establishing posts in far-flung areas across the state. The majority of these immigrants, however, didn't arrive until more than a century later, arriving in great waves in the early 1800s. More and more settlers came in the 1830s and in the next two decades, in response to a European food shortage.

While the Lower Peninsula has an array of immigrant nationalities—Dutch, German, African American, Arab, Indian, and more—the immigrants of the Upper Peninsula vary from the Lower Peninsula's as much as its topography does. The iron and copper mines lured many immigrants—from Sweden, Finland, Italy, and Cornwall, England—with promises of steady work and decent wages. (It came, however, at a price: job conditions were extremely difficult and unhealthy.) **Swedes** and **Finns** in particular took to the U.P., at home with the area's woods and rushing rivers.

There are still large Finnish and Swedish influences here, including (this might surprise you) active Finnish- and Swedish-speaking communities. Finnish names, foods, and the ubiquitous sauna can be found throughout the Keweenaw Peninsula, and Hancock remains largely Finnish, down to its street signs. Some 16 percent of the population up here is Finnish, and these counties in the northwest Upper Peninsula are still the largest Finnish-American population in the United States. You'll find Finnish influences in Marquette, too, and the Swedes have left their mark on Escanaba (you simply must go to the Swedish Pantry).

Arts and Entertainment

HISTORICAL MUSEUMS

Not surprisingly, many of the peninsula's museums cover the lore and legends of the Great Lakes and the state's maritime industry. Paradise, located in the eastern U.P.'s Whitefish Point, is home to the **Great Lakes Shipwreck Museum,** which includes artifacts from 13 shipwrecks, including an exhibit that features the bell from the *Edmund Fitzgerald,* the Great Lakes ship that sank mysteriously in 1975 and later became the subject of a hit song by Gordon Lightfoot. The museum does a fine job telling the haunting tale of the hundreds of ships that met their match in the area's frigid, turbulent waters. Also in the U.P., the **National Ski Hall of Fame** in Ishpeming chronicles the downhill and cross-country versions of the sport, while neighboring Negaunee is home to the **Michigan Iron Industry Museum,** an excellent state-run facility on the site of one of the state's first iron forges.

ENTERTAINMENT

The Upper Peninsula doesn't exactly have an abundance of what most people consider cultural entertainment: theater, music, dance, even a riotous nightlife. Which isn't to say there isn't anything at all. Plenty of towns host summertime music festivals, the biggest of which is the Pine Mountain Music Festival, hosting opera, symphony, and chamber music at various locations across the peninsula every summer. You'll be able to find theatrical production and musical performances at the peninsula's college towns, particularly at Northern Michigan University in Marquette. With the exception of community bars (there's no shortage of these), you'll find the entertainment and nightlife pretty well limited to what Mother Nature supplies.

Native American Gaming

If there is a form of entertainment that the U.P. *does* excel in, it's gaming. As sovereign lands, reservations often are able to offer high-stakes gambling that isn't legal elsewhere in the state. Michigan's first Native American casino opened near Sault Ste. Marie in 1984. The Bay Mills Blackjack Casino had just 15 blackjack tables and one dice table in a 2,400-square-foot room in the tribal center. While it wasn't Las Vegas or Atlantic City, visitors quickly displayed their love of gambling, pouring tens of millions of dollars into casino coffers. It started a gambling tradition that has escalated ever since.

There are several Native American casinos in Michigan, many of them in the Upper Peninsula. They range from small, simple gambling halls to glitzy showplaces; many are open seven days a week, 24 hours a day, and have become enormous tourism draws. The Vegas Kewadin complex in Sault Ste. Marie has added an interesting art gallery, which displays paintings, jewelry, and crafts by Native Americans. Not surprisingly, more and more tribes, many of whom live at or near the poverty level, are seeking to open casinos.

By the early 1990s, the state wanted in on the deal. In September 1993, Governor John Engler passed the Tribal-State Gaming Compact, giving the state eight percent of net win income derived from games of chance. Contributions total hundreds of millions of dollars. While providing the state government with easy cash, the success of Native American gaming has also given new power and influence to tribal governments.

While the pros and cons of gambling remain an ethical debate, there's no arguing the positive effect gaming has on the reservations' economies. Within the tribal community, gambling provides jobs and funds schools, health-care facilities, cultural centers, and all sorts of other resources. Many overlook the loads of economic benefits gaming provides to those outside the Native American community, too, creating jobs especially for the building trades and the neighboring tourism industry. Michigan residents and visitors, it seems, just can't spend enough on Lady Luck.

ESSENTIALS

Getting There

BY CAR

The only way into the Upper Peninsula from the Lower Peninsula by car is to cross the Mackinac Bridge on U.S. 75, which is an exhilarating experience for most and a frightening experience for some. It costs everyone a little bit of cash: $3 for every passenger car in 2009, although tolls will be making a long, slow climb until 2015. From Wisconsin, U.S. 41 will take you north of Green Bay into Menominee, while U.S. 141/U.S. 8 sneaks in near Norway and Iron Mountain. Moving west, U.S. 45 connects with U.S. 2 at Watersmeet, and both U.S. 51 from the south and U.S. 2 from the west meet in Ironwood.

That about does it for travelers who drive up from the Upper Peninsula's southern borders. Visitors from Canada will want to take Hwy. 17 (the Trans-Canada Highway) to Sault Ste. Marie, Ontario, and cross St. Mary's River into the other, smaller, American Sault Ste. Marie, via the cleverly named International Bridge. Passenger cars are currently charged a $2 toll. That's American dollars, or the Canadian equivalent. Go to www.xe.com/ucc/ for exchange rates.

BY BUS

After Greyhound decided to drop its contract as the Upper Peninsula's intercity bus system

© BECCA BISHOP

MACKINAC BRIDGE TOLLS

	2009	2010	2011	2012	2013	2014
Auto/Passenger Vehicle	$3	$3.50	$3.50	$4	$4	$4.50
Vehicles with trailers (per axle)	$1.50	$1.75	$1.75	$2	$2	$2.50
Commuter	$1.70	$1.80	$1.90	$2	$2.10	$2.20
Motor home (per axle)	$3.50	$4.50	$4.50	$5	$5	$6
Truck (per axle)	$3.50	$4.50	$4.50	$5	$5	$6

in January 2007, the Michigan Department of Transportation replaced North America's largest bus company with **Indian Trails** (800/292-3831, www.indiantrails.com), a Michigan-based company with regularly scheduled routes throughout the Upper Peninsula. Main routes go between Calumet and Milwaukee, Wisconsin, via Marquette and to St. Ignace and Ironwood via Escanaba. Contact Indian Trails for current rates and schedules.

BY PLANE

No surprise here: **Detroit Metropolitan Airport (DTW)** (800/642-1978) is the state's biggest and busiest—but it's in the Lower Peninsula. It's also a hub for Northwest Airlines (800/225-2525, www.nwa.com), so you can fly direct to Detroit from pretty much anywhere in the United States and then fly into most of the Upper Peninsula's commercial airports, including Escanaba, Marquette, Pellston/Mackinac Island, and Sault Ste. Marie. For flights into Houghton, you'll have to go through Minneapolis.

Still, flights to the U.P. are limited even from Detroit, and most airports have only one or two arrivals and departures each day. If you're flying in from other regional cities, try Milwaukee, Chicago, or Minneapolis–St. Paul. Contact your arriving airport to double check flight availability and schedules. The major airports for U.P. destinations are:

- **Pellston Regional Airport (PLN)**
  U.S. 31
  Pellston, MI 49769
  231/539-8441
  www.pellstonairport.com
- **Chippewa County International Airport (CIU)**
  119 Airport Dr.
  Kincheloe, MI 48471
  906/495-2522
  www.airciu.com
- **Delta County Airport (ESC)**
  3300 Airport Rd.
  Escanaba, MI 49829
  906/786-4902
  www.deltacountymi.org
- **Sawyer International Airport (MQT)**
  225 Airport Ave.
  Gwinn, MI 49841
  906/346-3308
  www.sawyerairport.com
- **Houghton County Memorial Airport (CMX)**
  23810 Airpark Blvd.
  Calumet, MI 49913
  906/482-3970
  www.houghtoncounty.org

© BECCA BISHOP

The *Ranger III* ushers visitors to Isle Royale National Park.

BY BOAT

Surrounded by zillions of miles of shoreline, Michigan's Upper Peninsula is easy to enter via the Great Lakes, and visitors who do find plenty of places to tie up the boat when they get here. The state's Parks and Recreation Division has established a network of protected **public mooring facilities** along the Great Lakes, a "marine highway" that ensures that boaters are never far from a safe harbor. More facilities are being added every year, with the goal of locating them so a boater is never more than 15 shoreline miles away from a protected public mooring. Mooring fees vary. For more information or a free *Michigan Harbors Guide,* contact the Department of Natural Resources (DNR), Parks and Recreation Division (P.O. Box 30257, Lansing, MI 48909, 517/373-9900, www.michigan.gov/dnr).

Getting Around

BY CAR

Roads in the Upper Peninsula are plentiful and, as long as you stay on the main byways, good. Along with interstates and federal highways, the state is crisscrossed with numerous state highways, marked on road maps by a number with a circle or oval around it. In conversation, they are often preceded by an "M," as in, "Follow M-28 west to Marquette." County roads are marked with squares on most road maps; county roads may be designated "CR."

Two routes traverse the peninsula pretty much east to west: M-28 is the northern route, passing through Marquette; U.S. 2 is the southern route, passing through Escanaba. If you're traveling all the way from the eastern end of the U.P. to Ironwood, M-28 is usually faster. Several state (and a couple of federal) highways running north-south link M-28 and U.S. 2—these include, from east to west, I-75, M-123, M-77, U.S. 41, U.S. 145, and U.S. 45, among others.

When planning a route in the Upper Peninsula, consult your map legend regarding road surfaces. Roads you might assume are paved may be gravel or dirt, which can make for very slow going. All state and federal highways are paved and well-maintained, as are most county roads and many more secondary roads. But just be aware. For construction updates, the Michigan Department of Transportation has a road construction hotline (800/641-6368).

Interstate speed limits in Michigan are 70 mph, unless otherwise posted. Most four-lane highways, and many two-lanes, have increased their limits to 65 mph.

For first-time visitors to the state, one of the most confusing aspects of driving Michigan's interstates is a turn that's found only here: the Michigan left. To put it simply, no left turn is allowed at an intersection where a Michigan left is in place. Instead, to turn left from the interstate to a crossroad, you'll have to continue straight past the intersection, then make a U-turn at the median crossover, double back to your intended street, and finally turn right. If you want to turn left onto an interstate, you'll have to turn right onto the interstate, then take a U-turn at the median and continue on your way. According to the Department of Transportation, these turns serve to relieve congestion and reduce the severity of crashes. The numbers of crashes at intersections with a Michigan left have dropped 30 to 60 percent overall, enough to make one wonder why other states haven't picked up the idea. Since these turns are usually installed at high-traffic intersections, there aren't many above the Bridge, but you can expect to find them by the U.P.'s larger cities, particularly along U.S. 41/M-28 near Marquette.

Finally, there's a long-standing joke about Michigan roads that goes something like this: "Michigan has two seasons: winter and road construction." Sure, it's a bit of an exaggeration, but there's enough truth to make it sting a little. It's a problem caused by the state's weather: temperatures swing from frozen to thaw and back to frozen, and the snows

bring with them heavy snowplows, sand, and salt. These road surfaces go through quite a bit and deteriorate quickly, so it seems as if the Michigan Department of Transportation works all the way from Easter through Thanksgiving to correct the problem.

Winter Driving

Michigan roads are generally very well-maintained in winter, plowed free of snow, then salted or sanded. (Salt does a better job of melting, but sand is less destructive to the environment.) During or immediately after a storm, though, don't expect smooth sailing; it's often hard for road crews to keep up with conditions. County and city crews have a well-established hierarchy, first taking care of interstates, state highways, major thoroughfares, and roads to schools and hospitals and such, then addressing less-vital routes. Smaller roads are a little different, especially in the Upper Peninsula. If a sign reads Seasonal Road: Not Maintained in Winter, that means it is not plowed or patrolled. To check winter driving conditions before you travel, call the AAA road conditions number, 800/337-1334.

If you're not used to driving in snow, don't learn on the road in a Michigan snowstorm. Drive slowly, allow lots of extra room between you and the car in front of you, and remember that it may take a lot longer to stop. If you don't have antilock brakes, tap your brakes lightly in succession to come to a stop; never stomp on them, or you'll send your car reeling into what high-school kids call "a doughnut." If you have the newer ABS antilock brakes, apply steady pressure instead, and let the system's computer do the work. Remember, too, that four-wheel drive may get you going better than the next guy, but it won't help you stop.

Chains and studded snow tires are not permitted on Michigan roads. Many residents do switch to snow tires, which have a heavier tread. If you have a rear-wheel-drive car, adding weight to the back end can greatly improve traction. Bags of sand or water-softener salt work well, and sand can be used if you get stuck.

Snow isn't the only hazard. Ice is considerably more dangerous, since it provides even less traction and stopping ability than snow. Be especially aware of "black ice," pavement that looks wet, but is actually covered with glare ice. Watch for icy roads as rain turns to snow (called "freezing rain"), especially on bridges, which freeze first, due to cold air circulating above and below the road. Ice also forms when lots of cars travel over a snowy surface, compressing it into super-slick hardpack. This often happens on heavily traveled interstates and state highways. On four-lane roads, the less-used left lane usually looks snowier but may actually be less icy and less slippery.

Equip your vehicle with a shovel, sand (kitty litter works even better), and boots, in case you get stuck. Throw the sand or kitty litter under the front tires for a front-wheel-drive car, the rear tires on a rear-wheel drive. Keep the tires straight and *slowly* apply the gas. Flooring it will only spin you deeper. Gently rocking the car forward and back, especially if you have someone who can push, works best.

Keep a flashlight, flares, blankets, and extra clothing in your vehicle in case you have to spend the night in your car. It could save your life. Especially in rural areas, help may not always be on the way. If you see a car hung up on a snowbank or in a ditch, by all means offer a push or a ride to town.

Driving and Deer

Several million deer inhabit Michigan, posing a significant threat to drivers. Several thousand contribute to automobile accidents each year, some of them fatal; in the U.P. alone, between 5,000 and 8,000 deer–vehicle accidents are reported each year, while many more accidents go unreported. Deer behave erratically and will dart in front of your car with absolutely no warning, popping out of the roadside ditch or woods like a massive, living jack-in-the-box. Be particularly alert at dawn and dusk, when deer are most active, and during hunting season in November, when they're really nuts. Yellow-and-black "leaping deer" signs warn motorists of roadways where crossings are common, but deer can appear absolutely anywhere.

Deer may come from the woods or from an open field, almost out of nowhere. If you see deer by the side of the road, slow down and get ready to stop. If you see a deer cross ahead of you, also slow down—where there's one deer, there are usually several. If you do hit a deer, notify the nearest law enforcement office immediately.

Car Rentals

Rental cars are available at most commercial airports around the peninsula. Even in the U.P.'s larger cities, you'll be limited to the big players like National (800/227-7368), Budget (800/527-0700), Hertz (800/654-3131), and Avis (800/831-2847). Any good local operators are mentioned in the appropriate *Getting There and Around* sections. It is highly recommended that you reserve a car in advance; small locales don't keep many on the lot. If you plan to do any exploration in the Upper Peninsula, ask about the rental company's policies regarding off-road driving. Many forbid you to leave pavement, which can curtail your access to a lot of U.P. sights.

ENTERING CANADA

U.S. citizens entering Canada are usually given little more than a perfunctory glance. Thanks to heightened national security after 9/11, the traditionally lax rules at the Canadian border crossing are becoming more and more strict. Gone are the days when a driver's license would be enough to get you through; as of June 2009, you'll need a passport or an equivalent travel document (visit the U.S. Department of State's travel website at http://travel.state.gov for a complete list of acceptable documents). Unless you're transporting plants or animals, you'll probably be asked a question or two about why you're visiting and then be waved through. Pets require proof of proper vaccinations; plants will be confiscated.

Canadians face similar rules. You'll need a passport to get into the United States. For all other travelers, security can be surprisingly tight. Visit www.usa.gov/visitors/arriving.shtml

or www.dhs.gov/xtrvlsec for up-to-date information and requirements.

Unless you travel from Michigan to Canada by boat, you'll do so by road bridge or, in the winter, ice bridge (exciting, isn't it?). The toll bridge connecting Michigan's Upper Peninsula and Ontario is the International Bridge from Sault Ste. Marie to Sault Ste. Marie ($2). If you do arrive by boat, you're required to check in at the nearest customs station immediately upon arrival. An ice bridge is usually accessible—at your own significant risk—from Drummond Island to Thessalon, Ontario, as soon as the waters freeze thick enough. Just follow the trail of old Christmas trees, then book it to the nearest customs station with your passport.

Recreation

NATIONAL PARKS AND FORESTS

Michigan's Upper Peninsula is home to two national forests and a national lakeshore: the **Ottawa National Forest** in the western Upper Peninsula covers 982,895 acres; the **Hiawatha National Forest** in the eastern U.P. adds another 860,000 acres; and **Pictured Rocks National Lakeshore** extends along 42 miles of Lake Superior shore. **Seney National Wildlife Refuge** occupies 95,000 acres of cutover logging land in the eastern Upper Peninsula, while **Isle Royale National Park** is in a world of its own, a 45-mile-long wilderness surrounded by the waters of Lake Superior.

Even in the Upper Peninsula, where national land is highly valued, you'll find that the parks are still notably secluded visitor destinations—except for maybe a few key attractions like particular waterfalls or beaches—yet they offer a remarkable quantity and quality of activities for anyone interested in the outdoors. **Hiking** trails tend to be little-used. **Campsites** are more secluded, more rustic, and usually lightly used. **Mountain biking** is permitted on miles and miles of federal forest land, and much of it is terrific (mountain biking, however, is often forbidden in state or national parks). Inland lakes can be a little difficult to reach with a boat trailer, so they tend to be ideal for those looking for a quiet **paddling** experience. You get the idea.

Contact the national forest headquarters to receive information on hiking, camping, paddling, and other activities: Ottawa National Forest, Ironwood (E6248 U.S. 2, Ironwood, MI 49938, 906/932-1330, www.fs.fed.us/r9/ottawa/); Hiawatha National Forest, Escanaba (2727 North Lincoln Rd., Escanaba, MI 49829, 906/786-4062, www.fs.fed.us/r9/forests/hiawatha/).

STATE FORESTS

Like national forests, state forests are a bit of a hidden gem for anyone looking for a quiet corner of woods or water. Much of the state's forest land was actually acquired by default, picked up after the Depression when its owners couldn't pay the property taxes. Their loss was the public's gain—much of the property is exceptional, comprising rivers, waterfalls, lakes, beaches, and, naturally, forest. Altogether, it encompasses 3.9 million acres of land, the largest state forest holding in any state east of the Rocky Mountains.

Visit the **Department of Natural Resources (DNR)** website (www.michigan.gov/dnr) or contact the following offices to receive maps and information on Upper Peninsula state forest camping, hiking, and more: Copper Country State Forest, Baraga (906/353-6651); Escanaba River State Forest, Escanaba (906/786-2351); Lake Superior State Forest, Newberry (906/293-5131).

STATE PARKS

You'll see it written probably a dozen times in this book: Michigan's Upper Peninsula has an outstanding state park system. They're well-planned and well-maintained, and they

Backcountry campers should be especially aware of safety precautions and leave-no-trace policies.

showcase some of the state's most diverse and most beautiful land. Some state parks were clearly set aside for public access—the state park beaches along the Lake Michigan shore come to mind—while others preserve historic sites and state jewels like the Porcupine Mountains and Mackinac Island.

The U.P. has 21 state parks and nearly 60 state forest campgrounds. The Michigan DNR Parks and Recreation Division (517/373-9900, www.michigan.gov/dnr) publishes a handy *State Parks Guide* that includes a map, a short profile of each park, and a chart that lists each park's amenities. You can get much of the same information from the DNR website.

All state parks charge an entry fee per motor vehicle: $6 per day or $24 per year for residents and $8 per day or $29 per year for nonresidents, no matter how many passengers are in the car. The annual sticker is good for all Michigan state parks. Senior citizens can obtain an annual pass for $6, but only with a vehicle registered in Michigan.

There is an additional fee for **camping,** which costs $6–9 per night for rustic campsites and $12–18 per night for modern campsites (with flush toilets, showers, and electricity), depending on location. Some parks also rent "mini cabins," tiny shelters that offer you a roof and walls to protect you from the elements, but little more, for around $32 a night. These book up fast, so reserve yours well ahead of time. A few parks, including Porcupine Mountain Wilderness State Park and Craig Lake State Park, rent rustic cabins, equipped with bunks and a stove or other cooking facility, for $25–65 per night. They're great if you have a group or if you're visiting when bugs are particularly fierce. These are *extremely* popular; if you hope to get one, call in January.

For a $2 fee, you can make a camping reservation at any park in advance by calling 800/447-2757 or reserving online at www.midnrreservations.com. You can request a specific site, but it is not guaranteed. Camping reservations are highly recommended in summer months at many state parks; this book indicates if a park is particularly popular.

HIKING

With its bounty of national parks, state parks, national forests, state forests, national lakeshores, and private land accessible for public use, Michigan's Upper Peninsula has almost unlimited offerings for hikers. Where you go depends certainly on your taste; this book will give you plenty of ideas.

For backpackers, Isle Royale National Park in Lake Superior is an outstanding choice, free of roads and other development. Rustic campsites along the way allow you to hoof your way across the 45-mile-long island; water-taxi services can get you back to your starting point. A little less remote, Porcupine Mountains Wilderness State Park in the western Upper Peninsula also offers great backpacking in a rugged backcountry environment one doesn't normally associate with state parks.

Michigan also has lots of linear hiking trails, like the Bay de Noc to Grand Island Trail, which bisects the U.P. And for those really looking for an adventure, the North Country National Scenic Trail traverses the Upper Peninsula as part of a national trail that, when complete, will stretch from North Dakota to New York. Many long segments of the trail crossing national forest land are already open to hikers in Michigan. Check with national forest officials for more information.

BICYCLING

With its rolling topography, shorelines, and ample country roads, Michigan's Upper Peninsula makes for a great bicycling destination. Some favorite areas for road riding include the quiet roads near Les Cheneaux and through the temperate Garden Peninsula. Check with local visitors bureaus for suggested routes.

Michigan leads the nation in its number of rails-to-trails, with 55 old railroad beds converted into multi-use trails. Some, like the Bill Nichols trail in the Keweenaw Peninsula, are very rough—they essentially removed the rails and left everything else, including railroad ties and sharp old mining rock. Some of these more

Like much of Michigan's Upper Peninsula, Mackinac Island is well-suited for biking.

© TOM BUCHKOE / TRAVEL MICHIGAN

primitive trails are appropriate only for snow-mobiles and all-terrain vehicles, but most are great for mountain bikes passing through wonderful wilderness terrain. (The Bill Nichols, by the way, is a gem.)

Unlike much of the Midwest, Michigan is kind to mountain bikers. Good technical mountain biking can be found in many state and national forests. In fact, you can pretty much look at the U.P. as a giant mountain bike park. Between the national and state forests, you probably have more miles than you could ever ride; then throw in hundreds of miles of old logging roads. Off-road riding in places like the Keweenaw and the Huron Mountains is the best you'll find between the Rockies and the Appalachians, and Michigan adds a little extra perk—some stunning Great Lakes views.

SKIING

The Great Lakes churn out plentiful lake effect snows, which drop onto some of the Midwest's hilliest terrain. That convenient marriage has made the Upper Peninsula the top ski destination in the Midwest. While you can't really call anything here mountainous, resorts do an admirable job of working with the terrain they've got, carving out 600-foot vertical drops and runs that wind through the pines or give you jaw-dropping views of the Great Lakes.

Though downhill ski areas can be found throughout the peninsula, they're concentrated in the western Upper Peninsula from Ironwood to the Porcupine Mountains.

Cross-country skiers have even more to choose from. Though they don't all offer lodging, several privately run Nordic trail systems call the U.P. home. Many of the downhill resorts, such as Big Powderhorn Mountain in Bessemer, also have notable Nordic trails. The national lakeshores and many state parks groom trails for skiing, and the state and national forests offer virtually limitless opportunity for backcountry skiing.

For information on both downhill and cross-country skiing, contact Travel Michigan (800/644-2489, www.michigan.org/skiing).

GOLFING

Turns out the U.P. has plenty of top-class courses, many that feature a diverse terrain of hills and water views that make for great golf. Drummond Island, Mackinac Island, and Marquette are home to some of the U.P.'s finest golf courses. Here, you'll find award-winners like The Rock at the Drummond Island Resort and Conference Center, The Jewel at the Grand Hotel on Mackinac Island, and Greywalls at the Marquette Golf Club. You'll find plenty of well-kept and challenging courses elsewhere in the peninsula, too. For more information, contact Travel Michigan (800/644-2489, www.michigan.org/golf).

BOATING AND FISHING

Michigan leads the nation in boat registrations—a whopping 940,000. There are an estimated 200,000–300,000 additional legally unregistered boats in the state, adding up to at well over 1 million watercraft in the state. Boaters cruise from port to port on the Great Lakes; sail along scenic shoreline like Pictured Rocks and along island chains like the one extending off the tip of Wisconsin's Door County; water-ski on thousands of inland lakes; paddle white water rivers and quiet waters; and fish just about everywhere.

Small watercraft like daysailers, fishing boats, and canoes are readily available in many U.P. communities. Contact the local chamber of commerce or visitors bureau in the area you plan to visit for more information. For larger sailboats or powerboats, contact the **Michigan Charter Boat Association** (800/622-2971, www.micharterboats.com). The Travel Michigan website (www.michigan.org) also has an interactive travel planner that can provide you with a list of charter operations in a given region.

If you'll be trailering your own boat, the DNR (517/373-9900 www.michigan.gov/dnr) publishes a list of public launch sites. (If you'll be arriving by water, see the *Getting There* section earlier in this chapter for information on Great Lakes public mooring facilities.) A Coast

Guard–approved lifejacket—known as a PFD, or personal flotation device—is required for each person on any kind of boat.

Michigan's Upper Peninsula is a paddler's dream. You can **canoe** down several national Wild and Scenic Rivers, **surf** waves along Lake Michigan's shoreline, **sea kayak** along Pictured Rocks or Isle Royale National Park, or run white water. For mellow paddling, the Sturgeon River is a favorite. The U.P. also has several notable white water rivers, including the beautiful Presque Isle River and the Ontonagon. For more information on paddling destinations and liveries, contact the **Michigan Association of Paddle Sports Providers** (www.michigancanoe.com).

Fishing is extremely popular in Michigan, deeply embedded in the state's psyche. It comes in all seasons and styles, too, from fly-fishing along a pristine stream to hanging out in an ice-fishing shanty watching the Lions-Packers game. The quantity of blue-ribbon trout streams is unrivaled this side of Montana— enough clear, swift, and rocky waters to make you weep on your Orvis vest. The Fox, the Chocolay, the Carp…you'll find most of the best ones in the eastern U.P.

"Deep-sea" charters on the Great Lakes go after the big chinook salmon, coho, and lake trout. Lake Michigan's Bay de Noc arguably offers the finest walleye fishing in the state, if not all the Great Lakes. Inland, literally thousands of lakes harbor walleye, northern pike, muskie, bass, and panfish. Some of the most popular spots are the Manistique Lakes chain and huge Lake Gogebic.

But to avoid the people and the whine of outboards, you really should head for the dozens of small lakes in the Ottawa and Hiawatha National Forests, which are peaceful, harder to get to, not heavily used, and teeming with fish. Some, like the Sylvania Wilderness, have special fishing regulations, so check with authorities. All Michigan waters require a valid Michigan fishing license. For fishing information, contact the DNR Fisheries Division (517/373-1204) or visit the DNR website (www.michigan.gov/dnr).

HUNTING

As the saying goes, there really are three major holidays in Michigan: Thanksgiving, Christmas, and Opening Day. With its abundance of wildlife, forests, and undeveloped land, Michigan's long history of hunting continues as strongly today as it ever has. And when most people think about hunting in Michigan, white-tailed deer tend to be the first creature that comes to mind. There are some 325,000 deer in the Upper Peninsula; of these, hunters take tens of thousands each year. In 2007, hunters killed around 58,000 deer.

While the sentiment and sympathies of many people tend toward the deer, this annual culling of the herd helps prevent much larger problems—among them deer–vehicle accidents and fatalities. When the statewide deer population peaked in the 1980s at about 2 million animals, signs of distress were seen in the herd: animals were perilously underweight and in some places as many as 6 out of 10 fawns died. Some 125,000 animals starved to death during a single hard winter; deer-vehicle accidents increased to 40,000 each year, killing an average of 5 people and injuring an additional 1,500 annually. Crop damage appeared and threatened significant economic damage as the urban and suburban deer population grew. Fencing, trapping, and birth control have proven far less effective in controlling the population than recreational hunting, which is the most efficient means of balancing the population and encouraging healthy cohabitation with human interests and the economy. Besides, as any Michigander will tell you, there's nothing quite like the taste of fresh venison.

The DNR has spent many years trying to strike a balance between scientific herd management and other considerations to maintain a healthy population, working with hunters and members of the agricultural industry to develop a mutually beneficial situation. The ideal herd size is around 1.5 million animals, with a buck population around 35 percent. Hunting rules and regulations change frequently in the ongoing management effort—special hunting seasons appear and disappear as needed, and specific rules balance the number of ant-lerless and antlered (more on these definitions in a moment) deer that can be taken by each hunter. There are plenty of general regulations in place, but you'll want to pay attention to the specific changes that occur in each season.

Hunting Licenses

The most basic rule for hunting in Michigan is this: You can't kill an animal unless you have the proper license. For Michigan residents, this is a fairly easy and inexpensive process, cost-ing $15 each for a firearm or archery license (allowing one buck during each season) and $10 for an antlerless license. Nonresidents will have to pay considerably more, at $138 each for firearm and archery seasons, and $100 for antlerless deer. It's a much steeper price, but given the abundance of deer and the quality of Michigan hunting, it's worth it. To apply for a license, residents need a valid driver's license or a State of Michigan ID card. Nonresidents have to get ahold of a MDNR Sportcard, a type of Michigan ID that'll let you hunt, fish, and trap in the state; they cost only $1 and can be ordered online (www.mdnr-elicense.com). Both residents and nonresidents born on or after January 1, 1960, must present either a hunter safety certificate or a previous hunting license or must sign their license in the pres-ence of a license agent. And carry the signed license—as well as the ID that you used to get it—any time you're hunting or trapping.

What type of license you get depends on how you like to hunt, and when or where you'd like to do it. Buck hunting regulations are a lit-tle different in the U.P. than below the Bridge and depend on the type of license purchased, so take your time and make sure you're buying exactly what you want. First, a note on antlered and antlerless deer, since that makes all the dif-ference. Any deer that has at least one antler extending three or more inches above its skull is considered *antlered*. Any deer without antlers or with the longest antler extending less than three inches above the skull is considered *ant-lerless*. Now, back to the types of licenses. You can buy a separate license for both archery and firearm season, which will limit you to only one antlered deer in the U.P. for all seasons combined. (You can, however, use the archery license to tag an antlerless deer during archery season.) The Michigan DNR also sells combi-nation deer hunting licenses, which consist of a regular and a restricted license. In the Upper Peninsula, both the restricted and regular li-cense have antler point restrictions. With the restricted license, hunters can take a deer that has at least one antler with four or more antler points, each at least one inch in length. The regular license can be used on deer with at least one antler with three or more antler points, each at least one inch in length. Both the reg-ular and combination license can be used for antlerless deer in the U.P.

Of course, deer aren't the only animals hunted in the Upper Peninsula. Hunters can go after both black bear and elk, although there is a lottery system and drawing for each of these animals. There are drawing systems for wild turkey, antlerless deer, reserved waterfowl, and special deer hunts, too. Rabbit and hare, crow, pheasant, quail, grouse, and squirrel can be hunted in Michigan. Fur harvesters and trap-pers can hunt fox, coyote, badger, beavers, bob-cat, muskrat, mink, and more.

Public and Private Land

The Upper Peninsula has seemingly endless acres of public land accessible to hunters; con-tact the Michigan DNR for a comprehensive list of locations. In addition to public land, the state has purchased public hunting rights to se-lect privately owned land, as well more than 2 million (statewide) acres of commercial forests. Hunters can also ask permission to hunt on pri-vate land—all you need is a verbal agreement from the landowner. A few tips for asking: Get permission well in advance, and approach the door with only yourself or one other person. Always, *always* leave your firearms behind. If you can't visit the landowner, write a letter ask-ing to meet in person or make arrangements by phone or mail. Provide your name and contact information, the dates and times you'd like to hunt, and exactly where on the land you plan on hunting. Ask if there are any areas off-limits to hunting, and respect any additional requests from the landowner (party size limits, ORV limits, safety zones, etc.). Leave the property exactly as you found it, or better. And always thank the landowner on your way out. Offer a portion or piece of game or venison (once it's been cleaned, of course).

Hunting Safety

It goes without saying that firearms and bows are deadly (that's the whole point, really) and dangerous, so carry and use them with utmost care. The state has a clothing requirement as a means of cutting down on hunting accidents and is pretty adamant about it, too: "You may not hunt with any device or trap with any firearm, on any lands during daylight hunting hours from August 15–April 30 unless you wear a hat, cap, vest, jacket or rain gear of highly visible orange color, commonly referred to as Hunter Orange." Pretty straightforward, that. The Hunter Orange garment must be the outermost garment and visible from all sides. Camouflage items that have at least 50 percent or more of the surface in Hunter Orange are legal. There are a few exceptions. The requirements don't apply to archery deer hunters *except* when hunting during the youth firearm season and the November firearm deer season. Waterfowl, crow, wild turkey, and archery bear hunters are also exempt.

For more detailed information (and it does get *much* more detailed) get a current Michigan Hunting and Trapping Guide from the Michigan DNR (www.michigan.gov/dnr).

BEACHES

The beaches of the Upper Peninsula have a completely different mood than most of the Lower Peninsula's sandy destinations—often wild and windswept, rocky and remote. Striped cliffs rise directly from Lake Superior at **Pictured Rocks National Lakeshore;** nearby, the **Grand Sable Dunes** and **Twelvemile Beach** provide enough sand to thrill even the most devoted beachcomber. You probably won't see many people along Twelvemile Beach, but you may glimpse a deer, or even a black bear, headed to the water's edge for a drink. While perfect for long, sandy walks, only a hardy (or foolhardy?) few actually swim in Superior—the water temperatures rarely climb out of the 40s.

The U.P. shares its southern shore with Lake Michigan, a winding border filled with bays and inlets. A favorite of anglers, it also has some good beaches—if you know where to look. Public access is a little more difficult here. The best spots are along U.S. 2 from Naubinway to the Straits of Mackinac, where rest stops and county parks point you toward nice sandy beaches hidden behind the pines. You'll find another good sandy stretch along Green Bay between Menominee and Escanaba, where **J. W. Wells State Park** and several county parks offer good swimming beaches.

DIVING

A century ago, the Great Lakes were like today's interstates—the fastest and most efficient way to get around. Commodities like lumber and iron ore were hauled from the forests and mines to Great Lakes ports; passengers traveled on steamships from urban areas around the southern Great Lakes to imbibe the fresh, cool air of northern resorts.

Of course, the Great Lakes also were known for shallow reefs and violent storms, which led to hundreds of shipwrecks. What's more, the fresh, cold, barnacle- and worm-free waters kept those shipwrecks from decaying. Many of them sit on the lake floor, undisturbed and almost unchanged.

A century later, all of this comes to the delight of divers. Michigan has set aside nine areas where shipwrecks were particularly prevalent as **underwater preserves,** protecting their historic significance and mapping and marking them for divers. Together, they cover 1,900 square miles of Great Lakes bottomland—an area the size of Delaware. Off the shores of the Upper Peninsula, underwater preserves are located off the Keweenaw Peninsula, at Marquette, Munising, and Whitefish Point on Lake Superior, as well as around the Straits of Mackinac in Lake Huron.

Most of the popular dive sites are marked with buoys in summer by volunteers of the Michigan Underwater Preserve Council. All the preserves are served by dive charters. For more information, request the booklet that describes each preserve and provides a list of dive charters and other services from the

Michigan Underwater Preserve Council (560 North State St., St. Ignace, MI 49781, 800/970-8717, www.michiganpreserves.org). You can also contact the chamber of commerce or visitors bureau near the preserve you wish to visit and consult the appropriate chapters in this book.

Accommodations and Food

LODGING OPTIONS

Yes, from Holiday Inns to Super 8s, Michigan's Upper Peninsula is well served by most of the big chains—don't expect to find a Hilton or an MGM Grand up here, though. If you prefer staying in a tried-and-true chain establishment, pick up a copy of its national directory to find current locations, rates, and services for its properties in Michigan. There's nothing inherently wrong with chains, but you've got plenty of other alternatives, too. All Michigan lodgings charge a 6 percent "use tax," similar to a sales tax. Many counties also have additional room taxes, ranging from 2 to 5 percent, to fund their visitors bureaus and other tourism-related services.

Camping

How exactly does one sum up camping in Michigan's Upper Peninsula in a paragraph or two? You can park an RV next to a pool with a waterslide, or you can pitch a tent in backcountry so remote you could go weeks without seeing another soul. Most of us, of course, seek out something in between. With tens of thousands of campsites in the state, you can probably find it, too.

This book lists many campgrounds, though it admittedly does shy away from highly developed RV-type properties. Many of the state park campgrounds are included, because they are almost universally good—usually the nicest campgrounds in a particular area. Some can get busy in summer months, though. You can reserve one ahead of time (and even request a specific site, though that's not guaranteed) by

calling 800/447-2757 or visiting www.midnr reservations.com.

State and national forests also tend to have nice camping facilities, often more rustic but in appealing, out-of-the-way locations. A directory of Upper Peninsula campgrounds is available from the Michigan DNR (517/373-9900, www.michigan.gov/dnr). Backcountry camping is permitted in many forests and commercial lands owned by paper and mining companies.

For a complete list of private campgrounds, view a free *Michigan Campground Directory* at the Association of RV Parks and Campgrounds of Michigan website (9700 M-37 South, Buckley, MI 49620, 231/269-CAMP, www.michcampgrounds.com) or order a print copy for $3. You can also order a free *RV and Campsite Guide* from the Michigan Association of Recreational Vehicles and Campgrounds (2222 Association Dr., Okemos, MI 48864, 517/349-8881, www.marvac.org).

For help in selecting public or private campgrounds geared to your tastes and destination, check out the interactive Travel Planner on the state tourism website at www.michigan.org.

Independent Motels

The combination of interstate highways and chain motels dealt a fatal one-two punch to hundreds of independently owned motels in the last few decades, as Americans proved their love for efficiency and predictability. The pendulum seems to be swinging the other way these days—interesting inns and distinctive lodges seem to be cropping up in the most unlikely places.

But we're not talking fancy here. We're talking about those good old mom-and-pop motels, places with a neon vacancy sign and a couple of lawn chairs out front, the kind of places now romanticized along Route 66.

Well, the happy news is that they never went away in the Upper Peninsula. Too out-of-the-way to attract the big chains, perhaps, many U.P. towns have several independent motels. They're still not fancy, and in some cases, those folks seeking predictability had a point—some *can* be kind of beat up and grungy. But on the other hand, many mom-and-pop motels are clean, tidy, and remarkably inexpensive, and they offer perks most chains don't—allowing pets, for example. Additionally, they're often pedestrian-friendly, located in town or along a waterfront, rather than stranded out along a highway. (One caveat: Some don't take credit cards, but if they don't, they will almost always accept a personal check.) Many are listed in this book, and you may discover many more. Don't be afraid to try.

Bed-and-Breakfasts

The Upper Peninsula has dozens of bed-and-breakfast inns. Some are the traditional, old-fashioned variety—a spare room or two in someone's quaint old farmhouse—but those have become the exception rather than the rule. Today's B&Bs run the gamut from large inns with amenities like pools and tennis courts to renovated lighthouses and other neat historic buildings. For a Michigan bed-and-breakfast directory, contact the Michigan Lake to Lake Bed and Breakfast Association (888/575-1610, www.laketolake.com).

Ski and Golf Resorts

Several of the U.P.'s ski resorts double as golf resorts in summer, ringed with lodging that ranges from motel-style rooms to condo units and townhouses with kitchens (which allow you to save money by eating in). Many also offer a number of other amenities, such as pools, game rooms, and fitness centers, so they can be a particularly good choice for families with active kids. While golf resorts tend to be pricey, ski resorts that *don't* have the summer golf draw can be great bargains. For information on golf resorts and ski resorts with lodging open in the off-season, contact Travel Michigan (800/644-2489, www.michigan.org).

FOOD AND DRINK

Throughout the Upper Peninsula, many Main Street cafés and bakeries serve up the pasty, a potpie creation of beef, potatoes, onions, rutabagas, and other vegetables. (Pronounce it PASS-tee, not PACE-tee). Brought to the U.P. by Cornish miners, the pasty made for a hearty and filling meal, one that was easy to transport deep into the mine and warm up later with their candles. The same concept works well today, if you're headed from town to your campfire.

Another Michigan food well worth tasting is its abundant fresh fish, from brook trout to Great Lakes whitefish. In Great Lakes ports, you'll often be able to find a commercial fishery operating a small retail store, usually down by the docks. They often sell both

---

PASTIES

Prepare your favorite pie-crust recipe, making enough for four nine-inch pans. Then mix together:

- 2 pounds cooked pork and/or beef, cut into half-inch cubes

- 2 cups onion, diced

- 1 cup rutabaga, diced

- 1 cup potatoes, diced

- Salt and pepper to taste

Roll pastry out and cut four circles, using a nine-inch plate as a pattern. On one half of dough, layer meat, then onion, rutabaga, potatoes, and more meat. Fold pastry in half, then roll and crimp edges tightly together. Prick with a fork three times. Bake on a cookie sheet for one hour at 400°F. Makes four large pasties.

fresh catch and smoked fish. The latter is absolutely superb with a bottle of wine and a Great Lakes sunset.

Wine and Beer

There isn't much in the way of wineries up in the Upper Peninsula. **Threefold Vine Winery** (5856 NN Road, Garden, 906/644-7089, www.exploringthenorth.com/threefold/vine.html) in the Garden Peninsula—where the winters are comparatively mild and the temperate weather allows for grape-growing—is

a notable exception. Instead, beer is the craft beverage of choice, and a number of breweries across the peninsula make a mean brew or two. Among the best are the **Keweenaw Brewing Company** (408 Shelden Ave., 906/482-5596, www.keweenawbrewing.com) and the **Library Bar and Restaurant** (62 North Isle Royale St., 906/487-5882) in Houghton, and **Hereford and Hops Steakhouse and Brewpub** (624 Ludington St., 906/789-1945, www.herefordandhops.com) in Escanaba.

Health and Safety

Every major city in the sparsely populated Upper Peninsula has a hospital, so odds are you won't be too far away from quality medical care—unless you're deep in the woods.

CONTAMINATED WATER

There are a couple of critters in Michigan worth mentioning. That crystal-clear stream may look inviting for a drink, but don't do it. Even many of the most pristine Michigan waters may be tainted with *Giardia lamblia,* a nasty little organism that is most commonly transmitted in the feces of beavers, moose, and other mammals. It is present in many lakes and streams in the Upper Peninsula. **Giardiasis** can result in severe stomach cramps, vomiting, and diarrhea. As one Isle Royale ranger says, "It won't kill you, but it may make you wish you were dead." Neither chemical treatment with Halizone nor a water filter will make water safe from giardia. You need a water purifier filtering down to 0.4 microns or less. Boiling is also effective, but make sure to get your water to a full, rolling boil for five minutes. Isle Royale waters also may be infected with the **hydatid tapeworm,** so they also require purifying or boiling.

TICKS

Wood ticks and **deer ticks** are found in U.P. woods and grasslands. The larger wood tick, about a quarter-inch long, attaches itself to

your skin and gorges on your blood. Gross, yes, but relatively harmless. If you find a wood tick on yourself, your companion, or your pet, grasp it as close to the head as possible and yank. Don't leave a piece of the animal embedded, or it might cause an infection. Ticks aren't super particular, but they prefer warm areas—the scalp, neck, armpits, or genitals. Ditto for your dog. On Fido, check under the collar and all around the ears, too.

Deer ticks are the more dangerous beast. They may transmit **Lyme disease,** a potentially debilitating disease. Lyme disease shows up as a temporary red rash that often resembles a ring, which slowly expands outward. Other symptoms as the disease progresses are sore joints, fatigue, and nausea; if left untreated, it can lead to arthritis and severe neurological and cardiac problems. Caught early, antibiotics treat it effectively.

To complicate matters, deer ticks are tiny—often hardly larger than the head of a pin. Like wood ticks, they burrow into the skin, especially in warm places. After hiking, check yourself and hiking partners carefully. If it's large enough, grasp the tick and pull it like you would a wood tick, or use tweezers. If you've been in a tick-infested area, watch for a rash within the next week and have anything suspicious looked at by a doctor promptly. Your best defense against ticks is to wear long pants and long sleeves and to spray yourself liberally with a hard-core repellent, such as those containing DEET.

Dogs are also highly susceptible to Lyme disease. Check your dog carefully and thoroughly for deer ticks by slowly running your fingers or a comb through his coat to get a look at the skin—a task that requires a lot of patience from you and your dog. Again, ears, necks, bellies, and genitals are favorite tick hiding places. Signs that your dog may have acquired Lyme disease include nausea, fatigue, and lameness that may come and go from different joints. If you see potential symptoms, get to a vet right away. Like humans, dogs respond well to antibiotics if the disease is caught early enough.

There is a canine vaccine for Lyme disease, but veterinarians are divided on how effective it is. There are some very good tick repellent sprays on the market. Use them.

BLACK BEARS

When it comes to bigger animals, deer are by far your biggest danger—they cause thousands of accidents a year on Michigan roads. But **black bears** certainly seem more frightening, especially when you're deep in the woods. Black bears are found throughout northern Michigan; the Upper Peninsula has an especially large population. They usually live in areas of heavy forest, but will routinely wander into open areas, especially for berries and other food sources. They're beautiful animals, and you should consider yourself lucky if you observe one.

Black bears are generally shy creatures that would prefer to have nothing to do with you. If they hear you coming down the trail, they'll likely run the other way. If you happen to see one before it sees you, make sure you've left it an escape route, then clap, yell, or bang pans. Give especially wide berth to a mother with cubs. There are very, very few documented cases of black bear aggression against humans, and theories vary on what to do if you should ever find yourself in such a sorry position. Most behaviorists believe that, unlike grizzlies, black bears will be intimidated by dominance behavior like shouting and waving your arms.

The biggest problems come when bears are lured into populated areas by human carelessness. It's always sad to see a bear relocated away from its home territory, but it happens frequently in campgrounds, where humans don't properly store food or do away with garbage. If you're car camping, keep all foodstuffs in your car (with the doors and windows closed!). If you're tent camping, keep everything in airtight storage containers if possible, and suspend the containers on a line between two trees, high enough off the ground and far enough apart to be out of a bear's reach. Latched coolers shoved under a picnic table are not only *not* sufficient to keep out bears, they're hardly even a challenge.

Clean pans and utensils right away, dumping the water well away from camp, and store them with the food. Never, ever keep any food (even gum) in your tent. Bears have an extremely good sense of smell and may be tempted to join you. Some say cosmetics also can attract them, so play it safe and store your soap and toothpaste with the food. You might want to leave your tent unzipped during the day while you're gone. Bears are curious, and if they want to check out your tent, they'll make their own entrance if they can't find one.

If you're at a campground, deposit garbage in the animal-proof refuse containers provided. If you're backcountry camping, pack it out. Never, ever attempt to feed a bear, no matter how "tame" it may seem. That goes without saying, right?

Information and Services

TOURIST INFORMATION

For general information on traveling in Michigan, your best source is the state-run **Travel Michigan** (800/644-2489, www.michigan .org, 9 A.M.–5 P.M. Mon.–Fri.). Your call is answered by a real person who can send or fax brochures and consult a vast database to field your questions about festivals, lodgings, and all kinds of other stuff. It's a much more helpful service than many tourism hotlines and is staffed five days a week.

You may find it even more convenient to surf the state tourism database yourself, at **www .michigan.org.** This is a terrific website, with an interactive menu that gives you specific information tailored to the parameters you set. Tell it you want to go charter fishing on Lake Superior in fall, and it will display a list of appropriate charters; click on each for a detailed description, rates, directions, and more. Currently, the site has categories for accommodations, attractions, camping, charter boats, communities, events, golf, restaurants, shopping, and skiing.

For information specific to the Upper Peninsula, you'll find the folks at the **Upper Peninsula Travel and Recreation Association** (P.O. Box 400, Iron Mountain, 906/774-5480, 800/562-7134, www.uptravel .com) particularly helpful, too.

The Michigan Department of Transportation operates seven **Welcome Centers** throughout the Upper Peninsula. These facilities are stocked with travel literature and staffed with "travel counselors" who are quite knowledgeable about the state in general and their region in particular. The Welcome Centers are open year-round.

You'll find Welcome Centers at major gateways to the peninsula and at a couple other "interior" locations. They're marked on the state highway map and with signs on the nearest highway. Hours vary.

BORDER CROSSINGS

You'll find this information elsewhere in the book, but it's important enough to bear repeating. It used to be that you could get across the border into or out of Canada with a verbal declaration of citizenship, but 9/11 changed all that. It's considerably more involved now. The easiest approach is to make sure you have a passport. There are other acceptable forms of ID—a passport card, NEXUS or other trusted traveler card, military ID, etc.—but a good rule of thumb is to simply pack your passport. You'll be stopped at the border (they do stop every car), where all of the passengers will have to present proper ID and answer a few questions. If you're traveling with a minor for whom you aren't the parent or legal guardian, you'll need

HOW FAR IS IT?

For some reason, visitors tend to think that the Upper Peninsula is a small place, but in reality it's anything but easy to drive around. The long, narrow stretch of land is about 320 miles across and 125 miles up and down, which makes the between-city drives considerably longer than you might expect.

Distance from St. Ignace to:
- Escanaba: 140 miles
- Ironwood: 320 miles
- Copper Harbor: 320 miles
- Marquette: 175 miles
- Sault Ste. Marie: 45 miles
- Detroit: 300 miles
- Chicago: 400 miles
- Toronto: 475 miles

Distance from Marquette to:
- Escanaba: 65 miles
- Ironwood: 145 miles
- Copper Harbor: 145 miles
- St. Ignace: 175 miles
- Sault Ste. Marie: 160 miles
- Detroit: 470 miles
- Chicago: 390 miles
- Toronto: 600 miles

© JOSH BISHOP

Yoopers are rightfully proud of their unique heritage and cultural identity.

a signed letter from the parent or legal guardian that grants permission for the child to leave the country and that includes a contact phone number. Travelers who aren't residents of Canada or the United States should have the proper travel visa and other documentation and be prepared for a more intensive experience.

You'll need to declare any goods purchased abroad, and you'll have to pay a duty on particular items (alcohol and cigarettes beyond those for personal use). If you're bringing firearms across the border for lawful sporting purposes (such as hunting), make sure you have the proper paperwork and declare your weapon at the border—failure to do so may lead to your arrest. Oh, and remember cash for the toll on the International Bridge ($2).

MAPS
Michigan's official state road map is one of the few maps of the state that doesn't parcel the Upper Peninsula into infuriating and impossible-to-follow pieces. (No, the Keweenaw Peninsula really isn't part of eastern Ontario.) Pick one up at a Michigan Welcome Center or request one from Travel Michigan.

For more detail, the DeLorme *Michigan Atlas and Gazetteer* provides great detail, with the state portrayed in 102 large-scale maps. Though the 15-inch-long format is unwieldy for hikers, it's a great resource for planning your trip, and it even identifies lighthouses, historic sites, waterfalls, industrial tours, and other points of interest. You can find it at many Midwestern bookstores for $15.95, or contact DeLorme (800/561-5105, www.delorme.com).

If you'll be exploring the backcountry, you're best off with an official topographical map produced by the U.S. Geological Survey. Michigan's national forests and lakeshores have topographical maps for sale at their visitors centers and ranger stations. Outside federal lands, you may find them (or other good detailed maps) in local outfitter shops, but don't count on it. If the shop you visit is out of the map you need, you may be a hundred miles from the next store that has it in stock. If you can, buy one ahead of time at an outfitter or map specialty store that carries topo maps; even if they don't have the one you need, they can help you figure out its number and can probably order it for you. You also can contact the U.S. Geological Survey yourself (800/872-6277) for a free map index and order form.

TIME AND MONEY

The Upper Peninsula is located in the Eastern Time Zone, with the exception of the four Upper Peninsula counties that border Wisconsin. Gogebic, Iron, Dickinson, and Menominee Counties are in the Central Time Zone.

Visa and MasterCard are accepted throughout the peninsula, except for in some of the smallest towns. ATMs also are becoming more and more prevalent, tied into the national Cirrus network. Having said that, there still are mom-and-pop motels that balk at charge-card fees and accept only cash or checks. (You might be surprised at how many small establishments are willing to take an out-of-town check and, in fact, prefer them over credit cards.) Cash is needed at self-registration campgrounds. As any wise traveler knows, never count on getting by with only plastic.

If you're traveling to or from Canada, you'll find currency exchanges at the border and at nearby banks in both countries. Used to be, you could use Canadian and U.S. money almost interchangeably near the border, especially coins. In recent years, though, the exchange rate has changed dramatically. Plan to exchange currencies when coming or going.

If you're a U.S. resident with Canadian money left over at the end of a trip, try to end up with bills, not coins. Many banks (especially away from border towns) will exchange only paper money, and with $1 and $2 Canadian coins, you can easily find yourself with $10 or $20 worth of heavy souvenirs.

EMERGENCIES

Most of Michigan's Upper Peninsula is tied into the 911 emergency system—all of it, in fact, except for a small pocket near Seney. Dial 911 for free from any telephone (including pay phones) to reach an operator who can quickly dispatch local police, fire, or ambulance services. This service also works from cellular phones. Be aware, however, that cell towers can be few and far between in rural areas. Much of the Upper Peninsula remains without reliable cellular service, not to mention digital wireless service.

Hospitals

In case you need it, here's a few of the major hospitals: **Mackinac Straits Hospital** (220 Burdette St., St. Ignace, MI 49781, 906/643-8585, www.mshosp.org), **Marquette General Health System** (580 W., College Ave., Marquette, MI 49855, 906/228-9440, www.mgh.org) and **War Memorial Hospital** (500 Osborn Blvd., Sault St. Marie, MI 49783, 906/635-4460, www.warmemorialhospital.org). Most of the Upper Peninsula's larger cities have hospitals and emergency medical care—see each chapter's **Information and Services** section for hospital listings.

RESOURCES

Suggested Reading

ATLASES

DeLorme. *Michigan Atlas and Gazetteer.* Yarmouth, ME: DeLorme, 2006. Covering everything from major highways and byways to the back roads, this is one of the most detailed atlases you can find. Topographical maps and GPS grids are included.

Sportsman's Connection. *Northern Michigan All-Outdoors Atlas and Field Guide.* Superior, WI: Sportsman's Connection, 2008. Detailed maps, supplemental information, and helpful advice make this a must-have atlas for anyone who wants to spend any amount of time in Michigan's outdoors.

FICTION

Harrison, Jim. *True North.* New York: Grove, 2004. Best known as the author of *Legends of the Fall,* Michigan native Harrison here explores the colorful—and often harsh—landscape of the Upper Peninsula. A tragedy, the book can be shocking and dark, but filled with beauty.

Hemingway, Ernest. *The Nick Adams Stories.* New York: Scribner, 1972. As encouragement for Michiganders to read and discuss the same book, Hemingway's *The Nick Adams Stories* "a literary masterpiece literally made in Michigan," was chosen as the Great Michigan Read in 2007.

Monson, Ander. *Other Electricities.* Louisville, KY: Sarabande, 2005. Raised in da U.P., Monson presents a melancholic vision of his native peninsula through this critically acclaimed collection of stories and lists. Highly recommended.

Traver, Robert. *Anatomy of a Murder.* New York: St. Martin's Press, 1983. The popular novel-turned-movie was penned by state Supreme Court Justice John Voelker (aka Robert Traver), about a love-triangle murder that took place in Big Bay.

GENERAL INTEREST

Emerick, Lon L. *The Superior Peninsula: Seasons in the Upper Peninsula of Michigan.* Skandia, MI: North Country, 1996. A collection of essays about and "love letters" to the big lake and its peninsula, categorized by season.

Peterson, Rolf O. *The Wolves of Isle Royale: A Broken Balance.* Ann Arbor, MI: University of Michigan, 2007. Internationally known wolf researcher Peterson has compiled a firsthand account of Isle Royale National Park's ongoing wolf study—and it's a delightful, informative read, filled with personal stories and powerful photographs.

Stonehouse, Frederick. *The Wreck of the Edmund Fitzgerald.* Marquette, MI: Lake Superior Press, 1997. The definitive (if there can be such a thing) discussion of the events leading up to this famous shipwreck and the various theories of what caused its demise.

Traver, Robert. *Trout Magic.* New York: Simon and Schuster, 1989. For anyone who agrees with Traver's introduction: "I fish because I love to; because I love the environs where trout are found, which are invariably beautiful, and hate the environs where crowds of people are found, which are invariably ugly."

NATURAL HISTORY

Black, Ted, and Gregory Kennedy. *Birds of Michigan.* Auburn, WA: Lone Pine, 2003. More than 300 of the state's birds are identified in this color-coded, well-organized book that's immediately accessible to casual and passionate birders alike. Filled with beautiful, clear, color illustrations.

Grady, Wayne. *The Great Lakes: The Natural History of a Changing Region.* Vancouver: Greystone, 2007. Part written history, part photographic record, this book would be a beautiful and informative addition to any coffee table in the Great Lakes region.

Kershaw, Linda. *Trees of Michigan.* Auburn, WA: Lone Pine, 2006. This is *the* guide for tree identification in Michigan. Nearly 300 species of trees referenced here, with color photographs and illustrations of the bark, leaves, flowers, and overall shape of each tree. Tips are included for distinguishing between similar species.

OUTDOOR RECREATION

DuFresne, Jim. *Isle Royale National Park: Foot Trails and Water Routes.* Seattle: The Mountaineers, 2002. The definitive guide to Isle Royale, filled with practical information about campsites, portages, fishing spots, and more. Small enough to carry along, and you should.

DuFresne, Jim. *Michigan State Parks: A Complete Recreation Guide,* 1998. Michigan outdoor writer DuFresne worked with the Michigan Department of Natural Resources to compile this handy guide, which devotes a couple pages to each of Michigan's state parks.

DuFresne, Jim. *Porcupine Mountains Wilderness State Park: A Backcountry Guide for Hikers, Backpackers, Campers, and Winter Visitors.*

Hansen, Eric. *Hiking Michigan's Upper Peninsula.* Guilford, CT: Falcon, 2005. Hansen set out to hike and map 50 of the Upper Peninsula's finest trails—many of them little-known gems—and he succeeded magnificently.

Hillstrom, Kevin and Laurie Collier Hillstrom. *Paddling Michigan.* Guilford, CT: Falcon, 2001. This exhaustive paddling guide covers routes and rivers in the Lower Peninsula, too, but more than half of the book's waterways are located in the Upper Peninsula.

Suggested Viewing and Listening

SUGGESTED VIEWING

Anatomy of a Murder, 1959. Based on the novel by local state Supreme Court Justice John Voelker, this movie is based on real events (and filmed) in Big Bay. Starring the late, great Jimmy Stewart.

Escanaba in da Moonlight, 2001. Starring, written by and directed by Jeff Dainiels, this off-beat comedy has taken some heat for its portrayal of the fine people of Escanaba. Some people claim it's spot-on. With a strange plot and plenty of potty humor, this film isn't for everyone.

Somewhere in Time, 1980. Although this film isn't a classic, it's has a cult following and a reputation as a timeless love story. Its stars, Jane Seymour and Christopher Reeve, are only overshadowed by the Grand Hotel and the Mackinac Island setting.

SUGGESTED LISTENING

Stevens, Sufjan. *Greetings From Michigan: The Great Lakes State,* 2003. When Michigan native Sufjan Stevens released his Indie ode to Michigan, people started to notice. Pay special attention to songs set in the Upper Peninsula: "For the Widows in Paradise, For the Fatherless in Ypsilanti," "The Upper Peninsula," "Tahquamenon Falls," "Sleeping Bear, Sault Saint Marie," and "Oh God, Where Are You Now? (In Pickerel Lake? Pigeon? Marquette? Mackinaw?)."

Lightfoot, Gordon. "The Wreck of the *Edmund Fitzgerald,*" 1976. From the album Summertime Dream, Gordon Lightfoot's folk retelling of the tragic sinking of the *Edmund Fitzgerald* during a Lake Superior storm immortalized the accident in popular memory.

Internet Resources

STATEWIDE INFORMATION

Travel Michigan
www.michigan.org

Michigan's official travel website ranks number one for a reason. The site is the number-one state tourism website in the United States, receiving more traffic than any other.

Upper Peninsula Travel and Recreation Association
www.uptravel.com

Upper Peninsula–specific tourism information and plenty of helpful links. Request the free (and indispensable) travel planner.

OUTDOOR RECREATION AND CAMPING

Michigan Department of Natural Resources
www.michigan.gov/dnr

The site for state park info, campground reservations, and information on all sorts of outdoor recreation, including fishing, hunting, and snowmobile registration.

Michigan Interactive
www.fishweb.com

A great resource for all sorts of outdoor activities in Michigan, including interactive maps for fishing, hiking, and snowmobile and off-road vehicle trails.

National Park Service
www.nps.gov

Official one-stop shopping for all of the national parks in the U.P.: Isle Royale, Keweenaw, and Pictured Rocks—plus the North Country National Scenic Trail.

U.S. Forest Service
www.fs.fed.us

Go here for information about both the Hiawatha and Ottawa National Forests.

TRANSPORTATION

Michigan Department of Transportation
www.michigan.gov/mdot

The best, most up-to-date source for information on tolls, Michigan lefts, lane closures, and various public transportation options.

WEATHER

Weather Michigan
www.weathermichigan.com

An easy-to-use collection of Michigan-related weather links, all in one place.

Regional Information

**Bays de Noc Convention
and Visitors Bureau**
230 Ludington Street
Escanaba, MI 49829
906/789-7862
800/533-4386
www.travelbaysdenoc.com

Delta County Area Chamber of Commerce
230 Ludington Street
Escanaba, MI 49829
906/786-2192
888/335-8264
www.deltami.org

Drummond Island Tourism Association
P.O. Box 200
Drummond Island, MI 49726
906/493-5245
800/737-8666
www.drummondislandchamber.com

Ironwood Chamber of Commerce
150 North Lowell Street
Ironwood, MI 49938
906/932-1122
www.ironwoodmi.org

**Keweenaw Convention
and Visitors Bureau**
56638 Calumet Avenue
Calumet, MI 49913
906/337-4579
800/338-7982
www.keweenaw.info

Les Cheneaux Tourist Association
P.O. Box 10
670 West M-134
Cedarville, MI 49719
888/364-7526
www.lescheneaux.org

Mackinac Island Tourism Bureau
P.O. Box 451
Mackinac Island, MI 49757
877/847-0086
www.mackinacisland.org

Mackinaw Area Visitors Bureau
10800 West U.S. 23
Mackinaw City, MI 49701
231/436-5664
800/666-0160
www.mackinawcity.com

Manistique Tourism Council
800/342-4282
www.visitmanistique.com

**Marinette/Menominee Area
Chamber of Commerce**
601 Marinette Avenue
Marinette, WI 54143
Menominee, MI 49858
906/863-2679
715/735-6681
www.marinettechamber.com

**Marquette Country Convention
and Visitors Bureau**
337 West Washington Street
Marquette, MI 49855
906/228-7749
800/544-4321
www.marquettecountry.org

Newberry Area Tourism Association
P.O. Box 308
Newberry, MI 49868
906/293-5562
800/831-7292
www.newberrytourism.com

**Paradise, Michigan,
Chamber of Commerce**
P.O. Box 82
Paradise, MI 49768
906/492-3219

**Sault Ste. Marie Convention
and Visitors Bureau**
536 Ashmun Street
Sault Ste. Marie, MI 49783
906/632-3366
800/647-2858
www.saultstemarie.com

St. Ignace Visitors Bureau
6 Spring Street, Suite 100
St. Ignace, MI 49781
800/338-6660
www.stignace.com

Tourism Association of the Dickinson County Area
600 South Stephenson Avenue
Iron Mountain, MI 49801
800/236-2447
www.ironmountain.org

Western U.P. Convention and Visitors Bureau
P.O. Box 706
Ironwood, MI 49938
906/932-4850
800/522-5657
www.westernup.info

Index

North Pier Light: 85
Norway Trail: 98

O

off-road vehicles: Copper Harbor 151; Escanaba 80; Grand Island: 189; Hancock-Calumet Trail 139; Huron Mountains 186; Huron Shore 245; Internet resources 286; Iron Mountain 98; Iron River 106; Ironwood 112; Marquette 178; Munising 194; Pictured Rocks National Lakeshore 204; Porcupine Mountains 121; Sault Ste. Marie 236; St. Ignace 46; St. Ignace to Manistique 66; Whitefish Point 224
Ojibway Tower: 16, 163
Old Depot Park Museum: 110
old-growth forests: Estivant Pines 144-145, 152; Hiawatha National Forest 78; Pictured Rocks National Lakeshore 201; Porcupine Mountains 117, 119
Old Mackinac Point Lighthouse: 20, 51, 53
Old Victoria: 119
Olson Falls: 194
Ontario Travel Information Centre: 234
On the Waterfront Car/Small Truck Show/Pedal Cars & Swap Meet: 45
Ontonagon: 15, 117-123
Ontonagon County Historical Museum: 117, 119
Ontonagon Lighthouse: 119-120
opera: 134, 136
Oswald's Bear Ranch: 221-222
Ottawa National Forest: 101-109; general discussion 270; recreation 103, 104-105, 107, 111-112, 114

PQ

packing: 12
Palms Brook State Park and Kitch-Iti-Kipi: 62-63
Paradise: 218-227
Paradise Inn: 24, 225
parasailing: Mackinac Island 35; Mackinaw City 54; St. Ignace 46
parks: Bailey Park 87; Bayshore Park 190, 192; Gould City Township Park 64; Great Lakes Marina Park 14, 85; Hebard Park 146; Henes Park 86, 87; Kleinke Park 87; Little Girl's Point 110-111; Locks Park 229; Ludington Park 8, 74, 76; Peninsula Point Lighthouse Park 76; Presque Isle Park 10, 17, 173, 174; Sac Bay Park 72; Tourist Park 85, 87; Van Cleve Park 79; see also state parks; specific national park

pasties recipe: 278
Paulding Mystery Light: 102-103
Paul's Plunge: 148
Peek-A-Boo Hill Cross Country Ski Trail: 246
Pendills Creek National Fish Hatchery: 229
Peninsula Point Lighthouse: 22, 76
Peninsula Point Lighthouse Park: 76
people: 262-263
pet caskets: 76
Peterson Falls: 112
Pictured Rocks Boat Cruises: 10, 18, 23, 199-200
Pictured Rocks National Lakeshore: 198-207; general discussion 270; trip planning 10, 18, 19-20, 23
Piers Gorge: 97-98
Pine Bowl Pathway: 234, 236
Pine Marten Run: 78
Pine Mountain Music Festival: 97, 176
Pine Ridge Nature Trail: 208
Pines and Mines Mountain Bike Trail: 104-105, 111
planning your trip: 8-12, 253; see also specific place
plant life: 256-257, 285
Point Iroquois Lighthouse: 229, 232
Point Louise Range Lights: 232
politics: 262
Pomeroy/Henry Lake network: 104
Porcupine Mountains: 8-9, 117-123
Porcupine Mountains Wilderness State Park: 15, 117, 285
Portage Bay State Forest Campground: 71, 73
Portage Lake Upper and Lower Entry Lights: 133
Portage River Light: 133
Potawatomi Falls: 106, 112
Presque Isle Falls: 121
Presque Isle Park: 173; lighthouse 174; trip planning 10, 17
Pretty Lakes Quiet Area: 222-223
pub crawls: 34
Quincy Mine: 16, 130, 132
Quincy Mine Hoist Association: 132

R

Rainbow Falls: 106, 112
Rainey Wildlife Area: 65
Range Mountain Bike Trail System: 176
Rapid River Falls: 80
Rapid River Ski Trails: 80
reading suggestions: 284-285
recreation: 270-277; see also specific type of recreation

List of Maps

www.moon.com

DESTINATIONS | ACTIVITIES | BLOGS | MAPS | BOOKS

MOON.COM is all new, and ready to help plan your next trip! Filled with fresh trip ideas and strategies, author interviews, informative blogs, a detailed map library, and descriptions of all the Moon guidebooks, Moon.com is all you need to get out and explore the world—or even places in your own backyard. As always, when you travel with Moon, expect an experience that is uncommon and truly unique.

MAP SYMBOLS

Symbol	Name		Symbol	Name
	Expressway		Highlight		Golf Course

Expressway   Highlight   Airfield   Golf Course

Primary Road   City/Town   Airport   Parking Area

Secondary Road   State Capital   Mountain   Archaeological Site

Unpaved Road   National Capital   Unique Natural Feature   Church

Trail   Point of Interest   Waterfall   Gas Station

Ferry   Accommodation   Park   Glacier

Railroad   Restaurant/Bar   Trailhead   Mangrove

Pedestrian Walkway   Other Location   Skiing Area   Reef

Stairs   Campground   Swamp

CONVERSION TABLES

$°C = (°F - 32) / 1.8$
$°F = (°C \times 1.8) + 32$
1 inch = 2.54 centimeters (cm)
1 foot = 0.304 meters (m)
1 yard = 0.914 meters
1 mile = 1.6093 kilometers (km)
1 km = 0.6214 miles
1 fathom = 1.8288 m
1 chain = 20.1168 m
1 furlong = 201.168 m
1 acre = 0.4047 hectares
1 sq km = 100 hectares
1 sq mile = 2.59 square km
1 ounce = 28.35 grams
1 pound = 0.4536 kilograms
1 short ton = 0.90718 metric ton
1 short ton = 2,000 pounds
1 long ton = 1.016 metric tons
1 long ton = 2,240 pounds
1 metric ton = 1,000 kilograms
1 quart = 0.94635 liters
1 US gallon = 3.7854 liters
1 Imperial gallon = 4.5459 liters
1 nautical mile = 1.852 km

MOON MICHIGAN'S UPPER PENINSULA

Avalon Travel
a member of the Perseus Books Group
1700 Fourth Street
Berkeley, CA 94710, USA
www.moon.com

Editor: Michelle Cadden
Series Manager: Kathryn Ettinger
Copy Editor: Teresa Elsey
Graphics Coordinator: Kathryn Osgood
Production Coordinator: Darren Alessi
Cover Designer: Kathryn Osgood
Map Editor: Kevin Anglin
Cartographers: Kat Bennett, Chris Markiewicz
Director of Cartography: Mike Morgenfeld
Indexer: Jean Mooney

ISBN-13: 978-1-59880-173-6
ISSN: 1946-312X

Printing History
1st Edition – April 2009
5 4 3 2 1

Text © 2009 by Avalon Travel.
Maps © 2009 by Avalon Travel.
All rights reserved.

Portions of this book are taken from Tina Lassen's Moon Michigan, 2e.

Some photos and illustrations are used by permission and are the property of the original copyright owners.

Front cover photo: © Lee Rentz / digitalrailroad
Title page photo: Pictured Rocks © Dave Vugteveen
Interior color photos: Page 4 © istockphoto.com/ Dean Pennala; page 5 © Becca Bishop (left, right), © Josh Bishop (center); page 6 © 123rf (inset), © Josh Bishop (bottom); page 7 © bigstock.com (top left), © Josh Bishop (top right, bottom); page 8 © Josh Bishop; page 9 © Josh Bishop; page 10 © Raymond J. Malace; page 11 © Charles Cook; page 12 © Raymond J. Malace (top), © Terry W. Phipps (bottom); page 14 © Vito Palmisano; page 15 © Becca Bishop (top), © Josh Bishop (bottom); page 16 © Travel Michigan; page 17 © Josh Bishop; page 18 © Carl Ter Harr/ Travel Michigan; page 19 © 123rf; page 20 © Becca Bishop; page 21 © Josh Bishop; page 22 © Becca Bishop; page 23 © bigstock.com/James Phelps; page 24 © Travel Michigan

Printed in the United States by RR Donnelley

Moon Handbooks and the Moon logo are the property of Avalon Travel. All other marks and logos depicted are the property of the original owners. All rights reserved. No part of this book may be translated or reproduced in any form, except brief extracts by a reviewer for the purpose of a review, without written permission of the copyright owner.

Although every effort was made to ensure that the information was correct at the time of going to press, the author and publisher do not assume and hereby disclaim any liability to any party for any loss or damage caused by errors, omissions, or any potential travel disruption due to labor or financial difficulty, whether such errors or omissions result from negligence, accident, or any other cause.

KEEPING CURRENT

If you have a favorite gem you'd like to see included in the next edition, or see anything that needs updating, clarification, or correction, please drop us a line. Send your comments via email to feedback@moon.com, or use the address above.